PSYCHOANALYTIC THEORY

PSYCHOANALYTIC THEORY

An Exploration of Essentials

George S. Klein

INTERNATIONAL UNIVERSITIES PRESS, INC.
New York

Klein, George Stuart, 1917-
Psychoanalytic theory.

Bibliography: p.
1. Psychoanalysis. I. Title.
BF173.K47 150'.19'5 75-18508
ISBN 0-8236-5059-6

Manufactured in the United States of America

Contents

Editors' Preface

When George S. Klein died unexpectedly on April 11, 1971, at the age of 53, he was deeply immersed in writing this book. The manuscript had occupied him for several years, the summer of 1967 being perhaps the initial and most concentrated work period, during which time he prepared the first drafts of Part II. That Klein was working on a critical reappraisal of psychoanalytic theory was known to his many friends, colleagues, and students; he had already presented and published his ideas concerning the "dilemmas and options" confronting psychoanalytic theory in a variety of contexts. It is some of these already published statements which constitute, as he had planned it, Part I of this book. But we eagerly awaited his proposed solutions, his "restatement" of the theory (that is, the contents of Part II of this book).

With his sudden death there was, intermingled with our profound grief and deep sense of loss, a growing concern about the fate of George's manuscript, the product of so many years of arduous labor. Was it sufficiently "ready" to allow its publication? Obviously Klein's own severe judgment would have been "No": the manuscript would need much more work before it was ready. Those who knew George's demanding work habits and his incessant rewrites, draft after draft, would surely have urged him to temper his perfectionism for the sake of publication, though they would in all likelihood have been unsuccessful in swaying his judgment.

Nevertheless, his friends and colleagues, after reading the most recent drafts of his manuscript and consultation with others, believed that it was worthy of publication even in its unfinished state. It is therefore being published as he left it save for extensive editing and the elimination of one chapter that had been roughed out in only preliminary fashion: entitled "The Anatomy of Psychoanalytic Meaning," it was the most philosophical of his writings and was intended to explicate further his central thesis that psychoanalytic theory is essentially a theory about the meanings of behavior. A chapter entitled "The Scope of Inquiry" was planned as the introductory chapter, outlining the aims, assumptions, and strategy of argument of the book. Since the chapter was in too rough a form for even heavy editing, we have instead selected and rearranged the most central statements from it (pp. 1-13) which, together with "Is Psychoanalysis Relevant?" (Chapter 1), ought amply to provide a general orientation to the book.

Klein would undoubtedly have acknowledged his intellectual indebtedness to the many colleagues who influenced his ever-evolving views of psychoanalytic theory. Understandably, he did not leave a list of them. He would of course have acknowledged his support from the National Institute of Mental Health, since he was a Research Career Awardee (No. K06 MH19728). He was also appreciatively aware of the fine editorial help of Mrs. Berta Tabbat, with whom he worked before he died and who, after his death, continued to work on the book. We also want to express our gratitude to Miss Sue Annin for her final editing of the entire manuscript in her usual outstandingly competent fashion.

It is with gratitude that we acknowledge the help, patience, and trust of George Klein's widow, Bessie Boris Klein, who chose us to look after the manuscript.

We add a few remarks about our own perspective on this book. It is by now fairly well accepted that a sharp distinction has to be made between Freud's two psychoanalytic theories. They may be characterized as one theory framed in terms of meaning and a second theory framed in terms of the material substrate or mechanism of mind, the latter theory supposedly explaining the former. Klein called them by their usual names, "clinical" and "metapsychological." We ourselves prefer "psychological" to "clinical," and would call the metapsychological—a natural-science theory—"neuropsychological." What remains in dispute is the relationship between the two theories and their appropriate roles in psychoanalysis.

The position Klein takes in that dispute is that metapsychology and the clinical theory belong to two different universes of discourse and that, important though a metapsychology or neuropsychology is for a comprehensive science of man, it is irrelevant to and obstructs the proper study of the data and explanatory concepts of psychoanalysis. The examination of the two different kinds of explanation, metapsychological and clinical, occupies the first two chapters of Part I.

Klein's position is to be sharply distinguished from another which has appeared in our literature, namely, the proposal to substitute for the present metapsychology a different natural-science theory; information theory, for example. This latter position still rests on the assumption that a natural-science theory is required to explain clinical psychoanalytic theory and must remain an intrinsic part of psychoanalysis. A volume of essays presenting various points of view in this dispute is soon to appear in *Psychological Issues*. It is dedicated to George Klein's memory and is edited by Merton Gill and Philip Holzman.

Klein realized that his position means that two major tasks must be faced. The first is the disentangling of the dense intertwining of the metapsychology and the clinical theory. He attacked this task in Chapters 3 and 4 of Part I of this book, in his reassessment of the psychoanalytic theories of sexuality and of the ego. The second task is a systematization of the clinical findings of psychoanalysis by a psychological theory to take the place of the systematization of psychoanalytic theory by metapsychology. It is this task that he assayed in Part II. He was under no illusion that his attempt was more than a beginning.

How was George Klein able to make such a critical and yet constructive reappraisal of psychoanalytic theory? We believe there are two main reasons. First, he was gifted with an independence and integrity of mind that could not remain satisfied with what he saw as accepted dogma, in unusual combination with a responsible generativity that demanded that what he rejected must be replaced by something better.

A second reason is that he worked both in the laboratory and behind the couch. His first training was as an experimental academic psychologist and his second was as a research candidate in the New York Psychoanalytic Institute. Like most pioneers who work in two disciplines he will doubtless be attacked from both sides. His accomplishment is an unusual one, since an innovative interdisciplinary approach ordinarily leads to a synthesis of the two disciplines, in this instance clinical psychoanalysis and metapsychology. But he followed his findings rather than his preconceptions, and boldly concluded that a disengagement rather than a synthesis is required.

We do not know what will be the fate of this incomplete effort to conceptualize the principles of a psychoanalytic psychological theory divorced from an only partially explicit neuropsychological metapsychology. But we do know that psychoanalysis is indebted to George Klein for having been in the vanguard of those who recognized that the task is crucial to the advance of the field. His early death at the height of his power and in the midst of his creative labor was a tragic loss to our science and profession. But we have no doubt that, despite the unfinished character of this posthumous work, it will be welcomed into the ongoing debate as a timely, exciting, and important statement.

Merton M. Gill

Leo Goldberger

INTRODUCTION

The Scope of Inquiry

In the present book I have attempted a new approach to the assessment and survey of psychoanalytic theory. My scope of inquiry is a search for the essential theoretical understructure that constitutes "clinical psychoanalysis." That such an inquiry is timely needs no demonstration; but it cannot be done through empirical effort alone. Certainly there is nowhere to be seen a systematic empirical sifting and choosing among the stronger and weaker concepts of psychoanalytic theory. Indeed, such a sifting itself depends upon some kind of ordering of the theoretical understructure. One aim of this book is to show what characteristics of the theory make such a summary difficult, that indeed two kinds of orientation to explanation exist, with concepts adjusted to both, but interpenetrating each other in such a way as to make systematization difficult.

My approach is anchored in the conviction that two modes of explanation distinguish the many strands of theoretical concepts in psychoanalysis. One is characterized by an attempt to read the experiences of a person and to account for them, that is, understand them, through concepts that state them as a manifestation of internal states, whose function is exhibited through these modes of experience and behavior. In short, the clinical theory tries to specify the patient's viewpoint in concepts describing both his experience and the functional reasons for the experience. I believe that Freud's main contribution to science was this new mode of explanation.

The essential properties of clinical explanation, then, in whose behalf the constructs of the clinical theory are developed, are the data of experience (encompassing both what is and what is not acknowledgeable in reflective awareness) and the postulation of internal states specified in terms of functions which enable us to describe, and also to explain, *directions* in behavior and thought. Clinical explanation, in this functional manner, does not therefore distinguish sharply between description and explanation; to describe a person's intention or aim is to say that what a person is doing is also why he is doing it. Or conversely, why a person is doing what he is doing is also to tell what he is doing. The clinical explanation, in short, to put it in another way, enables us to identify the action (directional) aspect of movements.[1] This is what we mean, then, by explaining in terms of the patient's standpoint.

The other strand of theory attempts both more and less. Its intent is to place psychoanalysis in the realm of natural science by providing an impersonal, nonteleological view of the organism as a natural "object," subject ultimately to the laws of physics, chemistry, and physiology. Teleological considerations—the patient's standpoint—are irrelevant to this level of explanation. Some concepts in psychoanalysis have an uncertain relation to the two strands of explanation, the ego and the structural point of view in general being one example.

Issues of causal explanation, impersonal causal processes and mechanism, the desire to establish interfaces with the natural sciences, and the theory of evolution and biology, reinforced in recent years by the momentum toward developing a "general psychology," not to mention the heavy medical origins of psychoanalysis, have all created a momentum for a mode of theoretical explanation quite different from the clinical mode, to the point where it is no longer clear which mode of explanation has priority in the development of the theory. Does one explain a motive as an injury to self-esteem, or as the discharge of a drive? The usual answer given is to strive for a "complete" explanation in terms of the five metapsychological points of view. However, so contaminated are these five levels of explanation that it is hard to find a "dynamic" interpretation, for example, that is free of the drive-discharge notion. Even more unfortunate is the fact that metapsychological explanations in causal mechanism terms have led to an

[1]*Editors' note.* There is a noteworthy similarity between this formulation and Roy Schafer's recent writings on an "action" language.

obscuring of the clinical phenomena that are to be the basis of observation and explanation.

From the standpoint of the clinical objectives of explanation—that aims and direction are uppermost, and the mode of experience involved and the role of consciousness in relation to them must be specified—psychoanalytic metapsychology is in large part, however interesting as a spur to neuropsychology, irrelevant, in the same sense that, if we are looking for an explanation in terms of *intention*, it is irrelevant to get a detailed account of muscular operations and the kinetic energy of the effort.

The difference between the two theories is not at all in terms of abstractness—as has sometimes been said. The nonphenomenological concepts of the clinical theory are just as abstract as the other. Indeed, insofar as a "meaning" is never observable in any direct way, it is always an abstraction from behavior, which is supposedly to exemplify it. The difference is not in degree of abstractness but in explanatory intent.

It is also sometimes said in defense of the metapsychology that the clinical theory is, after all, only a psychology of pathology, of interrupted development, of illness, of the normal gone bizarre. But the narrowing of perspective of the clinical theory to illness misses an important point—that there is a general psychology of the normal at the very basis of the clinical theory, and this is what the present book tries to emphasize and to articulate.

The general ingredients of the clinical mode of explanation are as follows: It is first of all a theory of motivations. It is concerned with the specification, the conditions, and the origins of motivations, their development, and their pathological miscarriages. Its concepts have mainly to do with tendency and direction. Second, it has to do with an accounting in terms of reasons and origins, significance and meaning, of behavior, rather than with the exact sequential linkages of events in the traditional notion of causation. Third, it is concerned with motivation in the sense of aims acted upon and lived out in interpersonal relations, object relations, rather than with "the discharge of a particular level of energy." Fourth, in formulating the distinctive clinical principles of psychoanalysis, we reach for formulations that make possible a more readily confirmable link to the experiences that are the data of the clinical situation. Fifth and finally, the principles should be formulated in a fashion that is consistent with the received, contemporary, nonpsychoanalytic psychology and responsive to changes in that psychology.

By this last point I mean that psychoanalysis is a part of psychology but by no means the over-all structure which incorporates the rest of psychology. Metapsychology does in fact try to encompass all of psychology, but this has been one of its chief sources of muddiness, which has obscured the distinctive aspects of clinical psychoanalysis as a theory. It is my belief that some of the log-jam of problems created by difficulties in the specification of the clinical principles could be broken by bringing them into relationship with the received psychology. Although attempts to formulate psychoanalytic theory should try to emphasize what is distinctive about psychoanalytic theory compared to others, progress consists in part in putting such issues of distinctiveness on the line for investigation and test against rival assertions. In this strategy the context of reformulation is the body of *relevant* received nonpsychoanalytic psychology—relevance here defined as involving concepts framed from the same orientation to explanation as that of the clinical theory. This orientation is no longer unique to Freudian psychoanalysis.

It seems to me it would be well both for psychoanalysis and for psychology to make psychoanalytic theory ever more explicit in respect to the distinctive hard-core clinical assumptions of the theory, to make more explicit its points of divergence from other theories. For a sharply delineated theory is a probe and a guide; it may prove in time to have been a misleading guide, but it is the business of science to settle the matter. Clinical psychoanalytic propositions have not yet been exposed to systematic examination. One of the sad things about the early experimental efforts to "validate" psychoanalysis is that they did so on the basis of the poorly articulated clinical theory. Before we can make precise confrontations with rival assertions we must see the clinical concepts in more systematic form that would allow us to make definitive testable statements.

Since it is only the broadest features of psychoanalysis that have been incorporated into psychology in a variety of different contexts, the narrower and more delimited powerful conceptions and implications are in danger of being lost. For example, this is what is happening to the theory of infantile sexuality. It has never really been investigated in academic psychology, and its essential, core proposition—a distinction between sensual experience and sexual behavior and its continuity from infancy to adulthood—includes many important systematically testable propositions. Academic psychology has rejected this quest by its de-emphasis of infantile sexuality in favor of the generalized importance of infantile experience.

Thus the present work takes the position that progress would be marked by a greater articulation of the fundamental critical principles, the axiomatic basis, of clinical propositions in terms of which meanings, motives, and aims are read in the clinical situation, both within psychoanalysis itself and in an integration of psychoanalysis with received nonpsychoanalytic psychology. In this effort my three guidelines are, first, an effort to point to the concepts that are constructed from the patient's standpoint; second, an emphasis on phenomenological experience; and third, an emphasis on the dynamic principles that account for this experience in terms of motive and aim.

The search for the fundamentals of psychoanalytic theory is of course based on Freud's writings, but there are two possible ways of proceeding. One could try to systematize what Freud himself had to say, winnowing and combining, reinterpreting, reconciling the inconsistencies in his thinking over time, and highlighting the consistencies. With this course, the chief test of success would be the parsimony of the integration, and its logical cohesion. The alternative procedure—which is the one followed here—is to select what seem to be certain root assumptions in Freud's thought as points of departure for an independent reformulation of basic psychoanalytic principles. These root assumptions may not have been what Freud himself saw, nor how he chose to formulate them. They represent what in my opinion, however, seem to provide a useful integration of the inductively derived major clinical propositions. It remains to be seen whether they are sufficient, whether others need to be added, and whether in fact the formulation is appropriate or adequate. It is a start, however, for others to continue.

Since my aim is not exegetical I have no hesitation in being selective about Freud's own thinking, in neglecting certain of his thoughts and emphasizing others, and in accepting still others not explicitly present at all in Freud—as long as they implement the goal of accentuating what is essential in the legacy of psychoanalytic clinical explanation, and serve the purpose of developing these principles into workable tools of understanding and research. The result is therefore to be evaluated as a contribution not to a systematic exposition of Freud's ideas but to the contemporary requirements of restructuring the field of psychoanalytic theory.

It is tempting to speculate on the relative importance which Freud ascribed to his clinical theory and his metapsychology. He wrote: "The assumption that there are unconscious mental processes, the recognition of the theory of resistance and repression, the appreciation of the importance of sexuality and of the Oedipus complex—these constitute the principal subject-matter of psycho-analysis and the foundations of its theory. No one who cannot accept them all should count himself a psycho-analyst" (1923, p. 247). This statement was published before the advent of ego psychology as a separate subdiscipline.

What was Freud opting for when he stated these requirements—the phenomena, the clinical theory, or the explanatory metapsychology? We see no reference to the libido theory that was developed to account for sexuality, or to the ego, or to the many other concepts of his metapsychology. I emphasize again that, to make an accounting of the clinical theory, the distinction I develop in Part I between two modes of explanation is crucial. The problem is to follow a course that will save the phenomena which Freud considered essential and at the same time to be sure we are not favoring a particular theoretical construction of processes or model or mechanism that is not essential to the functional intent of clinical explanation.

What does seem quite clear about Freud's statement just quoted is this: It is not a statement of dogma but an assertion of fundamental theories and basic principles, assumed to be interlocked in such a way that adherence to one means adherence to the others; and that they are exclusive and distinctive to psychoanalytic theory.

In Part I, the first four chapters of the book, I have tried to disengage the two strands of the theorizing that are pervasively interlaced in psychoanalytic doctrine—the clinical and the other, which is called "metapsychology." The latter might be better named the mechanistic or process puzzle approach. In Chapters 1 and 2 I try to specify some of the qualities of the clinical theory as a way of thinking that distinguish the psychoanalytic clinical approach. Chapters 3 and 4 are "case histories" of two important concepts in the theory—the theory of psychosexuality, and the concept of ego—through which are illustrated the confusing interpenetrations of the two trends of explanation and theorizing, and their consequences.

In any accounting of basic psychoanalytic principles Freud's theory of psychosexuality must hold a prominent part of the stage, or at least be confronted. Especially so is this the case for the point of view developed in this book which denies the indispensability of the energic point of view and the drive-discharge model in the account of motivation. Since the drive-discharge model is the most prominent derivative of this energic point of view, and since it is popularly regarded as the heart of Freud's revolutionary views on sexuality, the issue is joined.

It confronts us with the question of whether the price of excising the energy model would be to eliminate the importance of sexuality in personality development, neurosis, and all of the areas of motivation in which it is commonly invoked. This is a proper concern, and is one of the bases of the reluctance of analysts to dispense with the drive-discharge model; for it has seemed to them that such a course would result in a re-repression of the hard-won insights into the importance of sexuality.

The conclusion I draw in the chapter, however, is that a detailed examination of the essentials of the theory of psychosexuality from its clinical theoretical aspect leads to the pleasant discovery that, far from eliminating the key revolutionary aspect of Freud's theory, the disengagement of these propositions from the drive-discharge model freshens perception of the vitality of the clinical theory and opens new vistas for its exploration. It offers an opportunity for seeing how sexuality and pleasure can be viewed within a consistently dynamically oriented, that is, motive-oriented, way of looking at events.

Similarly, with respect to the ego I conclude that the attempt to see the ego as an "apparatus" has actually obscured considerations of motives and aims that the concept, in its clinical interpretation, is designed to get at or to encompass. The functional or regulative principles embodied in the concept of the ego have not been delineated in contemporary ego psychology. Thus one of my conclusions is that with the so-called "structural point of view" the ego has lost its distinctiveness as a clinical psychoanalytic concept.

Ego psychology as it is currently formulated is without dynamic foundations, a graft on the clinical concepts of psychoanalysis. For example, if, following Hartmann, the theory holds that drives are transformed in relation to ego *requirements*, it is silent on what are the dynamic principles—or requirements—according to which such a transformation unfolds. The formulation of such a dynamic of "ego" activity was one of David Rapaport's concerns in his postulation of a principle of activity and passivity. But in its current development without such a dynamic, and with its focus on specifying its "structure" instead, ego theory looks more like a potpourri, identical with many of the concerns of academic psychology and without any distinctively psychoanalytic clinical meaning.

It should be clear to the reader, then, that some of the traditional conceptions of what is fundamental in psychoanalytic theory are part and parcel of metapsychology, and are therefore here found expendable. They include the concept of drives and the notion of an energic quantity, both spelled out in a model of tension discharge, as well as the concepts of the structural systems of ego, id, and superego.

To deal with the phenomena which these concepts were designed to encompass I introduce from the received psychology the concepts of self[2] as a grade of organization, and of meaning schema as the unit of cognitive organizations as they exist internally as motives in a person.

As for "self," it seemed clear to me that, rather than starting from the assumption of an impersonal "structure" with implicit mechanism characteristics, I had to begin with the assumption of a single apparatus of control which exhibits a variety of dynamic tendencies, the focus of which is either an integration experienced in terms of a sense of continuity, coherence, and integrity, or its impairment, as cleavages or dissonance. I call this central apparatus the "self."

As for schema, I believe my path to it was by way of dealing with the basic biological tendencies which the concept of id was supposed to encompass. Again, with my point of departure being the experiencing person, I begin with that aspect of these biological tendencies which are pleasure experiences directly arousable and sought after. A distinctive quality of pleasure is aroused in a particular object relationship, and the pleasure so aroused invests the objects with signifi-

[2]*Editors' note.* This was written before the concept of self began to be so prominent in contemporary psychoanalytic theorizing. Klein's conception of self is not the same as that found in much of this contemporary writing. It has for him the connotations of "person."

cance in this respect. These are not reactive pleasures so much as "operant" in quality. The record of such arousal makes further reinstatement of these conditions desirable. The cognitive record of the experiences of sensuality constitute a schema of meaning. When sensual pleasure becomes recorded as such a schema, the fact that it can be persistently activated under certain conditions gives the schema its "drive" character. I am not, of course, restricting schemata to those concerned with sensuality.

In thus accounting for the pervasive motivational importance of sexuality I believe that nothing essential is lost by eliminating the libido concept. Eliminated at the same time are the problems that psychoanalytic theory acquired with the libido theory, of forcing the assumption that there is a separate sexual development independent of structure, of "ego," and of a social matrix. Also avoided are the problems that come with the assumption of a libido energy that requires a separate system of controls, and with the whole network of assumptions having to do with neutralization and defusion of energies.

Since self and schema are not themselves distinctively part of psychoanalytic theory, to those accustomed to the familiar concepts these divergencies of emphasis and concept will be strange enough to provoke the criticism that I have not so much reformulated psychoanalytic theory as constructed a new theory. I will let the reader decide whether I have succeeded in capturing the essentials of what the familiar concepts tried to cope with—the empirical phenomena critical for psychoanalytic explanation in terms of aims and motives.

I will mention in passing that the mechanisms involved in schemata, the structures of cognitive meaning, are, in my opinion, better dealt with by Piaget's theories of the assimilation and accommodation of structures in their activity in the environment than by a theory centered on discharge, but I do not explore this possible model for a causal-mechanism theory in this book.

In the light of my account in Part I, I try, in Part II, to reformulate what seems to me to be the essential structure of psychoanalytic clinical theory—the root principles that underlie any attempted formulation of psychoanalytic propositions. I try to find the invariants which distinguish psychoanalytic clinical theory throughout the vicissitudes of its history.

Six basic principles are cited in Part II, all related in one way or another through an assumed condition of self syntonicity and dystonicity. The first principle asserts the importance of motivation as expressing the resolution of incompatibilities; the second principle is the crucial importance of primary pleasure experiences in the development of motive structures; the third and fourth refer to two dynamic properties of self whereby integration is achieved—one by the maneuver of dissociation or splitting (repression), and the other via the active reversal of a passive experience; finally, fifth and sixth, two developmental principles issuing from these dynamic principles are described—fractionation and identification. These seem to me to be the core principles on which much of the analytic clinical superstructure is based.

One way to look at the general principles considered in Part II is as a restatement, in more clinically relevant terms, of basic tendencies that are often implied in the "structural point of view" of contemporary psychoanalysis. Thus they are a means of providing for what is implied in ego, id, and superego, the pleasure-unpleasure principles, and the five points of view of the metapsychology.

Although the principles I have stated seem to me to be consistent with the critical emphases in Freud's clinical thinking, I became aware quite late in the writing of this book that there is perhaps a point of serious divergence between my emphasis in this book and Freud's. The discrepancy grows out of the rejection in the present work of Freud's quantitative model of discharge. It seems to me that this model led Freud to emphasize impersonal forces that are not themselves conscious, rather than experience and awareness. Now it has been said that to emphasize conscious experience takes the dangerous step of denigrating the most critical factor in the substantive revolution wrought by Freud, namely, that unconscious processes have a preeminent role in thought and action. I am quick to insist, however, that that is *not* the case. The difference in emphasis deserves further comment, since certainly the emphasis upon "unconscious," for all of the importance of the ego in recent psychoanalytic work, remains a firm and central bastion of Freud's thinking.

Freud's emphasis on unconscious processes is intimately connected with his concepts of psychical energy and discharge. He wrote: "The concepts of 'psychical energy' and 'discharge' and the treatment of psychical energy as a quantity have become habitual in my thoughts since I began to arrange the facts of psychopathology philosophically [sic!]; and already in my Interpretation of Dreams I tried (in the same sense as Lipps) to establish the fact that what are 'really psychically effective' are psychical processes which are unconscious in themselves, not the contents of consciousness" (1905c, p. 147).

It is sometimes said that "ego psychology" corrected this emphasis. Actually, by stressing the fact that the ego too has "unconscious" aspects, ego psychologists have also tended to move away from an acknowledgment of the importance of conscious experience. I believe that Freud's metapsychology has resulted in a devaluation of the importance of conscious experience—that is, in what ways it is actually an effective aspect of action and thinking.

It seems to me that the appropriate emphasis on the role of conscious experience can be restored in the context of the contemporary concept of feedback. What Freud did indeed demonstrate through his overwhelming evidence of "unconscious phenomena" is that what we are conscious of is only the last phase of a process that goes on outside of consciousness. We are aware only of end products of thought and we are often moved by what we are *not* aware of. In this view the content of experience is only a reactive outcome, but the information received thereby has an influence on the next steps taken in thought and action. Following this image, a train of thought is dark, though it leads from one point of awareness to another. But what it is that *these points of awareness* themselves contribute to the train of thought is critical to clarify. For when one does focus on this contribution, one is not satisfied with Freud's statement that the only thing that is psychically effective is what is unconscious.

The informational model of conscious experience implied here will not be spelled out in this book but it is taken for granted. Its tacit acknowledgment makes it imperative that the qualities of experience as information-guiding aspects of thought and action be acknowledged, and by that fact it points up how properties of thought and action differ when awareness does or does not accompany a thought or action. Indeed, it is the contrast between consciousness and unconsciousness in this fasion that is one of the core principles spelled out in Part II.

The importance of conscious experience and the consequences of ignoring the experiential aspect of pleasure are nowhere better exemplified than in the chapter on the primary pleasures. Here Freud's central principle is asserted: "For man is a 'tireless pleasure seeker' . . . and any renunciation of a pleasure he has once enjoyed comes hard to him" (1905c, p. 126). But it is not drive and its discharge that is the goad or the desirable factor; I take the statement literally to mean that pleasure is an *experience*, and it is the pleasure or its absence under certain conditions that is determinative, not an impersonal imperious discharge of unconscious energy. So with affect experience generally. The considerable amount of work going on in psychology now on the powerful effect on behavior of feedback in awareness amply demonstrates this point.

Actually, all that I have said returns to an emphasis that Freud himself gave to consciousness early in his career in the "Project for a Scientific Psychology." To reassert this emphasis does not bring a loss, but a gain, in insight. It highlights the importance of repression and unconscious fantasy rather than detracting from it.

I distinguish three types of action which psychoanalytic theory must encompass. First are the actions linked to consciously avowed and premeditated aims. Second are the nonreflectively performed actions so automatically suited to a situation that we can justifiably call them operational rules. Third are the nonreflective actions which are carried out with a "deliberate" avoidance of anything that would betray awareness of their aims. The latter constitute the "Freudian unconscious." Psychoanalysis as a therapy is primarily concerned with identifying these aims and showing how action fulfills them.

One virtue in the exercise that I attempt in this book is to reintroduce simplicity into the theory. One of its problems has been an unnecessary complexity, and the diagnosis of psychoanalytic theory from which the present study was developed is that its overcomplexity results from intermingling two essentially different universes of explanation and their corresponding theoretical terms.

What is perhaps new in my account are these two points: First, the insistence that clinical theory must be anchored in the data of experience and behavior, and the attempt to construct this theory from the patient's standpoint; second, the disentangling of the concepts which are valid abstractions from human experience from the heavy and hopeless burden of the expendable metapsychology. My intent in doing so is to try to breathe new life into a way of thinking which revolutionized twentieth-century psychology but which has been overgrown by an obscurantist jargon, suffers the dry rot of overconceptualization, and is bedeviled by the intertwining of two incompatible modes of explanation.

PART I

DILEMMAS AND OPTIONS

CHAPTER 1

Is Psychoanalysis Relevant?

SOME PSYCHOLOGISTS, especially critics of psychoanalysis, will regard a concern with the continuing identity of the psychoanalytic body of thought as a reversion to schoolism. Aren't schools of psychology an anachronism in our maturing science of psychology? Aren't ambitious images of the "whole man" out of date? Besides, haven't the major principles of psychoanalysis been absorbed into the mainstream of American psychology? And aren't psychology and psychoanalysis both better off for the fact that psychoanalysis has gone the way of all schools?

Granted the many signs of absorption. Even in behavioristic psychology, defense, displacement, conflict, and drive are common coin. Within psychoanalysis itself as a profession the eclectic spirit has been so insistent that it is hard to trace the common thread among the diverse groups who pre-empt the label "psychoanalyst." And perhaps the most dramatic evidence of absorption is the change in common-sense psychology. Consider how much of yesterday's psychoanalytic jargon is today's lingo of everyday life. Even the young, among whom formal psychoanalytic theory finds little favor, would be tongue-tied without it.

But is there cause for satisfaction with this state of "absorbed psychoanalysis"? Does it speak for a maturing science of psychology which has separated wheat from chaff and arrived at a superior integration?

There are plenty of indications that the absorption has not actually been integrative, but rather a process that subtly obscures the stronger features of psychoanalysis; in effect it denies them by deflecting attention from their investigative possibilities, giving a net result, as Lindzey (1967) put it, that is perhaps "a more palatable but less powerful set of ideas." It is striking, for example, that the theory of infantile sensuality has never really been investigated systematically, either experimentally or naturalistically. The emphasis on infantile sexuality has become instead a generalized emphasis on infantile experience, important, but not *quite* the same thing. Far from a good reason for interment, therefore, "absorption" of the allegedly best parts of psychoanalysis calls instead for a fresh affirmation, for an articulate rediscovery of the center of psychoanalysis.

A perhaps more important justification for a revitalized appreciation of root psychoanalytic principles has to do with their relevance to the troubled cultural climate and to psychology itself as a science. Addressing itself to this context is a vital responsibility of psychoanalysis.

It is customary to describe our age in metaphors of explosiveness: Political revolution, family disintegration, population explosion, mind-blowing, generation gaps, are the order of the day. Certainly there is going on something akin to the Industrial Revolution of two centuries ago, which was called a revolution because it created a new environment—a new average expectable environment, and with it a revolution in aspirations and social values.

We don't have the words or the concepts of social change to characterize the present "revolution." But it doesn't take much probing to notice that among the major signs of its psychological impact are an impressive heightening of self-consciousness, a sensibility and savoring of what it means to be "myself." Never was the "self" more "in," or sideburns longer. The modern appetite is for pluralistic selfhood, in the insistence among the young on an ever more prolonged moratorium on commitment, of resistance to every structure, form, convention, and practice that edges us to singleness of view or option, or that forces us to accept this or that single role as the whole truth of our being. There is a longing to live one's life rather than to be lived by it, preferably for an indefinite young manhood, defined by psychological rather than biophysical time. There is a striving to feel time itself in different terms from those hitherto customary—an urge to shed linear time, before and after, cause and effect, historical understanding of events, even in our personal lives. There is a distaste for those views such as psychoanalysis that speak of hierarchical meanings, of experiences that point to meanings beyond them, of in-between experiences and consequent experiences linked in historical configuration, for to do so is to be insufficiently alive to the *Moment*; it is the Moment that we must savor, live into, and inhabit without thought of antecedent and consequent.

There is ethical aspiration in the rejection of past structures, as Erikson reminds us (1969), in the heightened sensibility to selfhood, the wariness of alienating commitment. But surely it must catch our concern in psychoanalysis that the distrust with which the intervention of intellect between self and experience is regarded has ominous aspects to be reckoned with, that abandonment of ethical positions, however justified, is invariably accompanied by regressions, hopefully only experimental. In this Babel of chaotic admixtures of the fresh and novel, the empty, the ugly, and the pathetic, by what perspective to man's nature are we to preserve the power to compare, and to choose?

Here the central strength of psychoanalysis as an orientation to psychical reality could not be more relevant. Freud's discovery of unconscious motivating and symbol-inducing processes was a discovery not merely of a new range of facts but a guide to self-knowledge. For voyagers into the inner reality that we live by he held out the warning that the occasions on which we to a greater or lesser degree misrepresent to ourselves what we are trying to do, and why, are much more common than we prefer to think, that we have an unconscious stake in disavowing self-knowledge even when we are pointedly striving for truth. The cornerstone discovery of Freud's method was, of course, resistance and repression—the breeding devices of self-delusion.

As a perspective to the social structure of Freud's own time, psychoanalysis brought to cultural historians the shocking insight that a European society which harbored the illusion that it was most enlightened tended to produce psychic cripples as a result of maimed instincts, that the individual life paid a psychical price for a secure adaptation and position in that society. Psychoanalysis thus opened the door to a search for the requirements of developmental integrity and the conditions that undermine it, a search which has certainly contributed to the poignant self-consciousness of this, the first generation that grew up "under Freud." Particularly timely, too, is an important suggestion from psychoanalytic ego psychology, that the craving for pluralistic selfhood may be a peculiarly contemporary transcription of the biologically rooted need to create and preserve coherence, continuity, and integrity of selfhood, and therefore that the quest for coherent identity is no less now than it was before, despite the avowed emphasis on plurality of selves; that behind the frenetic displays and regressions of self-expression there is a search for integrating values and integrative growth.

And what about our parent field of psychology; what is the climate there which justifies a renewed psychoanalytic identity? Contemporary psychology, particularly the version we find in academic departments, has been characterized by Koch (1961, 1969a) as a citadel of "ameaningful thinking." "Ameaningful" is not "meaningless" thinking nor is it nonsense; it is an orientation which severs thought and action from the thinking and acting *subject* and treats them as objects—"process"—in their own right, eligible for objective scrutiny on premises drawn from natural science, usually physics. The program of ameaningful science requires scrupulous avoidance of *why* questions—that is, explanations in terms of intentionality or directional tendency, which is considered to be "prescientific"—in favor of *how* explanations in terms of process and mechanism. Hence the popularity of models of mechanism.

Some behaviorists, especially since the "New Look" period of the fifties, began to suspect that maybe there is a psychological *subject* as well as psychological process after all. They talked of plans and "totes," of thinking, and even, well, ego, and these sometimes without quotation marks. Some have even allowed themselves the label "subjective behaviorists." If on balance, however, the first enthusiasms for models, fitted to animal behavior, tended to conclude that basically man is a rat or a monkey, there has not been much edification either from the later sophistications which tried to prove that a rat is basically human. While recognizing the need to dust off the acting person, psychology in the main simply has not been able to give up the image of studying him in a natural-science mold. So the strategy shifts to the engineering discipline: As Koch remarks, we not only get the observational methods of physics, but the answers from physics as well. We have seen a long succession of efforts to prove that man is a telephone exchange, a servomechanism, an analogue computer, a processor of input and output, and the like.

It is instructive to see how our natural-science bent in American psychology has tried to shape "absorbed psychoanalysis." Following Freud's first impact, the study of motives in psychological laboratories soon turned to a focus on motive from the standpoint of mechanisms; motives were and are studied in the laboratory very much as "objects." For instance, departing from the clinical meaning of repression as a concept that alerts us to reasons that a patient cannot avow, the mechanism viewpoint attempts to specify a locatable process of repression, permitting detached observation like the functioning of a pancreas.

In short, psychology has been and still is plagued by a phobic retreat from the psychological *subject*. It shies away from what should in fact be the first requirement of a psychology of human action: to find a language adequate to the description of disposition and intentionality as clued by testimony regarding the subject's own vantage point. It is precisely because an orientation to *intentionality* is its distinctive mark that clinical psychoanalysis fills a gap in contemporary psychology.

Behavior therapy is a showcase achievement of ameaning psychology because it has successfully sallied forth, with its rejection of person-oriented explanations, into the very sanctuary of the psychotherapist himself—the clinic. Behavior therapy challenges psychoanalysis both in theory and practice. It challenges its orientation to intentionality as a prescientific form of explanation, but even more important, it challenges its very relevance to the objective of bringing about effective changes of behavior. There is a crucial and basic difference here: Whereas for psychoanalysis behavior and experience are critical only for what they imply about what is hidden from view, for behavior therapists it is behavior itself that is the focus of interest. It is, after all, the painful behavior that is to be changed, they say, so why hover over "hidden," unobservable meanings? For the behaviorist clinician the point is to break into the tight chain of antecedent-consequent *behavioral* links of which a "symptom" consists.

When we turn to that growing sector of "humanistic psychology" which has acquired the label "Third Force," we find, curiously, that psychoanalysis is only slightly more popular. In fact, some proponents of the new humanism include psychoanalysis (Freudian) among the hated positivisms. This increasingly popular backlash against American behaviorism includes among its diverse forms an extreme version of existentialist doctrine which advocates exploration of the glow and shade of conscious experience in its every nuance as the royal road to psychological freedom. Translated into an approach to psychotherapy, the goal of therapy is experience known in its own moment-to-moment quality, texture, delight, or misery, rather than as a backdrop for wishes and intentions, conscious or unconscious, aborted and conflicted, or of repetitive iterations of fantasy. It is no accident that this offshoot of existentialism has become an ideological anchorage for many contemporary youth. However, from the psychoanalytic viewpoint, it tends to encourage the delusion that novel experience itself *is* insight and achieved selfhood, not in-between indications which along with action point to directive aims that, while not directly accessible to the subject's experience, have a molding influence upon it. It is this difference of emphasis that makes for a divisive departure from psychoanalysis. In this version, applied existentialism follows a route surprisingly akin to behavior therapy—to manipulate the person via exercises, drugs, and stimuli (tactile, gustatory, or whatever) into dramatically novel sensation and feeling. The *dominant* thrust of existential thinking seems to me eminently consistent with psychoanalysis. But in the zeal for seeing the here and now without gloss, to comprehend the subject in his own terms, to see him as a person rather than as an object, to see structures and situations as they emerge from *his* side and not simply from the observer's side, it may tend to bypass, even reject, interpreted meaning of experience and the question of therapeutic relevance of insight into such meanings (see Edelheit, 1967).

And lastly there is the movement of "social psychiatry," a relatively new venture that has crystallized from the increased responsiveness of clinics and hospitals to community appeals for prevention and rehabilitation. Community psychiatry at the present time is more an anguished response to social ills than a theory; at best it is a developing operational strategy. However, it inclines generally toward principles of etiology derived from social science; it tends to view even psychoses as a societal phenomenon. Actually, community psychiatry is not a declared antagonist of psychoanalysis, but it is clearly disposed to view psychoanalytic therapy as elitist, and generally to take a dim view of the one-to-one therapist-patient duality, doubting its practicality or even its theoretical relevance for understanding the "real" breeding ground of illness—"social systems." It is inclined to favor the idea that therapeutic effectiveness is better achieved through the treatment of families and other social groupings definable as "systems" whose principles are not a simple extension of individual psychology.

Now in drawing attention to the climate of mixed disenchantment and uninterest, coolness, even hostility which once again confronts psychoanalysis, I am definitely not advocating retreat to a Maginot line of psychoanalytic-institute bunkers identified by precepts hardened into dogma, unresponsive to challenge, and paranoidally resistive to change. It is perhaps too easy to take comfort in Freud's belief that it is the fate of psychoanalysis to suffer periodic cultural repression. I have even heard some psychoanalysts say, in a nostalgic backward look at the pioneering days when Freud's intimate coterie was creating a Movement, that they welcome the prospect of becoming once again an elite cultural corps.

But just as psychoanalysis gathered a certain momentum as a reaction to nineteenth-century psychiatry (an intellectual history of psychoanalysis will one day give proper recognition to this fact), so we should not ignore the possibility that further advances in psychoanalysis could be sparked by directly confronting these currents. Again, by responsiveness I don't mean dressing up psychoanalysis in the current fashions of what is "proper" science, or a leap to one of the system-mechanism models of mod psychology. There were those, you remember, who once prescribed for psychoanalysis an emetic purge with an S-R model—and they lost clinical psychoanalytic theory in the bargain; there are those who now trumpet the engineering models, and we can once again be skeptical that they will contribute much to the basic objectives of clinical psychoanalytic explanation.

Rather, I mean the kind of confrontation that is receptive to concepts from received psychology that are consistent with the psychoanalytic aim of understanding intentionality, and that offer genuine, perhaps superior alternatives on this level of explanation. There is a healthy reminder in such responsiveness that discovery and fresh conception are as possible in a science dedicated to the aim of reading intentionality as in one devoted to brain physiology and the mechanisms of systems, that development of this level of explanation need not have dried up with Freud's death.

At the same time, responsiveness and confrontation should be accompanied by a sense of continuity—a resolve to be wary of sophisticated forms of denial which pose as corrective change. We need to update the clinical theory, but in a fashion that would not leave behind insights of the past nor the empirical base of the original principles. If Freud's conceptual solutions are to be put aside, the phenomena they were meant to capture must at least adequately, and hopefully even more effectively, be provided for in the conceptual modifications.

Perhaps I can illustrate what I mean by a sense of continuity in revision by examining two short summaries of basic psychoanalytic theory offered by Freud. In 1923 and again in 1925, in a few terse sentences he capsuled the substantive center of clinical psychoanalysis. He wrote:

> The assumption that there are *unconscious mental processes*, the recognition of the theory of *resistance and repression*, the appreciation of the importance of *sexuality* and of the *Oedipus complex*—these constitute the principal subject-matter of psycho-analysis and the foundations of its theory. No one who cannot accept them all should count himself a psycho-analyst [1923, p. 247; italics added].

In a slightly different version he wrote:

> The theories of resistance and of repression, of the unconscious, of the aetiological significance of sexual life and of the importance of infantile experiences—these form the principal constituents of the theoretical structure of psycho-analysis [1925, p. 40].

I think it would be a mistake to dismiss these as formulae for detecting heresy. They summarize what Freud considered at that time to be fundamental in clinical *theory*, vital to psychoanalytic clinical explanation, principles interlocked in such a way that adherence to one required, in his opinion, adherence to the others; he regarded them as the distinguishing marks of *psychoanalytic* as compared to other conceptions of intentionality.

But that was 45 years ago, and certainly these cannot be the last words on the vitals of the theory—even perhaps as a fair distillation of the span of Freud's own career as theorist. To assess the adequacy of these principles would seem to be very much in order, if not indeed a sign of progress in psychoanalysis, and to replace them if need be but without losing sight of the empirical base of the earlier principles. For example, in speaking of the etiological significance of sexuality, Freud was able to relate such diverse phenomena as perversions and strong interests. In questioning his theory of psychosexual development—and there is plenty in it to question, especially his assumption of a libidinal energy—our responsibility is to find a viable conception of sexuality that provides for the observations that led Freud to suppose that there are such far-reaching extensions of sexuality; it would include an assessment of his original observations, refining them where necessary, and juxtaposing them with others made since Freud's time that are not easily fitted within his earlier framework of "sexual etiology."

Responsiveness could begin, then, with an attempt to define the sinews and bones of clinical psychoanalytic theory, its core principles, those fundaments distinctive to psychoanalysis which separate it from other existing theories. How are these seminal concepts dependent on each other and what concepts lead out from there? Do they require reformulation to accommodate developments in received psychology? And what of these developments *should* it accommodate? What other principles are needed? This sort of articulation has rarely been attempted; not even Freud tried it except in the terse summaries cited. The guiding consideration of change should be the objectives of psychoanalytic explanation, for it is these aims which underlie the substantive principles of clinical psychoanalysis.

But in reaching for this core of the theory we quickly find that our course leads back over not one but two lines of development in psychoanalysis. We must recognize now, some 70 years since *Studies on Hysteria* and some 30 years after Freud's death, that psychoanalytic theory itself has acquired a history in which it is not easy to separate genuine developments in psychoanalytic insight from ideological currents of the cultural context as well as elements of the scientific community's image of what is "real" science. The two lines of development express different conceptions of what psychoanalysis is and ought to be. If not exactly analogous to the Talmud and Kabbala of Judaic tradition, they represent the same kind of uneasy fit, sometimes in open conflict over which should prevail in tradition. To get to the core assumptions of clinical psychoanalysis (those fundamentals that are distinctively psychoanalytic) surgery is necessary—a theorectomy, so to speak, that separates one from the other so as to free the irreplaceable core concepts of clinical psychoanalytic theory for further exploration, application, and differentiation.

It seems to me that this objective is best served by our first being as clear as possible about the *kind of inquiry* that clinical psychoanalysis is, and the type of explanations of behavior that it sets itself the problem of delivering. The important difference between the two traditions of psychoanalysis is not the energy-discharge model of the one—the so-called "metapsychology"—which is absent in the other. The more profound point of distinction is that they derive from two different philosophies of inquiry and explanation. Each leads to different conceptions of what psychoanalysis is all about, of where efforts at discovery should be directed, how psychoanalytic knowledge should be systematically organized, on what problems and in what settings we should do research, what objectives of explanation should be served in doing research. The tragedy is that the two orientations have often been confounded, creating theoretical and empirical havoc.

It has taken us a long time and the efforts largely of certain philosophers of science to whom we owe a debt of gratitude—particularly R. S. Peters (1956) of the English school tracing to Wittgenstein, Ricoeur in France (1970), and in this country Kohut (1959), Apfelbaum (1965, 1966), Loevinger (1966), Holt (1965, 1968), and others—to become aware of the intricate confoundings of these contrasting orientations within psychoanalysis.

The central objective of psychoanalytic clinical explanation is the *reading of intentionality*; behavior, experience, testimony are studied for meaning in this sense, as jointly exemplifying directive "tensions," avowed, disavowed, repressed, defended. This orientation to explanation generates concepts that reflect a picture of individual development as a problem-solving, meaning-seeking, meaning-organizing venture, involving and resulting from the constant resolution of incompatible aims and tendencies. Applied to the understanding of symptoms, for example, such explanation consists in going back from a symptom not to the workings of a mechanism which is itself actually or potentially observable, but to a life-history context in which the symptom becomes intelligible as exemplifying an aimful solution.

Freud's rather confusing word "overdetermined" expressed this idea. From the clinical standpoint, it amounts to saying that a symptom is positioned in several configurations of meaning that make it intelligible as a solution, that at the time of its onset the symptom was not, so to speak, *externally* determined but represented a strategy of resolution, a compromise among inner tendencies felt to be incompatible.

Having this objective of answering "why" questions—the reasons of behavior—clinical explanation requires us, then, to identify not only the intentionality exemplified by a configuration of experience and behavior, but the history of such guiding directives in a person's life (the "genetic point of view"), to identify the milestones, crisis points, and conflicts in this development ("dynamic point of view"), and to see how certain capacities and functions participate in the logic of his intentional behavior (e.g., attention, intellectual capacities, cognitive style). Explanatory objectives of this type provide the base for the analyst's efforts to bring about behavior change in therapy; "psychoanalytic insight," and hopefully, change, depend on the shared understanding by patient and therapist of the patient's aims, goals, and beliefs.

A distinguishing mark of psychoanalytic explanation is that it aims at specifying the subject's own vantage point. All the explorations and probes as well as concepts of the clinical theory are dedicated to this effort. Having this orientation to inquiry and explanation, the analyst relies upon a perceptual process, still little understood, which Polanyi has called "indwelling" (1958), and Home "cognitive identification" (1966), in which the analyst reconstructs the subject's orientations by dwelling within his patient's experiences and behavior while standing back from them sufficiently to enable him to detect configurations of intention, especially disavowed ones, that the patient is living out in his experiences and movements. The patient's point of view is reconstructed by putting together the patient's avowed experiences of behavior with those that he cannot avow, or resists avowing. It is more a process of seeing pattern or "fit" than detecting causes in the patient's behavior, given his aims, goals, and beliefs as revealed in his behavior and conscious avowals. Questions of validation and rules of evidence are no less critical for this orientation to explanation in terms of meanings perceived by an observer and lived out by a subject. They are in fact a matter of great and neglected importance in psychoanalysis, but pursuit of this topic would get us off the track I have set for myself.

Cognitive identification or indwelling joins with existentialism's emphasis on the exploration of conscious experience. However, the analyst will not rest with the assumption that intentionality is exhausted in what the patient is able to avow consciously; he does not believe that he is abandoning the objective of reading the patient's own vantage point when he looks for directives which even the patient himself cannot admit or has a stake in not admitting. However, any account of such disavowed aims must encompass what the subject *can* experience or insists upon as *the* "real" reasons. For example, to an observer a person may be exhibiting the defensive maneuver of undoing. At the same time, the subject's avowed reasons for behaving as he does may give no hint of acknowledging a defensive intent, and may indeed even contradict this tacit reason. A complete accounting of the intentionality of his behavior, however, is obliged to relate the two by showing how the subject's conscious rationale is consistent with or may actually have been tailored to suit the defensive requirement of veiling certain wishes and the defensive intent itself. Thus, an analyst plunges into phenomenology, but goes beyond it to generalizations that connect accessible and inaccessible levels of experience in hypotheses regarding dispositions and aims. The process does not rest there, of course. Reading the patient's experience with the aim of perceiving intentionality in depth, he must then translate his perception back to the patient's own experience in a way that is meaningful to the patient, so that the patient comes to share in the discovery of the configuration.

The substantive concepts of the clinical theory are meant to aid the analyst's efforts to listen for directive tendencies and their vicissitudes. Although they vary in abstractness, i.e., in reflecting actual conscious experience, all are meant to aid the indwelling process by pointing to something in the mind of the patient which the patient does not experience but is part of his inner reality or psychical *Umwelt*. Such is the status of such concepts as resistance, repression, repetitive unconscious fantasy.

Now none of the clinical concepts nor their underlying explanatory intent have much to do with the "how" of behavior—its causal texture in the sense of mechanisms. For example, the conception of repression is useful and indispensable, but a model of the mechanisms of repression is neither crucial to the analyst's clinical explanatory objectives nor directly testable by the kind of evidence the analyst's inquiry produces—unless he takes up the vantage point of the engineer or the physiologist and leaves off being an analyst.

The second side of psychoanalytic metapsychology and theoretical aspiration draws a different bead on explanation. I have dealt with it elsewhere (Chapter 4), as have others (see, for example, Apfelbaum, 1965, 1966; Holt, 1965, 1967), and I will here confine myself to the contrast with clinical explanation. In this other side of psychoanalytic explanation, the terms of explanation have nothing to do with the subject's own vantage point; it is the person *observed as a physical process* that is the main objective. In pursuing this aim of detailing impersonal cause and mechanism, this strategy of explanation leaves the process of indwelling altogether and instead transposes data to an assumed model of mechanism. When this premise is made operational, the experience of the subject and his aims become "objects" for study. They are no longer aims and intentions within reach of the subject's experience, but structural facts of the psyche, "properties" of an object. In psychoanalysis this objective has been served by a model of mechanism and causation in the mold of physical science of half a century ago, but similar objectives are shared by proposals which reject this older model and would replace it with more plausible versions of hardware or software. Translated to these models, experience and aim henceforth become "representations," "bound cathexes," or "structures that can be cathected," or in more modish terms, "memory banks," "templates," "input and output channels," "feedback circuits," and the like.

The different explanatory aims have led to different theoretical constructions, and to different meanings of terms shared by the two contexts of theory. Within the clinical frame of reference, for example, the ego is a high-level abstraction referring to a class of aims or directional configurations of behavior and experience. Within the process-mechanism theory, however, ego is reified as a *system of regulation*. Similarly, both theories have concepts embodying genetic and dynamic viewpoints. In the clinical theory the genetic point of view refers to the fact that aims have a history, not in the sense of trying to specify invariable and unconditional antecedents, but in the sense of specifying an inner logic of development.

The concept of conflict is again differently interpreted from these two points of view. Within the energic or mechanical model, conflict (the dynamic point of view) is imaged as a clash of *forces*. The terms of conflict are conceived as agents that push against each other and against a reactive ego. But the clinical theory need harbor no such notion of the actual mechanism of conflict, although our training is so contaminated by the energy model that it is still hard to see the misplaced concreteness and attributes of positioned force, required by the other frame of reference but irrelevant to the clinical focus.

For the aims of clinical psychoanalytic explanation it is sufficient to assume that conflict is a state specified through a person's experiences and actions which reveal him to be living out an inner conviction that two or more directive tendencies are irreconcilably in opposition. (There may be such incompatibility in actuality, e.g., weaning involves the irreconcilability of the desire to be at the breast with a desire to be free of it, or the incompatibility may be merely so in the person's *fantasy*, out of, say, guilt about masturbation or fear of castration.) Conflicts have an underlying physiology, of course, perhaps representable in metaphors of hard- and software, or in a physiology of forces, but for the psychoanalytic clinical objective of explaining why a person is pointed toward the world temporally and spatially in the way he is, it is conflict viewed as the subject's way of understanding *his* world—a cognitive configuration—that needs to be understood.

If there exists a crisis in psychoanalysis, one aspect of it is in the question of which course to emphasize in theorizing and research. My point is that it is the clinical orientation to explanation, and the concepts anchored to it, that are the most distinctively psychoanalytic—more relevant to psychotherapy and more applicable to other humanistic endeavors in which reading the directionality of man's behavior is central. This kinship of explanatory focus links clinical psychoanalytic theory more closely to the humanistic disciplines than to natural science. The analyst's job of explaining has much in common with the historian's obligation of narrative construction and with the playwright's responsibility for depicting a logic of motivation. I am skeptical whether conceptions of mechanisms or physiological models, on the other hand, can lead deductively to concepts of intentionality of the sort that serve the aims of clinical explanation. They may win a researcher a Nobel Prize, but I doubt that they will make him a better analyst.

A clinician's interest in conceptual innovation, like that of any scientist, is likely to be guided by tacit criteria of relevance to his explanatory objectives. On this basis he judges "importance." The clinician's attraction will be greater for concepts that seem to issue from applications of the indwelling process in contexts such as therapy (but not only in therapy), where a human subject's engagement with his inner reality of aims and directive tensions can be reconstructed. A clinician is, therefore, less likely to be intrigued by the proposal that the ego is a "stimulation maximizer" than by a concept like "negative identity" which holds out the promise of disclosing to him still another vein of intentionality by which to explain a person's behavior.

This is not to deny the importance of models of mechanism nor the explanatory objective which is satisfied by nothing less than the specifications of a system's workings. Explanations in these terms are likely to be, in fact already are, of tremendous assistance in dealing therapeutically with behavior patterns that reflect system disintegration or failure, and where considerations of intentionality are irrelevant. It is still the better part of wisdom to recommend surgery for a brain tumor rather than a psychoanalysis. But it is the clinical side of psychoanalysis that is more likely to give useful guidance in a society which badly needs a viable guide by which to view the reasons men live by, their course, divergence, and miscarriages in an individual's life, as a psychological anchorage for theories of social change.

Core Principles of the Clinical Theory

I have paused over the tacit objectives of clinical psychoanalytic explanation. The *substantive core* of the clinical theory, the empirical fruit of this explanatory orientation, consists of certain root propositions about universal basic tendencies. Without these assumptions of human tendency psychoanalysis loses its identity in a rootless empiricism.

In the chapters that follow I have attempted a specification of these assumptions. Here I shall content myself with a brief summary of my own version of certain core principles.

In trying to come to grips with them I find it useful to think of them according to Scriven's (1964) notion of "normic statements," universals which specify lawlike regularities but not of the nature of cause and effect. A normic principle describes a basic mode of change undergone by dispositions and relationships to people and events as they become internalized as inner structures; these principles of transformation are posed as universally true but with no pretense of describing rigorously the antecedents and consequences that would enable one to speak of them as causal laws. They are, however, in my view, basic anchorages of the psychoanalytic way of thinking. Whether they are sufficient, and whether they can themselves be subsumed under others, or need to be supplemented, remains to be explored in fuller discussion. Seven such principles have emerged for me as fundamental.[1]

First, that psychical structure, whether in normal or pathological development, is an outcome of contrarieties—*the resolution of incompatible aims or dispositions.*

For a long time it was the resolution of a particular type of opposition, namely, a conflict between defense and drive, that occupied stage center in the theory. However, major changes have come about in the conception of the polarities that are constantly at play in the organism. A most important one is this addition: Where previously resolution of crisis was taken to mean resolution of conflict, equal emphasis is now given to the *developmental crises* that arise when adaptational modes of one stage are no longer suited to the unfolding requirements of an emerging biological potential, creating an urgency for adaptational change. In psychoanalytic conceptions of normal development, crises and dilemmas are inescapable, indeed, positive conditions of normal growth; neuroses are miscarriages of this process.

Thus Freud's original insight into conflict as a source of motivation is now better regarded as but one expression of a more general principle which holds that psychological growth is a product of continuing efforts to resolve incompatibility, crises, and impasse. Out of such felt or actual incompatibilities emerge structures of action and thought.

Second is a basic principle suggested but not adequately captured by

[1] *Editors' note.* Though Klein speaks here of seven principles, it should be noted that only five of these receive detailed treatment in the chapters of Part II of the book. The principle of selfhood (self-identity) is touched on throughout the book; the principle of regressive repetition is most specifically discussed in Chapter 9, pp. 305-310.

the conception of ego. The necessity of resolving conflict at any cost, and indeed the fact of conflict itself, imply a need for integration at all life stages, a requirement for coherence among dispositions and tendencies. Psychoanalytic theory thus carries with it an assumption, which has been more or less tacit up to now in the theory, of a developing *self* which is the referent of a sense of coherence, continuity, and integrity at every stage of life. Two components of selfhood must be recognized: a centrifugal assertion of personal autonomy, and a centripetal requirement for being an integrated and needed part of a larger, more encompassing entity or social unit. The reconciliation of this dual requirement as a condition for integrated selfhood itself creates one of the most basic sources of potential conflict. Exploration of the dynamics of this polarity seems to me a neglected area of psychoanalytic theoretical development.

A third key tenet of clinical psychoanalytic theory concerns the formative influence of *pleasure experience* and *anxiety* in the development of self-identity and in the structuring of motives. Articulation of this principle requires a thorough disengagement of the conception of pleasure from the bland and contentless form in which the pleasure principle has come to be known in psychoanalytic metapsychology. Doing so requires also that we free the notion of pleasure from the confines of the model of libidinal development which narrows considerations of pleasure to those of sensual experience alone (see Chapter 6).

Pleasure, even sexual, does not reflect something essentially external to the ego impinging on it as a "force" to be controlled, a "stimulus" to be dealt with, something to be disposed of, or to be reacted to. Rather, pleasure and anxiety are to be seen as two great and contrasting states of feeling, generated by contacts with things, events, and people. Both might be said to refer to states of selfhood, complimentary to each other: Just as anxiety is informative of estrangement, denoting threat or conflict, pleasure is informative of accord and well-being, of things and objects acquiring values of approachability and desirability. Anxiety and pleasure are motivating in distinctively different ways, the one to minimize experiences of threat, the other to reinstate and to sustain affiliative contact. Further specification of this principle of the structuring importance of pleasure experience must go on to delineate the prototypical *conditions* or classes of pleasure and the differing roles of these varieties of pleasure in the structuring of motives, relationships, and conflicts.

An accounting of seminal propositions could hardly omit the principle of *repression* or dissociative splitting on the one hand, and, on the other, what Loevinger (1966) has called the *active reversal of passively endured experience*—two distinct and equally basic modes of confronting and resolving conflict, impasse, and crisis. From these lead such indispensable concepts concerning inner structure as defense, introjection and identification, positive and negative identity. The principle that internalization of interpersonal relationships as schemata is accomplished in the form of introjects through repression, and identifications through active reversal, itself deserves separate recognition as a sixth basic principle of the clinical theory.

Lastly, there is the core principle of *regressive repetition*, which proposes that crises are occasions for the activation and enactment of earlier prototypes of conflict, pleasure prototypes, and earlier, proven modes of resolution.

A potential for repetition is implicit in all the core principles. That growth, and even life itself, is in critical ways a repetition is basic to psychoanalytic understanding and knowledge. For example, it is in the nature of pleasure once experienced that it is savored and thereafter sought in its prototypical forms (see, e.g., Chapter 6), and it is of the nature of a repressed conflict, because it is outside of the orbit of self-determined control, that it remains a potentially pre-emptive, though unconscious, basis of action and thought (see, e.g., Kubie, 1941). Such a tendency for regressive repetition is vital for the understanding of transference; transference phenomena are understood as the reliving of past prototypes in their conflictual wish-gratifying and defensive aspects.

Regression has come to be emphasized primarily as a maladaptive retreat rather than as also a setting of reconstructive growth; clinical observations have tended to dwell exclusively on stereotypic, passively experienced reiterations which remain "outside the ego." Consequently even in psychoanalytic writings regression has taken on a somewhat pejorative meaning. But as Loewald (1971) has pointed out:

> . . . this notion is no stranger to psychoanalysis, although "neurotic" repetitions have been stressed more in psychoanalytic writ-

> ings than repetition as a "normal" phenomenon. . . . The whole conception of psychosexual development, . . . of typical "traumatic" experiences . . . , of prototypical complexes and conflicts and imaginés, in determining the life course of the individual, undoubtedly contains the general notion of repetition, in one form or another, of prototypical events and complexes which took place and shape in the early days of the individual. Of equal importance in psychoanalytic thinking . . . is the concept of repetition as contained in the theory of identification and internalization [p. 64].

Of course, Kris's (1932-1952) concept of regression in the service of the ego has been a particularly useful formulation of the same point.

Loewald (1960, 1962, 1971) and Erikson (1970) must be singled out for having particularly drawn attention to phenomena of *normative* progression via regressive repetition. Such regressions seem to occur within a context of a relatively intact sense of personal causation (that is, of *willing* changes rather than of being compelled) and sense of future. Regression in this context is a form of experimental maneuvering toward the development of new ethical positions, ground rules, and values, which involves creatively repeating, in the present, prototypically crucial conflicts of the past and early levels of organized life experience; these are lived out within a sense of present realities and an experienced need for arriving at a new level of coherent selfhood. Passive, essentially duplicative reproduction of prototypes Loewald contrasts with this active, reconstitutive form of regression which he calls "re-creative repetition," and which Erikson terms "re-enactment." Loewald (1971) notes, for example:

> The dissolution (not repression) of the oedipal conflict, to the extent to which it succeeds, in its aspects of mourning and internalization of abandoned object-relations, with the erection of the superego as a new differentiation in the ego, is a prime example of re-creative repetition in the psychic field—in contrast to passive reproduction in the psychic field represented by the perpetuation of oedipal fantasies or pathological introjections [p. 60].

This expanded view of regression has extended the understanding of transference as involving both passive and active forms of regressive repetition (Loewald, 1971). Through his studies of Luther and, more recently, of patterns of dissent in the young, Erikson (1958, 1970) has shown how different forms of regressive retreat from abandoned ethical positions may actually reflect the gropings of self-articulation toward more viable standards of accepted self-coherence and identity.

Needless to say, all of these principles allow plenty of latitude for further delineation; changes and additions to them are undoubtedly in order. I cite them to illustrate the point that elaborations and modifications of such principles, pointed to the aims of clinical explanation, are more characteristically the mark of progress in psychoanalysis than are so-called interface concepts with natural-science disciplines.

Does "Classical Psychoanalytic" Therapy Have a Future?

My remarks have dealt almost exclusively with matters of theory and with an eye to the relevance of psychoanalytic method to theory, considered apart from the treatment situation from which the theory has evolved. Is such a separation possible? And what about the relevance of the therapeutic setting of "classical psychoanalysis"? I would like to touch briefly on an issue that is bound to affect its future.

This has to do with the persistent and unresolved dilemma of whether the long-term leisurely one-to-one classical format of analytic therapy, which has been so tremendously productive of insights into human tendency and personality, is also the most effective setting for *behavior change* and *therapeutic relief*. We really don't know to what extent the interventions, probes, and observations that have yielded such a vast store of explanatory insight have yielded the same gains in therapeutic effectiveness. Psychoanalysis has always had faith in the conjunction of these two aims; we still do not know if this faith is justified. Much as analysts would like to think so, the measure of the power of psychoanalytic theory has surely not been its achievements as a therapy in its "classical" mold. Even the basic assumption of psychoanalytic therapy that it is the shared insights by therapist and patient that produce therapeutic change is by no means solidly established. Freud chose not to tamper with the observational context of "classical psychoanalysis," possibly because of the incomparable investigative opportunity it offered; he looked with distrust on all attempts to manipulate the psychoanalytic situation for purposes of therapeutic advantage alone.

It is with this problem in mind that the challenges from behavior therapy, other humanistic therapies, and socially minded psychiatry must be faced. We hear much from these quarters about the "outdatedness" of psychoanalysis as a therapy, its eliteness and impracticality, even callousness in the face of pressing issues of social change and misery, and the uncertain outcomes of the one-to-one therapeutic context. From such considerations of *therapeutic* economy and effectiveness, it has not been uncommon for critics to imply, if not actually to proclaim, that therefore the substantive psychoanalytic principles themselves on understanding directionality in behavior and the methods and guidelines of its probes into such directionality, are inadequate at best or downright wrong.

If the classical psychoanalytic treatment situation is founded on dubious grounds of practicality and shaky evidence of therapeutic success, how to justify it? I believe we ought to retain the classical psychoanalytic treatment setting, but we must justify its retention mainly as an indispensable resource for the study in depth of personality and pathology, without leaning upon claims of superior therapeutic effectiveness. There is no sensible basis for denying the impracticality of classical analysis, whatever its virtues as therapy, as a routine recommendation for psychotherapy—even for those who can pay 50 dollars an hour, five hours a week. I believe, however, that there are plenty of grounds for claiming that as training experience in self-understanding the classical psychoanalytic procedure is unparalleled for anyone aspiring to a career as a therapist. Furthermore, as a context for the continued study of man the analytic situation, with its unique therapeutic pact, is surely one of the most extraordinary contexts of human observation ever invented, whose potential for generating further insights about directionality is far from exhausted. It used to be thought that the psychological laboratory would be the testing ground of insights gained in the consulting room. This is in my opinion a failed hope, and I think we are beginning to realize that the analytic *situation* is itself a kind of "laboratory," not, to be sure, for manipulative experiment of the standard kind, but for controlled naturalistic observation that is difficult to match in other observational contexts.

Thus, other therapies may be quicker and even more effective in getting a person through life's tasks and the relief of symptoms. Yet it would be a sad loss if the objective of understanding human intentionality and in depth could not avail itself of the intensive, long-term probe of an individual life which is made possible by the classical context of the psychoanalytic treatment situation. This setting has been a lifeline for the development of psychoanalytic theory; the theory that has emerged from it has in turn been a nourishing artery for the humanistic disciplines. A way of resolving the dilemma, therefore, is to look upon the future of classical psychoanalytic therapy as a limited and restricted enterprise, justified mainly for its importance in the *training of therapists* and as a *research context*; its justification would be primarily educative and investigative. Support for it, therefore, must be sought not in the usual fashion of a patient paying his doctor for services rendered, but from public and private foundations—resources dedicated to investigative and educative goals of scholarship.

If these are the ultimately important rewards for the psychoanalyst-researcher, he owes it to the patient (and his own conscience) to have a rationally confident belief that, for the patients he engages in such a long-term commitment, there is a better than fair chance of therapeutic benefit as well. It seems to me vitally important, therefore, for the psychoanalytic community to initiate efforts, involving the coordinated resources of psychoanalytic institutes over the United States, to see what kinds of people are especially likely to profit from the "classical" procedure and analytic setting—not compared with other therapies, but simply by the yardstick of criteria of success in psychoanalysis. The routine recommendation of analysis for nonpsychotic applicants who are able to afford it may have been justified earlier, when "classical psychoanalysis" was the only psychotherapy; in the present, when alternatives are available, even psychoanalytically oriented ones, it is irresponsible.

It is worthwhile to ask, in closing, what favors the psychoanalytic perspective to personality in this period when, as never before, other competing orientations have thrown a cold glare of disapproval upon its gaps, dilemmas, imperfections, and rigidities. Why psychoanalysis still? Other humanistic orientations have emerged, and the names Rogers, Maslow, Fromm, Heidegger, have gained popularity as "correctives" to the alleged sins of psychoanalysis. Let me affirm at least my own credo. The persisting strength of the line of tradition leading out from Freud is not only as a conceptual structure but as an orientation to self-truth guided by considerations of the human inclination for self-delusion. This general orientation has opened us to a many-faceted inner world of directional aims, conscious and unconscious, dissonant and convergent, which behavior and experience exemplify. This is the saving perspective provided by psychoanalysis which Schafer (1970) calls a "tragic view of man" as against the romantic view which typifies other humanistic ideologies.

In highlighting the dialectic of contrariety which is both stimulus to progress and context of failure, the psychoanalytic viewpoint keys us to the inescapability of conflict, the ineradicable fantasies of early years, the unshakeable ambivalences in human relationships, the terrible power of fixation, repression, regression, and repetition; it also tells us that these are the soil not only of hate, ill health, and failure, but the conditions of love, health, and achievement.

The essence of this outlook, and why calling it the *tragic outlook* is so apt, is that it captures the paradox that one's identity is shaped by the very distorting components one is trying to revise; the *patient* experiences it in his gradual realization that he himself has been the unconscious saboteur of his work and love, owing to guilt, and anxiety, and compulsively re-enacted early themes. For the *analyst,* the tragic perspective is the foundation and safeguard of his objectivity; it accounts for the special quality of his indwelling in the patient's experience and behavior. The indwelling of the analyst is *not* an intimacy of feeling of the kind that describes friendships, but awareness of the emotional and changing atmosphere of his relationships with his patient; as Schafer points out, it is an empathy nurtured and enlarged by the analysis of resistance and crisis and the working through of regressive yearnings.

The sense of the tragic in our humanness which psychoanalysis gives us is not an invitation to pessimism and despair. Pessimism and cynicism are products of a traumatized romanticism. Applied as a therapeutic perspective, the psychoanalytic probe is a goad to shed apathy and accept responsibility for one's one and only life, but with a strengthened sense of reality and with less frequent recourse to the anodynes of self-delusion. Its objective is an intensified sense of options and responsibility—not happiness, not adjustment, not a delusional psychedelic high, but a sense of self-rule and a rationale for it, and an anchoring within a sense of linear, irreversible time and future.

The vitality of this perspective to man and its orientation to explanation are well worth the continued commitment of the psychoanalytic psychologist to the future of psychoanalysis. They augur well, I think, for a distinctive psychoanalytic identity in a science of psychology.

CHAPTER 2

Two Theories or One?

PSYCHOANALYSIS IS UNIQUE, I believe, among psychological disciplines in containing within itself two kinds of theory, one clinical, and one metapsychological; or, as Rapaport has expressed this distinction, the "clinical principles" and the "general psychological theory." The distinction is exemplified in Chapter Seven of Freud's *The Interpretation of Dreams,* where his explanations are on a level entirely different from that of the first six chapters of the same book. I am referring to Freud's attempt to discuss the mental apparatus in terms of a quasi-thermodynamic energic system. In moving to that level Freud believed, and he is echoed by most contemporary psychoanalytic theorists, that he was on the most fundamental level of explanation.

When we follow this tradition we leave behind the particulars of the clinical situation and dwell in the realm of a hypothesized drive quantity. We say how the phenomena we are explaining show this or that vicissitude of "drive energy" in a state of "fusion," "diffusion," or "neutralization" (Hartmann's addition), and that traces have been invested with, or cathected with, this hypothetical energic quantity.

Theorizers in this metapsychological vein also assume that the activity of wish and psychosexuality is essentially economic, i.e., a process aiming at the reduction of drive tension. Rapaport (1951) worked this out in a series of conceptual models based on the economic point of view.

Psychoanalysts have tended to take their "clinical" concepts for granted, and to think of metapsychology as the basic theory. That is, they assume that the "clinical concepts" are those by which they actually work, by which they function as therapists; and they tend to think of metapsychology as *the theory* that explains those clinical concepts. To be sure, we also hear metapsychological theorists complain that many analysts are ignorant of metapsychology, that they resist theorizing, or have an antipathy to it, ascribing this aversion to the atheoretical bent of practitioners. I think what is actually the case is that many analysts resist metapsychological theorizing as unclinical, or impractical, while they unquestioningly accept clinical concepts as if they were actual, observed phenomena, while they are, in fact, themselves theory.

Those practitioners who resist metapsychological theory seem sometimes to be saying that clinical concepts, being closer to the psychoanalytical situation, are *less* theoretical, more descriptive of observed phenomena. This seems to me a grievous misconception, and harmful to the future growth of psychoanalysis. Clinical concepts are as abstract, and as theoretical, as metapsychology, and just as open to modification. They do have one point of distinction: They are closer to the activities of clinical observation and to the focus of the analyst's intentions; clinical concepts are, hopefully, more responsive to pressures imposed by data and hence potentially more capable of systematic modification. Moreover, being speculations about man's behavior and experience, the clinical concepts constitute a *general* theory of behavior, no less than metapsychology. More on this later.

Now it should give us pause to be told that metapsychology as exemplified in Chapter Seven is the most basic theory of psychoanalysis, for it is surely not the part of psychoanalysis that stimulated, excited, and revolutionized twentieth-century culture. It was the so-called "clinical" part of the enterprise which sparked the revolution. Psychoanalysis as a scientific system appealed to many people, including those outside psychology, because of its elegance and beauty in accounting for behavior. Relatively few simple principles enabled us to see meanings in the most varied and apparently incomprehensible or senseless behaviors, such as dreams, jokes, mistakes, and symptoms. Yet, as analysts came to formulate their ideas systematically, they abandoned this level and assumed the aims and mannerisms of natural scientists talking about energies, forces, cathexes, systems, layers, mechanisms, and physical analogies, rather than meanings. Thus, today, psychoanalysis presents itself in two guises: the psychology in terms of which Freud interpreted dreams and symptoms and slips of the tongue—the distinctive meanings that behaviors acquire when interpreted in terms of sexual and aggressive wishes, conscious and unconscious events, displacement of aims, transference, unconscious fantasy, and related principles; and on the other hand a theory—the theory of metapsychology—which explains that clinical theory. This is the only scientific specialty I know of with such a pretention. How did this come about? What are the implications of such a dichotomy? In what alternative directions might this divided commitment lead the psychoanalytic enterprise? I believe the issues involved are of crucial importance, affecting even how we conceive the training offered in our institutes.

The existence of two theories—the two cultures of psychoanalysis—is, I believe, a historical aberration traceable to Freud's philosophy of science. Freud's philosophy assumed: (1) that concepts of purposefulness and meaning are unacceptable as terms of *scientific* explanation; (2) that an acceptable *explanation* must be purged of teleological implications; (3) that regularities described with purposivistic concepts will ultimately be explainable through the use of purely psychological models, which disclose the causes of which the purposive principle is simply a descriptive expression.

When Freud made his first discoveries—and the germinal one was that unconscious wishes have a determining effect on behavior and in the formation of symptoms—his positivistic bent and training compelled him to make adjustments in the neurological models of his time so that they might encompass in impersonal causal terms the observations he was making clinically. What Freud was doing was to ask (very much in the manner of a contemporary neuropsychologist like Hebb), if there are phenomena like repression and defense, *how* do they occur? What is their mechanism? At this stage of Freud's thinking there was no issue of an independently causative psychic energy; he was thoroughly convinced that these phenomena could be specified in the nonpurposivistic terms of a neurophysiological structure.

There is no occasion for surprise in this. Freud was brought up in the by now well-documented tradition of the Brücke-Meynert scientific value system, which held it as axiomatic that no phenomenon was to be considered "explained" except in physical-chemical terms, "neurophysiological" being within this classification (Jones, 1953; Erikson, 1955; Holt, 1965). There is little reason to believe that Freud disputed this. For him, as for many of our contemporaries, to explain something meant to know *how* it worked. For Freud this meant (and he never wavered in this conception) that a "how" theory ought to be, or must eventually be, neurophysiologically grounded. He tried so to ground it, as we know, in the "Project for a Scientific Psychology" (1895).

But we also know that Freud discarded this project, did not, in fact, even publish it. He was clearly dissatisfied with it, though, I must emphasize, not with its *objective.* I find no reason to believe that Freud ever gave up the idea that neurophysiological modelizing was itself a good thing; he only believed that he didn't have the *right* model. Ernest Jones, after studying the early "Project," said that were Freud alive today, he would be quite sympathetic to cybernetic and information-processing models.[1] Freud might possibly have drastically revised, in favor of such models, the current so-called "structural" conceptions of ego, id, and superego which have features both of models of system operation and simple classification of functions. But despite his orientation, Freud shelved the "Project" model, for to resolve his dissatisfactions with it would have engaged his efforts at the price of ignoring the torrent of clinical discoveries unfolding to his view. The freshness and novelty of the grades of meaningfulness that Freud perceived seemed ever so much more interesting to him than attempts at squeezing them into an obviously grudging neurology.

"I have no inclination at all," he wrote, "to keep the domain of the psychological floating, as it were, in the air without any organic foundation. But I have no knowledge, neither theoretically nor therapeutically, beyond that conviction so that I have to conduct myself as if

[1] *Editors' note.* All Jones (1953) seems actually to have said is the following: "In the last half century since then that hope [that the terminology of chemistry and physics could be extended to psychology] seems to have remained fairly dormant, but of late it has revived under the stimulus of the new work being carried out in the field called cybernetics. It would be interesting to attempt a correlation between Freud's early attempt and the modern outlook" (pp. 369-370).

"It does not pertain to a biography, but I would throw out the suggestion that an interesting study could be made of a comparison and contrast of Freud's sketch of cerebral physiology sixty years ago, one he discarded as worthless, with the recent electronic theories of cerebral functioning as expounded by Hebb, Lashley, Penfield and Rasmussen, Wisdom, Wiener, Young, and others" (p. 393).

I had only the psychological before me" (quoted by Jones, 1953, p. 395).

Yet the issue of explaining clinical phenomena in terms of an impersonal mechanism remained an important one for Freud, as it has for the metapsychologists who followed him. Freud needed a "how-does-it-work" theory. Jones writes:

> The language of physics and cerebral physiology in the "Project" was Freud's natural one, to which he in great part adhered later even when he was dealing with purely psychological problems.... To wander away from it and embark on the perilous seas of the world of emotions, where all was unknown and where what was invisible was of far greater consequence than the little that was visible, must have cost him dear.... we may regard the feverish writing of the "Project" as a last desperate effort to cling to the safety of cerebral anatomy. If only the mind could be described in terms of neurons, their processes and synapses! How fond the thought must have been to him [pp. 383-384].

For Freud, then, positivist and determinist that he was, the mechanism of matter was all-important for understanding. But what to do in the face of an obviously inadequate neurology? In a characteristically grand manner, he developed a solution that has come to us as the famous Chapter Seven of *The Interpretation of Dreams* (1900). It was Freud's positivistic intent to develop a conception of "how" freed of the shackles of an inadequate neurology. The explanatory language was a new one. It was designed to tell, in impersonal terms, how the mind functioned, and to tell it without employing the language of purpose, as the purposes were the phenomena that were to be explained. This was the birth of the so-called economic point of view. Its terms were different from the neurophysiological terms of the "Project" model, but its intent was the same—to provide a nonteleological, causal account of the phenomena of purposefulness as these revealed themselves in the psychoanalytic situation.

Thus, the economic point of view was Freud's substitute for the neurophysiological model of the "Project." It is part of the general outlook of materialism, which assumed that phenomena are to be understood, and ultimately explained, in terms of their physical-chemical nature.

Contemporary psychoanalysts are inclined to dismiss Freud's neurological model in the "Project for a Scientific Psychology" as a temporary aberration, a passing indulgence in the same category as his views on lay analysis—an interesting curiosity, isolated in significance. They do not, I believe, sufficiently realize the extent to which Freud's philosophy of science, which motivated the "Project," persisted throughout his lifetime, the extent to which it determined what we call metapsychology, and the fact that the economic point of view is simply a veiled extension of that physiologizing effort.

Freud's philosophy of science implies a stand on the mind-body problem: that mentalistic concepts are temporary expedients, to be ultimately reduced to the terms of physiological mechanism. For Freud, teleology was anathema. He felt that descriptive concepts formulated in terms of purpose had no status as explanations of behavior. Hence his quantitative concepts of metapsychology with their impersonal, nonpurposivistic language. He replaced *neurons* with *instinct, excitation* with *cathexis*. He kept the impersonal terms of energy, tension, and discharge. In short, he constructed a theory of mechanism, of how the "apparatus" works. Moreover, the model in Chapter Seven of *The Interpretation of Dreams* is programmatically similar to the physiological model he discarded. It is a strikingly creative model, on the one hand spanning the "purely psychological," and on the other the to-be-hoped-for but not yet available neurophysiological understructure. This is a peculiar form of brinksmanship, you might say, a primitive kind of what Rubinstein (1967) calls a protoneurophysiological model, in the sense of pointing toward as yet unknown neurological processes as well as to psychological events.

Dissatisfaction with psychoanalytic theory usually centers on Freud's "metapsychology." Some of its critics have no objection to the *principle* of converting the terms of clinical observation into the terms of impersonal processes. Their arguments, rather, tend to demonstrate that Freud's veiled neurophysiology is either implausible or inefficient (e.g., Holt, 1967). In short, the objections are to the particulars of the solutions.

Much of this dissatisfaction is guided by popular canons of what an explanatory theory *ought* to be, and by the contemporary disposition—naturally congenial to *medical* psychoanalytic researchers—to use neurophysiological anchorages (either of the "dry" circuitry kind or of the "wet" chemical kind) for explaining the mentalistically stated phenomena of psychoanalytic observation. Other critics of the "metapsychology" prefer cybernetic or informational models for translation into impersonal terms (e.g., Peterfreund, 1971). The central inadequacy of Freud's model is deemed to be its assumption of psychic energy; it is held that if this conception were given up, we would be in a better theoretical position—not, mind you, necessarily to get a better *clinical* theory, but a better theory to *explain* a clinical theory. Without denying or questioning Freud's outlook, all of these critics are of a mind not to relinquish the metapsychological effort, but to replace the metapsychological model.

My own objection to the thermodynamic model of psychoanalysis, as well as the contemporary counterparts vying to replace it, is not their inherent implausibility; more to the point is that they are simply *irrelevant* to the clinical psychoanalytic enterprise. I believe it is possible to show serious incompatibilities between Freud's metapsychology and the interpretations of meaning and significance which constituted Freud's major clinical principles. The logical links between the two were never easy for Freud himself to draw. To take one example: in *Three Essays on the Theory of Sexuality* (Freud, 1905b) there is a long and quite obsessive rumination over whether the *quantitative* approach to sexuality is sufficient to cover the facts. He never could quite resolve the issue of viewing sexuality as a matter of increases and decreases of libido. Indeed, Freud's drive-reduction model itself (into which Rapaport [1951] tried to encompass all psychoanalytic conceptions) is more appropriate to a rat than to a human being, and is as congenial to violently antipsychoanalytical theories as to Freud's metapsychological ones. This example is particularly fitting because the favorite target of many objections to psychoanalysis itself is precisely this metapsychological assumption of tension reduction. That a drive seeks its own gratification is a banality; it is part of the definition of drive. To say that drive-instigated behavior reduces tension is not (as Holt [1965] rightly points out) necessarily a representation of the clinical phenomena of psychosexuality or motivation; it is not an inevitable deduction from clinically observed meanings of interpersonal relations. Thus, objections to psychoanalysis that emphasize the inadequacy of drive-reduction models are noisy distractions from the more fundamental, more constructive consideration of whether there is any validity, in the first place, in this conception of object relations as drives.

The essential *clinical* propositions concerning motivation have nothing to do with reducing a hypothetical tension; they are inferences of *directional* gradients in behavior, and of the *object relations* involved in these directions. They describe relationships needed and sought out, consciously and unconsciously, and how they are fulfilled through real and conceptual encounters, symbol, and action. The key factors, then, in the psychoanalytic clinical view of motivation are relational requirements, encounters, crises, dilemmas, resolutions, and achievements—not a hypothetical "tension" reduction (Apfelbaum, 1965).

Another example of incompatibility between metapsychology and clinical theory, and of its irrelevance to clinical conceptions, is the pleasure principle, or one of its alternate versions, the constancy principle—the principle that action and experience are directed by the requirement of keeping cerebral excitation constant. The pleasure principle is, strictly speaking, a physiological concept, for it is not the personal experience of pleasure that the term defines. Though Freud put forward this principle to explain mental events, the "mind" to which it refers is, in fact, regarded as a mechanical model. In this case the model is automatically self-regulating, but not, however, self-regulating for the fulfillment of personal aims; that would be an explanation in terms of psychological meaning.

Bear in mind that Freud needed to escape teleological explanation. Therefore, the personal "aims" of the clinical level of theory are translated in the pleasure principle of the economic point of view to mean the reduction of a quantity of excitation to a constant level. This is simply another version of the psychology for neurologists which Freud had supposedly abandoned in the 1895 period.

In short, Freud's metapsychology is not *distinctively* psychoanalytic. Moreover, it reduces human behavior to a conceptual domain which requires a kind of observational datum different from that available in the analytic situation. What neurophysiologist studies his datum by talking to it? Metapsychology throws overboard the fundamental intent of the psychoanalytic enterprise—that of *unlocking meanings*. Terms like cathexis, hypercathexis, bound cathexis are drained of psychological meaning, and inhabit a sphere distant from that of psychoanalytic psychology. The wholly impersonal and quasi-physiological terms of the metapsychology are entirely out of tune with the data of the psychoanalytic situation. This holds not only for Freud's metapsychology but for the neurophysiological, thermodynamic, and informational models that followed it. In Allport's words, "[Such models are] not telling us what behavior is; [they are] simply saying that man behaves *as if* he were something else. . . This is not theorizing; it is analogizing" (1964, p. 32). One may well ask: *Had it not been intertwined with Freud's basic psychology, would metapsychology have survived?*

Thus, metapsychology was not Freud's primary discovery, but an expression of his philosophy of science. It is neither essential to, nor expressive of, the fundamental effort of the psychoanalytic enterprise. It is simply a philosophical stance regarding what is true explanation and what is really "real." Secondly, metapsychology is not cognate to the obtainable data of the psychoanalytic situation. Thirdly—and this is the most critical point—physiological terms cannot substitute for psychoanalytic terms descriptive of the meanings of object relations; for it is these purely psychological considerations, not the physiological ones, which make behavior coherent to the analyst. Even if finer levels of physiological occurrences *were* measurable during the analytic hour, physiological theory would never be primary, for the *personal meanings* of such events—their psychological significance—require so-called mentalistic and teleological terms. I will return to this last point because it applies to any of the models that are being offered to replace Freud's metapsychology.

The "Clinical" Theory of Psychoanalysis

Once we take the position that there is only *one* psychoanalytic theory, not two, we face a more manageable job of systematizing and articulating the theory itself. If, on the contrary, we make a distinction between a general psychoanalytic theory and a clinical one, we imply that because the clinical theory is tied to the psychoanalytic treatment *situation,* it is something less than a general psychological theory. But, if transference accounts for phenomena in the clinical situation, is transference less applicable as a general principle to account for human behavior? Is the concept of an Oedipus conflict less a part of a general theory of psychology?

Once we reject this distinction, we come to realize that the terms of the clinical theory are just as abstract as the terms of metapsychology, and that they are remote, in varying degrees, from the observational process that governs the patient-analyst exchange.

The possibilities of observation are bounded by the objectives of the analytic situation, which is determined by the therapeutic pact and its standard conditions. While setting limits, these conditions encourage the emergence of phenomena that few experimental situations can rival, or dare to duplicate, because of ethical considerations. The therapeutic commitment, the relaxed yet therapeutic atmosphere, the interested yet detached analyst—to these elements of the situation we owe the emergence of resistance phenomena, varieties of defense, preoccupying unconscious fantasies, and transference.

A distinction that is likely to be more useful to the analyst than that between clinical and metapsychological theory is the distinction between experiential and functional concepts, i.e., between intraphenomenological and extraphenomenological concepts. The basic data of a psychoanalytic hour are the analyst's inferences about the analysand's experiences, including those the analysand may not be aware of having. These include inferences about (1) how the analysand sees himself, (2) how the analysand sees the analyst, (3) how the analysand sees the situation he shares with the analyst. The analyst's own self-perceptions are also involved. In general, the experiences the analyst attributes to the patient, whether the patient is or is not aware of them, are in the category of experiential, or intraphenomenological, concepts. For instance, the analyst will assume that the patient's unconscious fantasy is his basic way of experiencing himself and others. It is from his own assumptions about the patient's fantasy that the analyst will see the meaning of the patient's action and testimony.

Concepts like projection, introjection, and repression, which point to something in the mind of the patient which the patient does not experience but is part of his reality, are functional or extraphenomenological concepts. These are of the class of concepts which are meant to account for, or in some way to illuminate or elucidate, those experiences of the patient which are not accessible directly. Thus an analyst plunges into phenomenology, but goes beyond it to generalizations that connect accessible and inaccessible levels of experience. These generalizations almost always have to do with purpose, function, accomplishment. The analyst's extraphenomenological concepts are meant to illuminate, in these terms of purpose, function, and accomplishments, the *significance* of the experiences he infers and the actions he observes—not simply the existential meanings which are based on conscious experience, but also the meanings or significance of inferred unconscious fantasies.

The phenomenological concepts, the logic of the analyst's inferences, and the extraphenomenological concepts of function, purpose, and meaning of experience and behavior make up psychoanalytic theory. The upshot of this—and my major theme— is that *assessments of the importance of psychoanalytic concepts must be based more intimately upon systematic efforts to link these concepts to the observational data of the psychoanalytic situation, and upon the responsiveness of these concepts to modification by observation.* The logic and dependability of inferences from phenomenology crucially influence the validity of the extraphenomenological concepts. Unless those inferences are valid, the concepts refer to witches and unicorns. My second point is that in order to effect systematic and responsible changes in the theory, we must have a much more disciplined consideration of the nature of evidence than has been shown by psychoanalytic theorists since Freud's time.

I mention these distinctions, some of which may seem minute, mainly because I believe that the strategy of inference from data to lawfulness is a matter of crucial importance for the future development of psychoanalysis. I think we will find that metapsychological concepts as we generally know them—e.g., energy concepts—will be of little help in this regard because they are impervious to the type of data obtainable from the psychoanalyst's hour. However, the clinical concepts can and will change in systematic fashion.

I turn now to some of the characteristics which distinguish the clinical theory of psychoanalysis from other theories. I think we must go back to fundamentals, distressingly elemental ones—distressing because after some 60 years of development, the theoretical paradigm (Kuhn, 1962) by which we operate in the psychoanalytic situation still remains unclear. There is no escaping this journey backwards; the psychoanalytic journals reveal that a tremendous amount of energy is being wasted on theoretical questions that are fruitless for the psychoanalytic clinical situation.

Psychoanalysis, first of all, attempts to specify coherences in behavior in terms of purpose, not only conscious intention but also that arising out of the dynamics of aborted wish, conflict, defense, anxiety, guilt, and unconscious fantasy. When an analyst sees a pattern of behavior functioning as a "defense," for example, he is stating the *significance* of a pattern of behavior; he is making a statement about its purpose or intention. The coherences to which an analyst becomes sensitized are unique in their distinctive concern with purpose—aims frustrated, conflicted, aborted, regressed, defended against. This discovery of intention is the primary objective of the analyst in the psychoanalytic situation, and the primary function of his extra-phenomenological concepts of meaningfulness.

Traditionally, such discovery has been the province of the novelist, or of the great epistemological philosophers, who employed the methods of introspection. And it is still to these sources, more than to biology and physiology, that we are beholden for our hypotheses concerning the meaning of man's behavior. It is not a minor curiosity that the power of psychoanalysis for illuminating unconscious intentionality has been an enormously vitalizing force in contemporary literature, graphic arts, and drama. The reason is that art is itself a process of creating meaning, a contemplation on the state of man. The artist's concern complements the analyst's systematic concern with the same objectives.

This meaning-seeking orientation and the conceptual tools he uses for detecting purposeful dispositions enable the analyst to see regularities different from those other psychologists generally see when they look at the same behavior. I used to be puzzled by the quite common fact that an analyst can be wise in the goings-on of his consulting room and at the same time remain innocent, and even ignorant, of the details of perception, learning, and the other formal areas that constitute the Ph.D's basic academic psychology. The reverse is, of course, just as common, perhaps more so. How is this possible? How can the psychoanalyst be a poor psychologist in one sense and a wise one in another? I think for an answer one must look to the unique level of coherence he is tuned in on when he observes people's behavior. I have been impressed that when you confront the same wise clinician with the design or the data of a learning experiment, he is, in his innocence, likely to raise a surprisingly, and soberingly, sophisticated cluster of questions, all around *why* the subject is learning what he is, *why* he might be set to learn one thing rather than another—in short, hunches about the *why,* the *reasons* for his behavior, often completely ignored in the psychologist's preoccupation with the *what,* and *how,* the proximal causes of behavior. Similarly, the analyst's questions about perception and memory are likely to gravitate toward the significance or functions of the behavior shown, to its motivational and symbolic meanings. If an experimental psychophysicist tells us that three-dimensionality is a primary perceptual event, the analyst will not evince much interest. But he might be interested if you said that through the workings of this three-dimensional perception one can discern how a person symbolizes.

When psychology left philosophy to become "experimental," the "why" of behavior lost its status as the psychologists' primary objective. Problems of meaning and significance had been relegated to philosophy by the mainstream of experimental psychology. It was the genius of Freud that brought them back squarely into the psychologists' concern; he developed a taxonomy and a code for deciphering the meanings of personal relationships in their conscious and unconscious aspects. Psychoanalysis imputes meaning to behavior by showing the significance of myth in our lives, those inner phantoms of fantasy which render objects significant, and which lead us to establish and react to relationships.

The analyst's distal foci, then, to use Brunswik's term, are behavioral coherences that exemplify purpose and significance. The main point of psychoanalytic work is to unlock such meanings. Only in these terms can we appreciate the importance of a concept like transference. In 1912 Freud wrote: "This struggle between the doctor and the patient, between intellect and instinctual life, between understanding and seeking to act, is played out almost exclusively in the phenomena of transference" (p. 108). In the analytic enterprise there are, strictly speaking, no impersonal "stimuli"; there are challenges, crises, relationships, wishes, frustrations, values good and bad, varieties of pleasure and pain.

This fact about the primary focus of the psychoanalyst should determine the objectives of theorizing in psychoanalysis. Let there be no mistake: Psychoanalysts are theorists not on the "how" but on the "why" of behavior. Undeniably, some psychoanalysts are profitably engaged in "how" research; but you may note that they work *outside* the psychoanalytic situation, in the university or medical-school laboratory.

In its clinical task, psychoanalysis uses extraphenomenological conceptions of the dynamics of purpose. They have to do with trends in the development and changes of purpose over the course of a person's life—conceptions of *crisis, conflict, defense,* and *modes of resolution,* which determine the evolution of purposes in his behavior. These concepts include, among others, ego development, psychosexual development, repression, consciousness-unconsciousness, transference, identification, drive, fantasy. All of these concepts are crucial, in different ways, in pointing to units or coherences of behavior that without such concepts would not be noticed. They are aids to the psychologist's perception. None of them has much to do with an account of "how," or mechanisms. This is so even with the concept of anxiety—which is regarded clinically as a reaction to specifiable conditions having the significance of a type of danger or threat. We also find it useful, even indispensable, to invoke repression. But a model of the mechanism of repression is not crucial to the analyst's objectives; neither is it an issue to which he is equipped to contribute—unless he leaves the psychoanalytic situation.

A second focus of the psychoanalytic enterprise—perhaps only another way of stating the first, but with a different emphasis—is that psychoanalysis is a psychology of the *meanings and syntheses arising out of crises in an individual's lifetime.* Freud's central contribution was not only the discovery of sexual and aggressive determinants of behavior, though these were fundamental; it was also the understanding of behavior as *syntheses* which evolve from *conflict,* that is, of behavior as modes of *resolution of conflict.* This was the basic wisdom of the principle of overdetermination. That principle was not an escape hatch of weaseling explanation. It provided a new orientation for old questions. For example: If man is conceived of sexual and aggressive impulses, how, then, are the two creatively synthesized into the phenomenon of, say, friendship? If a man is both self-seeking and needful of others, how do we have a phenomenon like altruism? What are the forces that eventuate in taboos such as incest?

It was from Freud's consideration of the roots of conflict in the actual and fantasied involvements of patients that he developed his conceptions of motivated meanings of behavior. He emphasized not only the *terms* of conflict but their forms of evolution and of synthesis. He specified critical periods in libidinal development, and the qualities of thought in which these were expressed, calling them primary and secondary processes. He saw in behavior a descriptive language of symbol, wishful attainment, and defense.

The core, then, of the clinical psychoanalytic enterprise is in the meanings that emerge from the dialectics of the directed forces to which a person is subject; that is, the forces resulting in dilemma and conflict and the opposing conditions from which evolve patterns of behavior which are viewed as ego syntheses. Few other theories talk in these terms. Psychoanalysis looks upon human development in terms of milestones and of solutions occurring in a context of given limits. Again, psychoanalysis is, in this respect, most related not to biology but to the aims of the dramatist and novelist, for it parallels the intentions of dramatic structure and reflects the basic appeal of drama.

There *are* other psychologies of meaning and of development (e.g., Rogers, 1947); for example, monistic ego conceptions that start from the proposition that ego development occurs because man strives for mastery, or competence, or self-actualization. But these theories say little more than that ego development does occur. They state too little to be accounted substantial theories because they tend to leave out precisely the vital factors of the dialectics of conflict and resolution of crises. In contrast, psychoanalytic theory, in its clinical concepts, provides for the facts of development of interpersonal patterns through the dynamics of encounter, conflict, impasse, and resolution. In this respect, too, psychoanalysis is distinguished from various existential viewpoints, which consist of descriptions, often detailed and valuable, of the actual modes of experience of an individual, as determined by his anxiety. But such psychologies also lack dynamics; they lack a conception of the evolution of a person's life, with its interlacing of conflicting aims, both conscious and unconscious; they lack the attempt to view these experiences in the perspective of solutions. They have no provision for showing the polarities and gradients involved in developmental resolutions that produce different self-conceptions. They are simply a compilation of interesting phenomenologies.

The key, then, to the profundity of Freud's insights is in the effort to look at life as a problem-solving venture, a constant adjudication of incompatible polarities; behavior patterns are seen as syntheses of opposing tendencies, actual or fantasied, symptoms as solutions carried to pathological extremes.

Psychoanalytic Explanation

It is sometimes held that psychoanalysis is a biological science. However, the program psychoanalysis actually follows in the psychoanalytic *situation* consists of explaining behavior through meanings the analyst reads from the patient's inferred experiences; in terms of the functional capacities of the human system through which the meanings are realized. *It is through this program that psychoanalysis has achieved its triumphs of understanding.*

Psychoanalysis is, therefore, in the class of theories that concern themselves with the "why" of behavior, that try to state reasons rather than causes, that try to say that a behavior has a certain meaning, derived from the *history* of this meaning in the person's life, that try to speak of the psychical *functions* through which the meaning is expressed (e.g., Peters, 1960). Thus, to say that a wish is repressed explains a behavior without specifying *how* repression is accomplished. Do function statements of this type qualify as terms of explanation?

There are three points I want to make in this connection: (1) that an intention and a function are as directly observable, and as specifiable, as a neurological discharge, and in that sense are just as "real"; (2) that a statement of function or intention is as adequate a basis for explanation as a neurophysiological one; (3) that meaning and purpose—conscious and unconscious—define *principles* of regularity that are *translatable* to, but not *reducible* to, physiological and neurophysiological specifications. This last point deserved special emphasis. It is not simply that the psychoanalytic situation cannot provide the data for a physiological conception of psychoanalytic facts. It seems to me that no such data could ever substitute for the constructs of personal meaning which constitute psychoanalytic psychology, which is of an entirely different level of perceived order, involving different units of analysis. These cannot be known from, or deduced from, principles of physics and chemistry, or from mechanical, physiological, or cathectic models. Therefore it is of secondary, not primary, importance for psychoanalysts to concern themselves with translations to physiological models of explanation.

Yet one still hears that a physiological explanation is more real, more tangible, more basic than so-called psychological statements. This lingering notion is based upon "an epistemological fallacy that has had a paralyzing effect upon American psychological thinking ever since Watson popularized it" and has infiltrated the efforts of American psychoanalytic research to develop explanatory concepts. "This is the widespread belief that our perceptions of 'physical' situations and objects are somehow in better epistemological status than our perceptions of other people's psychological situations and objects; that seeing a cat's situation as frustrating is less secure *in epistemological principle* than seeing his physical environment as made of wood or glass" (Adams, 1954, p. 71).

It would help, I think, if we talked less about "psychological" and "physiological" levels and more about designatable *event units* or *coherences.* Then we come to realize that an intention is just as real as a physical property, and that an intention can be as directly read from behavior as a neurological discharge; moreover, it is in fact a level of coherence that *cannot* be inferred from the neurological data. In this view, a unit of reality is any *perceived and confirmable coherence;* this would include temporal as well as spatial coherences.

An array of events becomes coherent (1) when a leading element, an organizing principle of the array, can be specified, and (2) when the clues or carriers of this leading element—its mediation—can also be specified. In this way, it is just as possible to perceive intentions that are stable, in respect to the clues that specify these intentions, as it is to perceive a chair, in respect to the clues that specify a chair.

Indeed, around this capability there has arisen an entirely new field of perceptual psychology, which includes the study of causal perceptions (Michotte, 1963), affects, and intentions (Baldwin, 1967; Heider, 1958). Hochberg (1964) even speaks of a "grammar of intention." When an analyst perceives a motive in an array of disparate behaviors he is defining a coherence in the same class as these perceptions. A transference reaction is a coherence produced by an active wish or fantasy. It is specifiable from a patient's communications to the analyst and in the analyst's sense of his relationship with the patient. When we conclude that a patient "isolates" affect from idea because of anxiety, we are doing so from an integration of clues; we are perceiving patterns specifiable by these clues and these coherences we call "isolation." Thus realness is a property given partly by the perceptual referent of the coherence; the concept can then be used in stating the "reason" for the event.

We make an occurrence reasonable by explaining it. In this sense the coherence that we call a "chair" is actually *less* real for the microphysicist than is its atomic structure, for "chair" as an object to sit on has little pertinence to the physicist's domain of variables. Thus the same thing or comprehensive entity, as Polanyi calls it, can have different orders of reality, depending upon the focus, or the clue domain, we are looking *from*; this focus defines background and foreground in the act of looking.

Moreover, statements about meaning, purpose, and function—which comprise the bulk of terms used in psychoanalytic psychology—are often not easily commensurate with what is currently known about human physiology. But having no current neurophysiological explanation does not make these statements less "real" or less valuable in accounting for behavior. *We should be wary of defensiveness on this score.* Some psychologists may remember a time when the complete and final refutation of Thorndike's law of effect was the remark that the law postulated a retroactive effect of a later state of affairs upon an earlier one, and that this was physiologically impossible. Now that the principle of feedback and servomechanisms is available, we get along quite comfortably with the law of effect without becoming liable to the horrid accusation of vitalism; we need only call it "homeostasis."

The important conclusion from these considerations is that different varieties of coherence and levels of meaning reside in the same arrays of events. This fact rests on an important property of the process by which coherence is known and recognized, a property that clarifies the controversy over whether physiological or psychological explanations are more basic. Here I find Polanyi's (1965a, 1965b, 1966) description of the process by which coherence is perceived to be the most clarifying and indispensable guideline to a solution that I have as yet encountered.

Polanyi says that any perceived entity is a *focus,* derived from the clues which signify that focus. Any act of knowing proceeds from incidental awareness of the clues to focal awareness of the leading element of the entity. (Cf. Heider's [1926-1959] and Brunswik's [1956] distinction between distal and proximal.) When we look at an event as a clue it has a different meaning from when we look at it as a focus.

When employed as a focus, it no longer has a clue function; it now takes on a different level of meaning. That which we are aware of focally and aware of as incidental to the focus are logically disjunctive. Though the same *realm* of events is involved, the structured *order* of events, and therefore their meaning, becomes altogether different.

An important implication of this disjunction of levels of knowing—the clue versus the focal character of the event—is that different coherences and meanings are not reducible one to the other. Polanyi's example of a game of chess is much to the point. The strategies of chess cannot be accounted for in terms of the *rules* of chess; they refer to regulating principles which control the "boundaries" or the limits of applicability of the rules. The *rules* of chess permit a large number of such strategies; they leave open an indeterminate number of options of play, all of which *conform* to, but are not explainable by, the rules. These options are the boundary conditions of the game. The rules do not control these boundaries. The strategies controlling the applicability of the rules refer to different principles of order. As Polanyi puts it,

> Any particular application of the rules requires that these circumstances be fixed by some agency not under the control of that principle. The conduct of a game of chess is an entity controlled by a strategist and the strategem relies on the observance of the rules of chess. This relation does not hold in reverse, for the rules of chess leave open an infinite range of strategems. Rules of chess are therefore meaningless in themselves and their meaning lies in serving *jointly* the performance of a strategem.[2]

We may speak of function rules, machine rules, and physical-chemical rules in a hierarchy of principles. If we define the function of a watch we speak on a different level from when we define its mechanism, an arrangement that has a spring and a balance. However, we now have watches without springs and balances. There remains as its definition only the purpose of the watch (Polanyi, 1966). This does not mean that the watch does not operate according to the laws of mechanics or of physics. It means only that the attributed meaning of "watch" in terms of its function is *independently specifiable*.

[2] *Editors' note.* We have been unable to locate the source of this quotation.

In the same way, we may say that the machine aspect of the watch may operate in accord with the principles of physics and chemistry, but it cannot be accounted for by them. "... the operational principles of a watch ... define its construction and working, ... [but] these principles ... cannot be defined by the laws of inanimate nature. For no part of a watch is formed by the natural equilibration of matter. Physics and chemistry cannot reveal the practical principles embodied in a machine" (Polanyi, 1965a, pp. 134-135). The operational principle defining the structure of the machine is of a different level from the laws of physics and chemistry. The material of the machine is under the control of two principles, operational, and physics and chemistry. The machine would not function *except* for the laws of physics and chemistry, but this principle does not hold in reverse. Again, to quote Polanyi: "Pulverize a machine and its fragments will continue to obey the laws of physics and chemistry. The wrecking of the operational structure does not affect these laws, for they apply to the material of the machine in itself even when split into isolated bits of matter" (1965a, pp. 135-136). And so there is an upper comprehensive level which embodies the operational principles of the system, and a lower one controlled by the laws of physics and chemistry.

Mental versus Physiological Explanation

What holds for the ordering principles of a machine in relation to the laws of physics holds for the psychoanalytic principles of purpose, function, and significance in relation to the physiology of the organism.

Now we come to the key dilemma in current efforts to develop psychoanalytic theory, two conceptions of its task of explanation: whether to develop a theory of the mental apparatus through quasi-thermodynamic principles (including contemporary, more plausible physical analogies in this choice) or to confine theoretical effort to the enterprise of deciphering meanings, i.e., to remain on the level on which the discoveries themselves were formulated.

The view of a growing number of psychoanalytic theorists, coinciding with a behaviorist mentality that dominates American psychiatry and psychology, is that for true scientific understanding the qualitative statements of meaning and purpose could be, and should be, replaced by quantitative statements expressing physiological lawfulness. Investigatively-minded analysts seem increasingly to feel that their real function as scientists ought to be the pursuit of the physiological principles which underlie the psychologically stated rules of order of the psychoanalytic situation. They are expressing a view which holds that the "mentalistic" statements are merely a reflection of physiological counterparts—an isomorphism—and that the physiological is the more basic domain of data. The view seems even to imply that only by knowing the physiological laws will we get a more advanced psychological theory of purpose. The issue is critical, because preconceptions about what is the "right" kind of theory bias the way in which problems for research are formulated.

The resolution of the dilemma requires a clear-cut stand on the relation of "mind" to "body." What I would like to show, continuing the train of thought developed by Polanyi, is that principles of meaning perceivable in the psychoanalytic situation are on a level which is not deducible from a physiological schema, no matter what the physiological model.

First of all, let me say that on the mind-body relationship there is no issue over whether there is a physiological basis of mind. Of course there is. I am not saying that purpose and meaning are not physiologically implemented. Of course they are. Nor am I saying that a search for a mechanism is an inappropriate ambition for the psychologist. I like to play that game myself. Moreover, I would not underestimate the fact that a valid principle of motivational direction can be a tremendous incentive to the specification of physiological mechanisms. Coherences observed in clinical psychoanalysis have been an undeniable boon to neurophysiological investigation (see Adrian, 1946; Fisher, 1966; Hernández-Peón, 1964; Pribram, 1965).

However, a statement of the meaning of behavior is of a different level of coherence from a statement of physiological laws. There is no questioning that a meaning must be accomplished in a physiological setting, and that the most appropriate model is that of an open system. But, knowing only the physiological rules of operation of a machine or system, and without an observer who recognized its purpose, we shall look in vain for a "purpose" structure in the machine or system. I am not denying that we always operate within the boundaries of physiological "rules." I am saying that in the operation of this physiology an indeterminate number of principles are left unspecified, especially in the case of the human being. These indeterminate principles left open by the physiological laws are not specifiable in terms of the impersonal workings of the system per se. What the psychoanalyst perceives are *strategies* (functions) of the machine as determined by his own attributions of meaning and intention. Since purposes are personal and *relational,* the models appropriate to the search for purpose and intention cannot possibly be stated in terms of impersonal models of stimuli, triggers, physiology, etc.; such models are on the "lower level," while what are needed are models from the "upper comprehensive level."

What we call a "mental" concept is, then, the result of an observer's consciousness applied to the data of physiological events. Again paraphrasing Polanyi, *statements of purpose or meaning and principles of physiological regulation are two mutually exclusive ways of being aware of our bodily activities.* The somatic is to the mind as the clue is to the meaning. To put it another way, what we call "mind" or "mentalistic" consists of the meanings we as observers give to the workings of the body. The purposes or coherences that we read in the actions and experiences of another are actually not *in* the physiological events, any more than a transportation purpose is to be seen *in* the actual workings of an automobile. They are the products of consciousness applied to a domain of clues. The laws of physiology do not include the consciousness that perceives purpose. Therefore detailing the specifics of the machine can never lead to an induction of the purpose *from* the workings of the machine, any more than we can induce that the fox is chasing the rabbit from the facts that the fox's and the rabbit's legs are going in a northerly direction at different speeds.

The day may come when a patient will be able to come into an analytic hour, be fitted with frontal lobe implants, with electrodes on 10 different parts of his body, and have samples of his blood distilled into a processing center—all while he is free-associating. Even if we could solve the rather interesting transference issues these procedures would create, it is questionable whether any of this could ever supplant the specification of purposive organizing principles which are the stock in trade of the psychoanalytic enterprise.

The key point, to repeat, is that purpose principles and physiological principles are two mutually exclusive ways of being aware of our body and the workings of another's body. They require different foci of observation, and the terms in which they are cast reflect their respective foci. We may be able to define the *physiology* of aggressiveness, but the *phenomenon* of aggression is a *meaning* that we attribute to a physiological pattern; it must be *recognized* as aggression as a condition of its specification as a physiological unit. Where aggression begins and where it ends are not given by the pattern itself. Your knowledge that you are observing aggression precedes specification of the beginning and ending of the physiological unit.

If we focused our attention on the patient's bodily workings, thus converting them to *objects* instead of clues, we would lose sight of the patient's "mind." The bodily workings would then lose their value as clues of functions—of the meanings in relation to which they are *clues*. The relation between body and mind is, then, an instance of the relation between what is subsidiary and what is focal in the process of knowing. "A neurophysicist observing the events that take place in the eyes and brain of a seeing man would invariably fail to see in these natural events what the man sees in them" (Polanyi, 1965b, p. 807).

Investigative versus Therapeutic Orientation in the Psychoanalytic Situation

The effort to achieve a more economical psychoanalytic theory has been seriously impeded by the absence of concern for the rules of disciplined inference. When analysts remove the mantle of therapist and don that of researcher they behave in either of two ways. If they move to the laboratory, they naturally take on rigorous standards. If they remain with their observations of the analytic hour, they turn to a casual, impressionistic approach laced with elaborate metapsychological theory. Some analysts foster the impression that their major function is to develop links to metapsychological theory. But metapsychology is *not* an end in itself. The basic enterprise of science is the employment of *perception,* the search for coherences in the tumult of changing appearances. Einstein spoke of his elegantly parsimonious theory of gravitation as *tamed* metaphysics, meaning a theory leavened by knowledge—responsible knowledge. So whether our emphasis is on the perceptual aspect of science, or on the economical encapsulation of the known in the form of simple theories, it must be rooted in criteria of *responsible* knowledge. If we work with the perceptual aspect, we must avoid pseudo perception, e.g., the unicorn concept or the false biological clock, and avoid using concepts as substitutes for reality. If we are theory-making, we must have responsible standards for prescribing changes in the theory. If we use theory as a tool of such perceptual search, it must be supplemented by a discipline of observation and inference.

Here is cause for dismay. During Freud's lifetime, and since, there have been very many modifications and variations in theories, both clinical and metapsychological. Yet is it not astonishing that, except for a few recent faint stirrings (see, e.g., Luborsky, 1964, 1967; Dahl, 1972; Gottschalk and Gleser, 1969), there has not been, since Freud's time, a *single* advance in the investigative or research methodology used by psychoanalysts—not one advance in studying psychoanalytic protocols? We find the same impressionistic reliance-upon-authority type of statements, with only anecdotal reference to case reports. I have stressed that psychoanalytic discoveries are not likely to come from translations attempted through a metapsychology, since metapsychology requires another domain of data. In addition, I do not believe they can come from the continued use of the casual methods of observation that have characterized so-called research in the psychoanalytic setting. My point is that the process of investigative inference in the psychoanalytic community is too leisurely and inefficient, providing no means or standards for checking another person's work. We need quicker determinations of truth, more disciplined bases of restricting generalizations. If our task is to make theory more efficient, it cannot be done by logic alone, nor by relying upon the presumably more precise data of the laboratory. We must go to the source of the immediately *relevant* data—to the psychoanalytic clinical situation itself. This brings us to the issue of the appropriate methods for doing research within the psychoanalytic situation.

Among the sorriest clichés I have heard in psychoanalytic circles are the view that doing therapy *is* research and the related one that treatment *is* experimentation. Some years ago I had the temerity to write that the research process and the therapeutic intent of psychoanalysis are fundamentally incompatible. This view fired up one correspondent, who vehemently asserted that to do therapy is also to do research. Therapy has even been called one of the primary research *methods* (Lustman, 1963). This point of view, I believe, ought to be completely rejected. Therapy is the context from which we obtain the unique data of psychoanalysis. It must, of course, ever remain so, but therapy is not a *research* method. The error is in the failure to perceive the difference of focus between doing therapy and doing research. One source of confusion lies in not distinguishing between the *inference process by which an interpretation is derived,* and the *research strategy* for asserting formal lawfulness from the data. The first—the basis on which an analyst makes an interpretation—is what we might call a substantive problem, which is itself to be investigated. The second refers to the strategies of investigation themselves. The analyst must don a different mantle for each role, therapist or researcher. This is difficult, but it is necessary. A physician using a stethoscope does not pause to assess the reliability and validity of the stethoscope. He accepts its utility. When we use the Rorschach for diagnostic purposes, it is in the capacity of an observing tool, a *clue domain* for a diagnosis. It is something else to make the stethoscope *itself,* or the validity of the Rorschach, the objects of inquiry. Then it is no longer clue or tool, but *object.* The two operations require different approaches, different orientations, different training. The analytic situation produces coherent, perceivable regularities, which need not have any immediate or distant relevance to therapeutic intent, yet which are legitimate for study and may even have basic importance for psychoanalytic theory.

The training for research given in practitioner-oriented psychoanalytic institutes is woefully inadequate. It is not a task to be shunted off to the psychologist. It is a responsibility to be met by any psychoanalyst who aspires to an investigative career in psychoanalysis. The future of psychoanalysis as a systematic guide to investigation is at stake. The allegations that we have to preserve the psychoanalytic situation as a context for data collection, that we have to preserve the free activity of the analyst and the constancies of the psychoanalytic situation, are correct, but these requirements need not be incompatible with systematic research. The pedestrian tasks of methodology with complex multivariate data are the development of techniques of contingency analyses, scaling procedures, sorting, and the like, and the attempt, generally speaking, to specify the content of clues without serious loss of meaning, and these tasks confront all investigation-minded psychoanalysts.

It is wrong to imply that these are onerous or trivial chores. I believe that the discovery potential of such discipline has been shortchanged by analysts. We often hear that in science the statement of a problem or a theory precedes a search for method. This may be an easy pedagogical ploy for textbooks, but it just ain't necessarily so. Sometimes new methodological tools and methodological breakthroughs (which, like the microscope, really come down to providing new opportunities for looking) themselves open up possibilities of perceiving coherences that we had not before envisaged (e.g., the REM technique). Detailed concern with protocol analysis may well reveal regularities that slip through conventional clinical scanning. Even if these newly revealed regularities have no crucial or immediately discernible value for the therapeutic process, they can nevertheless be most pertinent to a basic theoretical issue. I will cite an illustration later. Thus, training in research ought to be considered essential to the analytic curriculum; but in no known psychoanalytic curriculum is there any provision for training in developing strategies for dealing with the unique kind of data obtainable from the psychoanalytic situation.

Therapy, then, is not research. Here I wish to stress that the induction of lawfulness from data obtained in the psychoanalytic situation can be conducted with a systematic rigor comparable to experimentation. Some say that the data of the analytic situation can only generate hypotheses, not "prove" them. But there is no basis in principle for denying that rigorous standards of demonstration can apply to the nonexperimental occurrences of the psychoanalytic situation.

Let us not confuse such clinical investigation with experimenting; I consider experimentation to be incompatible with therapy and objectionable in a therapeutic context. Experimentation is the reasoned control of conditions and the manipulation of alleged causative variables—not an easy thing to do in any case—but precluded in therapy. Experimentation is not the only source of controlled information. Nevertheless it is true that experimental psychology is at present far ahead of clinical psychoanalysis in the development of criteria of responsible knowledge.

The clinical researcher can use the model of the historian or the model of the biologist-naturalist. In either case, he works not by experiment but by demonstration in the manner of a naturalist, in which description is backed up by a method of disclosure, through which the focus becomes apparent and confirmable. (An exception is Gill's [Gill and Paul, manuscript] study of planned interventions.) In short, the researcher's responsibility in his research strategy is to develop ways of specifying the clues of alleged regularities. In the case of the biologist investigating a specimen, the aim is essentially a taxonomy of the structures of the comprehensive entity he is studying. In the case of the historian, a long-term sample is involved. In both cases, a confirmation strategy is called for. In the naturalist method, observations that serve as controls must be provided for; in the historical method, some strategy for developing internal consistency and validation of an inference must be provided for.

A problem that requires consideration is that of the preservation and recovery of the actual data of the analytic situation. Acceptance even of the recording of data has been only partially gained. This is a ludicrous obstacle when you stop to think of it. In no other field is it presumed that raw data can be carried around as part of one's memory, though this is often implied by analysts who—of all people—know how memory can be distorted by motives, including their own. I think that if we take an investigative attitude in psychoanalysis, we cannot ignore the requirement for some means of recording, whether it be sound tape, film, or other devices. At the least, we require notes, to be built in as a standard part of the psychoanalytic situation. As a *standard* condition of the analytic situation, recording procedures need be no more or less incongruous, and no more or less of an influence upon transference, than requiring the patient to lie on a couch.

True, beyond this first stage, the problems of recording and storage could become complex. Many research problems may well not be formulated until *after* the analysis has been terminated. This would require storing all analytic data, which may be impractical.

In general, we can distinguish five classes of investigative approach to phenomena in the analytic setting:

1. *Contingency Studies,* which attempt to discover regularities through a systematic specification of pattern.

2. *Critical Incident Studies,* which attempt to specify the conditions of critical incidents and in particular to link the critical incident to the context of associations.

3. *Construct Generality Studies,* which collect incidences and manifold expressions of such constructs as behavior typologies, cognitive style, fantasy theme, and defensiveness of language.

4. *Inference Testing,* in which deductions from a clinical hypothesis are implemented by accumulating instances of its verification and plausibility.

5. *Manipulation* or *Intervention Studies,* which attempt to predict the effects of such procedures.

All of these investigative approaches overlap in some respects; yet the classification seems to supply workable guidelines. Each of these aims will determine strategies and specific problems of methodology.

I mentioned above some recent stirring toward reducing the gap between theory and evidence by methodological innovation. An excellent paradigm applicable to many psychoanalytic problems is illustrated in a study carried out by Luborsky on momentary forgetting during free association (1964, 1967). It is not the specific intent of the study but rather the research strategy employed that is critically important to us. The study combines the qualities of dealing with a phenomenon unique to the psychoanalytic setting with the features of a rigorous research design characteristic of, but not identical with, experimentation. The subject phenomenon is that of momentary forgetting—the awareness, brief loss, and subsequent retrieval of a thought. Typically, the patient, while free-associating, says, "I just had a thought, but I can't remember what it is; it's gone." Luborsky developed a research design, *confined to the data of his psychoanalytic protocols,* by which he was able to answer such questions as whether all patients, or only certain kinds of patients, have this kind of momentary-forgetting experience in the course of treatment; whether the lost content is the same in all instances; whether there is a consistency in the surrounding context of thoughts; whether momentarily lost content is similar to the themes of a person's dreams, and, on the theoretical side, the connection between forgetting and the concept of repression.

It is interesting, and a lesson to be carried away from this study, that once Luborsky had become interested in the phenomenon and had a way of isolating it, he began to see it all the time. In our present state of casual research inquiry, how many such distinct phenomena we overlook! Luborsky collected 155 momentary-forgetting instances from 19 patients in the course of over two thousand sessions. The immediate thought context and the forgotten content were recorded verbatim or nearly verbatim. Classificatory devices made it possible to illuminate the meanings of the quantitative indices of frequency of momentary forgetting, to tease out consistencies in the content of the recovered thoughts, and to relate them to characteristics of the context.

Take the matter of consistency of content. Luborsky developed scoring categories by which to assess the content of the momentarily lost and recovered thought. He assembled 37 pairs of sessions, the forgetting session and a control counterpart. The control session was usually within a few sessions of the forgetting session, and was compared with the forgetting session. A statement in the control-session protocol having approximately the same number of words as the sentence in the forgetting session, and appearing at about the same point in the protocol, was chosen by a rational procedure as a pseudo-forgotten sentence. Out of this comparison of the paired protocols came such characteristics of content as "guilt," "Oedipal conflict," and the suggestion that the forgetting process involves a "momentary altered state of consciousness" producing a transitory weakening of synthetic functioning, even though the person is relatively wide awake.

Luborsky's investigation illustrates a systematic, naturalistic type of strategy for studying a phenomenon that could not possibly be observed *in its details* by the casual research methods currently employed by analysts. It illustrates how a particular problem can be investigated in the psychoanalytic situation and offers a way of coping with the inherent complexities of free-association data. And it is repeatable by others. I agree with Luborsky: "In this respect, the method stands in sharp contrast to many laboratory studies of forgetting and repression, since the variables relevant to the concept of repression, which are discernible in the psychoanalytic situation, are not easily discovered in the laboratory" (1967, p. 217).

A variety of problems seem to be approachable in this manner. For example, by this means we can study the function of metaphoric expression in psychoanalytic therapy by relating the occurrences of metaphor to the context of association in a given hour. The assumption is that since metaphor involves the choice of words which have a control as well as an expressive function, a metaphor is a way of handling simultaneous trains of thought *occurring at a given moment* in the course of free association.

Naturally, this or other methods are no substitute either for imagination or for the close definition of researchable problems. But the use of methods of this sort will, over the long haul, generate the painstaking regard for data that psychoanalysis sorely needs.

In summary, the core of my argument is this: The psychoanalytic enterprise and the therapeutic intent (whether intentionally or not) inevitably provide a clue domain pertinent to the search for *meaning, purpose, direction, aim* of behavior. This is singular to the psychoanalyst; no other scientist has the privilege of this kind of investigative situation—a situation made possible by the therapeutic pact between patient and analyst, in which the patient agrees to confide to the analyst everything that it is possible for him to confide. It is a unique research and researchable context. Within this situation, it becomes a rather empty enterprise for an analyst to speculate on issues of mechanism and to use models more appropriate to physiological data. I am not against such speculative enterprises if they provide useful *clues* to others who are themselves prepared to work with data *appropriate* to the terms of the model and its process questions. But when we have only the data of analytic protocols to work with, over-concern with questions of mechanism may throw us off our main track and dissipate our capacities for perceiving new dimensions of lawful purposefulness in behavior.

Charles Fisher said (personal communication) that analysts tend to be somewhat complacent, too willing to ignore the major discoveries in other fields, and have not produced their own core of research workers in the *biological field* to bring about the translation of psychological events into neurophysiological and physiological terms "that was Freud's ultimate goal." I have some misgivings about this admonition and this prescription. I agree with the accusation of complacency, *not,* however, because psychoanalysts ignore neurophysiology, but because they ignore the fact that clinical concepts are themselves theory requiring systematic research. I also share the hope that researchers in biology will translate psychoanalytic propositions into neurophysiological terms, but *not* because this was Freud's ultimate goal, not because this is in any sense a superior endeavor, but simply because it is part of the scientific effort to do so—to build bridges and discover coherence on any level. But I see no call for analysts to feel defensive because they are not enlisting molecular biologists to work in the interest of psychoanalytic theory, any more than molecular biologists need feel defensive about not enlisting psychoanalysts for their pursuits. It is nice when this sort of thing happens. It is another thing to bewail the fact that it does not. Our own backyard still has prior claim to our cultivation.

Let there be no mistake about the status of such translation to neurophysiology: The pursuit of meaning and significance, and the specification of their lawfulness, which are the special and unique focus of the psychoanalyst in his *situation,* can never be substituted for by neurophysiological data.

We may influence man's intentions, his aims, and his defenses by inducing somatic changes. This is indeed a large part of the attraction of physiological work. Physiological understanding may even improve our techniques of effective therapeutic change. However, the reading of intentionality, meaning, and significance will always be a special *and separate* level of observation. For the psychoanalyst there are no such things as stimuli and responses, but only "encounters" which have meaning. His is the intricate and intriguing job of deciphering that meaning.

CHAPTER 3

Freud's Two Theories of Sexuality

Many years I have wandered through the land of men, and have not yet reached an end of studying the varieties of the "erotic man". . . . There a lover stamps around and is in love only with his passion. There one is wearing his differentiated feelings like medal-ribbons. There one is enjoying the adventures of his own fascinating effect. There one is gazing enraptured at the spectacle of his own supposed surrender. There one is displaying his "power." There one is preening himself with borrowed vitality. There one is delighting to exist simultaneously as himself and as an idol very unlike himself. There one is warming himself at the blaze of what had fallen to his lot. There one is experimenting. And so on and on—all the manifold monologists with their mirrors, in the apartment of the most intimate dialogue! [Buber, 1929, pp. 29-30].

AN ANALYST I GREATLY esteem wrote to me: "Now you want to eliminate the concept of drives. . . . Did Rapaport try it?" This reproof made me anxious, naturally so, because I was brought up in the value system of "classical psychoanalysis," which recognizes the challenge "You are denying drives!" as an indictment, not an invitation to inquiry. A basic violation of catechism is at issue. (And in the offing, perhaps, that gentleman's pyre, intellectual isolation from the psychoanalytic community.) My testy defense was that frequent plea of the guilty, "No, no, you misunderstand!"

Here I recalled Freud's remark that conceptions of instinct are the mythology of psychoanalysis. What did he mean by this? Surely sexuality and aggression are not "mythological." It would seem, on the face of it, that holding a *theory* of sexuality and aggression which distinguishes its propositions from the *phenomena* of sexuality and aggression is an acceptable position.

This reassuring reminder revealed the have-you-stopped-beating-your-wife nature of the analyst's question. For indeed, to say "Yes" (I *do* want to eliminate the concept of drive) would imply that I am denying the importance of sexuality in neurosis and in the shaping of motivation, and surely I am not denying that. To say "No" (I do *not* want to eliminate the concept of drive) implies that I endorse the theoretical model which views sexuality as a *vis-a-tergo* force or stimulus upon the mind, one capable of building up a "demand" for "discharge" and the reduction of tension; and I do have great doubts about that theoretical model.

There is reason to believe that the psychoanalytic conception of sexuality exists in two versions. The first I will call the clinical theory because it is the one that actually guides clinical work. It centers upon the properties peculiar to sexuality, upon the values and meanings associated with sensual experiences in the motivational history of a person from birth to adulthood, upon how nonsexual motives and activities are altered when they acquire a sensual aspect, and vice versa.

The second version, which I will call the drive-discharge theory, translates this psychological conception into the quasi-physiological terms of a model of an energic force that "seeks" discharge. This energic conception is connected with Freud's fundamental belief upon which his entire metapsychology was constructed: that the source of all activity in the organism, perhaps even characterizing it as "living" altogether, is its tendency to deal with the energic influxes of "stimuli," to discharge them, to reduce the tensions produced by their energic quantity. This was the all-embracing precept that included the special theory of sexuality. It was designed to serve Freud's conception of his own scientific objectives of "explanation," which have become the conventions of psychoanalytic metapsychological theorizing. Through the concepts of metapsychology, developed from this basic precept, he sought to create interfaces with other disciplines, particularly with physiology, and to relate his conceptions of human psychology to the theory of evolution.

I wish here to make the two versions explicit by contrasting them. When they are so contrasted we can see that they are on different logical planes; that they are not reducible to one another; that they require different data for confirmation; and that they are, in critical ways, inconsistent with each other. It is the clinical theory that was Freud's revolutionary contribution. The data of clinical psychoanalysis are more pertinent to investigation of the clinical theory than of the drive-discharge theory. Despite this, theoretical writings since Freud's time have put greater emphasis on the drive-discharge theory than on the clinical. It is now time to give fresh attention to the clinical theory.

Despite their differences, the two theories have become confounded in psychoanalytic discussion. (It is unlikely that Freud himself thought of the two theories as distinct from each other; there is no evidence that he did.) Indeed, the drive-discharge version of the theory of sexuality has acquired the spurious status of *the* theory of sexuality. Writers on psychoanalysis almost universally assume that the drive conception is a more abstract, more general version of the theory of infantile sexuality, an attempt to place that theory within the framework of a "pure psychology." There exists, then, the curious state of affairs in which the clinical propositions remain largely inarticulated *as theory,* even while guiding actual psychoanalytic treatment. The model that dominates theoretical reflections on clinical work is the drive-cathexis-discharge model. "Squeezed through the eyelet of the drive-discharge model" is perhaps a more appropriate expression, for I hope to show that that model is unable to encompass the propositions of the clinical theory.

So ingrained and unquestioned is the assumed identity of drive theory with the clinical theory of sexuality that, to cite a recent example, Waelder (1966) could entitle a paper "Adaptational View Ignores 'Drive,' " meaning, as we discover in the body of the paper, that the theory he is questioning ignores sexuality. I hold no brief for the adaptational theory Waelder was criticizing; I point only to the assumption of identity expressed by the title. Were sexuality and drive not identical in Waelder's mind, why should it matter that a theory ignores the concept of drive, if it does not ignore sexuality?

The drive-discharge model of sexuality has so long been a part of the climate of psychology that it retains its hold even on those who reject it; for this rejection is automatically considered a denial of the motivational primacy of sexuality. Neo-Freudians have agreed on this equation. Expressing their dissatisfaction with the drive model, they usually conclude by disputing the importance of sexuality in the structuring of personality. On the other hand, the assumption of interchangeability is so universal that when some theorists have referred to drive *without* giving specificity to sexuality, it has gone unnoticed. For instance, Rapaport (1960) held such a notion of a generalized drive, in which sexuality loses its distinctive position among the "drives" and is relegated to a lesser status than it had for Freud.

Perhaps the failure of traditionalists to distinguish between the two theories comes from a tendency to regard the clinical propositions not as theory but as confirmed fact, and to regard its concepts simply as descriptive tools. Many analysts feel that they downgrade the conception of infantile sexuality when they regard it as a *theory,* to be investigated, tested against rival assertions, and subject to revision. As a result the propositions of the clinical theory have remained oddly static; since Freud's time there have been precious few additions from psychoanalytic sources to our systematic knowledge of sexuality. At the same time, applications of the drive model have been long on words in "explaining" clinical data, but short on actual testing with clinical data. The drive model, being constantly invoked to "explain" clinical observation, distracts from the necessary tasks of exploring, enlarging, and pruning the clinical theory, which is closer to clinical observations.

In order to appreciate Freud's revolutionary views on sexuality, we must separate the clinical propositions from the drive model. To this task I turn first.

The Sensual Dimension of Human Sexuality

1. *Capacity for Sensual Experience*

The crux of the clinical propositions is Freud's radically novel view of the essential nature of human sexuality, which enabled him to see human relationships in a fresh light. The observations that led Freud to reconceptualize sexuality have been reviewed many times. Since my aim here is to highlight the principles that emerged, I shall make only sketchy reference to these observations: (a) Indications of sexual intent in hysterical symptoms. (E.g., he wrote: "According to a rule which I had found confirmed over and over again by experience, though I had not yet ventured to erect it into a general principle, a symptom signifies the representation—the realization—of a phantasy with a sexual content, that is to say, it signifies a sexual situation" [1905a, pp. 46-47].) (b) Indications that the traumatic nature of nonsexual experience was traceable to sexual encounters in early childhood. (c) Pathological and "perverse" sexuality, where sexuality has no connection with reproduction, as in people in whom sexuality is directed exclusively toward the same sex and as in other people who seek sexual satisfaction and find it without any assistance from the genital organs or their normal functioning, as, for instance, in sexual fetishism. (d) Evidence that children, a much greater number than one would imagine, show an interest at an early age in sexual matters and find pleasure in them. (e) Finally, and perhaps most important, Freud's insight into the universality of the incest taboo, a fact which made him ponder the power of impulses that would create such a universal taboo.

Some of these observations suggested that sexual conflict can occur much earlier in life than anyone had before imagined. They brought into question, too, whether sexuality is essentially dependent upon the matured capacity for reproductive behavior. They all seemed to converge upon the conclusion—strange to the mind even now—that sexuality must originate long before puberty, and *must have a bearing upon how sexuality will manifest itself in puberty.* Freud confronted a paradox that called for solution. There seemed to be common to children and adults a sexual capacity that would justify the idea of developmental continuity in sexuality, yet would be independent of *procreation.* Freud believed it was essential to identify a property of sexuality which manifests itself long before puberty but is not synonymous with an individual's particular sexual behavior. His solution was a conception of *what is common to sexuality in all its adult and infantile behavioral manifestations.* He proposed an invariant of sexual development, across different forms and manifestations of sexuality, that can be postulated to exist in children.

This invariant—the shared factor of infantile and adult sexuality—is a capacity for a *primary, distinctively poignant, enveloping experience of pleasure* that manifests itself from early infancy on (exactly *when* is an empirical issue). It is a *primary* pleasure because it can be evoked from direct stimulation of the dermal surface of the body; it has its own requirements of stimulation, its own thresholds, and its own qualities, compared with other forms of cognitive, knowledge-seeking, and sensory experiences. Sensual experience is *not simply the result of the removal of unpleasure*, or of tension as defined in the drive theory; it is directly tied to conditions of arousal specific to itself. Sensual experience is a positive aspect of a distinctive excitatory process of a body zone; it is different from the pleasurable experiences of satisfaction and reward. That is why it deserves the special designation of *sensual.*

It is unfortunate that, except for passing references to "sensual sucking," Freud did not refine his terminology to bring into sharper focus this critical feature of his reinterpretation of sexuality—the distinction between the sensual experience itself and the behavioral modes and regions through which it is obtained. He used the term "sexuality" to refer to both the experience of pleasure which even infants can have and the behaviors of genital sexuality which mature only in puberty. The word sexual, burdened by the older limited meaning, tended to obscure the *experiential* aspect he was pointing to. *Sensuality* might be a more natural designation for the particular pleasure component of sexuality. Moreover, reference to *sensual* pleasure distinguishes sexual pleasure from other forms of pleasurable affects, a distinction important in theory. The term "libido" as noun and adjective has been used to convey this distinction, but the absorption of the libido concept into the drive-discharge model causes difficulty in using the term for this purely classificatory purpose, so I prefer the term *sensual pleasure*.

In Freud's proposal, the sexual pleasure experience differs in specific ways from other forms of pleasurable experience. For example, here is how Freud distinguishes the sensual aspect of sucking from sucking in eating:

> The baby's obstinate persistence in sucking gives evidence at an early age of a need for satisfaction which, though it originates from and is instigated by the taking of nourishment, nevertheless

> strives to obtain pleasure independently of nourishment and for that reason may and should be termed *sexual* [1940, p. 154].

Sensual sucking involves:

> A complete absorption of the attention and leads either to sleep or even to a motor reaction in the nature of an orgasm. It is not infrequently combined with rubbing some sensitive part of the body such as the breast or the external genitalia. Many children proceed by this path from sucking to masturbation [1905b, p. 180].

Freud's assumption that this experience is in a category of affect unto itself seems contradicted by his later metapsychological theory which identified *all* pleasures as libidinal. This lost for the theory a certain power, for, as we shall see, that distinction between sensuality and sexuality is important for another critical proposition, namely, that sensual pleasure can serve various *functions* that are not in themselves specifically or *primarily* sexual. For instance, the search for sensual pleasure can come to be a means of eliminating unpleasure of nonsexual origin, as when sensual pleasure is used as a means of reducing the pain of an experience of failure.

The recognition of this distinction between sensuality and sexual behavior was a fundamental point separating Freud from his contemporaries, and it still separates the psychoanalytic from other conceptions of sexuality. While sensual pleasure is elicitable from infancy on, its arousal is characterized by a varying and systematic progression of behavior manifestations; this was the justification for speaking of sexual *development*. Before Freud (and in many theories even today) sexuality was synonymous with genital behavior; it was viewed exclusively in relation to the reproductive function and the phylogenetic requirement of procreation. When Freud proposed a distinction between sensual experience and the behaviors through which it is elicited and expressed (the genital modality being but one), he presented the possibility—for the first time—of nongenital but nonetheless sexual stages of development.

Freud's defining of this distinction was revolutionary; it meant that human sensual experience is not locked in, as in lower species, to the behavior pattern of reproduction. Freud proposed something that may well be characteristic of human sexuality alone—the existence of an extended period of time in which the sensual pleasure experience is separable from reproductive sexuality. The two aspects of sexuality, the sensual pleasure experience and the modes of its evocation, eventually converge on the genital pattern. But this convergence is by no means inevitable in man; it is a *guided* process, one in which societal sanctions, values, and encouragement are vital.

From this premise—that the capacity for and means of sensual pleasure undergo systematic development—Freud evolved a conception of how this development is affected by a person's symbolized record of interpersonal encounters through which he has been sensually aroused. His theory includes assumptions about the role of their sensual significance in how relationships evolve and about how the meanings that have accrued to sensuality are also expressed in the form of symptoms. The recognition of continuity also made it possible to understand certain phenomena, such as fixation on or regression to particular modes of sensual gratification.

2. *Sensual Arousal*

We assume that sensual arousal results from appropriate patterned stimulation of the body's erogenous zones. With the proper stimulation, these areas are not only capable of sensation but also of producing feelings of poignant pleasure. A hard swipe on the buttocks produces pain, but it can also produce tinglings of sensual pleasure. In Freud's view, given the proper patterning of stimulation, the capabilities and possibilities of arousing sensual pleasure are multiple. In addition to the stimulation of the especially responsive dermal areas, other stimuli elicit sensual pleasure. Aerial movements, muscular exertions in play, seem capable of eliciting sensual excitement. Fathers have excited their sons by flinging them into the air and catching them, by rocking, by sitting their youngsters astride their knees, with pleasures to both not fully acknowledgeable by either.

The nature of the somatic mobilization required for the stimulation of and the experience of sensual pleasure is hardly better understood than at the time of Freud's first formulations, and is still unclear. Compared with the study of other sensations, this one has been neglected in psychophysical laboratories and still awaits investigation. The faint beginnings of a psychophysics of sensuality is suggested by Pfaffman's (1960) solitary paper on the "pleasures" of sensation. Freud offered many leads toward such a psychophysics, e.g., that different zones have different thresholds of sensual arousal. The significance of such differences for development and motivation is unknown. No one really knows, for example, how the pattern of stimulation necessary for sensual arousal in the oral region compares with requirements for the anal region. Nor have the pleasures of bowel retention and expulsion been subjected to systematic study. It also seems reasonable to assume that there are genetic differences among children in the potential of different zones for arousing sensual experiences.

3. *Sensual Arousal through Nonspecifically Sensual Modalities*

Although all body zones have in common the capability of eliciting sensual experience, some of these zones are not specifically sexual in function (Erikson, 1963). Moreover, the stimulation required for erotic arousal in one zone is different from the requirement of another zone. The stimulation required is quite specific to and dependent upon the form of responsiveness—i.e., the modes—of the zone, for example, the sucking and biting capabilities of the mouth. In this view, a zone is a perceptual and behavioral system, and sensual arousal is manifested in the behavioral activity of its modes. Gibson (1967), for example, writes of the mouth:

> For the infant mammal it is an apparatus for sucking as distinguished from eating. Hence, it is originally a means of feeling the mother's nipple and causing the mother to feel the infant's mouth—a means of mutual stimulation. This is perhaps the earliest kind of social interaction in animals of our sort. In man, the mouth remains an organ of sexual-social contact throughout life, as the act of kissing demonstrates.
>
> The mouth is also an organ for haptic exploration in the infant, often with the cooperation of the hand. . . . It is much used for auto-stimulation in the sense of information-getting, and the baby appears to practice mouthing—to be interested in the regularities and possibilities of it. He drools and blows bubbles and sucks his thumb and learns how the mouth feels and what noises can be made with it [p. 135].

In short, the mouth is a versatile apparatus of information seeking and getting. It is a perceptual system.

Now the intimate conjoining of informational potential and sensual pleasure obtained through a perceptual system is important to the psychoanalytic theory of sexuality. The act of "receiving" serves for gaining both sensual pleasure and information about what is received. Presumably, the pattern of modal activity in erotic arousal is different from that of nonsensual experience, though this is again a largely unexplored issue. Recent studies suggest that differently patterned sucking movements of the mouth serve different aims; for instance, the sucking patterns of searching and attending may differ from those of eating (Bruner, 1968). Freud's propositions regarding sensual sucking suggest that there may exist still another pattern which is specific to sensual experience.

This conjunction of sensual and nonsensual functions, fulfilled through the same behavioral modes, is profoundly important for the development of a person's motivation. The fact that sensuality does not have its own "organs" but can be elicited only through modalities for learning and adapting insures the interlocking of sensual experience with nonsensual aims in development. Not only is sensual pleasure aroused through behavioral means that serve learning and adapting and thus acquires meanings tied to these systems; but it also becomes possible for the pursuit of nonsexual ends to be complicated by sensual connotations. Thus, affects and frustrations associated with the mouth's pleasure-giving capacity can have reverberations in its use generally as a system of control. Erikson (1963) speaks of *social* modalities, e.g., general attitudes of trust or mistrust, as being rooted in the configuration of manipulation and pleasure experiences that evolves in a person's history of modal experiences. In short, the negative and positive valuations associated with the control of sensuality in a mode also become aspects of the structural record of experiences obtained through a zonal behavioral system. In Freud's words:

> . . . we are led to the suspicion that all the connecting pathways that lead from other functions to sexuality must also be traversable in the reverse direction. If, for instance, the common possession of the labial zone by the two functions is the reason why sexual satisfaction arises during the taking of nourishment, then the same factor also enables us to understand why there should

> be disorders of nutrition if the erotogenic functions of the common zone are disturbed. . . . A good portion of the symptomatology of the neuroses, which I have traced to disturbances of the sexual processes, is expressed in disturbances of other, nonsexual, somatic functions; and this circumstance, which has hitherto been unintelligible, becomes less puzzling if it is only the counterpart of the influences which bring about the production of sexual excitation.
>
> . . . we must end with a confession that very little is as yet known with certainty of these pathways, though they certainly exist and can probably be traversed in both directions [1905b, pp. 205-206].

In this assumption of the two-way traversability of connections between sensual arousal processes and nonsexual informational functions, one may seem to recognize the familiar version of drive-discharge theory which holds that all motivations are circumspect forms of sexual "discharge." Critics of Freud's sexual theories have made this a target of particularly vigorous attack. But the clinical proposition makes no assumption about the primacy of "discharge"; it does not assume that the pathways of connection between erotic sensibility and nonsexual functions are erotic "discharge opportunities" for the former. Freud is affirming the ready ties between sensual experience and the *instrumental* processes serving nonsexual functions; he is proposing that the means of pleasurable sensual manipulation are also the means of manipulating and regulating things, and that values accruing to the sensual potential of a mode's activity can affect the mode's functioning generally. In the system of regulation he is picturing, sensual experience acquires affective-cognitive meanings from the context of actions and relationships in which it occurs; and, conversely, the activities of a mode may acquire erotic meanings. In theory, eating is capable of stimulating sensual pleasure. The reverse can happen as well; sensual arousal may evoke auxiliary desires for food. Disturbances in sensual experience may have reverberations in the normal nonsexual uses of a mode—a factor that loomed large in Freud's understanding of hysteria. For example, Freud suggests this possibility: ". . . If we know that concentration of attention may give rise to sexual excitation, it seems possible to assume that by making use of the same path, but in a contrary direction, the condition of sexual excitation may influence the possibility of directing the attention" (1905b, p. 206).

4. *The Record of Sensual Experience as a Basis of Sensual Craving*

A critical proposition is that the nature of sensual pleasure is such that *once experienced it continues to be savored; the record of its occurrence is hard to relinquish*. It is proposed that sensual experience is distinctively etched in memory and concept. The occasions of sensual experience in modal activities, and the values, positive and negative, which such experiences acquire, are recorded in a cognitive structure or *schema*[1] whose activation ever after helps to shape sensual experience.

The schema includes memories of the context of past sensual arousals and also an affective record of the success or failure that attended them. The sensual pleasure of the breast is recorded in the context of the mother's responsiveness to the feeding process itself. When a mother gives signs of disapproval of the smearing of feces, her disapproval becomes associated with the sensual pleasure in the smearing. It is this cognitive matrix that carries the symbolic meaning of sexuality for each person.

The evolving cognitive record of sensual experience is thus both a product of past sensual experience and a framework which shapes the content of current sensual experience; experienced through that framework, the current sensual occurrences gather meaning beyond simply the affective sensual tone. Freud assumed that early in infancy the capacity for sensual pleasure already has some degree of internal representation. The child discovers early that sensual pleasure can be autogenically evoked; before long, he reaches down searchingly and finds the genitalia. Presumably, shortly after birth the cognitive

[1]The concept of *schema* used here is that of Bartlett's original definition "... an active organization of past reactions, or of past experiences which must always be supposed to be operating in any well-adapted, organic response. Whenever there is any order or regularity of behaviour, a particular response is possible only because it is related to other similar responses which have been serially organized, yet which operate not singly as individual members coming one after another, but as a unitary mass" (1932, p. 201). For an account of further developments of the concept see Wolff (1963), who relates it to Piaget's theory of the development of intelligence.

schema of sensuality has affective and motor components, but almost no conceptual component. There is simply the zone and its mode. As development occurs, the conceptual scope of sensual experience comes to include representations of the actions and relationships through which the pleasure is won or thwarted, of restraint and controls, and of self-related meanings. Thus, the meaning *taking in* by mouth and lips becomes a conceptual aspect which colors sensual experience that is aroused by stimulation in the oral zone. "Holding back," "retaining," "expulsion," and the like, become conceptual affiliates of sensual experience through the anal zone. These developments occur in complementary response to the normal developmental shifts in the dominant zone of sensual capability. According to Freud's clinical theory, sensual experience has not only a *zone* of dominant focus but a *time* of dominant origin.

The meanings that can envelop sensual pleasure can be illustrated in regard to anal sensuality. The sensations of both a full rectum and of emptying the bowel can be primary sources of sensual pleasure, as Freud said. Associated with these can be the satisfaction of performing a function desired by the parents. But they can also acquire meanings of defying authority, of refusing to do one's job at the pot, and therefore of postponing the pleasure of emptying the bowel. In such fashion, through its embeddedness in a cognitive schema, the poignantly pleasurable sensual experience comes to acquire both high potential as an experience to be revived and sought, and connotations of an experience to be afraid of, ashamed of, held in check, or even quashed in its arousal.

The importance of the cognitive framework in structuring sensual experience is illustrated by a phenomenon to which Freud first drew attention (1898): that a zonal experience which at its occurrence had relatively little conceptual meaning as sexual (i.e., was not understood as such by the child) can retroactively acquire such a meaning at a later time when an enlarged cognitive capacity and increased sensual capability of the zone have raised the zone to prominence. Thus a recorded early genital experience may at puberty become coded with a significance it did not previously have and acquire influence in the current life situation.

The cognitive matrix of sensual arousal has much to do with what is commonly thought of as the "driving" force of sexuality. Actually, it is closer to the clinical meaning to say that the need or wish for sensual experience does not itself "drive" a person, but that he seeks sensual experience because of meanings that have become associated with it in the course of his development. Signs of "urgency," e.g., the excitement of anticipation, and fantasy, commonly regarded as the peremptory drive aspect of sexuality, are, in the clinical theory, manifestations of the cognitive schema in a state of continued or repetitive activation. We will have more to say later about the nature of "intensity" and "force" of sexual motivation.

5. *Development*

It is as an evolving cognitive structure, not as a disembodied "blind" energic force, that sensual experience is understood in the clinical theory. Sensual pleasure elicited by sucking at one period may later be elicited by biting as well as by sucking. The anal region, particularly the junction of the skin with the anal-rectal mucous membrane, becomes a prominent locus of sensual arousal. Although zones and modes of sensual arousal are not immutable at any one period, there is a pattern of dominant and recessive zones and modes characteristic of each period, and this pattern varies from one period to another. As time passes, the cognitive aspects of the sensual experiences of one stage are subordinated to those of the next, but are nevertheless carried over to affect the next developments.

Normally, the arousal of sensual experience comes to be dominantly linked to the genital, reproductive aspects of sensuality, but these two aspects, the genital and the sensual, never do become identical. To assure this development, restraints must be internalized (i.e., learned) and connected with the arousal of the sensual experience itself. Thus the cognitive record of sensuality, of its arousal and expression, includes guiding rules and reinforcing affective associations. It is as part of this guidance that early forms of sensual experience come to be couched in terms of shame, disgust, and other affects, positive as well as negative. Early preferences for sensual pleasure are carried forward to affect later preferences. A mother's facilitation or inhibition of sensual pleasures may affect a child's subsequent sensual aims and objects. Preferred modes of early sensual pleasure may remain fixated, and in times of stress regressively emphasized. Freud describes a girl who continued thumb-sucking right into puberty, and who never achieved the sensual satisfaction from kissing that she obtained from sucking.

Conversely, the maturing of sensual potential in a newly dominant zone, the learning and internalizing of societal sanctions associated with the various zones and modes, and a person's own traumatic and other impressive experiences may retroactively organize already recorded experiences. Earlier experiences, recorded for the zone and mode that were at the time recessive, and that had little or no conceptual significance at that time, may acquire sensual significance later, when the erogenous capabilities of the zone, and the child's cognitive abilities, have matured. A memory that had a relatively benign sensual aspect may take on ominous importance through a traumatic sensual encounter that subjectively resembles the earlier occurrence. In short, continuity in sensual development, both mobilization and inhibition, is made up of changes in the zone-mode media of sensual pleasure on the one hand, and a matrix of cognitive and affective values on the other.

6. *Plasticity*

The aspects of erotic sensibility and behavior described so far indicate a general property best described as "plasticity." Sensuality is "plastic" because it can be aroused by various means; at all stages of development its stimulation can be autoerotic, heterosexual, or homoerotic. It is "plastic" in the changes in the course of development in sensual capabilities of different body zones; in the variations, within each stage of development, in what is sensually stimulating and gratifying. Another aspect of this plasticity is the possibility of disjunction between meanings associated with sensual experience on the one hand, and specific modal behaviors, including genital sexual behavior, on the other—for example, sexual activity unaccompanied by sensual pleasure, as in hysterical frigidity and in certain kinds of sexual promiscuity.

But these qualities of plasticity are a source of danger in which society has a very large stake. Freud's attention to this fact makes his interpretation of sexuality a profoundly biosocial theory. This plasticity raises problems of control; the individual in our society must be guided to the goals of procreation and heterosexuality, and, within this general direction, it is mandatory that choice be guided away from societally destructive commitments. With great insight, Freud pointed to the paradox that the biologically plastic potentialities of sensuality include no built-in protection against societally destructive incest.

For a long time the most accessible, perhaps even the most satisfying, sexual objects to a child are those in relation to whom society must impose unequivocally inhibiting sanctions against mature sexual behavior. The very nature of sensual pleasure—a poignantly desirable experience that is hard to relinquish and hard to forget, with a record of its first arousal a potential basis of motivational direction—requires that the means of gratification be efficiently regulated, requires that regulated choice and sanctions be internalized as operational rules, and that they become part of the developmental record, the cognitive schema, of sensuality.

As Laing has pointed out, a good deal of effort in all societies is given to deciding which bodies may be joined with which on which occasions and at what age. Persons in all cultures are governed in their actions by an intricate web of injunctions about whose bodies of what sex their own bodies should come into contact with (1960). This is a learning experience that begins at an extremely early age, and one of the most difficult, in view of the inherent desirability of sensual experience itself and of the fact that the most natural directive principle of its satisfaction is propinquity. Very young children may respond sensually in situations that, in our moral belief, appear perverse, simply because they have not yet learned to avoid certain stimuli that are taboo, "or may never have learned to respond positively and exclusively to certain approved sexual stimuli."[2] It was this recognition of the social consequences of plasticity that opened the way to Freud's showing how many

> impairments of individual and group life . . . stem from the meaningless management of sensuality. . . . He found that neu-

[2]Ford and Beach (1951, pp. 258-259) make an interesting point in this connection: "Men and women who are totally lacking in any conscious homosexual leanings are as much a product of cultural conditioning as are the exclusive homosexuals who find heterosexual relations distasteful and unsatisfying. Both extremes represent movement away from the original, intermediate condition which includes the capacity for both forms of sexual expression. In a restrictive society such as our own a large proportion of the population learns not to respond to or even to recognize homosexual stimuli and may eventually become in fact unable to do so." This may be regarded as an illustration of an inevitable inference from the assumption of plasticity in sensual development, in the psychoanalytic clinical theory.

> rotics and perverts are not only infantile in their attitudes toward their fellow men, but also regularly impaired in their genital sexuality and given to overt or covert gratifications and comforts from other than genital body zones. Moreover, their sexual impairment and their social infantility are all systematically related to their early childhood and particularly to clashes between the impulses of their infantile bodies and the inexorable training methods of their parents [Erikson, 1963, pp. 64, 60].

7. *Inevitability of Conflict*

The key element in the social regulation of sensuality and in the shaping of erotic behavior consists of the internalized values that configure sensual experience, governing its arousal, instrumentalities, and objects. One might say that Freud's theory is not simply one of a biological appetite, but is, in the most profound sense, a "superego" theory concerned with the developmental structuring of the meanings, affects, and motives associated with this plastic organismic phenomenon.

The plasticity of sensuality creates a potential for conflict that distinguishes sexuality from all other psychosomatic cravings. Inevitable, also, are developmental crises created by the necessity of resolving incompatibilities between the established patterns of gratification of one stage and the potentialities of an emerging one; success in accommodating the new hinge on making obsolete the old. The resolutions of these conflicts and crises become part of the internalized value structure—the cognitive meanings—of sensual experience and sexual behavior, and are carried forward to affect sexual development. Compared to animal sexuality, and compared to all other sensory and affective dispositions in man, this predisposition to conflict is one of the most distinguishing characteristics of human sexuality.[3]

Since its arousal as well as the instrumentalities of its satisfaction are subject to control and socialization, all aspects of sensual experience and behavior are potentially subject to conflict. Here we see an

[3]Freud's concept of "moral masochism" is an example of a proposition concerning one form of conflictual involvement of sensuality: "Again, masochism creates a temptation to perform 'sinful' actions, which must then be expiated by the reproaches of the sadistic conscience . . . or by chastisement from the great parental power of Destiny. In order to provoke punishment from this last representative of the parents, the masochist must do what is inexpedient, must act against his own interests, must ruin the prospects which open out to him in the real world and must, perhaps, destroy his own real existence" (1924, pp. 169-170).

important difference between sexuality and such "primary drives" as hunger and thirst, with which sexuality is often compared. Most sexual rules concern admonitions and foretastes of consequences, hence the very arousal of sensual experience can be hedged by conflict. With hunger and thirst the internalized rules have much more to do with the choice than with arousal. When you become hungry, there are alternatives with respect to what you should do or eat. When sensuality is involved, social rules govern not only choice, but arousal itself. What you must not do, *lest* you become sensually aroused, is also part of the rules, as well as how to control and direct sensuality once it is aroused. There are, of course, taboos connected with eating and drinking, but the fantasies concerning such taboos are not a problem. On the other hand, the nature of taboos against sensuality necessitate anticipatory control of its arousal, means for its suppression and for its redirection—capabilities provided by the very plasticity which necessitates the controls!

By far the most important factor in the conflict potential of sensuality is the previously mentioned point that tabooed pleasures are so often associated with persons who are both the easiest, most convenient means of sensual gratification and sources of other important types of pleasure as well, for example, reward and the relief of distress and tensions. Heterosexual choice within the family would be the easiest and most congruent alternative for most people, because, as Lindzey (1967, p. 1056) expresses it, the organism seems to be "wired for sexual choice along dimensions of proximity and similarity." However, the child encounters a society necessarily programmed for inhibition and destruction of these tendencies. It is precisely against such choices that one of the most powerful taboos, the incest prohibition, is directed.[4] The child encounters this opposition at a time when he is poorly equipped to devise compromising patterns of response. He must learn to isolate and control the sensual pleasure mutually elicitable with mother, father, and siblings, and to internalize tacit canons of acceptable conduct.

Complicating the learning problem is the fact that the mother is a source of both sensual and of permissible nonsensual pleasures (e.g.,

[4]The prohibition of inbreeding transcends cultures, and Lindzey gives persuasive arguments for believing that the taboo is the product of strong evolutionary reinforcement, a biological necessity for survival of a hardy human species.

rewards and satisfactions), and these have early to be distinguished by the child. A mother gratifies in all sorts of ways, but beyond a certain age one must not acknowledge her as a specific source of sensual experience. Other pleasures, as for instance what White (1963) calls "effectance" pleasure, are probably never subject to so severe a rule of severance. These distinctions pose an uncommonly difficult task, one that is often complicated by the mother's own conflicts, and emotional stake, in blurring these distinctions. It will happen, therefore, that the child's feelings about his relationship with his parents and about their attitudes toward his body and person will become deeply divided.

Preparations for the required, eventual taboo on heterosexual relations between parent and child long precede the actual maturing of the child's genital sexuality. This matter deserves more study than it has received, but there is good reason to suppose that a mother's handling of the infant boy is from the beginning different from her handling of a girl, guided by a subtly inbred, culture-supported premonition of the inescapable sensual estrangement that is to come.

Given, then, the plasticity of sensuality, in which a natural tendency toward erotic arousal by and culmination on tabooed objects is ever present, "the operation of. . .negative sanctions against an almost equally strong countertendency could well constitute a psychological dilemma of enormous consequence" (Lindzey, 1967, p. 1056). Bringing this dilemma to light for the first time was one of Freud's monumental achievements; it is at the center of his clinical theory of sexuality; and it is a point which separates psychoanalysis from other theories of sexuality. From this discovery emerge conceptions of the types of conflict that originate in this basic and ineradicable dilemma, and of the various forms of their resolution, and therefore the discovery of a range of motivations unknown to other theories. The conception of the Oedipus complex, of course, and many propositions concerning sexual conflict in psychopathology, are linked to these assumptions.

We often hear that the importance Freud gave to sexuality was simply a reaction to the Victorian inhibitions of his time, and that in today's climate of sexual freedom his theory loses importance. But that sex is so freely discussed and its various forms openly tolerated does not minimize the profundity and relevance of the main point of Freud's theory. The dilemmas created by the plasticity of sensuality are as insistent now as in Freud's time. Although the requirement for control is differently resolved by different societies, and the range and nature of tolerance vary from period to period and from society to society, the requirement for control itself remains invariant; it is secured by the universal incest taboo and by the necessity for guiding and insuring the joining of sensuality to appropriate heterosexual expression. The plasticity of sensual arousal in a context of inevitable social guidance will always make the problem of sexuality a primary one in motivational development, and, through the inevitability of Oedipal stresses, an inevitable participant in the drama of generations.

Sexuality in Motivation

Motive refers to the directional aspect of action, the objective for the sake of which movements and choices are made. In this view, to understand the motivational aspects of sexuality is to assess the functions of sensual pleasure, the reasons for seeking or avoiding it. The clinical theory distinguishes the appetitive aspect of sexuality from the aims involved in the seeking of sensual experience and behavior. Sensual pleasure may have multiple functions; sexual gratification per se may be an immediate but not a primary aim of sexual activity; the requirement for gratification may be the instrumental expression of a variety of motives.[5] A person may be drawn toward sensual pleasure and conditions that arouse it because they give comfort, help to blot out reality, make him feel more manly, or even, perhaps, because they have repressed incestuous meanings.

In the drive-discharge theory the issue of aim is strictly limited to the process of discharge: Whatever contributes to discharge is construed as the aim of sexuality. Therefore, on the level of the economic point of view, which speaks of sexuality as the vicissitudes of the libido quantity, the distinction between drive and motive is blurred. But this

[5]To my knowledge Lichtenstein (1961) was the first to raise pointedly the question of what could be the *adaptive* function of *infantile* sensual pleasure. This question seems to have escaped notice even though it is one that follows directly and uniquely from Freud's theory. For if sensual development *culminates* in a joining of the sensual pleasure capacity with the procreative function, what adaptive function is served by sensual experience in the earliest infantile stage? Lichtenstein offers the hypothesis that sensual pleasure has a critical role in the establishment of self-identity. I can give only passing mention to this intriguing idea since my objective in this section is to deal with the functional plasticity of sensuality generally.

is not the case in the clinical theory, which emphasizes the cognitive matrix—the meaning—of sexuality. The clinical theory, indeed, assumes that the symbol and its appetitive-motor aspects, learned in a psychosocial process, are more important than the purely instinctual aspect of sexual capacity. It is the symbolization it acquires at critical periods that is crucial in shaping sexual responsiveness and crucial even in the arousing of sexual "need"; and it is this symbolization that accounts for sensuality being both a source of conflict and a means of resolving conflict.

Being a pleasure experience that is inherently desirable, sensuality is likely to be sought. In this sense there is a point in saying, as Koch (1956) does, that sexual activity is its own reward, that the pleasure in sexual behavior is also the reason for it. It would be foolish to raise the question whether the existence of a house is separate from or identical with its bricks and the fitting of its windows, so Koch argues in speaking about the inherent "value properties" of sexuality as "intrinsically motivating" and requiring no reference to "extrinsic" motivating conditions. It is true that pleasure resembles an end in being a reason for action; however, pleasure is not an end as it does not itself terminate action since we cannot identify it separately from the pleasurable activity.

Sexuality is therefore not only *regulative*, but *regulated*. It is a major point of the clinical theory that sexuality is responsive to different motivations. A remarkable feature of sensuality is that people will often go through hell for the sake of it; but this feature cannot be set in its true light by the fact that people *say* they are merely seeking pleasure. Although sensual pleasure may be experienced without a sense of ulterior motive, the experience can be an instrument of, the route to, other sought-for experiences, of the sort Buber describes in the passage quoted at the beginning of this chapter. Saying that pleasure is one's motive is confused with being motivated by pleasure in most popular accounts. The clinician, then, must distinguish between the motive of pleasure and other motives that are to be attained through the pleasure, but are not known to the patient. People may be able to acknowledge doing things for the sake of pleasure, but, simultaneously, through the pleasure, they may reach for aims they often cannot, even must not, acknowledge; for such acknowledgment might impair the quest.

A variety of motives involving sexuality originate as resolutions of conflict. The structural consequences may appear in defensive, substitutive, and exaggerated actions, which point either to the pleasure itself or to the modes in which it is elicited. Depending upon the circumstances, conflicts may be resolved by intensifying certain avenues of sensual pleasure, by deflecting or inhibiting sensual arousal and choice (they may result in fixation in respect to modes and aims of sensual arousal), or by regression to early forms of sensual gratification.

Another class of motives emerges from the serviceability of sensuality to a person for getting rid of unpleasure and for helping to achieve essentially nonsexual aims. In these roles, one doesn't defend oneself against sexuality, but, when under threat, uses it as defense, as part of one's repertoire of reparative and self-renewing devices. In such cases we might more accurately define the motives as sexual*ized* rather than as specifically sexual, as the immediate sexual action is ancillary to other aims to be achieved through it.

Because sensual pleasure is directly and even autogenously stimulable, resort to it is useful at all ages when a person seeks to rescue himself from unpleasure, pain, denigration, or humiliation. To give one example: There is accumulating evidence that in early life the reaction to separation is a powerful organizing motive centering on the unpleasurable experience induced by the absence of the familiar. In relation to this aim, sensual pleasure is a valuable option of action in two respects. It is a pleasure which counters the unpleasure of experienced isolation and separation; second, it is itself an experience of intimacy. Given the potential for sensual pleasure, one could expect its arousal and intensification to be greater when a person is experiencing isolation and separation. Segal (1963) writes that "sexually impulsive behaviour, precipitated by imagined or real object loss, is a desperate restitutional measure ... Continuing contact with such patients... [reveals] that they manifest extreme sensitivity to imagined or actual separation or loss of a currently needed person." He describes promiscuous women whose sexual activities include bodily contact, caressing and kissing, but in whom coitus is rare and provokes disgust. This behavior serves, he says, as "a screen for a more basic desire, ...the need to be closely fused with the mother in a symbiotic relationship" (p. 407).

Thus, for clinical purposes, assessing the motivational importance of sensual experience is not a matter of measuring appetitive strength; it is a matter of examining the functional significance of the sensual appetite, its cognitive values, positive and negative—how sensuality is internally represented for the person. These value aspects are the crux of its motivational importance.

This psychoanalytic clinical view should not be confused with the reductionist position of the drive-discharge theory that sees the structural consequences of sensual arousal as alternative "discharge channels" of libido energy; neither is it a version of the pansexual generalization which views all motives as "transformations of libido." Put in broad terms: The clinical theory of sexuality does not reduce motivations to a sexual history; rather, it locates sexual and nonsexual processes and their motivations in the one history they both express, which is that of the social existence of a developing self.

Relation to Personal Identity

An essential point of the clinical theory, then, is that sensual pleasure is not an autonomous experience sought after simply for its own sake. Sensual mobilization is an organismic event whose motivational importance arises from the requirement of a developing self that seeks always to perpetuate and preserve its unity, integrity, and coherence. Encounters and relationships that have linked sensual activity to self-conception and self-esteem are retained as part of the cognitive record of sensual pleasure and are thereafter very much part of the stimulation of sexual activity. Consequently, the stimulations and gratifications in every sensual experience reverberate to affect self-conception, self-identity, and self-esteem. Conversely, crises in these very respects affect the search for, the choices of, and the circumstances of sensual pleasure. In such instances, anxiety is not necessarily associated with erotic wishes per se, but rather, the erotic wishes are responses to the state of anxiety. The responsiveness of sensuality to experiences of danger and of profound loss (not specifically sexual deprivation) is well known to clinical observation. Sensual pleasure can be comforting; it helps temper the pain of social failure and deprivation. In such a case it can itself become a special kind of need to a developing selfhood, one aroused not necessarily by a specific requirement for sexual release but by an interpersonal deprivation to which an erotic value has become attached.

It is, of course, a biological fact that in pubertal development there is an accentuated association of sensual experience with the genitals. But the meanings of this association are entwined with the nature of one's self-identity at that point of development. The boy's sexual orientation is focused on the phallus, and a feeling of genital inferiority can affect his feeling of pride and growth and locomotion. Erikson describes the modality that is specific to the phallic stage as "making," in the sense of enjoyment of competition, insistence on goals, and pleasures of conquest. The boy attaches his first genital affection on the mother and develops his first sexual rivalry with her possessor, so that the rival with whom he is competing is usually his father. Sensual and aggressive fantasies about the parents may contribute to a disproportionate sense of guilt which affects the meanings that accompany sensual arousal.

Sensuality is, thus, never released from the claims and crises of self-identity, and has different meanings in different contexts of self-conception.

It is this relation to selfhood and to attitudes toward other people as objects that distinguishes sexuality in man from that in animals. Indeed, the more human sexuality is divorced from this centeredness in self-development, the more it resembles the mechanical, non-symbolic character of animal sexuality. As Merleau-Ponty (1945) expressed the matter:

> . . . the significance of psychoanalysis is less to make psychology biological than to discover a dialectical process in functions of thought as "purely bodily," and to reintegrate sexuality into the human being. . . . Insofar as a man's sexual history provides a key to his life, it is because in his sexuality is projected his manner of being toward the world, that is, toward time and other men. There are sexual symptoms at the root of all neuroses, but these symptoms, correctly interpreted, must symbolize a whole attitude, whether, for example, one of conquest or of flight [p. 158].

The Force of Sexuality

The main justification for viewing sexual behavior in the language of "drive" and for explaining it in terms of drive discharge has been the compelling hold that sexual craving can have on thinking and behavior. Man's sexual desires, active not only periodically, as in animals, can engross a great part of his activity, frequently at the expense of constructive activity, with which it can be in conflict. Such cravings certainly make one feel implacably steered toward objects that are satisfying sexually, as *if* an alien pressure were developing from within.

All theories of drive direct themselves to this experienced peremptoriness of sexual need. The solution of the drive-discharge model is to postulate an actual impulsion, taking the phenomenological fact as a model of the mechanism of the sensual craving itself. It is part of the craving that one feels helpless to the desire; it is natural then to think of it as outside the self, because what one calls "self" are body-connected functions and experiences under one's control.[6] The drive model redefined this state of feeling possessed to literal possession by forces independent of the ego and operating outside of consciousness. In the drive model, the force is outside in the sense of coming from the soma without control from "above" (the brain), which is the locus of the self. The drive is regarded as a stimulus upon the central nervous system, creating an affective state ("tension") that "stimulates" a "wish," the consummation of which is the reduction of the tension and pleasure. Drive motivation refers to a condition of dammed-up libido; the force of motivation is a direct function of the quantity of libido to be discharged. In this view all sexual behavior is an expression of this impulsion.

The clinical theory makes less drastic assumptions about the unobservable impulsion. The organized appearance of a sensual appetite lends itself to metaphoric description as the reflection of an implacable force; but it is misleading to take the experience of forcefulness as the process of sexual arousal per se. The clinical theory is not obligated to assume that the appetite is itself the consequence of a peripheral condition (a "drive") independent of itself. Its focus of inquiry is the motivational context. In the clinical theory, sexuality is viewed as appetitive activity within a reticulum of motivational meanings rather than the manifestation of a linear force impelling itself against a barrier. In the clinical theory, the structural nature of

[6]The point is vividly illustrated in the following report by Penfield: "When the neurosurgeon applies an electrode to the motor area of the patient's cerebral cortex, causing the opposite hand to move, and when he asks the patient why he moved his hand, the response is: 'I didn't do it. You made me do it.' . . . It may be said that the patient thinks of himself as having an existence separate from his body." [*Editors' note.* We have been unable to locate the source of this quotation.]

sensual craving is not that of a flow of something but of an activated schema—a cognitive structure in action. Fairbairn (1952, p. 150) says, " 'impulse' is not, so to speak, a kick in the pants administered out of the blue to a surprised, perhaps somewhat pained, ego, but ... a psychical structure doing something to something or somebody." Thus, whereas the drive-discharge model invites Newtonian metaphors of the motion of the particles, the clinical theory implies a system lending itself to description in value terms, for example, actions that are permissible or not in relation to self, that have meanings of must, must not, ought not, and the like; of comfort, of power, of self-aggrandizement, and such. Sensual experience always involves such value meaning to self.

Thus, in terms of the clinical theory, the language of force is replaced by the language of activity and relationships. From this perspective, need has a special meaning. A need is a state of thwarted tendency. It is misleading to picture such an active but interrupted tendency as an impersonal energic concentration separated from the ego. The need is an ego-world relationship in a state of active but aborted actualization. When the tendency is lived out, so to speak, when it is unimpededly realized, we do not speak of it as a need. Only when such a directional tendency is blocked in its course do we have a need. Gratification of a need amounts to finding ways of circumventing an obstacle. Defining a need in this way, one can say that how varied and complex are a person's needs reflects the complexity of relationships he is able to entertain with the world, and whether the actualization of these relationships encounters obstacles. Since needs are personalized projects or tasks, need satisfaction ends not only in pleasure or discomfort but also in ego-involved success or failure.

When a need involves sensual experience and sexual behavior—especially when the sensual craving is pre-emptive and nagging—the clinican suspects the active presence of a pre-emptive and nagging self-world value, and he suspects that the immediate sexual aim represents some more encompassing need in which self-conception and self-status are at issue. In such instances what hurts and disturbs is not the tension of unreleased sexual energy but the failure to actualize the self-value which has come to be symbolized through sexual accomplishment. As we have seen, the plasticity of sensual capacity makes it uniquely serviceable to various motivational aims; sensual and/or sexual gratifications can become subsidiary objectives within different motivational settings. It is these rather than the specifically sexual requirement that are in the therapist's focus.

In the clinical theory, then, felt intensity is regarded as the symptomatic expression of a motive or motives to which sexual arousal and gratification have been recruited. Desire for sensual gratification—the purely appetitive aspect of sexuality—is not the whole or even the main point of motivated sexuality. According to analytic clinical experience, in even the most flagrant cases of compulsive sexuality, the seemingly quantitative aspect of intensity involves supportive stimulations of sensuality by symbolic meanings. Therapy is conducted on the premise that if such meanings are brought to light, the intensity can often be reduced. The clinician is not misled by the patient's experience of impulsion to ignore its embeddedness in issues of self-identity, controls, and values. Compulsive sexual acting out presents the therapist with the problem of identifying the motivational matrices that govern the appetitive experience. The pertinent questions are: How easily is sensuality aroused in relation to what motivations, and what are the corollaries of sensual experience? In short, the problem is that of determining the functional requirements (meanings) that are making for persistent and repetitive sensual arousal.

When we view erotic activity in its cognitive aspect, we can more easily understand that the pursuit of sensual pleasure can become especially insistent because of its relationship to an insistent issue of self-identity. Take the phenomenon of sexual craving aroused in a state of grief. Here arousal and the efforts to gratify it are by no means the whole or even the crucial story, but rather what Kubie (1952) calls an effort to "close a circuit." The sequence of meanings encompassing sexuality under conditions of grief would be explained not as the workings of a sexual drive which builds up to intolerable intensity, but rather as a cognitive configuration in which grief leads to loss of security, to impotence, and in turn to renewal via sexual gratification. A series of interlocked purposes is involved here. As long as the grief persists, so does the sexuality. Thus, the explanation of persistence would be not in the tension produced by arousal of the sexual drive, but in the cognitive structure of grief. The motive of sexual behavior is described by the clinical statement, not by the drive-discharge model;

it would be inane to assert simply that the aim of a drive is to achieve its own satisfaction.

To illustrate in detail the difference in emphasis, let us take an example developed by Erikson (1963) to illustrate this point. Peter has retained his bowel movements for a whole week. Erikson writes: "He looked miserable, and when he thought nobody watched him he leaned his bloated abdomen against a wall for support." He has reveries in which " 'I wish I had a little elephant right here in my house. But then it would grow and grow and burst the house.' " And a bad dream in which monkeys are after him trying " 'to get into me' " and bees who are trying " 'to get at the sugar in my stomach' " (pp. 53, 54). A number of other indicators converged on several themes involving erotic sensibility. "I no longer doubted," continues Erikson, "that this little boy had a fantasy that he was filled with something precious and alive; that if he kept it, it would burst him and that if he released it, it might come out hurt or dead. In other words, he was pregnant" (p. 55). Sexuality is undoubtedly involved in the above example, but not in the sense that drive-reduction theory would have us believe. The terms of this fantasy express what Alexander (1935) aptly called an "emotional syllogism"—a rule or premise, expressing the logic of affective values, which guides behavior and thought.

From the therapeutic standpoint, the conscious and unconscious accessibility of the syllogism must be taken into account. Since the eroticism involved in this example is not simply a specific sexual wish, it is not clinically helpful to refer to the tension experienced in this instance as an anonymous drive energy that is clamoring for discharge. Rather, to alleviate the erotic intensity of the fantasy the meanings of the eroticized fantasy must be unraveled, as in Erikson's interpretation: "There was no doubt, then, that once having bloated his abdomen with retained fecal matter this boy thought he might be pregnant and was afraid to let go lest he hurt himself or 'the baby' " (p. 56). Thus Erikson told the child, " 'This,' I said, 'some children do not know. They think that the bowel movements and the babies come out of the same opening in animals and in women' " (p. 55).

Of course, there was more to the unraveling of the syllogism. Why the retention? It turned out that an abrupt separation and loss of his nurse was crucially involved. Sensual experience was doubtless part of the tie the boy felt. The relationship had included innocent sensual approaches that were dealt with playfully, perhaps enjoyed, by the nurse. That it was a conflicted tie for the boy, however, is suggested by the fact that the approaches were noticed with clear expressions of unease and even disapproval by the mother. In this context, during a period of budding, provoked, and disapproved masculinity, the nurse's leaving was disturbing. Further, the nurse subsequently wrote to the boy that she had to leave the household because it was her custom to stay only as long as the child was a baby, because "I like best to tend babies." Subsequently, he became babyish and dependent; it is better to be a baby; and in desperation, lest you lose more, you hold on. Part of the configuration of thought evolved in the effort at repairing the loss was that "the boy identifies with *both partners of a lost relationship*; he is the nurse who is now with child and he is the baby whom he likes to tend" (pp. 57, 58).

In this instance, conflicted values associated with a source of sensual contact received expression in the symptoms described. The erotic components could not easily be described as consisting only of specifically sexual wishes nor the symptoms classified simply as efforts to reduce "libidinal tension." It seems more faithful to the events described to say that sensual experiences were configured in a complex of positive and negative meanings of which the fantasy construction of a baby held on to was a symptomatic by-product.

Diverging Paths of the Two Theories

We often hear that the drive-discharge model is only a general, more parsimonious version of the clinical theory, given in terms that intersect with other fields of data, particularly physiology. It is useful, therefore, to bring the two into closer juxtaposition, to see just how faithfully drive theory mirrors the clinical propositions, to see where the theories are difficult to reconcile or are even at odds with each other. I will not retrace the ground covered by others (Holt, 1965) who have convincingly described the deficiencies of the drive-discharge model as a general paradigm for motivation, but will confine myself to the problems presented by the drive model in dealing with the clinical assumptions regarding sexuality. We will want particularly to see whether the drive theory does, in fact, encompass the range of phenomena to which the clinical concepts are explicitly tailored, and in what respects therapeutic prescriptions are affected by the two ways of looking at sexuality.

Let us first review the essentials of the drive-discharge model.

Drive is conceived as energy generated from within the body. Being energy, it is in movement; being limited in its amount, and varying in respect to the locus and the amount of its accumulation, it exerts different intensities of force, which create a momentum for discharge when a threshold of tolerable intensity is exceeded. Since the discharge is controlled cortically, the energic build-up constitutes a "stimulus on the mind." In this model the essence of sexuality is not an experience but a contentless physiological event, one could say the radiated energy of a source, extrinsic to the psychical event produced by its cortical impact. The psychological aspect of this stimulus, expressing the momentum for discharge, is the *wish*. A motive is drive energy that has acquired such structure. To the degree that motives involve drive energy, they are pressures for discharge.

One aspect of the above account should be made more explicit. There is a difference between the concept of libido and this drive-discharge model. The notion of libido is not by itself a theory of sexual motivation; it was a term Freud early employed to set apart the experiences and behaviors of sexuality from other kinds of activity, and he did this by assigning special properties to the energy involved in sexual activity. "We distinguish this libido in respect of its special origin from the energy which must be supposed to underlie mental processes in general, and we thus also attribute a *qualitative* character to it" (Freud, 1905b, p. 217). In this strictly classificatory meaning the term libido refers to an unspecified physiological substrate of all sensual experiences; the fact that it is seen as an energy could have been simply an early stage of the practice of referring to physiological processes as yet undiscovered.

Freud made these other assumptions about libidinal energy: It is generated within the soma, but its action is like that of an external stimulus because its movement—its stimulus impingement—is outside the realm of voluntary thought and action. As with an external impingement, control must be brought to bear upon it; to dampen it, deflect it, reduce its impact. But being generated from within the organism, such stimulation is particularly difficult to control compared with external stimuli; for example, escape is impossible.

The force of its flow requires an especially strong counterforce, which is therefore a drain on the organism's total energic supply. A good deal of structural growth emerges from this effort, and from the attempts to conserve the supply of energy available for adaptive effort. For this reason, Freud said, instinctual (libidinal) drives are the most important bases of psychological growth. (Rapaport made this proposition the foundation of his theory of learning, though it was a general drive, rather than libido, which Rapaport proposed.)

But Freud went a step beyond this, postulating a model in which this energy is converted into sexual motivation. The model of drive discharge is not specific to sexuality, but refers to a more general regulative process concerning what Freud considered to be the basic aim of the nervous system, the discharge of excessive energic accumulation. Since libido is a "*quantitatively* variable force which could serve as a measure of processes and transformations occurring in the field of sexual excitation" (Freud, 1905b, p. 217; italics added), it seemed readily adaptable to the drive model. Although sexual energy is a particular kind of stimulation to be discharged, it shares with other types of energy the properties required by the drive-discharge model; it is in fixed quantity at any given time; it presses for discharge; the vicissitudes of its deployment and discharge lead to motivation. Thus the drive-discharge model purports to explain how libido energy leads to motivation; but it describes the workings not simply of sex, but of any drive, and in this sense it is a graft on the theory of sexuality. In short, the drive model was part of a theoretical strategy of linking psychological activity to the body through the conception of a process of discharge—the return to an optimum quantity in a region where energic pressure had risen.

We must note the distinction, because just below the surface compatibility there is a serious incompatibility between the libido concept and the drive model in their construing of the central event of sexual activity. Libido gives distinction to the specifically sexual aim; it implies that the primary event is a distinctive pleasure. This is not by any means the same as a reduction of tension, the central event in the discharge model. The pursuit of sensual pleasure may, in fact, involve tolerating a high degree of tension. In the drive-discharge notion, sexual motivation is synonymous with one aim alone, that of modulating the energic level that is felt as unpleasurable. There is even an implied difference about what the essential pleasure of sexuality is. If one looks for a phenomenological principle in the drive-discharge model, it might be that pleasure experience is to be construed as the subjective correlate of the discharge of excessive stimulation, and that this pleasure is in direct proportion to the degree of unpleasure that the "excessive stimulation" had provoked. That pleasure is certainly not a directly elicitable, specifically sexual pleasure. The quantitative aspect of the libido contains no problem for the drive model, but the qualitative assumption of the libido concept of a distinctive pleasure is anomalous with the notion of a discharge origin of the pleasure experience. The drive model has no room for the idea that libidinal activation involves, in its very nature, a distinctive pleasurable experience.

Instinct and drive are quite different concepts. Instinct can simply refer to capacity, to potential activity. A drive definitely implies a quantitative force. Thus, within the clinical conception, we may speak of sexuality as an instinct, without implying the drive model.

These distinctions have become less and less evident in the psychoanalytic literature, and have merged into the by now almost automatic tendency to describe the clinical events of sexuality in the metapsychological terms of energy, tension reduction, drive, and discharge.

The conceptions of the biological substrate differ notably in the clinical and drive conceptions of sexuality. In the clinical view this substrate is a propensity for a distinctive kind of pleasure experience, directly elicitable, having different modes, loci, and developmental phases of arousal, which constitute a pleasure system. The events that affect the mobilization of this pleasure experience, or its inhibition, are its central concern—the motivational aims to which the appetitive experience lends itself, and the ways in which the experience and its modal expression are responsive to these aims. In the drive model the substrate is the need to relieve somatically instigated pressure. Assuming this, the drive model has no easy means, or even need, of regarding the values associated with sensual pleasure as factors which affect its arousal, and color the experience.

The fundamental difference in orientation is: In the drive-discharge model sexuality, conceived as "drive," is something to be disposed of, by consummation or sublimation. In the clinical viewpoint sexuality is a pleasure experience to be elicited or pursued, with variations of aim.

We now turn to some specific points of divergence of the two conceptions.

1. *"Intensity" Interpreted as Experience or as Energic Pressure*

We have already seen how the clinical theory deals with the issue of force. We shall draw upon these points in reviewing how the two theories consider the intensity of sexual motivation. In the drive model's quantitative interpretation, drive strength is viewed as the concentration of energy at a point of potential discharge. Persistent sexual preoccupation is seen as the subjective counterpart of unrelieved pressure of the quantity of drive energy upon a channel of discharge.

One perceives demands in the external environment; but it is misleading to say that the external environment *is* demanding. Murray (1938) used the term "press" to underscore this cognitive reaction to the environment—the environment perceived as pressureful. This is helpful in thinking about sexuality. Sensual wishes can be experienced as implacable, but to infer an "internal environment," external to the self, which is demanding distracts from the psychological meaning of the felt urgency. The clinician accounts for such sensual wishes in terms of the functions served by sensual arousal, in terms of the meaning of such arousal to the self's aspirations and efforts of coping and defense, since sexual experience always has such reverberations. In accordance with the conception of need previously stated, the experience of feeling impelled or driven reflects a directional tendency (motive) enacted abortively but repetitively via the sensual pleasure system.

In conceptualizing sexuality as a peripheral force, the drive-discharge model obscures the clear implication of the clinical view that sensual arousal and mobilization are as much activities of the so-called higher centers as of lower ones. From a physiological standpoint, intense arousal involves central events; arousal is not an intrusion from the gut upon higher centers. Basic to the clinical theory is the premise that the nature of the record laid down by sensual experience has much to do with sensual arousal and inhibition of the appetitive expression of sensuality. Sensual pleasure being an exceptional experience, it is to be expected that it will leave a record that will occupy an equally exceptional role in the controlled arousal and regulation of a sensual system. Why a sexual motivation becomes a not-to-be-denied impulse would then be answered by specifying the components of the cognitive schema actively associated with the sensual system.

The clinical view of motivational intensity reflects a general outlook on psychologically intense experiences of all kinds, for instance, slight versus violent anger, weak versus strong fears, a twinge of jealousy versus its obsessional extremes, etc. In the search for criteria of intensity that cover all of these emotions, and also those of sexual cravings, two stand out: (a) The first criterion is the extent and violence of bodily changes—physiological arousals—of general or specific variety. This is the one which theorists implicitly use when they explain motives on the basis of the energetics of drive. (b) The second criterion is the persisting influence of an emotion on thought and action over a comparatively long time. This is the perspective which guides the clinical viewpoint. According to this criterion, the strength of an emotion depends on how much of a man's conscious, volitional behavior can be explained by reference to it.

Note, however, that these criteria are not merely different sides of the same coin, for they may yield contradictory conclusions about intensity. As Kenny (1963) points out, if we measure a man's fear of heights by the number of times he has such a feeling, we may get a result different from the result obtained by measuring the strength of the fear by the pervasiveness of its effect on his thinking and actions. By the first criterion, a repetitive sexual craving that is relegated to the background by requirements of duty and obligation and is preoccupying only when realistically achievable is no less intense than a more intermittent craving which blots out all other motives when it occurs; but by the second criterion it is less intense. The second criterion is essentially a qualitative view of intensity.

Even if precisely measurable, the bodily phenomena of the first criterion are not identical with the phenomena of intensity of the second criterion. To account for the experience of craving the clinical theory looks to the aborted motive tendencies that are sustaining arousal. The physiological vehicles of sexuality are not themselves motives of sexual arousal. The clinical theory recognizes an intervening connection to self in the links between sexual arousal and its object, whereas the quantitative physiological criterion of the drive model lacks this element of intentionality.

2. *Distinction between Sensual Experience and Sexual Behavior*

The drive-discharge model, being focused on the presumed end state of discharge alone, not only has little to say about sensual experience but assigns no importance to it. This lack renders it insensitive to many clinical phenomena. Indeed, its only link to the phenomenology of sexuality is through the proposition that discharge is felt as pleasure. But this is in conflict with the clinical theory's assertion that sensual pleasure is not an outcome of some tension-modulating process, but is directly elicitable. It does not deny that tension-modulating events can be pleasurable; but sensual pleasure is unlike other affects, even other pleasurable ones, in being directly invoked by stimulation appropriate to the receptive potentialities of a zone. It is not a derivative of other forms of experience. That relief of any tension—not just sexual—is pleasurable is certainly supported by many findings, but that sensual pleasure and tension relief always coincide, or that the pleasure is the same, is questionable.

Freud himself was troubled by the incapacity of the drive-discharge model to provide for the pleasure aspect of sexuality, and proposed a distinctive kind of energy, libido, to explain it. That is why he spoke of libidinal drive, and not simply of drive. But accommodating the phenomenology of sensual feeling to the drive model through the conception of libidinal tension was no easy feat, and the strain did not escape Freud's notice. In one place he wonders "how it can come about that an experience of pleasure can give rise to a need for greater pleasure." "If an erotogenic zone in a person who is not sexually excited . . . is stimulated by touch, the contact produces a pleasurable feeling; but it is at the same time better calculated than anything to arouse a sexual excitation that demands an increase of pleasure" (Freud, 1905b, p. 210).

These considerations call attention to a useful distinction that the clinical theory makes possible, but that the drive-discharge model obscures: the difference between the pleasure principle and the pursuit of sensual pleasure. The pleasure principle, which holds that the organism both avoids unpleasure and seeks pleasure, is a basic regulative principle. The clinical theory clearly implies that the pleasure motivations of the pleasure principle are *not* synonymous with the seeking of sensual pleasure. At the same time sexuality, as a systematic organization, is itself responsive to motives arising from the pleasure as well as other regulative principles. It becomes possible to interpret some sexual behaviors as in the service of the pleasure principle, as when a particular unpleasurable state, such as grief, leads to sexual appetitive behavior. At one time Freud took pains to underscore this distinction, referring to the independent sexual instinct as the weak link in the development of the pleasure principle into the reality principle (see 1911). But he obscured this distinction in his later dual instinct theory of libido and aggression; he then tended to speak of the energies in all motivations governed by the pleasure principle as themselves libidinal and aggressive (1924).

The assumption that sensual pleasure is distinct from the pleasure of tension reduction, and from other pleasurable affects, such as those accompanying experiences of rewards and satisfactions, has barely advanced beyond its first formulation by Freud. It is by no means clear how sensual pleasure differs from these other forms of pleasure, or how infantile sensual experience differs from that of adult sexuality, or how people differ in erogenous and other forms of pleasurable excitability. Our ignorance reflects one of the unfortunate effects of the libido drive-reduction theory—to deflect interest away from the experiential properties of sexuality itself.

One other aspect of the quantitative emphasis of the drive model deserves notice. The coupling of sexual hunger with food hunger and thirst under the seemingly parsimonious conception of drive obscures the differences which are vital in accounting for the prominence of sexuality in Freud's theories. A critical difference lies in this paradox. Although sexuality is a valued and poignant source of pleasure, sexual deprivation can, nevertheless, be suffered with a tolerance far exceeding anything ever demonstrated for hunger and thirst. Moreover, unlike hunger and thirst, its arousal and consummation can be accomplished autogenously. Out of these differences in plasticity emerges the most crucial difference: In neither hunger nor thirst do we see the magnitude of associated values of guilt, sin, licence—the superego valuations generally—that are characteristic of sexuality. Experiences that elicit such valuations tell the clinician that he is in a realm of phenomena easily caught up in conflict. This potential for conflict, as distinguished from frustration, separates the sexual appetite from appetites serving bodily survival.

The clinical theory is helpful in preparing the analyst for possible disjunctions between sensual experience and sexual behavior. For example, sexual intent and behavior without accompanying pleasure is symptomatic of repressed ideas. Thus, sensual pleasure may be subject to repression because negative connotations of fear and anxiety stimulate its inhibition. Or again, the arousal of sensual pleasure may occasion nausea, expressing a repressed sensual involvement marked by humiliation or guilt or shame. The theory prepares the practitioner for a phenomenon such as promiscuous sexual behavior unaccompanied by sensual pleasure, as if the patient were following a syllogism of action whereby sexual indulgence is permissible provided the pleasure is not experienced. The point the clinical theory emphasizes here is that sensual experience itself is symbolized in a cognitive matrix.

The clinical propositions also provide for the expectation that the symbolic elaboration of sexual experience (for example, that of orgasm) will be different in men and women. The cognitive context of sensual encounter is framed by the presence of a penis in a boy and its absence in a girl, by the presence of a cavity in a girl (that, in Erikson's words, is destined to be filled) and its absence in a boy. The detection of these anatomical differences is a vital aspect of the different developmental tasks of each sex; the successes and failures in which they figure will color the sensual experiences closely bound up with them.

3. *Phenomenology of Infantile Sexuality*

Freud's reinterpretation of the psychological meaning of sexuality, the distinction between sensual experience and the modes of its expression, and the proposition of continuity from infancy, all contradicted the traditional view of a seuxal instinct linked to procreation as the only inherent aim of the sexual "drive." The main tenet of Freud's revolutionary reinterpretations of sexuality was that the bond between sensual pleasure and genital orgasm specifies a developmental stage, but is not itself the prototype of sexuality. But in construing sexuality as a discharge phenomenon at all ages, Freud came curiously close to reverting to the traditional view, which identified sexuality with the mode of genital orgasm. He was simply pushing the matter back by speaking of earlier stages with different discharge aims.

It is evident, by now, that the drive-discharge conception is inadequate to encompass even the phenomenology of adult sexuality, not to speak of the observations of infantile sexuality.

Seeing genital sexuality in others, as well as such phenomena as sensual play, sensual handling, sensual rhythms and movements, may arouse sexual feelings. These seem more in the nature of excitatory events that evoke distinctive experience than build-ups and discharge of sexual energy. Discharge is easily imaged for the genital mode, but it is exceedingly difficult to make it fit the phenomena the clinical theory regards as prepubertal sexuality. Particularly in young children sensual pleasure is variable in its forms in the manner of its arousal, and in the aims for which it is sought, with the genital aim and modes least prominent at these stages. Cases of prepubertal coitus are known, but they are unlike those of full maturity. Again, these phenomena seem more in keeping with a system conception of sexuality through which sensual experience can be evoked, by body movements and contact in particular zones—indeed by appropriate manipulations of an excitatory mode of the "sensory systems," for example, touching or being touched, manipulating or being manipulated, smelling or being smelled, listening and being heard, seeing and being seen.

Although the forms of experience of childhood sexuality are not equivalent to adult sexual feelings, the two are continuous; that was Freud's main point. At all stages of development sensual experience has properties that stamp it as uniquely different from other forms of experience. This assumption of a class of experience, sensual pleasure, which is invariant over the course of development, although with variations in the shape of sexual desire, made it possible to account for transfers forward and regressions backward in the course of sexual development.

4. *Conception of Conflict*

In the drive model, an enforced delay in the flow of drive energy intensifies the pressure for discharge. Since the model represents only those impediments to discharge which create a condition of mounting drive tension, it does not distinguish conflict from frustration. In the clinical theory, however, it is important to know whether an obstacle to sensual gratification is of the nature of a frustration or is symptomatic of a conflict. A conflict involves simultaneously active but contradictory tendencies which are innervating the sensual system; identifying these tendencies is a critical therapeutic task. Thus in the clinical theory it is not the tension resulting from a conflict that is the focus of effort, but the incompatible meanings which simultaneously prescribe and proscribe sensual experience and behavior. These meanings are of key importance in the clinical theory; they tell us that the valuations attached to sensual experience, including internalized parental convictions which act as a demand structure, become extremely important in arousal itself, in shaping the aims of arousal, the choice of objects and modes of gratification, and inhibitions in all these respects. Since such values owe their origins in part to conflicts, therapy requires a probe of this history. Such considerations of value or superego components of the system of sensual arousal, and its genesis, are very difficult to capture with the purely quantitative terminology of the drive model.

Why sexuality is universally a focus of conflict is thus brought into the foreground by the clinical theory, but is virtually irrelevant to the drive-discharge model. As we saw earlier, the clinical conception tries to explain why the plasticity of the sensual pleasure system makes inevitable a societal structure which is programmed for deflecting and inhibiting tendencies of sensual arousal and choice; therefore it makes equally inevitable the conflictual confrontation which is guaranteed by the interaction of sensuality and society.

5. *Equation of Sexual Activity with Primary Motivational Aims*

The drive model equates discharge with motivational aim. Since erotic manifestations are viewed solely as the release of libidinal energy, the relief of sexual tension is likely to be taken as the primary motivational objective of all instances of sexual activity.

The clinical theory proposes that much more than release is at stake, and is sought, in sexual activity; that associated value properties of sensual experience color its arousal and expression. It holds that sexual motives are based on learned expectations regarding the consequences of experienced sensuality. To bring about this experience again is a sexual motivation, but its aims, most of the time, extend beyond the relief of tension. Anticipation of sensual pleasure stimulates behavior, but this anticipatory excitement can be a "response" *by-product* of other aims. The motivational significance of an erotic need is revealed by the role sensuality may play in the aims of coping and mastery at the moment—an interpretative guideline which directs attention not so much to the immediate sexual arousal as to those aims which have recruited sensual experience in their behalf. As a functional system, sexual arousal is possible in situations of boredom, of emotional stress and frustration, as a means of replacing an unpleasurable experience with one more desirable and less damaging to one's sense of identity and self-coherence, where these are being threatened.

Correspondingly, the clinical theory does not have to assume that the motivations provoked by repressed ideas are necessarily primarily sexual in objective. The example of Erikson's young patient whose bowel was distended illustrates this point. There was no sexual appetite, or specific wish, clamoring for discharge. The bowel retention reflected a complex emotional syllogism originating in eroticized relationships which accounted for the specific erotization of the bowel. Effective therapeutic aid required the unraveling of this syllogism, not the satisfaction of a sexual wish or intent.

6. *The Issue of Sublimation and Displacement*

Both the clinical theory and the drive model provide for circumspect sexual activity through substituted aims and choices which do not have a primarily sexual intent. In the libido drive theory the sexual tendency is a potential of a certain amount of energy; this energy remains active until its release, but this release can be effected through activities of an utterly different nature from obvious sexuality. This is the essence of its notion of displaced sexuality. Sublimation is a special form of displacement which refers to the diversion of sexual energy and its discharge through higher, more socially acceptable activities that, in their adaptive aspect, are nonsexual.

The clinical conception, too, provides for alternative activities originating in enforced deflections of sexual aim and choice. However, an important distinction implicit in the clinical conception, but not deducible from the drive model, is the difference between substitutes *for* sensual pleasure and alternative means *of* sensual arousal.

From the assumptions of plasticity it is evident that erotic pleasure is potentially achievable in a variety of ways. The mouth, anus, genitals are in large measure interchangeable as sources of excitation, while potentially satisfying objects may range from auto- to homo- to heteroerotic, including even inanimate objects (fetishes). However, the clinical conception also recognizes that there are other sources of pleasure besides sensuality, and therefore that pleasure aims are substitutable. A deflection in aim from sensual pleasure can occur in the form of reinforcement of another pleasure aim. A critical point of difference between this and the drive model is that it is not necessary to assume that it is specifically sexual pleasure that is experienced in substitutive activity that has been generated by the thwarting of a sensual aim. It is thus within the bounds of the clinical conception that erotic sensibility may stimulate interest in subject matters in which a sensual experience is no longer an immediate objective. In the framework of the clinical theory, the nature of the pleasure aim in the substitution is an all-important consideration in analyzing substitutive behavior.

There are, indeed, activities not socially identified as sexual that do actually evoke sensual pleasure, and these may be emphasized alternatively to specifically tagged sexual outlets, for example, picking one's nose, as a masturbatory equivalent. Although not socially labeled as sexual, the sensual pleasure aroused is the main point of engaging in such activities. But it is incorrect to say that they represent what is ordinarily meant by sublimation. Actually, one finds that such permissible, available means of sensual stimulation lead to intensification of the activity, as when nose-picking becomes compulsive to the point of causing bleeding. If the substitutive activity is actually sexually stimulating, the appetite for it may increase, and the problem of control will be worsened, not alleviated. Such activities do not fall into the category of what is usually called sublimation.

But there are other activities which may indeed result from the frustration of sexuality but which in themselves are truly nonsensual, that is, they neither enhance nor relieve the sexual appetite. Thus satisfaction in another area may be great enough in a variety of ways to lessen the need for sensual gratification, not because "sexual energy" is "discharged" in an alternative channel, but simply because the role of sexuality in the motivational economy has been rendered relatively less insistent by another class of pleasurable satisfactions. Work, esthetic gratifications, and the like may have this function. This does not rule out the possible phenomenon of erotization of work itself; we find indeed that when this occurs it generally interferes with work. I am suggesting only that the mere conjoining of reduced sexual need and heightened nonsexual activities is no evidence whatsoever that the alternative activity is a surrogate sexuality—an avenue of libidinal discharge as drive theory holds.

Here we may recall Freud's proposition regarding the two-way traversibility between the sexual and nonsexual systems and the proposition that just as the sexual system is capable of serving nonsensual needs, other pleasure systems may be invoked in lieu of sexuality, perhaps even to participate in inhibiting its activity. We earlier discussed instances of the substitution of sexual activity for other, nonsexual aims which are frustrated. Sublimation is the other side of the coin; other pleasure systems may serve in lieu of sexual pleasure. Despite this possibility, howver, there are difficulties in achieving such true sublimations; the clinical theory also tells us that the promise of sensual pleasure is not easily deflected by other aims and other forms of pleasure, is certainly not easily stilled, owing to the cognitive record of its unique poignancy, which is unmatched by other forms of pleasure.

The drive model has no room for the distinction just described. Here, the shift from the original sexual object to the secondary social object is not simply the substitution of the one by the other, but is an actual displacement of the same libidinal energy now discharged in a new direction: and this holds for all displacements, including those qualifying as sublimations. The drive model has no place for substitutions, provoked by sensuality, that are not themselves sexual in aim; it holds the substitutive activity to be a specifically sexual discharge.

7. *Rapaport's Solution: Drive without Libido*

Some students of Freud, Rapaport prominent among them, were caught in the dilemma created by the libido drive theory of how to attribute qualitative as well as quantitative attributes to sexual energy. Rapaport resolved the problem by replacing the libido concept with a generalized conception of drive energy which is nonspecific in aim. Between the aspect of the drive theory that tried to account for sexual aim (libido) and the aspect of it that chose to deal with force (the discharge model), Rapaport chose the latter. To him the libido concept was expendable but not the drive-discharge model. Consequently, his solution was on the side of believing that the most important aspect of sexuality—its motivational aspect—could be construed in terms of the mechanics of tension alleviation and of structures resulting from the control of tension level and of discharge.

Rapaport believed the main characteristic of drive to be its peremptoriness, interpreted as tension produced by an energic pressure—a purely quantitative matter—and he felt he could save this factor within the drive-discharge model. Hence in Rapaport's model the critical terms were quantitative, such as cathexis, tension, binding, and discharge; they invoked no assumption of a qualitatively different kind of energy that was specifically sexual.

However, in speaking of mounting drive tension in the abstract, Rapaport actually ignored Freud's account of the motivational properties of erotic experience. In effect, he ignored one of the greatest of Freud's contributions, one which distinguished his theories from all other psychological theories of his time, namely, the unique conflict-inducing potential of sexual experience compared with other motivational sources. It may be that the libido theory is expendable, but surely the clinical propositions regarding sexuality that it tried to embody are not.

The net effect has been that Rapaport's version of drive theory has no clear line to clinical data; it is not intimately tied to clinical observations which in Freud's theory took on a new meaning as "sexual." In his model, sexual phenomena have no more uniqueness than the motivations of a nonsense-syllable learning experiment, their identifying mark as drive being only peremptoriness, like an urgent bowel movement. Eliminating considerations of the human aspects of sexuality and emphasizing a wholly quantitative concept of motivation, Rapaport's model is no longer specifically psychoanalytic.

8. *Different Assumptions about the Physiological Substrate*

The clinical and drive theories offer differing perspectives of the physiological substrate of sexuality. In the clinical theory, sexuality is not a drive of relatively fixed quantity, small or large, but an appetite of variable quality, adjustable in different contexts. Its propositions imply a system conception of sexuality—an appetitive structure responsive to arousing and inhibiting activations, including those which emanate from cognitive structures (schemata) in which concepts and memories of sensual experiences have been organized. If at one stage of development the child reacts sensually to a stimulus in one way, and at another age in exactly the opposite way, one must realize that there is an internal structural change which decides each reaction.

A system conception seems a more congenial framework for the clinical assumptions of an evolving and changing structure than a flow model of drive. Such a sensual system would be an open system, subject to differentiation and modification in the forms in which sensual pleasure is experienced. This open system, the theory of sensuality, would encompass the person's experiencing of the world, the formation of his images of the world and of his relationships. A system conception of sexuality also embraces the proposition that the modes which are capable of yielding sensual pleasure are also the means of its control and inhibition. The functioning of the system would be organized around rules of operation, subject to developmental change, regarding sensuous mobilization and inhibition—rules which specify, at each stage of development, the do's, can's, and must not's, and express the conflicts which surround sexual experience.

The cognitive activity of such a system also seems to be more congenially conveyed by the notion of a schema to which the sexual system is responsive. As we have seen, sensual pleasure is savored through activation of the record of previous arousals and reinforcement. The peremptoriness of sensual cravings has much to do with the persistent activation of this cognitive structure. It can activate the *adient* tendencies of search, moving toward, embracing, merging, and so on, which promise or afford and maintain sensual pleasure. According to the motivational context to which it is itself responsive, the schema is also capable of inducing *abient* responses of withdrawal in relation to sensual arousal. It is through the schema that memories and accumulated conceptions of sensuality thus become capable of invoking sensuality or inhibiting it.

In its early stages of development such a cognitive schema of the sensual system could scarcely extend beyond the capability of experiencing sensual pleasure (i.e., responsiveness to appropriate conditions of sensual stimulation). As sensual encounters occur, and with the emergence of capacities for anticipating (structures capable of utilizing the record of sensual encounter), there appears the potential for experiencing sensual need. It would be foolish to say that the baby from the start seeks sensual pleasure. The experience of needing, and therefore of seeking, presumes a cognitive record, not simply a contentless build-up of tension.

In the imagery of a system and schema conception, force would refer to the cognitively elaborated experience of sensual pleasure and to the extent of its pre-emption of thought and behavior. Certainly the circumspections of which sexual expression is capable, its deflections and even disavowal, are among its most remarkable features, but we need not refer these to an implacable, not-to-be denied linear force. What we actually observe—the data behind references to a sexual force or delay of drive discharge—is a pleasure that is permitted to occur or not, activities one is drawn toward for their promise of affording this experience or that are avoided for the same reason, and the capability of these tendencies of being stirred to repetitive arousal (peremptoriness) by a variety of motivational aims to which the system as a whole is responsive. If the term force is to be used at all within such a system approach, it would refer to the repetitiveness and pervasiveness of activation of the schema of sexual meanings—memories and concepts—in sensuous mobilization. It would lose its drive-model meaning of an uncoded energic quantity from the soma which moves the organism toward sexual behavior.

Obviously this is hardly an adequate account of the attributes that need to be assumed in a full-scale conception of sexuality. My purpose is to underscore the point that the drive-discharge model is essentially independent of the clinical theory, which is capable of, indeed requires, another physiological interpretation. One of the important holds of the drive model on theorists has been its seeming promise of a point of intersection between psychoanalysis and physiology, in spite of the fact that the physiological plausibility of the discharge model has been repeatedly and convincingly questioned (see, for example, Kaufman, 1960).[7]

[7]Kaufman concludes (p. 324): "... it seems to me that we need no longer postulate that the panorama of sexuality as we know it in man is derived from an inborn biological urge or force pressing inexorably for discharge. Rather, we may view the manifestations of sexuality in terms of an ontogenetic development of inborn sensori-motor patterns, achieving a maturational, hierarchical, unitary structure by progressive synthesis of components through a series of transactional experiences, in the course of which the goals and thereby the drive are acquired."

It should be noted that in Freud's work there never was any data that directly supported the idea of a drive quantity; there was only data about the cognitive and affective matrix of erotic activity. Freud's earliest formulations of sexuality, which antedated the drive concept, included an ideational structure which he called a "wish." Even later, in his drive theory he implicitly assumed that drive always occurs in a cognitive matrix, in this fashion distinguishing wish from *Trieb* (drive). But Freud never carried his thinking about this cognitive format beyond his formulations in Chapter Seven of *The Interpretation of Dreams* (1900).

This last point is especially important. In 1900 the theory of a developing sexual structure had not yet come into being, and Freud's notion of sexuality was still tied to the conventional one referring only to genital sexuality. The cognitive aspect of sexuality was conceived solely in relation to how genital modes and aims are hemmed in by conflict, with the thwarted genital impulse being revealed in symbolic ways. Therefore, his model of the activity of the sexual wish, indeed the very notion of "wish," was couched in the terms of genital functions.

The concept of "wish" more easily encompasses the cognitive aspect of *genital* sexuality than that of the sexual activity of early developmental stages and the correlative phenomena of fixation and regression as proposed in the later theory. Nor can it encompass the variety of motives which include but can also take forms other than genital wishes or even forms other than wishes at all (for instance, erotization of functions).

For the later theory, the issue of immediate and remote aims of sensual gratification was crucial; it brought into the foreground the possibility that sexuality can itself serve other motivational ends. Clinicians were alerted to the possibility that wishes themselves can have extended cognitive meaning, that a craving is the visible indication of converging facilitative arousals upon the sexual system. For instance, Jacobson (1967) describes a man struggling with a crisis of threatening dissolution of self, who experienced surges of sexuality and widespread erotization of behavior. She accounts for this on the principle that sensual pleasure has various functional properties, in this instance that of serving a defensive or restitutional function.

Thus the concept of sexual wish seems a structural unit too narrow to encompass the cognitive involvements of sexuality. Indeed, it was the anachronistic persistence of the early genital wish concept as the sole means of representing cognitively elaborated erotism that contributed to the pansexual extremes to which psychoanalytic interpretations were often carried.

Summary

I have tried to disentangle the psychoanalytic clinical propositions regarding sexuality from the propositions of the drive-discharge model. In the clinical view, the critical identifying mark of sexuality, at all ages, is a distinctive class of pleasure experience that differs from both sensory experience and from other pleasurable affects. The word *sensual* rather than *sexual* underscores the central importance of the experiential aspect of sexuality in the clinical theory, as an experience directly arousable through various forms of contact, principally involving human interaction, but also through self-initiated stimulation, and associated with a variety of adient behaviors. Anatomically, the equipment for its arousal is the same as the equipment for *doing*.

It is this potential for sensual experience that Freud proposed as the critical, invariant component of sexual development from infancy to adulthood. Sensual encounters and the maturing cognitive capacities form an evolving structural record of this class of experience; this record provides a schema of facilitative and inhibitive directives—canons or rules—governing all aspects of sensual sensibility. The subjective pleasure aspect of sexuality, the forms of its direct arousal, and its symbolizations encompass what is distinctive about human sexuality. For Freud they were the starting point for understanding the pervasiveness of sexuality in human motivation.

A crucial point of this radical reinterpretation of sexuality, which made it possible for Freud to conceive of stages of sexual development, was that the capability for sensual pleasure is not exclusively associated with the modes and behavior patterns of reproductive sexuality; this led to the idea that sexuality can be manifested in a wide variety of ways accompanied by sensual pleasure, and to the idea that preferences in these respects can be fixated or regressive. As an appetite of variable quality, adjustable in different contexts, it lends itself to many means of satisfaction and to many means of facilitation or inhibition.

Being plastic in respect to the modes and objects of its arousal, sensuality acquires a variety of motivating functions for the person's developing self-identity, particularly for dealing with unpleasure. Through its principle of plasticity, the clinical theory offers a profound, if also complex, view of the necessity for and possibilities of control of sensuality, and of the inevitability of its provoking developmental crises and conflict.

In contrast to the clinical theory which emphasizes the meanings of sexuality, the drive-discharge theory is one of ameaning. The critical difference of emphasis between the two viewpoints may be summarized in the statement that in the drive theory pleasure is derived not from the pursuit of drive but from the getting rid of it. Condensing the issues of sensual experience, modes, and sexual motivation to a process of discharge of tension, the drive-discharge model fails to make contact with the qualitative propositions of the clinical theory, militating against even acknowledging such a subjective state as sensual experience.

The drive-discharge model served Freud as an interface concept, to fill the gap in physiological understanding created by his revolutionary clinical conceptions, which no physiological model of his time could encompass. For many analysts, this still seems to be the great virtue of the drive-discharge model. Indeed, it is usually to physiology rather than to clinical data that analysts look for confirmation of the drive model. But almost all such efforts at confirmation by physiology turn out not to involve actual tests of the model; rarely, if ever, have physiological studies been designed as tests of Freud's conception of drive. Attempts, therefore, to draw sustenance from physiological studies for the drive model amount to a tranquilizing potion, self-administered in the dosage necessary to dull sensibility to the model's clinical inadequacies.

Actually, it is questionable whether the concepts of the drive model allow direct tests against clinical data. No method has ever been devised of constructing the appropriate intermediate terms that would reduce the distance between the drive concepts and clinical observations. As Rubinstein (1968) has aptly pointed out, the drive-discharge theory has been developed on data not appropriate to its concepts; it has drawn upon the same observational domain as the clinical propositions, but by unspecified steps of inference. The data that would be specifically suited to more direct test of the drive model would have to be quite different from those available through clinical observation. It needs data that lend themselves to the specification of an energic unit according to some specific standard of quantity, chemical or physical. Such data could not be those of clinical psychoanalysis; its units are cognitive ones of meaning. In this sense, the drive model is irrelevant to clinical psychoanalysis.

The consequence of the unchallenged pre-eminence of the drive model has been a notable failure to test the implications of the clinical propositions within the context of clinical observation. That is to say, there has been a failure to regard the clinical propositions as theory, as hypotheses to guide deductive investigation, and subject to revision. Psychoanalysis can grow only by pitting its theories against rival assertions, and primarily through the use of its own clinical data. The clinical propositions of sexuality, being readily referable to clinical observation, lend themselves to such confrontation.

The situation is, then, that a theory capable of exploration through clinical data lies more or less fallow, and a theory incapable of such development is constantly used to explain these same data. As yet there has been no extensive or rigorous attempt to explore the clinical propositions. Obviously, much remains to be done, too, about specifying the theory's propositions in forms that can be tested empirically.

Guardians of Freud's heritage generally discount repudiations of the drive concept as merely an effort to repress hard-won insights about sexuality. And so the static condition of the theory is solemnized. In the light of the wide gap that exists between the drive model used for explaining sexuality and the propositions of meaning by which analysts in their consulting rooms in fact make sense of sexual phenomena, we can see that the drive-discharge model imposes a kind of stultifying scientism on the clinician's efforts to articulate his understanding and to enlarge its scope.

CHAPTER 4

The Ego in Psychoanalysis: A Concept in Search of Identity

THOUGH THE TERM "ego" has meanings that go back to the beginnings of philosophy it is only its place in psychoanalytic theory that is our concern here. We must first rid the term of its popular nonpsychoanalytic meanings. The ego is not simply intelligence; it is not an inflated sense of one's own importance. It does not refer to its traditional philosophical meaning of self-consciousness. Freud did not mean it to be strictly a phenomenological concept. Neither is the ego simply the *subject* of experience, in contrast to the objects of experience; nor is it one's own person (self) in contrast to others. These exclusions are not arbitrary; they eliminate meanings irrelevant to psychoanalytic theory.

The concept of "ego," as shaped by Freud's continual efforts to coordinate it with the parent body of psychoanalytic theory, is that of the "representative of reality" within the personality. In Freud's last and most fully developed conception of the ego, self-feelings, the capacity to reflect on such feelings and on oneself as a person, and the capacity to experience distinctions between self and others are *functions* within the ego system, part of the ego's adaptational repertoire of controls and defenses as a subsystem of personality. For Freud, the fundamental meaning of ego was that of a hypothetical array of processes standing, generally, for survival and self-preservation, and concerned with the structuring of purposive action in relation to various aspects of reality.

Of course, psychoanalytic theorists are not always clear and consistent in their usage of the term. Sometimes "ego" is merely a taxonomical term referring to defensive and adaptational motives and their instrumentalities. Sometimes "ego" has the more ambitious connotation of a distinctive subsystem of the personality, one whose functions include the regulation of subsystems, superego, and id. In this sense it becomes more an independent variable that has a role in "affecting" behavior; it is not simply a taxonomy of motivational phenomena or of functions, but an entity whose parameters, mode of operations, and functions are potentially capable of specification in some model of self-regulation.

Confusion in psychoanalytic usage developed from the fact that while the ego concept had been present from the very beginning of Freud's theory, it underwent a number of changes and shifts of emphasis in response to developments in psychoanalytic theory at large, a fact which Freud sometimes neglected to acknowledge. Freud was not given to regular stocktaking. The lure of the next bend behind which new discoveries might appear was always distracting him from the labor of taking theoretical inventory. Part of the intent of this review is to draw attention to the invariant meanings that have clung to the term throughout its history in psychoanalysis, as well as to the changes of emphasis. Of equal concern will be the logical place of the ego concept within psychoanalytic theory and its distinctive character as a framework for explaining behavior. From what model of man's behavior did the concept arise? Which phenomena came within its sphere of meaning? What considerations compelled revisions? The history of the ego concept has been described several times (e.g., Hartmann, 1939; Kris, 1951; Rapaport, 1958b), so I will touch on historical considerations only to indicate how changes in the ego concept reflected the state of the parent body of psychoanalytic theory. These changes were, particularly, the gradual emergence of the ego concept from its setting within a theory of illness to one also concerned with normal development, and its further emergence to its present status as a concept constituting a distinctive field of psychoanalytic enterprise called ego psychology. A final and important consideration will be an assessment of its current status in psychoanalysis.

THE EGO IN FREUD'S EARLIEST MODEL

From the start, Freud needed a concept of ego. Indeed, it is a curious fact that his ego concept antedated even his theory of psychosexual drives, generally considered to be the cornerstone of psychoanalysis. We may reasonably assume that Freud's early theory of the mind was unavoidably dependent on a concept of ego, just as his later theories were dependent on a concept of instinctual drives. Believing that he had discovered the primary etiological basis of hysterical symptomatology—a psychical "lesion" traceable to a traumatic sexual experience in childhood—Freud, in the enthusiasm of discovery, envisioned the mechanics of neurosis within a comprehensive neurophysiological model of normal behavior. In a work published posthumously as a "Project for a Scientific Psychology" (1895), Freud developed his first systematic account of the fundamental forces in man's behavior. Behavior, he said, is ultimately the expression both of the discharge, through appropriate actions upon the environment, of the accumulated pressures of internally and externally generated tensions, and of structural complications that develop in the organism in the course of its efforts to find the most effective means of this discharge. He called these the primary and secondary functions of psychical structures.

There are two main peripheral sources of energic inflow, exteroceptive and enteroceptive, the enteroceptive being of endogenous chemical origin (later to be known as "libido"). A basic premise of this conception was that survival is contingent upon the maintenance of an optimal level of energic tension within the organism. Energies arising beyond the tolerable level require discharge. While the tension produced by such energic pressures "demands" modulation, survival dictates that the discharge be effective, and even that tension be tolerated until there appear realistic indications that the discharge will benefit the organism (e.g., discharge through hallucination may be satisfying over the short haul, but is not ultimately profitable). The secondary function of psychical processes not only represents the reality that must be recognized, but also defines the means of adequate drive discharge, to develop means of restraining the precipitous and sometimes dangerous discharge. All the functions of thought—perception, judgment, and reflection—are ultimately the instrumentalities of this secondary function, outcomes of the individual's encounter with the "exigencies of life," as Freud termed them. The constant requirement of finding means of discharge is ultimately the most important source of momentum toward the complicated developments that take place in thought and action.

The ego was conceived as an essential structural means of accomplishing the secondary function of effective discharge, one that could respond simultaneously to the demands of energic tension and to environmental conditions suited to tension reduction, one that could monitor motoric instrumentalities of discharge (because effective discharge is achievable only through action), and that could be implemented by perceptual-cognitive operations which guarantee the proving of reality, or "reality testing." The ego, then, was a coherent organization of capacities for controlling energy flow, and which operated in coordination with processes concerned with the "representation of realities"—thought, perception, judgment, reflection, etc. Freud even specified a latticelike arrangement of neurons with special capabilities of retaining excitation and directing energic transmission. In the "Project," defense, which later became a dominant property of the ego, was construed in both a broad and a narrow sense, as part of the secondary function: in the broad sense, as an inhibiting but adaptational process which directs the course of discharge, and in the narrow sense, as a specific form of inhibition or "repression." This is of interest, because for two whole decades following the "Project" the narrow sense of "defense" pre-empted all other meaning of "ego." In this remarkable document, which merits more detailed study than is possible here, Freud spells out the functions of the ego, which he was not inclined to do again in as systematic a way for some 30 years.

Status of the Concept: 1900-1923

The period following the "Project," 1900 to 1923, during which he produced *The Interpretation of Dreams* (1900), is generally regarded as the second and main period of Freud's writings. During this time, although ego frequently appeared as a necessary descriptive term, Freud's interest in a theory of the ego waned. Functions that in the "Project" had been specifically assigned to the ego now were dealt with separately, without being explicitly associated with the ego. The term had a variety of descriptive usages, sometimes connoting "conscious inhibitive control," sometimes meaning "motivations concerned with self-preservation" (i.e., "ego drives"), sometimes in the sense of "the internalized ideals and values of identification figures," and sometimes meaning "feelings of self." Mainly, however, it seems to have had the narrower connotation of "an instrumentality of *defense*," and specifically of repression. As such, the ego appeared variously as the conscious acceptable mass of ideas which took part in the conflict, as the ideals which precipitated the conflict, as the resisting force in conflict, the agency of the repressive process itself. In Freud's earlier as well as later conceptions, these were all *partial* attributes of the ego concept. The idea of a comprehensive, coherent system of control was put aside.

Several reasons have been put forward for the generally unsystematic way in which Freud used the concept in this period. In part, this was Freud's style of theorizing. He tended to emphasize the theoretical implications of his immediate empirical concerns, ignoring their sometimes dissonant juxtaposition with earlier formulations. He also wanted to discard the neuronal model, which he considered a failure, and with it went his early strategy of trying to encompass pathological phenomena within a comprehensive model of *normal* functioning. Instead, Freud now devoted himself entirely to the observations of phenomena he was most immediately confronted with—illness, symptoms, and conflict. He not only moved toward a physiologically "neutral" form of theory, but became preoccupied specifically with the dynamics of *illness*, and less with the task of a comprehensive *general* psychology of adaptation. This development impelled him toward concern with a theory of the genesis of illness in conflict, and to focus on the roles of sexuality and instinctual drives. In the "Project" he had tried to view issues of discharge and control not simply in relation to sexual wishes and tensions, but in the broader perspective of a general biological enterprise of adaptation to stimulation. There the secondary function of defense was broadly construed; now it became identified with the ego in the narrower sense of repression produced by conflicts in which sexual wishes were preeminent. The mental lesions—obsessions, hysterical symptoms, perversion, and the like—and their treatment took stage center. Elaboration of the principles of neuroses and conflict, and the relation of both to sexual bases, became the core of Freud's theoretical enterprise. Two developments were of monumental importance in setting the direction of his work for the next two decades: his retraction of the etiological importance he had given to sexual trauma in childhood, and his altered views of the nature of the conflictual bases of neurosis.

Freud's original conception of the importance of sexuality in the causation of hysteria (1896) was that the memory of an actual traumatic sexual experience in childhood (e.g., seduction) was central. In this view, the memory of such a prepubertal experience becomes especially pathogenic in the later period of genital sexuality, creating the condition of neurosis-inducing conflict.[1] However, Freud later became convinced that the disturbing idea in hysterical neurosis was not a memory, but a *fantasy* of seduction woven out of a tabooed sexual wish, and he gave up the conception that the critical etiological event was an actual seduction.

This development jolted the very fundamentals of psychoanalytic theory, for now one had to ask how such a fantasy and the wishes involved in it came about. The three main sources of neurotic illness—the sexual core of conflict, the unconscious wishes, and the unsuccessful repressive defense against these wishes—henceforth became the main themes of Freud's theoretical efforts. He systematically investigated continuities in sexual experiences at different stages of development, and their pathological miscarriages. His clinical data pointed to the autogenetic connection between early infantile needs and bodily functions and the later development of genital gratification.

Because of these observations, the theory of instinctual sexual drives became a critical anchorage of Freud's thought; it became all-determining, the "reality" to which adjustment must be geared. An internal stimulus, being periodic, peremptory, and inescapable through flight, creates a continuous, unrelenting source of striving that must be discharged through appropriate "objects." The other

[1] "The outbreak of hysteria may almost invariably be traced to *psychical conflict* arising through an incompatible idea, setting in action a *defence* on the part of the ego and calling up a demand for repression . . . the defence achieves its purpose of thrusting the incompatible idea out of consciousness . . . if the idea that is to be repressed can be brought into logical or associative connection with an infantile experience of that kind" (Freud, 1896, p. 211).

vital appetitive instincts like hunger and thirst were deemed to contribute little to an understanding of neurosis. By far the most important source of motivation and of individual development was the sexual drives and the conflicts engendered by their momentum toward gratification. Moreover, the sexual drives underwent developmental changes in relation to changes in their aims (wishes) and in their potentialities for possible gratification (objects); indeed, they were the primary momentum toward growth. Their structuring power seemed so great that Freud at times tended to believe that character development itself is patterned exclusively by fixation upon different aims and modes of drive gratification. Environment was accorded little significance in the development of instinctual drives, but figured rather in the conflicts generated by the drives. Family life and rearing were considered as creating obstacles to the discharge of drives, necessitating indirect forms of discharge or total repression.

For Freud, the most crucial discovery was that of infantile sexuality—the revelation of a developmental continuity in requirements for sensual gratification from infantile modes to the usual adult forms of sexuality. He wrestled with the formidable problem of how to fit into a uniform theory the facts of an erotic momentum: its seeming continuity in development, its interchangeability of sensual aims and modes of gratification, and its pathological deflections in perversion, fixations, and regressions. His theoretical solution was that of an active principle of sensual development, involving an energic quantum, with distinctive qualitative and directional properties; he called it libido. The aims of libidinal discharge develop in an implacable course, progressing by stages. At the same time, within each stage, libido is capable of some degree of transformation and displacement regarding objects of discharge. For example, "conscientiousness" could be a transformation of "anal libido"; for the little girl the genital drive had to be displaced from mother to father. Libidinal discharge became for Freud the most important single basis of motivation. He believed that the requirements for the relief of libidinal tensions, the shifts in distributions of libido, the conflicts to which tensions gave rise, and the deflections in their discharge were not only the main factors in neurosis but the paradigm of normal motivational development.

Through the simplification achieved by attributing direction to a distinctive type of energy, Freud had an attractive and seemingly efficient means of coordinating the complex facts of sexual development and the autogenic heightening and lessening of the desire for sensual gratification in each period. Through the *quantitative* attributes of libido, the theory could account for the intensity of drives, for the pressureful momentum of sensuality; through its *qualitative* attributes of directionality, it could account for the selection of the objects which can elicit its discharge. Libidinal energy in its various drive forms had characteristics usually associated with animal instinct; at the same time it had the crucial property of displaceability, which distinguished it as specifically human. Thus the forms of transformation from oral to anal to phallic and to genital stages are inherited, as is the momentum of transition from one phase to the next; but within each stage the options of gratification are considerable. Note, however, that the distinction between the energy or activation aspect of sensuality and the executive actions that form it into drives was obscure in Freud's formulation; the relationship of the quantitative and directional assumptions of the libido theory are still unclarified, and to this day remain in uneasy coexistence in psychoanalytic theorizing. Note that Freud was also sharply veering away from his early emphasis on the importance of environmental (exteroceptive) stimulation. (In the "Project" it was conceived as one of two crucial sources of tension increase requiring discharge.) Although at a cost of narrowing his perspective from adaptation processes generally (including those independent of the pleasure principle) to a process in which the environment was significant only in relation to the pleasure principle, Freud's libido theory helped him to elaborate, as had no one before him, on the role of sexuality in the structuring of thoughts and actions, both normal and pathological.

Sharing the spotlight with libidinal drives at this time was the nature of conflict in neurotic disturbances. Before, a traumatic event was considered to be the source of a symptom or "lesion." Now, Freud viewed symptoms as attempts to resolve the actual or fantasied incompatibilities existing in wished-for gratifications; symptoms were the outcome of the clash between the claims of drive-derived wishes and the claims of internalized representations of an obstructing social reality. For Freud a key factor in neurotic conflict was repression—the blocking of a wish and its derivatives and associations from conscious understanding and action. Symptoms of conflict were an outcome and a manifestation of repression; they reflected a strategy of resolving conflict, arising out of the impasse which repression imposes upon gratification. The narrowing of Freud's interest to the one adaptational function of defensive repression reflected the momentum of the logic of his theory; it led to, and was continually fed by, particular emphases of clinical observation. It is also true, however, that therapeutic necessity demanded clarification of the dynamics of repression. For according to the theory, the goal of therapy is to uncover the repressed; therefore, priority must be given to observing indications of the return of that which had previously been repressed and to means of overcoming the ill effects of repression.

Although the ego was present in this conception, it was a curiously vague entity, identified most of the time, but not exclusively, as the agency of the repressive force. Or was it an entity at all? Certainly Freud's interest in the concept of the ego was dominated by his preoccupation with the role of repression in conflicts. The most frequently recurring interpretation of the ego was an agency of repressive control. Emphasis was given to its function of *resistance* to drive and wish, and to its function of *inhibition*, rather than to its capacities for promoting effective gratification. It was identified not only with the repressing force but with the body of ideas—internalized value structures as well as consciously accessible and acceptable ideas—which instigated resistance to drive discharge. Freud also tended to link capacities for conscious experience and will with the ego, but this was loosely developed and does not easily fit with the notion of the ego as an agency that promotes elisions of consciousness through repression. The absence of any detailed regard for how these oppositely effective functions are related within the ego is an example of Freud's disinclination, in this period, to systematize the ego conception.

The reduced importance of a specific environmental etiology of neurosis may possibly have diminished Freud's interest in the ego, even though it remained a necessary part of his over-all conception of psychical structure. The purely adaptational aspect of the ego became less compelling.

Freud saw parental behavior and family life as significant aspects of the environment, but only as potential impediments which produced conflict and provoked defense. The possible supportive importance of the environment as a molding and implementing influence on normal drive functioning was not a natural fulcrum of interest for libido theory and so received little attention.

One also wonders if premonitions of contradiction with the libido theory contributed to the stasis of the ego concept in this period, since Freud's account of the structuring and motivational force of libidinal drives included attributes that he later, under the pressure of observation, imputed to the ego.

As for motivations specifically attributable to the ego, Freud spoke about them only in relation to the ego's role as an instrumentality of the pleasure principle, and mainly in its role of defense. He did for a time speak of "ego drives" but he gave up that notion, possibly because of difficulties in making it compatible with the libido theory. It seemed necessary to emphasize only reactivity to instinctual drive and containment of drive by defense. Indeed, this emphasis is common even today. Clinicians are still inclined to regard the ego mainly in the light of its participation in conflict and in its partnership with instinctual drives pressing for discharge.

Despite scant attention to adaptive functions of the ego as a system, Freud had much to say about the adaptive as well as drive-related aspects of thought processes; but he did not organize them into a single concept of an ego system of control. His epoch-making distinction between primary-process and secondary-process thought appears in *The Interpretation of Dreams* (1900). Primary-process thought is wholly in the service of drives, of promoting peremptory discharge; in marked contrast, secondary-process thought shows characteristics that follow the precepts and rules of logic, maintaining an identity or coordination with reality structures and events. The distinction implies that there is an "objective reality" and that secondary-process thought is capable of representing it without distorting it. However, Freud left the developmental origins and nature of the secondary process largely undescribed and unexplained. In fact, it never again received the attention he had given it in the "Project."

It is possible that some of the difficulties that have persistently clung to the ego concept since Freud's time can be traced to the fact that the secondary process and its reality-testing functions were not explicitly a part of the ego theory in this period. Its status as a means of implementing effective drive control, as well as a means of representing reality relationships generally, was implicit but not developed. Also, the question whether the mechanisms of symbolization, condensation, and displacement of the primary process are best viewed as ego manifestations is to this day unresolved. To have confronted such questions—and that of making primary and secondary processes comprehensible within a conception of ego—would have drawn attention to the crucial issue of the independence of ego processes from libidinal control. Moreover, there was something contradictory in the view of the ego as primarily a reactive, defensive agency whose vital biological mission is to insure self-preservation. There are, in Freud's writings, any number of hints that it was difficult to avoid the assumption of an autonomously active force in the ego. The critical point is that Freud did not consider in detail the problem of instrumentalities of control in general, whether in the service of drive or other adaptations. Had he done so, we would have had a psychological conception more consistent with the preoccupation of most psychologists in Freud's time, as well as in our own.

It seems reasonable to conclude that during this 1900-1923 period the assumptions of his libido theory suppressed Freud's interest in an interaction of adaptive motivations and environment as a major motivational source of behavior. Only after repeated indications that the theory of libidinal drives was clinically inadequate did Freud expand the ego concept to embrace these phenomena.

Later Development: 1924-1938

The decision to confront, more directly and systematically, the position of the ego in psychoanalytic theory was gradually forced upon Freud. (Actually, this renewed interest picked up themes of the early "Project.") The issue was forced largely by clinical observations and considerations; he was faced with an accumulation of facts and special theoretical formulations that had no specific status in the general theory as it then stood. We shall consider several of these: (1) Phenomena of unconsciously manifested resistance in psychoanalytic treatment. (2) His radically changed appreciation of the meaning of anxiety. (3) The role of unconscious guilt and internalized parental commands and morality. (4) Observations of psychotic breakdowns of thought functions.

Unconscious Resistance

Freud became increasingly impressed with the peculiar resistance to being understood or helped that patients manifested. The patient would proclaim with conviction his willingness to participate in the treatment, but there were many indications that he was undermining it in a variety of ways. The patient seemed not only to resist knowing the repressed ideas but, more significantly, to resist knowing and acknowledging that he was repressing them. The resistance seemed to operate quite unconsciously, indeed seemed even to gain in force by not being conscious. These revelations profoundly affected the strategy of therapy, and moved Freud toward a reformulation of the ego concept.

Accordingly, a great change eventually came about in psychoanalytic therapy—an emphasis upon working with defenses themselves, and with resistances; a great deal of attention was now given to their various forms and vicissitudes in treatment. No longer was analysis considered to be simply the uncovering of repressed memories through catharsis. The conception of repression had changed. Repression is a process that not only disturbs memory, but disrupts the awareness of associations linked to the conflicts underlying the neurotic symptoms. Such "splits" produced by repression have various behavioral manifestations. Thus, even the meaning of uncovering repression had changed; it could mean not only recovering a memory, but also the re-establishing of a conscious appreciation of causal connections among ideas.

The phenomena of resistance seemed also to point to an active principle in the structuring of behavior, independent of, and rivaling, that of instinctual drive. Defense could not be simply a reaction to repeated frustrations of drive discharge, modeled upon the discharge modes of instinctual drives. Moreover, the unconscious aspect of this seemingly drive-resistive force cast doubt on the logic of Freud's previous tendency to associate all unconscious determinants with instinctual drives alone.

The New Theory of Anxiety

Freud revised his views of anxiety, and his new conception had reverberations throughout psychoanalytic theory and therapeutic practice. Freud's previous resolution of the question whether anxiety is a reaction to danger or a transformation of libido was by what seemed a parsimonious solution in terms of libido theory alone: Anxiety was a product of libidinal drive blocked from discharge, an overflow of libidinal energy which induced a passive reaction of inchoate restlessness and diffuse feelings of fear. However, a number of clinical considerations—among them the facts of resistance and the problem of how repression itself is initiated—compelled him to assign an active role to anxiety in a regulative system of response to danger. He proposed that a small quantum of anxiety was utilitarian, a signal of impending danger, in response to which defenses are alerted. Thus, anxiety became associated with a directive function distinct and separable from libido, and able to determine the course of behavior independently of libido. He emphasized the separation from libidinal drive discharge, but avoided confronting the issue (if it did not originate from libido, whence the energic basis of anxiety?) by making it an ego function and part of the ego's regulative system of defense.

The importance of this new view of anxiety can hardly be overemphasized. It brought into the foreground an anticipatory capacity in the schema of regulation. Effective regulation meant functioning guided by anticipated danger. The anxiety signal is more than a realistic response of fear to actual danger. It reflects a regulatory system capable of initiating defensive action on the basis of a premonition; it indicates a system capable of the developmental feat of turning passively experienced, full-blown anxiety into a finely tuned means of anticipatory defense. Moreover, the anxiety signal is capable of mobilizing a great variety of defenses in this fashion.

The new theory also emphasizes the qualitative or configurational aspects of anxiety, in contrast with the earlier, purely quantitative energic conception. In general, anxiety is indicative of a state of mind in which a person is preoccupied with preserving rather than with gratifying himself. Anxiety is likened to internal representations of danger situations and fear. These prototypical dangers differ at the various stages of psychosexual development, producing correspondingly different anxiety configurations. For example, in the infant separation can provoke an experience of loss of love, which is internalized as a potential danger and is therefore an occasion for anxiety. Separation and object loss are especially potent sources of anxiety in the period of infant helplessness; later, the dangers of retribution, castration, and loss of potency become sources of anxiety. Freud thus implied that the controlling system which embodied the anxiety signal had a developmental aspect coordinate with, and separate from, libidinal development, one in which different focuses of anxiety at different ages result in correspondingly different defensive patterns. This theory also led to a further elaboration of neurosis as the retention and reactivation of past or obsolete conditions of anxiety—for example, loss of love, castration, etc.

The importance now attached to developmental circumstances that promote anxiety broadened psychoanalytic concerns to include the bases and content of ontological insecurities, their epigenesis, and relation to social development. It turned attention to the patient's personal construction of reality—that is, reality as he interprets it, whether of environment or of drive. This development had great impact on psychoanalytic therapy, and helped to redirect it. Now, in addition to asking what the patient desires, one has to ask what he is afraid of and what he does if he is afraid. Only by understanding the configuration of his anxiety and the modes of control associated with it can one get a comprehensive picture of his conflicts and fears.

But the new conception posed a difficult problem for the existing instinctual-drive theory. Since the link between anxiety and libido theory had been weakened by attributing anxiety's essential quantitative factor only vaguely, if at all, to libido, how does one relate anxiety to the parent theory? Freud resolved the issue not by revision but by addition: by broadening the ego conception to include properties of activity that he had not before ascribed to it, and by including anxiety among its signaling capacities. He thought that by endowing the ego with its own energy he had an expedient solution which accommodated various observations that had stubbornly resisted interpretation, which seemed to retain its explanatory usefulness, and which did not threaten the existing edifice of psychosexual theory.

Unconscious Moral Strictures and Guilt

With the assumption of a regulative capacity independent of instinctual libidinal drive, the theory could encompass observations of the phenomenon of guilt, and of patients who hold on to suffering out of a need for punishment. The fact, too, that the claims of conscience can be effective without being conscious emphasized the inadequacy created by Freud's former predilection for considering one party to a conflict conscious and the other unconscious. He now assigned motivational importance to this facet of regulation and termed it superego. The superego gives commands; it is an internal "must" system which can exert urgent motivational pressure. However, after internalizing and elevating the motivating forces of a morality system, Freud had to conceive another system that was responsive to it, one that was responsible for modulating and implementing its demands. He called upon the ego concept to provide the supplement; the activity of internalized moral values and strictures became part of a general system of ego control which is coordinate with the id, and which is capable of imposing restraints, of staking out the range of permissible drive discharge, of determining different forms of conflict, and of bringing about their resolution.

Psychotic Thought Disorders

Psychoanalytic experiences with psychotics pointed to impairment of adaptive capacities and to defective constructions of reality as primary problems. For example, the difficulties that psychotics have in sustaining emotional investments (transference) seemed to Freud to indicate a fundamental adaptational deficiency in the affective sphere. This deficiency was itself a precondition, rather than a result, of the breakthrough of drives into cognitive forms (primary-process thought). Clearly, clinical observations increasingly pointed up limitations of the existing model, which regarded libidinal drives as the dominant forces in determining behaviors, counterpoised by a vaguely defined inhibiting ego.

Expansion of the Ego Concept

In confronting the insufficiencies of the general theory, Freud could have revamped his conceptions of psychosexual (libidinal) determinism, conflict, and defense. Instead, he broadened the ego concept; he converted it into a hypothetical system of regulation, endowed with its own activity principle, one coordinate with instinctual drives. The adaptive aspects of all processes of selectiveness of thought and action were assigned to it. No longer was the ego simply an *ad hoc* passive outcome of impulses meeting implacable external barriers to discharge. This seemed to accommodate the new data, providing for adaptational motives and for choice, decision, and integration. Control of drives was now viewed as but one aspect of the organism's development. Moreover, the new schema brought to psychoanalytic theory a symmetry that it had previously lacked, for now the two main regulative principles, the pleasure and reality principles, were unequivocally coordinated with two corresponding structuring instrumentalities, the pleasure principle with the id and the reality principle with the ego (and superego) system. Freud stated his final conception of the ego as follows:

> Here are the principal characteristics of the ego. In consequence of the pre-established connection between sense perception and muscular action, the ego has voluntary movement at its command. It has the task of self-preservation. As regards *external* events, it performs that task by becoming aware of stimuli, by storing up experiences about them (in the memory), by avoiding excessively strong stimuli (through flight), by dealing with moderate stimuli (through adaptation), and finally by learning to bring about expedient changes in the external world to its own advantage (through activity). As regards *internal* events, in relation to the id, it performs that task by gaining control over the demands of the instincts, by deciding whether they are to be allowed satisfaction, by postponing that satisfaction to times and circumstances favorable in the external world, or by suppressing their excitation entirely [1940, pp. 145-146].

Through the critical functions of inhibition, detour, postponement, and integration through thought and action, the functions of defense, of realistic drive implementation, and of adaptation were joined to a single regulative system, coordinate with the drive itself. Perhaps the most critical capacity attributed to the ego was an autonomous integrative function (developed more explicitly by Hartmann) that specifically cast the ego in a much more active role than Freud had ever before accorded it. According to Hartmann: "The most incisive change which took place in Freud's model of psychic personality... [was] its representation as a (more or less) integrated whole, subdivisible in centers of mental functioning—these substructures being defined by their functions, and their demarcation being based on the fact that empirically he found greater coherence among some functions than among others" (1951, pp. 146-147). This reference to "centers of mental functioning" represents the "structural point of view" in psychoanalysis.

Adjustment, control, and integration and not simply the direct and indirect forms of drive discharge, thus became the main concerns of psychoanalytic theory. The achieving of harmony, balance, and general equilibrium, as well as the equilibria which result from conflict-determined defensive maneuvers, became a legitimate and even necessary focus of psychoanalytic observation. There is even a hint that the ego is not only coordinate with drives but also organizes drives, is a kind of omnibus regulator in the personality. Freud did not carry very far this hint of a model of self-regulation. Although this conception was framed solely in terms of the "functions" of the ego, the above-quoted summary implies that he saw these functions as interrelated in a single system of self-regulation. This fundamental idea enabled him to gather into a single coordinating concept of an ego system the various partial meanings which he had at different times identified with the ego. Freud's view of the ego was bringing the theory closer to conceptions of a self-regulating system and also, one might add, closer in spirit to his earlier physiological model of 1895.

A key change from Freud's previous conception of the ego, however, was his recognition of an active principle independent of libidinal drive energy, which involves the turning of *enforced* responses into *ego-initiated* processes. The motivations that develop from this activity are "ego motivations" as distinguished from "drive motivations." As Hartmann (1956, p. 292) remarks, the ego's dominion over the pleasure principle became a possibility—one that was unthinkable in the earlier theory. The new conception brought into the foreground the proposition that the motivational matrix of human behavior cannot be limited to unconsciously active instinctual drive; it was the first explicit recognition of this in Freud's thinking.

Indeed, so far did Freud go in his appreciation of the regulative power of the ego that, in a later reflection on negative therapeutic reactions in analysis, he even proposed that there might enter into a person's ego development a peculiar deformity that predisposes it to conflict—manifested as an inherent tendency of the ego to promote conditions of conflict. Clearly, he implied that the ego has a degree of organizational independence that enables it to motivate behavior independently of drives.

Although Freud intended to solve problems in the general theory, it is ironic that his respect for the organizing momentum of ego activity actually created a dilemma in psychoanalysis, raising the critical problem of identifying the energic basis of the ego's autonomy.

Freud's hint that the ego was energized by a "neutral" nondrive quantity sharpened the issue of incompatibility with libido theory which his expanded ego conception was intended to resolve. It has raised questions about the tenability of his drive and energic conceptions as explanatory tools. We shall return to these issues.

Freud's final conception of the ego created a new field of psychoanalytic endeavor concerned with ego development. It drew attention to a primary biological fact: a protracted period of helplessness in the child, which greatly influences the development of adaptational apparatuses and controls. Psychoanalysts were urged to consider in greater detail the gradual emergence of internalized values and controls that are attached to relationships, and the manner in which these become means of regulation. Thus the purely ego aspect of "object relations" became an area of possible study.

Freud's final conception, although clear enough in its outlines, was hardly more than a series of programmatic hints, and was ambiguous in several respects, such as: (1) The distinction between conflict and adaptational problems was by no means clear. The ego, in the new conception, was seen as an active participant in adaptation, implying that neither all encounters nor all impasses necessarily involve conflict. But the distinctions between disequilibrium and conflict—and for that matter, between the varieties of both disequilibria and of conflict themselves—were not clear. (2) Although the new conception implied a distinction between specifically defensive encounters and other modes of adaptational controls, Freud still tended to emphasize the ego's regulation of conflict through defense, although it was an ego working with "its own energies." The new conception, however, encouraged the broader view that behavior has a "multiple function"—that the person is responsive to a complex array of "realities," not simply to drive-defensive polarities of conflict. But as yet Freud had little to say about the varieties of adaptation to encounters or about developmental "tasks" other than those involving instinctual drives.

(3) There was still no explicit recognition of "self" as a grade of ego organization with distinctive organizing functions and motivations. (4) One could justifiably say that Freud still tended to view the ego's functions in relation to reality mainly from the perspective of an environment that embodied actual and potential dangers and frustrations. The ego's functions in the positive role of creator, rather than as defender or adjuster, were only hinted at. (5) Finally, the issues of the nature and bases of the ego's autonomy were left hanging, as was the problem of how one might now conceptualize the ego's development independent of drive development. This incompleteness was reflected in a curious ambiguity that remained in Freud's notion of the anxiety signal: The new conception of anxiety did not distinguish libidinal from nonlibidinal sources of anxiety, although it implied that there was such a distinction.

Post-Freudian Developments

The concepts of the new ego psychology were amplified and systematized by Hartmann and were supplemented by Kris, Loewenstein, and Rapaport, the torchbearers of the new ego psychology. Also pertinent are Erikson's efforts to delineate the biosocial conception of adaptational development, although he does not explicitly use an ego-psychological frame of reference. Erikson's work, in fact, diverges from the trends of ego psychology in important ways and highlights certain difficulties in ego psychology's attempts to distinguish between drive "structure" and ego.

Hartmann perceived the central importance of Freud's assumption of an autonomous activity principle (he calls it the synthetic, or organizing, function of the ego); he made it the key feature of his conception of an ego system which undergoes a development that is coordinate and interactive with that of drives, yet remains distinctive. Within Hartmann's scheme the ego emerges more clearly as a general adaptational "organ," coping with "realities" in the broad sense as well as in the narrow sense of serving the pleasure principle. He views the ego in a problem-solving role, not simply as the mediator of conflict; responsiveness to conflict becomes but one aspect of the ego's function in the adaptational tasks of "fitting in" with an "average expectable environment." Even the scope of conflict itself is greater than the clash of drive impulse and defense. As a self-regulative system, the ego responds to the requirements of different types of "disequilibria."

A central theme of Hartmann's is his conception of the autonomy of the ego's functions—that is, the degree of independence of ego activities from drives and from involvements in conflicts. Phylogenetic development has ensured that the human child will come into the world with an array of functions potentially adaptive to an average (expectable) environment, provided adequate environmental opportunity is supplied. These functions derive from the basic capacities of the organism: the abilities to perceive, to learn, to remember, to think, to move, and to act; also inborn gifts of all kinds, as well as dispositions to organize, to synthesize, to achieve balance from disequilibrium. The development of these functions also appears to be relatively independent of drive, and is guided largely by the necessities of contact with an environment that supports the actualizing of these potentials. (Relevant to this is the great difficulty experimenters encounter in demonstrating consistent effects of needs on perception.) The assumption of conflict-free structures is extended even to functions that are responsive to parental and social realities. For instance, there is a conflict-free superego aspect of ego development. This framework makes it possible to accommodate such nonpsychoanalytic developmental theories as that of Piaget, for whom stages of the development of thinking are essentially the outcome of interactions of perception and of actions accompanying cognitive operations.

These assumptions of primary autonomy of functions signify recognition of a range of phenomena whose essential form seems independent of psychosexual influence. Hartmann is careful to point out, however, that "conflict-free" does not mean "drive-free" and that actually many ego functions are moulded on the pattern of such instinctual drive manifestations as taking and giving, introjection and projection, holding on and letting go. In these instances the ego functions have their analogue in the modes of motor functioning of the various erogenous zones. Obviously, the issue of the participation of drive and, more generally, of libido in ego development has now become a troublesome matter.

For Erikson, this issue has been a departure point for developing a psychosexual conception of drives. For example, each of the zones that successfully attains a place of principal importance in the discharge of drive tension has one or more modes of operation that are basic for dealing with reality. The mouth lends itself to getting (i.e., receiving) and taking, the anus to holding on and letting go, and so forth. A critical point is that there takes place a process of estrangement, or autonomous separation, of the modes from their origin in zones. They become, then, general ways of approaching the world. Erikson offers clinical examples from play configurations, dreams, neurotic symptoms, social behavior, etc., which show the utility of this way of viewing consistencies in behavior.

It should be pointed out that Erikson's mode-zone conception is actually more a reformulation of drive theory than an extension of the new ego conception of autonomy, for the core of his theory is that the kinds of functions associated with autonomous ego functions in the Hartmann scheme (e.g., perception, motor, etc.) are present as a part of drive structure from the very first. It is no solution—nor is it meant to be—to the dilemma, created by Hartmann's notion, of how much primary autonomy could be ascribed to ego. Erikson proposed that drives are always implicated in psychosocial adaptational modes, being themselves shaped by the modes and having a formative influence on the modes as well. But this, in contradiction to Hartmann's view, seems to undermine the conception of drive-autonomous development.

In Hartmann's schema conflict remains an important condition for the emergence of new varieties of motivation and action structures. However, his view of the relation of conflict to development has two distinctly novel features. One is his proposal that structures of regulation can undergo a "change of function" from defense to adaptation. A regulative process that developed as a means of coping with conflict can be used for purposes other than defense. A defense such as intellectualization or denial may turn into a means of nondefensive adaptation. It becomes, as it were, a generalized mode of cognitive control suited to a range of encounters requiring resolution. These are examples of secondary autonomy; although they originated from conflict in the service of drive control, they developed into effective instrumentalities of adaptation generally. Secondary autonomy is a reminder that the conflict-free realm of primary autonomous functioning can be enlarged by the development of new structures. The natural course of development is seen, then, to be enlargement of the conflict-free sphere, building, on the base of the primarily autonomous structures, additional structures that serve to contain the drives, slow them, and harness them to useful work.

A second novel feature of Hartmann's views has to do with alternative origins of defense itself: the possibility that primary autonomous structures predispose the person toward certain modes of defense when he experiences conflict. In Freud's earlier views adaptive modes of control (usually termed character defenses) themselves originated in defensive reactions and/or fixations on one or another mode of drive gratification. Now Hartmann is saying that characterological style and adaptive control may not only be fashioned from defenses, but that the reverse is also possible—defenses may be patterned on an autonomous behavioral tendency. Thus, a special talent may affect the distribution of libidinal and aggressive energies; it may itself be useful as a means of resolving conflict, and therefore become a factor in determining habitual forms of defense. This principle incorporates the relationship between special sensitivities of infants and subsequent development of defenses in neurotic conflict; it suggests the importance of cognitive controls that are not *primarily* defensive in their regulative aim (i.e., controls which do not require activation by anxiety signals).

The developmental momentum of the conflict-free functions constitutes a source of independent motivation for contacting the environment and of developing adaptive controls—a "third force," on a par with drive and social reality. For instance, one source of motivation arises from the appearance of an anticipatory capacity which makes possible what Erikson calls time-locked motives. Hartmann attributes great importance to the anticipation function in ego development. Drives by themselves cannot guarantee adaptation to reality; neither is a heightened appreciation of reality enough to guarantee success for the ego's primary role, nor is the renouncing of an immediate pleasure enough to secure a greater and more certain one in the future. Fear of pain, or the lure of pleasure for that matter, is not in itself a precise indicator of direction and selection. It is necessary to assume a factor for anticipating the future, for orienting actions according to it, and for correctly relating means and ends to each other. This effort, if successful, yields pleasure secondarily. Thus integrative efforts become themselves a source of motivations for contacting the environment and for developing interests and talents—motivations not being derivable directly from drives.

Hartmann's formulation thus gives a place in psychoanalytic theory to pleasure in functioning—that is, the intrinsically pleasurable aspects of the sheer exercise of functions—as a motivational source. Indeed, there is a hint that such motivations and the search for opportunities to exercise these functions, without drive discharge as their basis, are even necessary to normal development. Such intrinsic activity motivations guarantee, in Rapaport's view, the "stimulus nutriment" required for growth; Rapaport suggested that the seeking of stimulus nutriment is the basis of many activities that come under the head of "curiosity," "search for novelty," and such. Incidentally, another implication of these views is that growth itself, and motives that stimulate activity, depend to a great extent on the environment, not on the instinctual drives, that contact with the environment seems to be essential for the development and persistence of certain psychological structures. The pleasures of such contact—and particularly of successful and effective contact—enlarge the person's repertoire of motivations beyond those originating in instinctual drives alone.

In enlarging the picture of the sources of human motivations, Hartmann has also produced a more complex picture than ever before of the potential conditions of, and participants in, conflict. For instance, motivations having to do with function or intrinsic activity of the type mentioned above are not always consonant with motivations which derive from drives or from internalized values. The subject of the disequilibria arising from within the ego system itself as well as from the conflict over drives becomes, then, a matter of concern to psychoanalysis. Through his insistence on the importance of processes of adaptation to reality, Hartmann focuses attention on conflicts within, as well as between, systems; between drives and superego, between ego and superego, and between ego motives themselves.

The contemporary emphasis on the ego as a synthesizing, balance-inducing system reflects a broader perspective of motivation than the earlier view, which saw it as a system for reducing tensions. Resolving the conflict of drive and superego demands is only one such task of the ego. The basic motivational conditions are still regarded as disequilibria, but these are not always assumed to involve drive nor do they always imply the reduction of tension. Indeed, some conditions of balance and harmony may require an increase in the tension level of the organism.

Because in a condition of disequilibrium the ego's synthesizing function is essential in modulating tension and achieving balance, the ego is established as the prime—in fact, only—regulative system of the psychic apparatus to which the claims of drives and of superego are subordinated. The new ego psychology has irresistibly moved away from the tripartite model of control to a single control system in which the id and superego are forces controlled by the ego. The ego becomes the embodiment of all active purposive realignments of behavior. In the new scheme "loss of control" connotes "ego deficiency." While the dominance of the ego system is not an acknowledged precept of the Hartmann, Kris, and Rapaport conceptions, it is a logical implication of their views.

Ego functioning seen as a developmentally autonomous process extends psychoanalytic interest to the study of particular functions, such as perception and memory. A program for the analysis of thought functions encompasses the ways thought and behavior become alienated from reality, the conditions of drive investment and conflict that determine this alienation, and the behaviors that characterize it. For example, one might ask about the conditions under which, and the forms in which, perception develops adaptively to give rise to effective psychical representations of reality; under which conditions might it become sexualized and aggressivized (drawn into conflict); what is the role of perception as helper or opponent of drives—that is, in drive facilitating or in defensive forms—and its modification in achieving equilibrium for superego motivations.

Pathological phenomena can be conceptualized through consideration of conditions which produce a loss of "ego autonomy"—that is, a loss of the ego's integrative capacity when drive and superego demands are beyond the person's tolerance. This presupposes that ego autonomy is always relative, never absolute, that drives and their traces can invade thought organization and action.

The possibility that ego autonomy can be lost in conditions of intense drive pressure or weakened ego functions or, in Rapaport's (1957) view, in altered states of consciousness, provides for the fact that adaptations can take regressive, as well as progressive, forms. At the same time, the efforts at adaptive synthesis and mastery (an ego motive) may result in a temporary abeyance of ego control and may yield unique and novel forms of integration and insight into environmental realities. Kris (1932-1952) brought this conception into prominence while attempting to determine the conditions necessary for artistic creation.

Two other contributions toward expanding the significance of the ego construct should be noted. One is Rapaport's attempt to reinstate consciousness as a decisive force in selection and action to a high place in the ego's repertoire of regulative functions. While Freud underscored the distinction between conscious and unconscious forces, he was not especially interested in delineating the functions of consciousness in adaptation and in the motivation of behavior. In the early period of the "Project," consciousness was more or less identified with the ego and was assigned adaptational importance; but later, when the ego became virtually synonymous with defenses, consciousness receded in significance in theories of the determining forces of behavior. However, the anxiety concept did reopen the general issue of the independent motivational importance of conscious states of feeling and affect and of modes of experience generally. The qualitative distinction between conscious and unconscious cognitive activity again assumes importance. This concern is exemplified, for instance, in Freud's view that ego functions have different behavioral consequences in different states of consciousness.

Rapaport has described a variety of types and states of awareness and their behavioral effects. Perhaps his most important proposition is: the smaller are the capacities for vigilance, for reflective awareness, and for directing attention at will, the more do thought processes take on passive characteristics (i.e., show evidence of the primary process), and the less effective is secondary-process thinking.

The Emergence of Ego Psychology

Having emerged as a distinctive field of inquiry, ego psychology bears witness to the radical changes of orientation that have occurred in psychoanalysis. These changes are perhaps best described as the development of psychoanalysis from a theory of psychopathology and illness—that is, from a theory of the miscarriage of functions—to one that tries to encompass all psychological "disequilibria," whether specifically psychopathological or not. These basic changes of emphasis in the parent theory deserve a brief review because they are the background of a crisis in contemporary ego psychology.

1. *From Narrow Concern with Conflict to Concern with Dilemma and Crisis*

Psychoanalysis from the first dealt with the dialectics of opposition of incompatible intrapsychic tendencies. Its propositions, distinguishing it from other theories, have mainly to do with how behavior reflects efforts to resolve and synthesize such oppositions. Deriving from this view was Freud's conception of symptoms as *solutions*, a central proposition in his theory of neurosis.

For a long time it was the resolution of a particular type of opposition, namely, a conflict between defense and drive, that occupied stage center in the theory. However, a major change has come about in the conception of what polarities are at play in the organism. Hartmann, for instance, refers to conflicts within as well as between systems; it is also recognized that not all conflicts are psychosexual in nature. Even more important, however: Where previously the resolution of crisis was taken to mean the resolution of conflict, equal emphasis is now given to *developmental crises* that arise when adaptational modes of one stage are no longer suited to the unfolding requirements of a succeeding biological stage, and that create an urgency for adaptational change. It is now a recognized principle in the psychoanalytic theory of *normal* development that crisis and dilemma are inescapable, indeed, they are *positive*, conditions of normal psychological growth, and not only of psychopathology.

Thus Freud's original insight into conflict as a source of motivation is now better regarded as only one expression of a more general principle which holds that psychological growth is a product of continuing efforts to resolve incompatibility, crises, and impasse. Out of such felt or actual incompatibilities, including conflict in the earlier, narrower sense, there emerge motives of action and thought.

2. *From Concern Primarily with Defense to Concern with Adaptational Controls*

The concept of defense originated within the framework of the theory of neurosis. With the recognition of varieties of conflicts and crises, it is logical for the theory to assume that adaptational control is multifaceted, with defense only one of its forms. This change is reflected in the shift from the ego conceived simply as an instrumentality of defense against sexual and aggressive drives pressing for discharge, to the ego as a system for dealing with a variety of adaptational tasks and therefore defense being but one of its regulatory accomplishments.

3. *From Concern with Sexual and Aggressive Drives to Concern with Motivation in General*

Few analysts will insist nowadays that all motivated contacts with the environment are derivatives of what before were regarded as the main driving "causes," namely, sexuality and aggression. The important question of motivational genesis—that is, how did the patient's aims and goals come to be what they are?—often turns out not to involve sexuality, no matter how far the conception of drive is strained.

The broadened outlook on motivation is reflected in such formulations as an "activity" or "effectance" principle in ego development (White, 1963), mastery motives (Hendrick, 1943a, 1943b), an inherent disposition of the ego for synthesis (Hartmann, Kris, and Loewenstein, 1945-1962), in Rapaport's (1960) idea that "intrinsic motivations" arise from the requirement for what he called "environmental supplies," and in Hartmann's (1939) notion of "secondary autonomous defenses."

The recognition of nondrive motivations is an uneasy one in contemporary psychoanalysis and a sensitive issue among theorists. Confronting psychoanalytic theory is the problem of embracing this recognition without repressing the hard-won realization that sexuality does have a unique plasticity and power which put it on an entirely different plane from hunger and thirst and any other class of motivations (e.g., its properties of displaceability and its incomparably higher potential for becoming involved in conflict). The reverberations of sexual conflicts in a person's life must not be lost sight of in the comprehensive motivational theory of the future. At the same time, it is doubtful that traditional libido theory is capable of effecting this reconciliation; in fact, the uncritical acceptance of libido theory within the newer current of ego psychology brings into sharp relief one of the focal dilemmas confronting psychoanalysis.

4. *From Explanatory Priority of Unconscious Activity to Explanatory Parity of Conscious Intention and Purpose*

The polarity of consciousness-unconsciousness was always significant for Freud, but his emphasis was mainly on consciousness as *reactive* to unconscious forces, particularly in his early formulation of the Consciousness (Ego) system. Due mainly to Rapaport's (1957) efforts, the causal importance of states of consciousness is gaining increasing respect in psychoanalytic theorizing. One aspect of the emphasis being given to consciousness is the role of affects, an outcome of the anxiety-signal theory. Before, affects were vaguely conceptualized as some sort of backflow of undischarged libido, or deflected drive discharge. With the break from libido theory implicit in the new anxiety conception, a new set of possibilities opened up in respect to the importance of affects in the motivation of behavior.

This change of emphasis in contemporary psychoanalysis is well illustrated by Edward Bibring's (1953) reinterpretation of depression, intended to replace the traditional theory. The older theory assumed that guilt over oral and aggressive striving was central in depression. Bibring's theory considers depression as primarily an ego phenomenon "representing an affective state of helplessness" which comes about because two incompatible sets of ego cognitions are simultaneously active: feelings of lowered self-esteem along with unrealized aspirations and a not yet relinquished sense of potential. Low self-esteem, inhibition of ego aspirations, and helplessness are the important focuses of the syndrome. Bibring assigns a peripheral role to the drive factors that are central in the accepted theory; drives may precipitate or complicate depression, or be exacerbated as a result of the *ego state*, but they are not primary determinants of depression, the crucial factor being the ego state. This is truly a radical reformulation in several respects: (1) Priority is assigned not to instinctual drives but to an affective state of the ego. (2) Importance is assigned to motivations and goals that are explicitly of the ego and not of drives. The incompatibility is "intrasystemic" and does not involve the id. (3) Conscious experience—the experience of helplessness—is assumed to be an active force in determining behavior. (4) The dynamic principle of conflict is broadened to one of dilemma. (5) A determining influence—even as a "fourth force" in addition to id, ego, and superego—is accorded to a grade of ego structure concerned with self-esteem.

(6) Overlapping with the above, instinctual sexual drives and aggression are regarded as complications, but not prior determinants, of the depressive state.

This expanded conception of the psychoanalytic enterprise is virtually the program of the field of inquiry now called ego psychology. The newer emphasis on the ego has been both vitalizing and humbling. It has brought into psychoanalytic theory a broadened appreciation of social and cultural influences and of varied adaptational modes and styles. One of the achievements of ego psychology has been to generate attempts to correct the earlier de-emphasis of cultural forces while avoiding a simple environmentalism. Psychoanalysis has come a long way from its beginnings, when the ego was a contravening agent against id and against the culture.

Moreover, ego psychology has affected, in a profoundly positive way, the objectives and techniques of psychoanalytic therapy. The analyst no longer defines his main task to be that of uncovering unconscious memories. The therapist's sensibilities must be tuned to the many facets of conflict and crisis, to the complex interweavings of motivations, and to the various forms of subjective reality that behavior expresses. With the shift in focus away from simply uncovering repressed memories, the goals of psychoanalytic treatment have become more ambitious and more difficult, and the hopes of success consequently more modest.

The proddings of ego psychology have opened fresh questions about the events of therapy. Just one example: If cognitive controls other than defenses are implied in the organizing activity of the ego, they may also determine the effectiveness of therapeutic interventions, and the conduct of therapy generally. How do the cognitive styles of therapist and patient affect transference? It has been customary to interpret every impasse in patient-therapist exchanges as resistance, as a reflection of the intrapsychic drama of drive and defense. However, an important contributor to instances of such stalemates may be a disharmony between the cognitive styles of analyst and patient which impedes the kind of "identification" that Home (1966) considers so vital to analytic understanding.

Some psychoanalysts have cast a jaundiced eye on the current ego psychology, viewing it as a retrogressive attempt to undo the importance of sexuality and of aggression—to re-repress the insights gained from Freud's long period of concern with instinctual drives. It is true, I think, that ego psychology does try to deal with motivations not previously accounted for in the libido-drive-discharge model, and perhaps it is this very attempt that raises the hackles of traditionalists. But I also think that expansion of the ego concept often reflects a diehard attempt to hold fast to the libido drive theory of psychosexual discharge by providing a means of absorbing its embarrassments. It is this effort, indeed, that is alone one of ego psychology's most vulnerable spots, and I will return to this point too. At any rate, the *explicit* aim of ego psychology is not at all to brush aside phenomena of conflict, defense, transference, regression, fixation, unconscious fantasy, and screen memories, all of which require proper understanding of the powerful forces of sexuality and hate, but to make them part of a larger framework.

Now this seeming vitality and broadened perspective in psychoanalytic theory ought to be a good omen. Ego psychology would appear to be a vigorous new development on the psychoanalytic scene, one of increasing explanatory promise. Unfortunately, this conclusion must be questioned. For all of the incentive given to investigation by ego psychology, there are grave doubts about its viability as *theory*, in its present form. Indeed, the picture presented by the field of ego psychology is more to be likened to an organism caught up in conflicting directions, uncertain objectives, even defensive denial. In short—and this is the point of the title of this chapter—it has all the earmarks of a crisis of identity. In the rest of this chapter I would like to point out three symptoms of this crisis or, shall we say, three areas of irresolution, within ego psychology.

1. *Is the Ego an Entity or a Classification?*

One difficulty of current formulations has to do with confusion in the descriptive language of ego psychology. This is traceable to divergent and not easily compatible views of what the ego *is*. In some accounts it is a *system*, a not-so-hypothetical mechanism of self-regulation; in others, it is simply a taxonomic term, referring either to a classification of *motivations*, or, in a variant of this view and the most common interpretation, of "functions." These three conceptions are often commingled, and confusingly so. In the first meaning, the ego is literally some kind of structure in the "hard" sense; it definitely has the ring of reification. Here is one statement that clearly implies this: "[From] the undifferentiated phase ... of needs, impulses, and behavior patterns which can hardly be attributed either to an ego or to an id ... the ego grows and develops into a *specific organ* of adaptation and organization, and the id becomes a partly separate *system* with its specific characteristics" (Hartmann, 1948, pp. 80-81; italics added). Such an interpretation as this is likely to emerge when the ego is used not simply descriptively but in causal or process explanations, as when it is implied that the ego *determines* behavior. However, for such explanatory ambitions something about the *operational nature of the system*—a model—needs to be specified. Yet there is little doubt that such specification at present exists only in the form of a promissory note.

Believing that such model building is inescapable, some theorists (Rubinstein, 1967; Peterfreund, 1971) have been urging that this is precisely the direction ego theory ought to take—to improve the uncertain metapsychology of mechanism implied by reference to the ego as a "system of control." We find some ego psychologists toying with the language of information theory, game theory, or physiology. Such attempts put ego psychology squarely in the business of mechanics or the workings of the "black box," with borrowings from biology, physics, or engineering.

Now many, perhaps most, psychoanalytic theorists are understandably reluctant to move in this direction, for to do so is surely to take on a commitment to a data language not easily applied to the psychoanalytic *clinical* theory, and even requiring data of an entirely different order from what is obtainable in the clinical situation. Moreover, it is even doubtful that such models could generate new clinical insights, or be anything more than translations of the directional concepts of aim, purpose, and meaning that comprise the clinical theory into a language of process and mechanism.

From such doubters we hear that no reification of the ego is intended anyway, or necessary, and that therefore such models of the black box are irrelevant to the real meaning and utility of the ego concept in psychoanalysis. They like to point out that when we speak of the "existence" of the ego we are simply using a convenient metaphor. Waelder puts it this way: "Thus the reality of the ego is more a conceptual reality, referring more to its usefulness for description than to an actual entity that we should eventually hope to find through direct observations in a microscope."[2] This seems to be the viewpoint of those who hold to the so-called "structural point of view" (which really should be called the "functional point of view"). Ego psychology is said to be the study of behavior from the viewpoint of the *functions* through which reality-adaptive efforts are carried out.

But there are plenty of troubles with this conception. Take the summary of ego functions offered by two spokesmen for the new ego psychology:

> (1) consciousness; (2) sense perception; (3) the perception and expression of affect; (4) thought; (5) control of motor action; (6) memory; (7) language; (8) defense mechanisms and defensive activity in general; (9) control, regulation, and binding of instinctual energy; (10) the integrative and harmonizing function; (11) reality testing; and (12) the capacity to inhibit or suspend the operation of any of these functions and to regress to a primitive level of functioning [Arlow and Brenner, 1964, p. 39].

Has anything in the standard subject matter of university psychology laboratories been left out of this list of functions allegedly specific to the "ego"?

One trouble here is in distinguishing the ego's functions from those of other systems. We quickly discover that there is little in ego theory to help us set limits on what is to be included, or that indicates any kind of hierarchy among the "functions." Moreover, in referring to the ego as a *group* of functions, this viewpoint comes mighty close to assuming a mechanism or a system which brings about coherence or organization. Never acknowledged is the problem of determining why and how certain functions collaborate and not others. So it turns out that even the attempt to speak only of "functions" implicitly leans upon a model of processes that is never acknowledged. It does not help matters to brush aside the problem by offering patronizing cautions about the dangers of reification or to attribute it to Freud's "unfortunate" predilection for metaphor.

Adding confusion, and testifying to the absence of helpful theory, is the fact that several quite different meanings of function are used interchangeably and confounded: Function in the sense of *phylo-*

[2]*Editors' note.* We have been unable to locate the source of this quotation.

genetic utility for survival; function in the sense of individual motivational *aim*; function in the sense of nonmotivational *capacity*, such as perception, memory, motor capability, etc. For instance, sexual potential may serve the phylogenetic function of contributing to survival, but this is not particularly enlightening in accounting for the motivational aim of sexual behavior. But perhaps the most unfortunate interpretation of function—and unfortunately almost the most popular—is the tendency to consider it in an entirely *nonmotivational* sense—as, for example, in referring to the "organizing function of the ego," or in referring to "perception" and "memory" as ego functions. Here function refers to a capacity or faculty or apparatus, without reference to the *aims* of the "organizing," the motivational point of perception or memory.

Thus current references to the ego's "functions" seem to be heading back in the direction of an old and unlamented faculty psychology. For example, in discussions of "ego strength" we may find statements of how good or poor are perception or memory or reality testing, these being conceived as kinds of instrumental hardware whose capabilities are assessable independently of their embodiment in actions expressing aim, purpose, intention. This is a throwback to the time when perception was studied for its own sake and never mind the motivational context.

Is the "primary autonomy" of perception simply the capacity to register the environment through the senses at all? Or is more meant—the capacity to register reality accurately? What then of individual differences in perceiving? Is perception ever autonomous of the organism's intentional life, conscious and unconscious?

2. *Ambiguity of the Ego's Relation to Drive*

Ego psychology assumes that certain functions undergo a development outside of conflict. At the same time, ego theorists are heard to say that "conflict free" does not mean "drive free." This uncertainty about the relationship of ego to drive generates a confusing fog in descriptive and explanatory applications of the ego concept. To say that drives are "structured" carries the implication that drive development itself has an ego aspect, involving the instrumentalities of perceiving, motor behavior, etc. But then in what sense is a drive an *independent stimulus* on the mind having a momentum toward discharge which must be controlled? If the instruments of this independent control are the very functions that enable us to speak of a drive's *structure*, how do we conceive of drive as both independent of ego and yet involved in ego development? This paradox remains unresolved in the theory.

At this point it might be well to remind ourselves of origins. The concept of an ego came about at an early time when Freud had only a most general concept of drive as one of two sources of energy, whose quantity the organism had to find means of controlling and channeling. The concept of an ego originated in the assumptions that (1) there is "blind" drive energy to be controlled and (2) this energic force is *independent* of the controls themselves. Without having given up these assumptions, contemporary psychoanalysts hold the later, radically different view that drives *develop*, and that drives have *structure*.

The ego concept is much more plausible in the earliest version of Freud's drive concept than in the context of his later theory of libidinal drive development. In the early theory which required an ego concept, drive was simply blind force needing control, a flow of energy from the gut impinging upon the mind as an uncoded stimulus. If you have a flow of something, you have to conceive of a counterforce, a means of controlling this flow, of giving it direction. For this early model a controlling force was an *inevitable* postulate—to specify the means by which the uncoded stimulation is made cognitively *sensible* and given direction. The concept of an ego—an agent for controlling the blind drive—suited this requirement. That is why the concept of ego in psychoanalysis dates from exactly the time when Freud postulated an endogenously generated, energic "stimulus" on the mind.

But this picture of drive changed in the libido model, and with it came a chronic problem of bringing drive into a logical and harmonious relationship with the ego concept. The notion of a quantity was retained (now called libido) and so was that of "discharge." But drive in the libido version is *not directionless*; it is *specific sexual* energy. "Specific" here means that it is of the libido's nature to have not only impetus but *aim*, a kind of selectiveness in the ways in which, and on what, it is discharged; in fact, it has its own development in these respects, and maybe even its own special mechanisms (e.g., displacement). Moreover, how could this "structure" come about if not through the activities of perception, retention, etc.—the well-known "ego functions"? In short, it is by no means a *blind* force. And so we have the problem of how to reconcile such a libidinal drive *structure* with the *old* assumption, kept intact from the first days of the theory, of an ego governing the direction of discharge of a blind force. This was and remains a real stickler for psychoanalytic theorists.

For a time, the problem was more or less swept under the rug by giving the ego the restricted status of being strictly the instrumentality of drive. Thus the ego's scope was narrowly construed; it had simply the functions of *defense* and of *implementing "drive discharge."*

Coexistence problems began to mount in earnest, however, with accumulating indications of motivations that could not easily be called sexual. What to do about these? The choice could have been to recast the whole theory of motivation to provide for them, involving a modification of the libido theory itself. Freud's solution consisted, instead, of simply *broadening the ego concept,* keeping the libido theory intact (1940). He converted the ego into a hypothetical system of regulation presumably with an activity principle of its own (a matter he never really clarified), a system coordinate with instinctual drives. No longer was the ego simply an *ad hoc* passive outcome of impulses meeting implacable external barriers to discharge. All processes of selection of thought and action in their adaptive aspect were assigned to it. This seemed to take care of the new data—providing for adaptational tendencies, for decision, choice, and integration. But it left untouched the problem of how to think of an *independently developing* libidinal drive structure.

By now the tendency is almost automatic to relegate nonlibidinal phenomena to ego psychology. The result is an ever-increasing estrangement of ego psychology from psychoanalytic drive theory. Ego psychology has had to take account of the plasticity of behavior, of such phenomena as cognitive "autonomy" from stimulation, of capacities for choice and volition, and of the development of abilities and intelligence. It has become an exceedingly acrobatic feat to relate these to libidinal drive development that has its own *directional* mechanisms prior to an ego, while assuming at the same time an independent ego agency whose main function is to control the workings of highly structured drives! As long as the ego was definitely secondary to drive, its satellite as it were, no intolerable difficulty was present. But with more and more evidence of nonsexual motivations, not easily linked to the basic drives, and the need to incorporate adaptational motivations other than those of defense and the implementing of drive discharge, the theory really breaks apart. It is to Hartmann's great credit that he did not gloss over the motivational phenomena that do not easily fit libido theory. But it seems clear that his solution of trying to make a home for them by enlarging the scope of ego theory has created a heterogeneous occupancy, and a difficult one to manage. The strategem of making the ego concept ever more inclusive is not theory; it hides the absence of theory.

One of the fundamental problems, then, confronting psychoanalysis is that of integrating the phenomena of psychosexuality with nonsexual motivations in a single comprehensive theory. We need something better than such question-begging solutions as "neutralization," which proceed from the assumption that the drive-discharge model must be salvaged at all costs. We need an entirely different theory of sexual development to replace the libido drive concept. Let me add that I believe the clinical theory of psychosexuality does offer the basis for such a revision, but it is the clinical theory *sans* the drive metapsychology. It still occasions some surprise to say that Freud's conception of psychosexual development—the clinical theory—is *not* synonymous with, and even does not *require*, the libido drive concept. Freud's propositions regarding the pervasive influence of sexuality in psychopathology and his formulations regarding developmental continuity in sexuality were the *bases* of, but are not identical with, the drive-discharge model. The conception of a libido *energy* which is inherently directional and has an inherited developmental course is a special theory, a graft upon the clinical one, designed to encompass, in one grand simplification, all the propositions regarding the development of sensual pleasure and sexual behavior. Confirmation of the developmental continuity of sexuality would by no means be confirmation of the concept of libido energy. Nevertheless, there is extraordinary resistance to making the separation, even though it has been demonstrated many times that the libido theory actually far from suffices even for the clinical data on sexuality. But all this is another story for another time.

3. *Explanation in Terms of Process versus Explanation in Terms of Motivation*

Psychoanalysts waver between two ways of explaining behavior, and ego theory reflects this uncertainty. One kind of explanation uses such impersonal terms as "tension reduction," "equilibria," "discharge." This is *process* explanation. In the other kind of explanation, descriptions of *direction* or *aim* are primary. Despite the fact that everyday clinical work is nothing if not an investigation of the purposes, motivations, and directions of behavior, when it comes to theoretical explanation, theoreticians turn to process explanations, represented by the side of psychoanalysis called metapsychology. This inclination traces to Freud himself. For the early Freud, only nonteleological explanations were satisfactory, and when he failed to accomplish such an explanation in a neurophysiological model he kept on trying with a neutral language of energy, cathexis, delay of discharge, and the like. This model persists to this day, and with it the conflict between the clinical parts of psychoanalysis, i.e., its bias toward motivational explanation, and its nonteleological impersonal focus on alleged processes. In the process model, various regulative principles are proposed, each with its own alleged equilibrium requirements that produce dispositions and motivations—e.g., the reality principle, the pleasure principle, the Nirvana principle, the repetition-compulsion principle. In these "regulative principles" the causative principles are tension, discharge, and *equilibration*, and all lean heavily upon the energic drive model.

Two different theoretical enterprises are implied in these two modes of explanation. Current ego psychology tries to straddle them, with no gain to either. The confusion in its explanatory focus is evident in the way in which ego "functions" are conceived. In *process* explanations, talk about ego functions focuses on perception, memory, learning, in their *formal*, operational aspects, but *not* on the aims, purposes, and intentions to which these functions are put and the settings in which they are involved. Proceeding in this direction, ego psychology becomes almost indistinguishable from traditional academic psychology in its concern with intelligence and cognitive processes; it is certainly not distinctively psychoanalytic.

The issue of explanatory commitment is crucial in that the two goals of explanation establish emphases in observation and make different claims for data. To the extent that we pursue process explanation, we are distracted from the need to improve upon psychoanalytic propositions regarding the aims, motives, and goals of behavior, their conscious and unconscious aspects, their epigenesis in a lifetime, in connection with life's tasks, problems, conflicts, and crises, and their consequences in psychopathology. This latter alternative certainly seems the more natural program for psychoanalysis, since it is closely linked to clinical objectives. It provides the sorely needed basis for distinguishing ego psychology more clearly from a psychology of intelligence and cognitive functioning.

When the two levels of explanation are mingled in ego psychology, the result is often unhappy. Take the conception of "the autonomy of the ego" as developed by Rapaport (1958a). Autonomy in Rapaport's concept is not meant in an experiential or phenomenological sense as Erikson (1963) uses it (as a "sense of autonomy" which characterizes self-identity); it is a purely hypothetical condition of equilibrium of an energic drive quantity. If one chooses to dispense with the notion of a directionless drive energy that banks up against dikes and flows to its discharge, Rapaport's autonomy notion really holds little appeal. It has little descriptive value as a means of designating motivational behavior. It is a variation of Freud's old notion of undirected drive energy which must be discharged. And, just as in Freud's original model, the "environment" becomes essentially a matter of "demands" and noxious impingements that one ought to be rid of, that is to say, become "autonomous" from.

To sum up: There is little reason for satisfaction with ego psychology as a body of theory within the psychoanalytic framework. Rather, contemporary ego psychology is a reminder to psychoanalysis of theoretical tasks hardly begun. We owe it, of course, to ego psychology that the language of psychoanalysis has become enriched with references to nonsexual factors in motivation, but it has not yet become a theory of such motivations. As Loevinger (1966) has remarked, what Hartmann and his collaborators have done in acknowledging conflict-free processes is to give such processes a name within systematic psychoanalysis. This is an achievement, but it is not yet integration of ego psychology into psychoanalysis. Merely to acknowledge the ego's functions is not to account for the logic of their grouping and the dynamic principles by which functions cohere and differentiate. Acknowledging a "synthetic" function of the ego is not to state a dynamic principle by which "synthesis" activity can be explained. Ego psychology has yet to articulate an active principle of development independent of the model of libidinal drive energy. Yet in assuming *non*libidinal motivations, it cries out for a theory of such a dynamic principle. We may justifiably wonder if ego psychology, lacking such theory, has not actually served merely as a kind of conceptual strategem to encompass the insufficiencies of the libido drive model.

Moreover, the effort to hold on to a dubious model of *drive* discharge as a paradigm of motivation has retarded theorizing about motives, at the same time saddling ego psychology with a foggy language of cathexis, neutralization, and discharge. This burden will remain as long as the present psychoanalytic theory, of which ego psychology is a part, continues to hold to the view that there are independent "blind" forces to be controlled and that there must be an agency of such control.

It seems likely that the difficulties of meshing libido theory with ego psychology will be resolved neither by further expansions of the ego concept nor by the invention of bridging concepts such as neutralization, but through a theory of psychosexual development which will make it unnecessary to speak of either libido or ego. Erikson's conception points the way. Erikson's is a configurational, rather than an energic, conception of psychosexuality; qualitative aspects of mode (apparatus) and zone are fundamental. If one were to look at these in the conventional psychoanalytic framework, one would have to say that such mode-zone applications are simultaneously ego-drive structures. But, obviously, the latter terminology and the tripartite model of ego, superego, and id, whose sense rests on the assumption of distinguishable energic forces, simply do not suit such a schema as Erikson's, in which the configurations of mode-zone relationships *are* the "drive structure."

Finally, ego psychology is torn between two objectives of *explanation:* It offers a half-hearted and half-annotated commitment to explanation in terms of purpose on the one hand and to mechanism on the other. It faces the choice either of trying to sophisticate a conception of a regulatory mechanism, building into it ever more detailed assumptions of processes to implement its heretofore implied reifications, or of frankly restricting the scope and the terms of ego theory to the level of motivational explanation that brought psychoanalysis into being in the first place—an endeavor exclusively concerned with understanding behavior in relation to psychological dilemma, conflict, task, and life history, an enterprise that explores, in Waelder's (1936) terms, the "multiple functions" of action. This is the shoemaker's last of the psychoanalyst. Sticking to it and pointing his theorizing in this direction, the psychoanalyst would shed all pretense of offering a nonteleological, mechanistic picture of ego processes, such as is implied by such impersonal terms as homeostasis, equilibrium, cathexis, energy and its modifications, and the like, which imply and require a different domain of data.

PART II

TOWARD RESTATEMENT OF THE CLINICAL THEORY OF PERSONAL ENCOUNTER

CHAPTER 5

The Resolution of Experienced Incompatibility in Psychological Development

True change is a matter of worthwhile conflict, for it leads through the painful consciousness of one's position to the new consciousness in that position [Erikson, 1964, p. 30].

FREUD'S REVOLUTION reoriented psychological perspective: it revealed and established a *genetic dimension* in the understanding of behavior. It is difficult now to appreciate the full impact of this revolution upon psychological study, since it has become so taken for granted by the psychoanalytic clinician, and, in this general form, even in doctrines ideologically far removed from psychoanalysis.

For psychoanalysis proper the genetic dimension provided a context for etiological explanations of symptom formation. In psychoanalytic theory it led eventually to the significant distinction between, on the one hand, *psychological* growth, and on the other, biological motivations and cultural conditions, on both of which psychological growth is contingent. Thus it provided for diversity of development within the constraints of biological essentials. Second, it gave rise to the notion of a persisting "psychical reality," encompassing fantasy, dreams, mythology, and persisting motives and attitudes, all knit by a special language of imagery and the combination of elements in the unconscious. Third, it entailed the assumption that phasic crises and conflicts leave a residue of persisting themes which are periodically re-enacted. Pathological development—and the issue of the origin of symptoms—was the initial focus of the genetic emphasis, but a more general orientation to conceptions of development subsequently became the main focus of the genetic "point of view."

The genetic emphasis took shape within the confines of a strategy Freud had evolved for dealing with an illness that had defied understanding. It originated in a doctor's attempt to cure an illness regarded as incurable. Up to this time, the "hysterias" were seen as either degeneracy or weakness—a constitutional deficiency of capacity (mainly in women). Freud sought lawfulness within the tradition of his training of looking for forces equal in dignity to physical and chemical ones, as in the "Helmholtz oath." His strategy combined what we now call a dynamic formulation and a genetic orientation. His ideas of the causes of hysteria changed in time, but one assumption persisted: that a structural residue of the past (at first assumed to be an actual seduction experience, later an erotic fantasy, later a wish) persists as a selective organizing principle of behavior and thought. Looking for "sense" in the heterogeneous array of hysterical symptoms, we perceive that the causal forces are in the person's history. The crucial elements of this history are the dynamic forces emanating from a critical "event," actual or fantasied, carried into the present. The notion of what the "clashing forces" were did indeed change, but this principle did not. We should not be distracted by what has become a familiar account of Freud's "self-acknowledged error"—namely, his early conception that the critical etiological event is a seduction by a father tyrant. In retrospect the seduction theory was only an overstatement of the more seminal insight: the critical nature of conflicted wish involving a willful parental influence, the theme of exploitation of young by old, and the residues in memory and concept of actual and fantasied encounters exemplifying this exploitation in various ways.

In short, Freud opened up a view of the epigenetic character of development, its normative course and its phasic pathology, the clarification of which is still an empirical matter, and the notion of successive transcriptions of early conflicts into later ones. The following chapters describe different aspects of this view in contemporary psychoanalytic clinical theory.

The subject of this chapter, the structuring role of conflict, is one important anchor of the genetic emphasis. The concept that intrapsychic order and the motives governing action arise from *experienced* disorder is basic to psychoanalytic theory, and continues to distinguish the pyschoanalytic conception of development from others.

Throughout the changes of emphasis in psychoanalytic thinking, the most invariant principle has been that the structures guiding action originate in attempts to resolve breaches of integration. Psychoanalytic propositions mainly concern how behavior reflects efforts to synthesize and resolve incompatible tendencies that produce crises of integration. Such crises are of two general kinds—phasic and intraphasic. It is assumed that motive structures arise as resolutions of such experienced incompatibility, that such experiences are inevitable throughout the life cycle, and that their resolutions have either growth-inhibiting or growth-fostering consequences. Development itself is conceived as qualitative change emerging from crises. As Peller (1965, p. 82) expresses it: "Inner conflict occupies as central a position in our psychology as the struggle between organisms and environment does in the Darwinian theory." Action and thoughts are seen as reflecting the adjudication of conflicting tendencies. Freud's conception of symptoms as solutions, as expressions of a state of inadaptive integration, was derived from this view.

What makes psychoanalysis a dynamic theory is the attempt to establish and specify the terms of *incompatibility*, its genetic context, its *structured* representations that constitute a "psychical reality," the strength of its components, and the forms of its resolutions. The history of psychoanalytic theory is in part one of shifts of emphasis in conceptions of incompatible tendencies, the relative importance of different classes of incompatible experience, their sources in development, the classes of resolution that grow out of them, and how these in turn contain the seeds of new crises of incompatible tendencies.

In Freud's first formulation of experienced incompatibility, it was not the principle of *normal* development; rather, it accounted for the origins of symptoms. Incompatibility was conceived as an *interruption* of normal development rather than as an inevitable and even necessary aspect of it. In this early form, the incompatibility, or rather the breach of integration, most emphasized was trauma, with its pathological outcome a symptom. The focus was on symptoms as attempts at solution, attempts to cope with a "blow" experienced as a threat. The notion of a "blow" was later broadened to include events which produced a surge of inner tendency—a wish or impulse—that had to be controlled. In this conception the impact of an outer event is heightened by its effect of arousing such a tendency, the latter constituting the "force" or psychical impact of the event. Thus, in his very first case, Anna O. (treated in 1881-1882 by Breuer; see Breuer and Freud, 1893-1895), Freud was impressed with the fact that the patient's first hysterical attacks immediately followed and seemingly were precipitated by nursing her fatally ill father, to whom she was passionately devoted. The content of the attack (the patient's behavior and utterances) seemed to be a partial re-enactment of an event; subsequent attitudes were apparently derived from repetitive variations of this event. These repetitions were essentially unsuccessful efforts to deal with painful experiences by inhibitive efforts. Freud saw the symptoms as a means of containing the painful emotions involved. This general interpretation of symptoms as strategies of affective control became the basis for understanding hysteria, and indeed all neuroses were seen as having "traumatic" origins.

In a crucial later modification of his theory, Freud considered the "traumatic" origin to be a conflict, the critical incompatibility being a wish which cannot be relinquished but is denied because it violates moral standards. In this view an event is "traumatic" in either awakening or reviving a conflict, and the critical "opposition" is a clash of inner tendency with outer restriction. In the "Preliminary Communication" (Breuer and Freud, 1893-1895), the opposition was between environmental restrictions and sexual wishes.

Quite soon, however, the entire conflict was viewed as an *internal* configuration; the "outer restriction" was conceived as itself a psychical event, an internalized set of values against which particular wishes must be assessed. This conceptualization of incompatibility as a conflictual, wholly psychical state led to the important place psychoanalysis has ever since accorded to "psychical reality." The conflicts that have to be adjudicated, including the interpersonal conflicts, are recreated intrapsychically. In psychoanalysis, the emotional-cognitive meanings of such experiences of incompatibility, the solutions that arise from these experiences in the form of new wishes, beliefs, attitudes, and roles, are much of the substance of man's development. The resolution of an incompatibility takes the form of a cognitive-emotional schema which frames the form of perceptions and actions; this psychic reality is no less substantial than outside events since it calls for and limits possibilities in thought and action. The person is changed by his solution of a conflict; the nature of change is an *internal, structured, altered direction* of *motivation* and *aim*. Such an "internal environment" may be construed as a kind of internal structuring of rules of relationships which thereafter must be taken into account whenever an impulse is aroused. In this view, then, "environment" was a participant in conflict in the sense of being an internalized, inhibiting societal stricture. As for symptoms, their primary accomplishment was not the control of the environment per se, but the inhibition of inner tendencies in conflict with the "environment."

Very early, Freud hinted that the structuring role of efforts to resolve incompatibility was important not only in understanding symptoms but as a general principle of human development. It was characteristic of Freud to herald conceptual leaps by *en passant* remarks. For example, in distinguishing his own theory from Breuer's, he remarks: "I had taken the matter less scientifically; everywhere I seemed to discern motives and tendencies analogous to those of everyday life. And I looked upon psychical splitting itself as an effect of a process of repelling, which at the time I called 'defence'" (1914, p. 11). The stuff of conflict was seen to be no different in normal people than in neurotics; indeed, "the depth psychology revealed by psychoanalysis was in fact the psychology of the normal mind" (1925, p. 56). Little Hans's (1909) phobia, for example, was a solution to the conflict between dangerous impulses and tender feelings toward the parents: hostile and sensual impulses toward the parents were displaced onto a symbol of dangerous impulses, an animal. But similar conflicts can have *other* than neurotic solutions, as in children's redirection of hostile impulses in *play*, in the *imagination*, and in other forms of cognitive restructuring of motivations and intentions. At the same time, broadening the principle to embrace normal development has its consequences for the theory of neurosis: that neurotics are characterized by conflicts is no longer crucial; what is critical is the question, Why does a conflict produce neurosis in one case and not in another?

That the structures guiding action originate in attempts to resolve breaches of integration is, then, the cardinal assumption of psychoanalytic theory. In this view, psychological growth, in the sense of differentiated affective and motivational structures, has two main bases. First, there is the development of conflict-free motivations (involving basic pleasures derived from the actualization of potentials in appropriate circumstances); second, there is conflict. Motivational and affective structures emerge when the primary pleasure sources become involved in conflict with other tendencies. These conflicts are signaled by painful experiences of estrangement from self, internal dissonance, and incompatibility. For a long time, the essence of conflict was seen as a particular configuration of opposition: namely, the conflict between "drives" (wishes) and defenses (internalized values); this conflict occupied stage center not only in the understanding of symptoms but in normal development. Conflict became a basis for understanding personality development: a person's cognitive and motivational richness owed much to his continuing efforts to resolve conflict.

The structured direction of behavior, aims, and motives at different ages was seen as the outcome of conflicts specific to critical developmental periods. In this respect Freud tried to conceptualize certain universals in normal development. For example, with his view that drives themselves undergo development, the theory became increasingly sensible to the inevitability of particular conflicts at different psychosexual stages; getting through these stages and their critical conflicts was an unavoidable part of development. The crucial importance of the Oedipal drama emerges within this orientation. Here the notion of drive was fundamental; for example, granting motivational force to "aggression" means that it can be independent of objective circumstances and can take different forms in "seeking its own satisfaction." It is this characteristic of drives that makes certain conflicts inevitable, e.g., conflict between drives themselves (leading to ambivalent relationships), between drives and moral constraints, between drives and realistic possibilities (ego), as when the same object both dispenses pleasure and causes frustration inviting hate. Freud very early emphasized that conflicts between the affiliative attachments produced by pleasure drives and the countering tendencies of aggression were critical in moulding personality. The concepts of defense, regression, fixation, repetition, became critical in specifying the nature of the efforts at resolution, and the structural solutions that grew out of conflict.

Different conceptions of the most critical incompatibilities, and of the nature of the antinomies involved in experienced conflicts at different stages of development, have prevailed at different periods in the development of psychoanalytic theory. For instance, formulations vary according to the conception of the "clashing forces." Moreover, the terms and nature of incompatibility have been formulated on different levels of abstraction: the conflict principle has been expressed as the tension between the pleasure principle and the reality principle, in terms of generalized forces such as love against hate, libidinal versus aggressive drives. Several aspects of the changes in the conception of "incompatible tendencies" are noteworthy:

1. The conception that many motives are "conflict-free" in origin (Hartmann, 1939) acknowledges a source of development other than conflict, e.g., maturation, or imprinting. The recognition that "ego functions" have a development outside conflict and that there is "pleasure in functioning" that makes for motivational structuring did not alter the basic principle that the solution of incompatibilities is a critical source of motivation. But the status of such conflict-free development has a certain ambiguity. When Hartmann drew attention to this source of motivation, his point of reference was the specific view of conflict according to which the critical clash is between drive and defense. The extent to which the development of "ego functions" is conflict free in *this* narrow sense of conflict does not answer the question: To what extent does their development involve crises of incompatibility in a wider sense? At any rate, recognition of ego-function development inspired a broadened view of development generally, without minimizing the central importance of conflict and its resolution as a pervasive aspect of the normal human condition. Indeed, says Hartmann, the absence of conflict "can be associated with failure" (1939, p. 12).

2. The ego's role as an active participant in conflict, rather than as a mere reactive instrument, has been increasingly recognized. With the development of the structural point of view, the variety of possible conflicts was greatly broadened. There can be not only intersystemic conflict (between ego and id—adaptive aims versus basic tendencies; and superego and drives), but also "intrasystemic" conflict (Hartmann, 1950), as, for example, between one purpose and another. Thus considerable changes have occurred since the early formulations in which, to quote Rapaport (1960, p. 889), "the conflict was con-

ceived of as between the memory of the traumatic event and the *dominant mass of ideas* of the person, or as the conflict of the ideas and affects present in the traumatic situation with the moral standards of society." The greatly broadened range of possibility is exemplified in Freud's shift from the early assumption that the basic conflict is between a wish and a control to his later emphasis on the importance of the resolution of the Oedipus complex and its consequences for the structure of the superego, and his conception of the repetitive re-enactment of earlier conflicts and earlier forms of resolution. The following assumptions about the essential characteristics of conflict have nevertheless remained invariant: that every conflict involves incompatible *aims*; on the one hand a persisting desire for gratification, and on the other hand a countertendency which, for dynamic reasons within the person, is incompatible with the gratification. A dynamic state of conflict is a trend toward gratification which is unsatisfied but which persists. For instance, the concept of the Oedipus complex is actually a series of propositions concerning the dynamic interplay of such persistent wishes and counterwishes in relation to fantasied consequences, and concerning the manifestations of this interplay in motives. There has been no basic change regarding the importance of conflict as a factor in the growth of a hierarchy of motivations and emotion.

3. But an important change is the relatively recent recognition that, just as not all motives originate in conflict, so not all states of experienced incompatibility are to be construed as conflicts. Not all crises of incompatibility involve the pleasure tendencies that are always involved in conflict. Conflict involves circumstances in which the gratification of a desire would increase the likelihood of a loss of security and an experience of threat to integration. The problem posed by conflict is that of evolving a means of gratification that will eliminate such experiences of threat. But not all experienced failures of integration consist of this kind of dilemma; they may consist, for example, of deprivations of function, environmental crises, and developmental crises involving sociobiological functions. We defer further discussion of the varieties of incompatibility experiences to later.

4. Another key change was a shift in emphasis in the conception of conflict or other incompatibility from the opposing systems or forces

(id, ego, and superego; aggressive versus libidinal drives) to the state of the person's self-integration. Clinically, the emergence of the ego as an active participant in conflict has made it evident that the critical focus of any conflict or incompatibility is always the person in a crisis of integration, not a class of specific functions or tendencies. On the theoretical level, the integrative activity of the "ego" received belated recognition. In the earlier conception of conflict, the ego was no more than a "buffer," a barrier to drives. This change of emphasis is critical because it implies that there is no *inherent* conflict of forces, and that every conflict, insofar as it poses a problem of resolution, exists in the context of self-integration: whether there will be a conflict at all seems to depend as much upon "ego organization" as upon the inherent properties of drives. Thus the more critical condition for conflict is not inherent opposition between tendencies but whether a tendency is incompatible with ego integration. This recognition helps to clear up a certain illogic that has always clung to the earlier conception of conflict. Take, for instance, the assumption of intrasystemic conflicts, such as between drive and drive. Such a conception of "id" conflicts contradicts the idea that "in the unconscious, drives are inherently compatible with each other" (the dictum that the unconscious knows no contradictions). The assumption of incompatibility in relation to an "organizing center" clarifies this issue. Similarly, in the case of so-called "superego" conflicts, it is difficult to see how a moral value could attack or defend another value: the superego cannot choose. The ego, however, can. What emerged was the recognition that conflict occurs only in relation to an integrating organization that is capable of *self*-observation, *self*-criticism, and choice, and that can regulate emotional needs and their expression.

This newer viewpoint, however, accentuates a gap in classical psychoanalytic theory. To give the ego critical and prior status as the determining *locus* of conflict creates a problem: If an "ego aim" is in conflict with a "drive," how can the ego itself *create* the conflict, and what would be the criterion of adequate resolution? Some provision is necessary for an integrating center *beyond* the ego, in terms of which "ego functions" and aims are recorded as compatible or incompatible with each other. In other words, we have reached the point where conflict is seen as a state of the organism calling for the solution of a task: conflicts involve the adjudications of aims—ego aims, superego aims, or "pleasure" aims. We now require a concept that provides for the *integration* of aims and for sensibility to contradictions among them. The notion of *self*, to provide what is lacking in the concept of ego, now seems indispensable.

This theoretical necessity will be clearer if we pause over Waelder's (1936) classic formulation of the problem of conflict. Waelder's formulation of the "principle of multiple function" epitomizes, more than any other, the broadened view of conflict in clinical psychoanalytic assumptions. It comes close to the meanings of the principle of incompatibility that we have outlined, stopping short of the fourth change mentioned above—postulation of an integrating locus from which the experience of incompatibility emanates. In Waelder's formulation, every human action is both an organized expression of biological tendencies by which man appears to be impelled to function, and a purposeful activity. Every tendency must "pass through the ego" to become organized or to become an action. An action therefore expresses both drivenness and purposefulness. "Even in the extreme case of an action carried out under the pressure of impulse which may seem at first to be driven purely by the instincts, the ego contributes its part" (p. 46). Since there are various impulses, the ego is faced with problems of adjudication; each of man's actions is thus an attempt to solve a problem.

What, then, are "those problems...to whose solution the ego is consecrated" (p. 46)? The ego faces four impulse-determining, aim-setting sources of motivation: (1) the id drives, (2) the "outside world," (3) the superego, and (4) a biological "compulsion toward repetition." These basic sources of tendencies and aims place before the ego the problem of finding ways of meeting their demands, that is, the problem of finding solutions.

It should be noted that for Waelder the ego, id, and superego are not simply three sets of impersonal forces or "systems." They are classes of intentionality of the person toward objects and toward his functioning in the world. They represent a person's potentialities for deriving *pleasure* and the impulses to bring about these pleasures; they represent aims that reflect moral and ethical evaluations of one's self and others, reflected in attitudes of punitiveness, cherishing, or indifference; the concept of ego represents the person's sense of realistic purposefulness. The meaning of the ambiguous concept of a "compulsion to repeat" is not central to the present discussion; here we can accept it as another "biological disposition" that must "pass through the ego."

All of these classes of tendency make claims on the ego for gratification. Waelder goes on to say, however, that "the ego has more to do than merely to take orders and care for their execution" (p. 47). It develops "its own peculiar activity," that of "*striving to hold its own* and beyond this to assimilate in organic growth the outer world as well as the other agencies within the individual" (p. 47; italics added).

> Evidently, the ego has then also an active trend toward the instinctual life, a disposition to dominate or, more correctly, to incorporate it into its organization. . . .
>
> The function of the ego is therefore not limited to finding attempted solutions for problems which are placed before it by the outer world, by the compulsion to repeat, by the id, by the superego, but in addition it assigns to *itself* definite problems, such as overcoming the other agencies or joining them to its organization by active assimilation [p. 48].

The ego's "definite problems" are mastery and overcoming danger, including the requirements and demands of the other agencies. The ego's efforts toward mastery extend even over the biological disposition to repetition. When Freud introduced the concept of the "compulsion to repeat" he emphasized that the ego *uses* repetitions "imposed upon it" by this deep-rooted disposition, in order to overcome a menacing drive.

Thus psychic life seems to be directed by a general principle which Waelder names the "principle of multiple function." According to this principle there is no possible solution of a problem which does not at the same time, in some way, represent an attempted solution of *other* problems. Each action, therefore, can and must be conceived as a simultaneous attempted solution of eight classes of problem, four set by aims which make claims upon the ego for satisfaction, and four more for the ego, which must gain control over these agencies with its own aims. Every action, then, has a multiple *meaning* in terms of these requirements for gratification and control.

However, a complete, simultaneous solution of these eight problems is impossible. The first class of problems is at variance with the second (domination and control), and there are other oppositions, as between the claims of the id and those of the outer world or the superego. It is also probable that some pleasure dispositions are more or less contradictory with realistic possibilities in the outer world. Actions are, therefore, *compromises.* Such compromises vary in success and in the gravity of the consequences of failure.

> They mean that a person is successful in loving or working (that is, in solving the respective problems) only when other specific impulses are thereby simultaneously gratified. . . . Sublimations, for example, can definitely be termed. . . successful solutions of the problem of adaptation to the outer world or of mastering the outer world, as simultaneously and in accordance with another meaning which they carry, they represent successful gratifications of strong impulses [p. 53].

The principle that psychical action constitutes a compromise or solution was the seminal psychoanalytic premise behind the specific theory which explained neurotic symptoms. "Perhaps," says Waelder, "this affords us a possible clue to the understanding of that sense of perpetual contradiction and feeling of dissatisfaction which, apart from neurosis, is common to all human beings" (p. 49).

Finally, each solution is a basis for further development of the inner reality which itself creates the condition for new tasks requiring solution. Such a revised inner reality and its complications of aim sets the terms for new confrontations and new problems which call for solutions: ". . . we have the fact that each attempted solution issuing from the ego already carried within itself the tendency to its destruction, for scarcely is it fixed than it no longer constitutes a solution" (p. 60). In sum:

> The whole phenomenon of the multiple function and of the multiple meaning of each psychic act. . . is not. . . to be understood through any sort of conception of a summation of stimuli and threshold values, but. . . is to be understood as the expression of the collective function of the total organism [to bring about integration within itself]. Since the organism always reacts in its entirety and since all these problems are constantly living within it, each attempted solution of a problem must be conjointly determined, modified and arranged through the existence and the working of the other, until it can serve, even if imperfectly, as an attempted solution for all these problems and thus necessarily preserve its multiple meaning [pp. 51-52].

Waelder's contribution cannot be overestimated. In articulating the change in clinical theory that had taken place—a view of conflict in the perspective of adaptational problems and solutions *centered in the ego*—and in giving *autonomy* to the ego as a distinguishable class of active aims, he significantly advanced the psychoanalytic conception of oppositional tendencies. However, the tripartite model of id, ego, and superego shows strain under the burden that Waelder assigns to this ego. The ego is not only an *instrumentality* of gratification, a set of aims, but also the *locus* of integration, which sets the requirements of intrapsychic compromise. The strain is reflected in the assertion that the ego "assigns itself tasks": traditionally, the ego's "tasks" were defined in terms of the "pleasure principle" and the "reality principle." Waelder's extension of the ego concept seems to include an organization that not only *implements* aims but also *sets aims by its own standards*. But we get no clear picture of what these autonomous aims are—that is, the aims of integration of the systems which the ego brings about, what rules of integration the ego itself is responsive to. These are evidently independent of adaptation (the reality principle) and gratification (the pleasure principle). We have only the inconclusive statement that the ego tries to "hold its own." Within Waelder's scheme there is no easy means of considering the ego as both instrument and "judge." A further extension of the theory is needed to clarify the nature of incompatibility as a crisis of *integration*, and of the principles that govern compromise.

Selfhood as Source and Objective of Experiences of Incompatibility

Tendencies are not *inherently* opposed to one another: the opposition of tendencies testifies to a self-structure in relation to which they are incompatible.

In the later development of the ego concept, Freud gave prominence to the ego as an organizing "system." As we saw in Chapter 2, the ego is a center of "functions" in the service of the reality and pleasure principles. However, the psychoanalytic conception of drives as "blind forces" that need to be controlled has trapped the ego concept: the ego is pictured predominantly as a controlling agency, and in the service of the "reality principle"—essentially an impersonal causal system. Hartmann carried forward the conception of the ego as an independently active system with the idea that a person strives toward unity within an omnipresent context of potentiality for inner conflict. But to maintain continuity with the idea of drive as a *separate* internal environment which is subject to the ego's control, Hartmann construed the activity of the ego as "synthesizing" or organizing. Thus the ego "and its forces" operate in relation to distinguishable other "forces"—the drives. Even for Hartmann, a conception of the person as a psychosocial and historical unity eludes specification.

As became evident in Waelder's synthesis, the conception of the ego as a mediator and synthesizer of the tendencies of competing systems does not acknowledge the responsible "agent" of the "synthesizing" function, which "agent" sets the terms of experienced unity and integration. To what is the ego as a "set of functions" responsible in setting about its "synthesizing function"? It is partly to answer this question that Hartmann (1950) seems to feel the necessity for a further "grade" of personality organization, the "self."

In psychoanalytic metapsychology the separation of "drive forces" has tended to obscure clinical assumptions that make for a way out of the dilemma. For example, viewing repression in terms of the mechanical control of forces is consistent with the conception of the ego as a mechanical system of homeostatic balance. But from the clinical standpoint, this is by no means a necessary assumption. What is *repressed* is not an energy quantum; it is a wish or desire. When a conflict is resolved through repression, the person attempts to maintain integrity among his acknowledged and accepted aims, motives, and values by disavowing responsibility for a desire. The unacknowledged impulse is *unconsciously* retained as "mine," however, and remains an active aspect of the personality which may show itself in behavior. The disturbing character of the conflict originates in the fact that both wish and constraint belong to the *same* personality.

Thus, embedded in and obscured by the concept of the ego as an impersonal entity with "adaptation-implementing functions" is the powerful wisdom contained in Freud's identification of conflict as a principal source of motive: the person always strives to function as a unit; that is, action proceeds from a sense of identity which signals compatibility or incompatibility. The possibility of inner conflict is therefore ever-present.

Integration and experiences pertaining to it seem to us better provided for if, with Hartmann, we distinguish more explicitly another grade of organization of self-identity in relation to which "functions" are developed. Lichtenstein's (1964) formulations are also pertinent: the self is a source of experience of integration and of failure of integration. The *instrumentalities* that make possible such experiences, and promote integrative activity, may still be called the "ego." A concept of self-identity is better suited to the ways in which phenomena of conflict and motives are understood clinically. Clinical phenomena have to do with experiences of unity and dissonance in respect to self, of relating one's actions to a responsible center, of "owning" and "disowning" them. Such attributions to a responsible self were always implied by Freud's distinction between ego and id; in this sense an assumption of self was always a part of Freud's concept of ego. When Freud wants to describe goings-on that can be considered a man's *actions* and his reasons for them, he speaks of ego; when he wants to say that a person *suffers something* or is "driven," he speaks of id (Peters, 1960, p. 69). In this usage, the ego is the agent of control as well as the responsible locus of control. He is distinguishing action related to the self from action without the self as a center.

The concept of self draws attention to the establishment of identity and its maintenance as a basic biological principle that defines a person's development. In man, a sensibility for identity may be inborn, but the identity structure itself—its contents—is not inborn; it is an artifact, a creation which emerges. The human lacks the environment-locked instincts of animals, and his biological development is a process of creating an identity, not necessarily consciously or intellectually. Loss of identity is a specifically human danger; maintenance of identity is a specifically human necessity. Erikson has emphasized the critical emergence of identity as a factor which dominates consciousness in the adolescent period, but it is plainly a factor throughout development, receiving a special emphasis, perhaps, in adolescence. What is invariant about development in this respect is the requirements of such a sensibility and such a self-identity structure; but this structure itself undergoes development, shaped according to the instrumentalities and sociocultural conditions of each period of life. It is this invariant of development which concerns us here.

Since identity is a distinctively human issue, the understanding of identity formation is a distinctively human science, perhaps the distinguishing factor of psychoanalysis as a general psychology. From this point of view, psychoanalytic interest in psychological development is not so much in the instrumentalities of the ego, the emergence of ego functions, or "drives," but in the development of motives and aims in relation to a sense of self-integration, which we call a sense of identity. The components of self in relation to which a sense of identity functions merit closer scrutiny.

Sensibility to identity refers to two aspects of self. One is an autonomous unit, distinct from others as a locus of action and decision. The second aspect is one's self construed as a necessary part of a unit transcending one's autonomous actions. "We" identities are also part of the "self." "A sense of identity implies that one experiences an overall sameness and continuity extending from the personal past (now internalized in introjects and identifications) into a tangible future; and from the community's past (now existing in traditions and institutions sustaining a communal sense of identity) into forseeable or imaginable realities of work accomplishment and role satisfaction" (Erikson, 1954, p. 53).

This second aspect deserves special emphasis, for it brings into the foreground a gap in psychoanalytic concepts of ego; these concepts cover only that aspect of self which concerns separateness from others; they fail to convey a sense of "belonging to," of "we-ness." We might say that psychoanalysis has lacked a concept of "we-go."

The aspect of "we-ness" in selfhood reflects a fundamental fact about the structure of units generally. Usually a "whole" is considered something complete in itself, needing no further explanation. But, as Koestler has put it, "wholes and parts in this absolute sense just do not exist anywhere, either in the domain of living organisms or of social organizations. What we find are intermediary structures on a series of levels in an ascending order of complexity. Each unit is Janus-faced: one is the face of the master, the other the face of the servant" (1968, p. 48). Like any biological "organ" or "part," the organism is—and must feel itself to be—both separate and a part of an entity beyond itself. The terminology of subject and object has contributed to misleading conceptualizations of selfhood and especially to obscuring its "we" aspect. The traditional view of man as becoming gradually aware of himself as "subject" confronting others as "objects" may be applicable *morphologically* but it does not describe dynamic wholes. Identity must always be defined as having aspects of both separateness and membership in a more encompassing entity, and as developing functions that reflect one's role in and relationship to that larger entity.

This aspect of identity—*we-ness*—has its earliest prototype in the mother-child unit. The infant *Umwelt* can be considered as a kind of prolongation of the mother-child symbiosis; the mother "pole" is the surrounding total organism, and the infant is an organic "part" within this totality. The actions of the infant occur within this mother-child sphere. From this symbiosis emerges a feeling of being part of a larger identity.

The primary condition of identity in man is a sense of disunity in respect to being either a differentiated unit or a part of a larger one, and in an integration of the two aspects. An identity is *not* defined in terms of the breaking up of this unit. Rather, the aspect of being part of a larger unit is a continuing presence and a molding factor in the life of the self. The person can experience deprivation in relation to either or both aspects; if deprivation is felt in respect to the one, he feels a need to be autonomous; if in respect to the other, he feels a need to be needed.

These requirements of selfhood constitute a large part of motivational development. Autonomy requirements may manifest themselves as ambition, competitiveness, aggressive or defensive behavior. Affiliative requirements may be expressed through familial and societal bonds; or the person may crave surrender to the higher entities of god and cosmos. The requirements of separateness and independence on the one hand, of cooperation and dependence on the other, may be served by motives and emotional commitments that run the gamut from constructiveness to destructiveness, good to evil. Affiliative needs can be reflected in *esprit de corps* or clannishness, in loyalty and devotion to duty or in contagious mob behavior and group violence. If we can be punitive to our own ego, we can also hate the group to which we feel bound; conversely, we can be as narcissistically committed to our "we-ness" as we are to our "I-ness"; we can be we-gotistical as well as egotistical. In both aspects, we jealously preserve our "identity"; and we want feedback that will sustain and confirm both. "It is in the reciprocal nature of the statement of identity, in the need for echo . . . to confirm one's own being, that lies the root of the Hegelian paradox: the need of one living entity for the presence of another, and the fear and hate engendered by that need" (Steiner, 1969, p. 7). "We-ness" is also promoted by language; our tongue tells us early who "we" are—again a jealously guarded identity.

Selfhood distinguished from "otherness" has, then, two aspects, and there is no contradiction in saying that "we" is as important a part of self as "I" in defining its distinction from "other." If these are the two main structural divisions of self, a sense of identity involves a sensibility to integration within and between them. We refer here to the assumption that at each stage of development the person must acquire means, consistent with the existing selfhood, of response to signals of nonintegration—a capacity for experiencing "messages" of the meaning of actions in regard to the requirements of integrated selfhood. The parameters of these sensibilities seem to be what may be called a sense of the *continuity*, the *coherence*, and the *integrity* of one's actions and thoughts in respect to autonomy and we-identity. *Continuity* refers to the sense that one is not an *ad hoc* evolving entity but is continuously evolving in the face of change; that what I am today is continuous with, even though different from, what I was yesterday and what I will be tomorrow. A sense of the *coherence* of actions, encounters, and relationships refers to their compatibility with the autonomous or affiliative aspects of selfhood. Coherence is constantly reinforced by emotional signals of compatibility or incompatibility; incompatibility can occasion crises and dilemmas. Finally, *integrity* refers to a sense of *moral truth* concerning what one does and feels. Here, perhaps, is where crises of simultaneously maintaining the autonomous and the affiliative aspects of selfhood are especially severe. It is perhaps also true that, developmentally, the most advanced aspect of a sense of identity is a sensibility to issues of integrity/falseness. Crises of integrity appear to be particularly virulent in adolescence; Erikson describes them as the first subject matter and preoccupation of the capacity for reflectiveness which develops at puberty. Thus issues of one's state in the world become particularly important in this period. The other two parameters—continuity and coherence—appear to have earlier origins and manifestations.

Dissonances and conflicts which affect any or all of these parameters of a sense of identity call for resolution. Experiences of fractured identity, as when a person feels a break in his continuity, coherence, or integrity, strain existing motivational structures and provoke a crisis of aims. Resolutions of such incompatibilities will thereafter persist as structures, and themselves become modes of resistance to change (Pine, 1970).

In this view, man is essentially a conservative organism, adhering to modes that preserve integrity, but equipped with the capability of motivational change through which experienced cleavage can be resolved. Implied, too, is that in building up cognitive structures the child and man try to find out not only how things are and how they factually relate to each other but also how they ought to be.

The often-noted paradox that man is both a conservative organism that resists change and one for whom stasis is anathema and who therefore always seeks out change, becomes understandable. The root of the paradox is the sense of integrated selfhood and the responsiveness of the sense of identity to experiences of incompatibility; this makes for a relationship of meaningfulness and meaninglessness. To hold on to cherished assumptions may produce dissonance and incompatibility; and a sense of incomplete identity, a sense of chasm between one's self and something else, can become the basis of efforts to change, to cope with novelty, and to make the novel familiar. Both tendencies can go to extremes. Man can even act against physiological needs in order to conform to his usual way of conceiving things. Confronted by such a challenge of incompatibility, the organism can go either way—along the path of assimilating the unintegrated, or toward an active restructuring that accommodates the new. In any case, whether through change or through more conservative assimilation, man is reaching for reasons and norms; that is, he develops motives that are responsive to the sense of fractured selfhood. Motives, in this view, are not conceived as derivatives of physical forces blindly discharging into motor action. A motive is always organized; it is a synthesis-inducing activity. Whether a "motive" is regressed, or a new, adaptive, creative solution, an effort to rectify an experienced cleavage is at its source. The maintenance and continuance of unity seems to be an innate developmental objective.

Associated with the requirements for coherence, continuity, and integrity is a tremendous human intolerance for meaninglessness. Meaning has two aspects—logical and emotional. Undoing a cleavage experienced in thought is one of the incentives of logical thinking. But something logically meaningless may nevertheless have emotional significance—conscious or not—and be held on to. What is emotionally relevant is likely to be particularly significant for the maintenance of selfhood. If meaning is not provided by the conventions of language or habit, it will be provided out of one's imagination. We see a camel in a cloud, a face in the foliage of a tree. We cannot help interpreting nature as an organization of parts within parts, because all living matter has a part-within-part structure.

If, then, we take not an impersonal "ego system" but self-identity as the referent of responsible actions, the preservation of this identity becomes a basis for understanding the logic of motivational and structural change in development. Motivation as a matter of "discharge" and structures as representing "delay of discharge" is too narrow a conception; rather, motives arise from crises of incompatibility. This broadened view reflects a principle of development, a gross tendency that begins in infancy, in which preservation of self-identity is as much a potential as "drives." The "imbalances" that make for motivational change are not the results of instinctual drives disciplined to the "exigencies of reality"; they come about from a state of maladaptedness to new requirements. Paradoxically, the effort to achieve and preserve unity gradually produces an ever more differentiated, complex hierarchy of motivations and aims. Integration is the preferred state; a threat to identity is a "blow" that requires reparative efforts. Proceeding from this view, the analysis of the meaning structure of an action would be the specification of how it is a solution consonant with self-identity; the positioning of this aim within the configuration of current crises and conflicts; and the discerning of the logic of its genesis in the development of selfhood.

Taking selfhood and its identity as a context in which experiences of incompatibility and conflict develop, let us restate the psychoanalytic conception of the tasks and solutions of encounter which Waelder formulated within the traditional id-ego-superego triad.

First of all, the self is pictured as a receptive and responsive structure to which instrumental structures—ego—are responsive. This conception of the ego is considerably narrower than the usual ones, but it establishes closer contact with the phenomenology of conflict and of other conditions that reflect a sense of disunity. To capture the idea that incompatibility and solutional tasks occur in crises of self-integration, we refer to self-identity as the locus of such experiences of incompatibility, and therefore of motivational solutions. Information coming from within or from without becomes the basis of assessments of compatibility or incompatibility. Thus conflict is not inherent in "impulses" or "values," or in the "functions" of the ego, but represents an *experience of assessment* issuing from an adjudicating center from which develop experiences of incompatibility.

Information, in the modern sense, is any input which informs the organism, that is, reduces its uncertainty. Input which does not reduce uncertainty is irrelevant; it conveys no information and is referred to as "noise." Information about the progress of an action or operation constantly flows back to the controlling center, which must constantly adjust the course of the operation in accordance with the incoming information. Without such homeostatic devices we should be in constant danger of disaster, unless we were always on the alert to correct voluntarily what is normally corrected automatically. This is the principle of feedback control, an important part of the instrumental apparatus which serves self-identity, and which may be designated as the adaptive "ego." Experiences in which the organism's continuity, integrity, and coherence are at stake will bring these functions to bear. Such ego "mechanisms" will continue to interest psychoanalysis, though they are necessarily secondary to the issues of meaning to self and the functional meaning of aims and tendencies.

Also pictured are potentially arousable aims and tendencies in relation to which the person must "hold his own"; that is, intrapsychic tendencies that can become involved in experiences of incompatibility. Freud stressed conflict as the primary structuring dynamism of motivational development; motivational structuring can, however, originate in other types of challenge to self-identity. For example, traumatic experiences of real loss, deprivation, disaster, estrangement, or threat to selfhood do not originate in conflict but nevertheless call for resolution, as they involve threats to self-identity. But as conflict is an especially powerful source of imbalance, when actual loss or deprivation is linked with unconscious conflicts and fantasies the crisis for selfhood becomes that much more intense and significant.

The aims pictured refer not to blind forces but to developmentally emerging sources of pleasure (sensual and other) as well as to environmental-cultural rules that have been internalized as tendencies to be satisfied in appropriate contexts. Aims, then, refer to pleasure tendencies, values, and precepts, organized in cognitive-affective schemata (see Chapter 6). For example, an experienced pleasure becomes a basis for motivation in that it leaves a record of its gratification, to which is added a record of its frustration and conflict in the interpersonal context. There are, then, three classes of "intentions" in terms of which the person is oriented in his world. Activated in the appropriate context, they must be responded to, that is, they become motivational: (1) wished-for pleasures; (2) the evaluation of aims or objects (including one's self as an object), either aggressive or penalizing, cherishing or neutral; (3) the experiencing of one's self as *determining* one's actions, rather than being determined. These classes of tendency tend to be in independent operation or in collaboration according to how they are integrated into the schema of self-identity.

In this view the traditional conception of id and superego as autonomous "forces" which exert pressure on the ego for "discharge" is a misleading metaphor. The traditional model implies that the pressures and incompatibilities are localized in the drive energies themselves. Moreover, the quantitative emphasis of the drive-discharge model narrows motives to discharges of tension. In the revised model, self-conception is what makes aims compatible or incompatible, and this self-conception is not inevitably a product of the tendency of drives toward discharge.

In the revised model, conflict is not reduced in importance. Indeed, the recognition of other classes of incompatibility brings out the special impact of conflict as an organizer of action throughout development. Conflicts involve tendencies that persist although blocked from direct and avowed gratification. Eissler had described the aim of the symptom as the concealment of a "secret" (1965, p. 116). The persistence of conflicted infantile wishes was a basis of Freud's conception of neurosis, and of the great importance he attributed to the "pleasure principle" as a factor in development (see Chapter 6). According to Kubie, the critical point about conflict is not that one tendency is blocked by another, but that the blocked tendency persists, and is repeatedly stated in behavior because it is in fact never consummated (1941, p. 32). Elsewhere we have shown how such blocked yet active ideational schemata constitute parallel trains of thought that can have an impact on cognition and action (see Klein, 1967). An important aspect, then, of the psychoanalytic principle of conflict is that the component tendencies of a conflict are embodied as an unconsciously sustained structure (unconscious fantasy) which may be repetitively enacted throughout life. Indeed, psychoanalytic understanding lies precisely in the recognition of themes "which we have never completely lived down, nor successfully outlived."

Experiences of incompatibility, including experiences of limitation and deprivation, can provoke particularly intolerable emotional experiences, which in turn provoke strenuous efforts at resolution. In psychoanlytic theory conflicts or experienced incompatibilities are therefore not necessarily negative influences, but may engineer change and development. We might say that in the psychoanalytic view change and new motivational structures have a basis of discontent. Creativity is seen as an effort to transcend limitation, elevating and contributing to self-regard and self-identity. A partial disintegration of old aims may be essential for a new integration through the formation of new aims. Each attempted solution carries within itself the tendency toward its own destruction and the creation of new problems, necessitating new methods of solution (Waelder, 1936, p. 60).

The inevitability of conflict implies a tragic component to life in that failure is in some respects inevitable. As Kaufmann says, "the hero (as in tragedy) is in a situation in which he cannot possibly satisfy all legitimate claims and is therefore bound to incur some great guilt, whatever he does" (1961, p. 345). A sense of human limitation was therefore an inevitable aspect of Freud's theory. But to say that Freud's view invites pessimism and passive resignation would be to ignore the other aspect of the paradox of man's development: that failure can be a condition of development, that man is capable of ethical growth and of self-ennobling efforts which are all the greater occurring as they do in the face of inevitable failure.

The remaining pages of this chapter round out these features of the principle of growth through the synthesis of incompatibilities: the varieties of incompatibility that arise, the types of experiences that signal conditions of selfhood, and the varieties of resolution that can eventuate from them.

Varieties of Experienced Incompatibilities

1. *Conflict*. We weaken the dynamic importance of conflict if we see it too broadly and equate it with other varieties of incompatibility. As the concept of conflict became more sophisticated and complex, it was expanded to encompass *any obstacle* to the gratification of a tendency. For instance, according to Rapaport, the prototype of conflict is a drive meeting an obstacle in reality that makes a satisfying object unavailable, producing "tension" and enforced "delay of discharge." But not all circumstances of acting reluctantly, of enforced delay of action, or of inability to act at all are conflicts. Psychoanalytically, conflict is not simply any occasion of frustration. If I must stay at home during my vacation because I have no money, I am doing what I do not want to do, but there is no conflict. If I am torn between vacationing at resorts A and B, I am of course in a position of having to make a choice, but whatever the outcome I cannot say that I did what I did not want to do. The dilemma did not involve a basic counteraction of one tendency demanding "satisfaction" by another tendency also demanding satisfaction; nor did it involve an incompatibility of a tendency in regard to self-identity. Aims cannot be said to be in conflict if they can be satisfied seriatim or if both are consistent with self-identity. Otherwise, any tendency could be said to be in conflict with, for example, the tendency to "sleep." Nor does a substitute gratification necessarily indicate conflict. When the meaning of conflict becomes so inclusive, it loses its descriptive importance.

Recognition of the complex combinations of tendencies that may exist in conflict has been expressed in the conception of *intrasystemic*, as well as "intersystemic," conflicts. But aims are not inherently in opposition to one another; they are so only in the structured experience of the person, in relation to a self responsive to experiences of dissonance.

To say that sexuality is inevitably caught up in conflict is not to say that it is accounted for by some inherent incompatibility of sexual energy (libido) and aggressive energy; rather, a person is confronted by a situation that arouses an aim incompatible with his self-conception. The "inevitability" of sexual conflict refers to the fact that, for example, no person can evade the Oedipal situation or the incest taboo in relation to which sensual aims must be structured. Similarly, where the superego is concerned, one cannot say that one value attacks or defends another value. Again, it is the center of responsibility—the self—that brings about an opposition of values.

The tendency to see conflict as an opposition of forces or impersonal systems obscured the critical point that conflicts have their source in an inner reality. It is not that conflicts *produce* disturbances in identity; rather, conflict is a "symptom" of imbalanced identity.

It seems advisable to return to a narrower conception of conflict, but one that would provide for its complexities. Conflicts, in the psychoanalytic sense, involve conflicting attitudes toward an aim, one pole of which is gratification, the other, control, which is reactive to signals of threatened self-identity. As Jacobson (1963) summarizes: ". . .in terms of conflict, we fear the voice of temptation, the voice of reason, and the voice of conscience." She points out that basically the distinction between id, ego, and superego refers to experiences of intentionality—aims. A conflict involves not mutually exclusive *goals* but mutually exclusive *aims* which the person refuses to relinquish. This is the essential focus of the clinical view of conflict. Perhaps the key point in this view is that conflict involves issues of authenticity. The organism's signals of authenticity or inauthenticity are accomplished by affects, such as anxiety. The emotional experience of incompatibility in respect to aims is the hallmark of dilemmas, of an incapacity to act, of difficulties in concentration and intense, obsessive self-preoccupation that so often characterize acute neurotic disturbances.

In this point of view, conflicts are wholly an *inner* construction. We cannot assume, therefore, that the specific character of conflict is the same in all people.

For true intrapsychic conflict to occur a certain level of cognitive development must be assumed, i.e., cognitive representations of pleasures and their values must have taken place. As cognitive structures mature, the requirements and conditions for synthesizing emerging tendencies also become more complex, and with this the potential for conflict becomes greater.

In its conception of conflict, psychoanalysis proposes a continuing, open-ended, empirical program regarding the terms of incompatibility, the emotional signals they generate, and the modes of their resolution. It leaves the study of the specifics of contradictory aims and their context to the investigation of special clinical conditions.

2. *Nonconflicting trauma.* Not all experienced incompatibilities

refer to conflict: self-identity can be challenged from other directions. Such nonconflictual threats—traumas—also call for resolution.

In the development of psychoanalytic theory the possibility of traumatic events or encounters became obscured by the conception of trauma as exclusively intrapsychic, events being traumatic solely in relation to an internal representation of conflicting aims. But there is ample evidence that the two varieties of trauma should be distinguished. Experiences can be traumatic when a critical component of the encounter is a feeling of being *passively* overwhelmed. In such cases the person feels a profound helplessness, a feeling of having had no hand in causing whatever it is he is overwhelmed by, that nothing he could do or desist from doing would avert the danger to which he is forced to respond. Such extreme experiences may be met by reparative and reconstructive efforts or by extreme inhibition of function and constriction.

Vulnerability to trauma in this sense may vary with the stage of development. The meaning of the trauma depends on the context of the feeling of helplessness. In the early stages of development, separation from the mother can be so profoundly anxiety-arousing as to result in an everlasting sensibility to separation. Freud described a series of such potentially "dangerous" experiences at different stages of development.

Although Freud early believed that external events alone may bring about such a situation of helplessness, he later concluded that a situation becomes traumatic only when it reverberates with internalized experiences of danger. Thus a situation becomes traumatic because it is recognized and expected to evoke an experience of helplessness as in earlier analogous circumstances.

3. *Conflict-involved trauma.* Freud seemed to give, alternatively, equal weight to two varieties of trauma: trauma as a stimulus or encounter involving an increase of energic input too powerful to be dealt with in a normal way; and trauma as a situation *elaborated* into an experience of threatened existence. Whether feelings of helplessness can indeed be induced without first having been elaborated in an unconscious fantasy has been a somewhat moot point in psychoanalytic theory.

In the second class of trauma-induced experiences of incompatibility, an external event is traumatic because of its relatedness to conflict. Perceptions of little importance to some people may cause others to faint (e.g., the sight of blood); precocious sexual excitement may become lastingly traumatic for one child but not for another. Such differences would presumably be created by the mobilizing of a premonition of extreme danger in one person but not in another. A critical aspect of the experience is that it has aroused a tendency or wish which is interdicted, taboo, and threatens punishment. Such a traumatic experience need not be massive from an energic or quantitative standpoint. The traumatic aspect of the perception is its portentousness.

Waelder (1967) points out that the latter kind of traumatic experience results particularly in extreme inhibition of functions. He also suggests that traumatic experiences involving underlying fantasies make for deeply carved memories or imprints; this factor particularly disposes such traumas toward chronic re-enactment.

4. *Circumstances provoking experiences of finiteness and of disassociation of self.* The structure-forming influence of experiences of finiteness is another incompletely developed aspect of psychoanalytic theory. At each stage of development the person is confronted with experiences that induce a vivid awareness of limitation and the threat of nonbeing. Feelings of discontinuity in both autonomous and affiliative aspects of selfhood arise in some form at each stage of development, and have an organizing impact on thought and actions. Preoccupation with finiteness has its precursors in a wide variety of experiences of helplessness associated with separation, loss of love, being cut off from a larger unity, of having no "place" in transcendent units. Taking refuge in yearnings for immortality is the reverse side of this preoccupation. The apparent contrariety of looking for immediate sensual gratifications, of being impervious to the passage of time, of total unconcern with the future, are other aspects of the profound dissonance arising from anxiety about finiteness.

5. *Developmental crises.* Traditionally, crisis was equated with conflict or trauma in the senses outlined above. The conception of incompatibility was dominated by the model of contradictory aims and resolution in defenses, as a natural corollary of the notion that "environment" and inner nature are inherently hostile to one another. Primarily through Erikson's developmental conception of the life cycle and Hartmann's more general recognition of conflict-free develop-

ment, it is now recognized that developmental crises are an inescapable aspect of normal psychological growth. Crises of development arise when the adaptational modes of one stage no longer suit the requirements of a new stage, and adaptational change is necessary. There are, then, critical periods of ascendance of adaptational modes. For instance, an infant will show something like autonomy from the time of birth, but not until the second year does he "manage the critical conflict of becoming an autonomous creature while continuing to be dependent" (Erikson, 1968b, p. 287).

In this view crisis connotes "not a threat of catastrophe but a turning point, a crucial period of increased vulnerability and heightened potential" (p. 286). Unfolding maturational potentialities, in the kinds and sources of gratification and their interaction, encounter social institutions created to receive the growing individual within traditional patterns. The weaning of the baby from the bottle or breast, the requirement that heterosexuality be the preferred adjustment, the setting of limits on the gratification of anal withholding, are all inevitable crises; an imposed limitation requires a transformation of structures. Each such phase-specific developmental crisis poses a problem that must be solved; the solutions, successful or unsuccessful, are presaged in previous phases and worked on in subsequent ones. A solution may be a pathological constraint or residue of estrangement. But even adaptive solutions become in time the setting for new crises; an adaptive mode may become a rigid orthodoxy, calling for new breakthroughs, followed by another period of consolidation, and a new orthodoxy; and so the cycle repeats itself. This principle of undoing and redoing is a critical one in development.

Affective States in Experiences of Incompatibility

In the various situations of incompatibility just summarized, the primary subjective event is one of discontinuity, of a threat to integration in respect to one's identity. This subjective state in respect to one's identity has been called *anxiety*. Anxiety connotes a variety of experiences signaling a threat to selfhood (Fingarette, 1963, p. 70). Subjectively the experience is akin to helplessness, and to meaninglessness, a failure in feeling anchored in a context that gives one's self meaning and is meaningful in relation to self. According to Riviere, the anxiety of helplessness "constitutes the fundamental pattern of all subsequent anxieties" (1936, p. 402), and is even the foundation of all later psychical developments: adaptations to the external world and to the changing needs of the organism are simultaneously measures of protection against this primordial danger situation which is ever-present in "the depths of the ego."

In this view the original occasions of anxiety are infantile experiences of helplessness: persistent nongratification and separation from a source of gratification. Anxiety is the first subjective experience and first objective message of helplessness; later it comes to be reproduced in the danger situation as a subjective signal for help. Analogous circumstances that connote separation, loss, or deprivation become occasions of an anticipatory anxiety "signal," a premonitory sign of the negative significance of situations.

At different stages of development certain situations are particularly ominous harbingers of self-disintegration.

> . . . Each period of the individual's life has its appropriate determinant of anxiety. Thus the danger of psychical helplessness is appropriate to the period of life when his ego is immature; the danger of loss of object, to early childhood when he is still dependent on others; the danger of castration, to the phallic phase; and the fear of his super-ego, to the latency period. Nevertheless, all these danger-situations and determinants of anxiety can persist side by side and cause the ego to react to them with anxiety at a period later than the appropriate one; or, again, several of them can come into operation at the same time [Freud, 1926, p. 142].

Such situations come to be recorded as signals of danger; the record includes both the wishes and the anxiety experiences and the modes of dealing with them. This record remains as an internalized form of what Melanie Klein calls the "bad object," and may be reactivated in analogous situations throughout life.

The emotional message of danger, like its cognitive record, becomes differentiated with development. Anxiety thus has a variety of qualities, each stage of development producing an addition to the repertoire of qualities of experienced threat.

It seems reasonable to suppose that emotional experiences of threat are differentiated so as to reflect the self's appraisal of its own state. Since the record of the "danger situations" is cognitive, the specific way in which circumstances reflect threat should be conveyed by an informative emotional appraisal which would "accurately" reflect such distinctive conditions, the kinds of danger that are latent in the situation, whether the situation of threat is being caused by the person or imposed upon him. It should be affected also by his appraisal of his ability to cope with it (e.g., pessimistic, moralistic, negativistic evaluations of his self). The record would include also whether regressive or active solutions have been of avail in the past, i.e., coping with it via dissociation or by active reversal and mastery. As the record changes, so the anxiety signals gain a number of meanings. It would be a necessary factor in continued development that at different ages there exist varying degrees of capacity to experience a range of emotions informative of threatened selfhood: affective signals of helplessness and hopelessness, of loss and deprivation, of pleasure tendencies frustrated, aborted, and conflicted, of undermined autonomy, of estrangement and alienation (apartness and isolation), of limitation and finiteness, and of threatened nonexistence (nonbeing) itself. Threat to experienced unity, integrity, and continuity come to be revealed in affective qualities of anxiety indicative of the particulars of the crisis to selfhood. Such states of experienced incompatibility may run the gamut from puzzlement, disquietude, shame, discontent, guilt, rage, and fear to panic and despair. All point to a temporary breakdown of integration and are the experiential indicators of a crisis which calls for resolution.

Affective experiences are critical for the selection of reparative efforts or for giving up altogether. Such anxious experiences carry other messages as well—of possibility of change (hope) or of ennui, resignation, or despair (hopelessness). For example, deprivation is critical insofar as it affects the child's sense of limitation. It is these emotional experiences that are the *immediate* stimuli to action; they are the signals of whether there is to be action at all. It is not the deprivation per se that is the motivation, but the experience provoked by it—as for example, a sense of profound limitation—the *form* of the *incompatibility experience.* Fraiberg (1967) describes the poignant situation of chronically deprived children who no longer seem to "care."

Affects thus exemplify different varieties of incompatibility; at the same time they are functional and are linked to the possibilities of purpose and of change, which depend upon the capacity for responsiveness to the conscious experience. To have such an emotion implies a belief; to feel fear, for instance, is to believe something is dangerous. Emotions connoting incompatibility become a way for the self to acquire understanding or sense its position in the world. They are the occasions, as well as the outcome, of the reactive and adjustive motivational structuring. Anxiety always involves a perception and conception of danger to the self; it occasions responses to the nature of the danger—responses either regressive, fixated, or reconstructive. The anxiety signal may lead to a further change in the organismic state. For instance, a patient may feel unreal because he is anxiously warding off some danger. (As Arlow [1963] points out, it is a mistake to assume that he feels anxious because he is having feelings of unreality.) Depersonalization, derealization, and similar states of unreality are themselves different kinds of reflections of attempts to ward off a conflict; they are varieties of anxiety. In these instances the anxiety signal shows itself in the form of a change in the organismic state. Thus a state of unreality is a manifestation of anxiety provoked by a conflict or other form of threat.

Structural Outcomes of the Resolution of Incompatibility

Freud was the first to propose that the coexistence of polarities is the basis of dynamics and change; their coexistence calls for efforts at resolution. The terms of incompatibility and the solutions adopted to reduce the incompatibility are internal structures which state themselves as themes, affective positions, and styles of action and thought. The structured residues of incompatibilities are dynamisms, which organize the aims of behavior. Structurally, they are meaning schemata.

The composition of such persisting structures and their activity were long considered mainly in relation to conflict and psychopathology—naturally enough, in view of Freud's original aim of accounting for pathological interruptions of growth and stasis of adaptation. Freud opened a new pathway for the study of psychopathology by showing how symptoms reflect efforts to resolve incompatible tendencies via disassociation and repression—a story still developing. Symptoms were regarded as manifestations of conflicts resolved maladaptively, either through an inhibition of functions or through various modes of withdrawal, regression, and fixation. The solutional aspect of symptoms lay in the fact that they provide the covert expression of conflicted wishes.

But a symptom is not simply aberrant behavior; it is a motivational structure. It entails an aim and selective principles of engagement in relationships. In this sense a phobia exemplifies a "rule" or relationship. For instance, in obsessional neurosis, Freud proposed that a prematurely experienced sexual pleasure is subsequently responded to with moral self-reproaches which thereafter obstruct the pleasure seeking; the ability to give up the remembered pleasure conflicts with the moral reproaches associated with it, leading to maneuvers designed to provide a resolution. Such maneuvers become habituated as *motivations.* Thus all circumstances in which both the wish and the reproach are simultaneously activated will institute the obsessional maneuver.

Although maladaptive, symptoms share with "defenses" the property of being solutions. (It is not inaccurate to speak of them *as* defenses, though to do so risks the implication that defenses are necessarily symptoms, which they are not.) From the early insight into symptoms as solutions, it was a logical step to the assumption that conflicts may be resolved through defense motivations, a conception which has loomed increasingly large in psychoanalytic theory. Freud invoked the concept of defense to account for the fact that if it is necessary to speak of unavoidable desires, there must be some factor which explains why the tendency in question is resisted. A defense originates in a conflict between standards of self-identity and a challenge to these standards. Whatever its specific form, the accomplishment of a defense is the dissociation of a tendency, a conscious disavowal of it. Resort to repression testifies to a stasis in self-identity, to the self's insistence upon the status quo. Repression implies that the meaning schema of a conflicted wish becomes active in a fashion which wards off an aim or goal from all possibility of reflective acknowledgment. Thus the unconsciously desired goal must enter into any accounting of defensive behavior, even if the desire itself is not apparently acted upon. This dictum was—and remains—one of the basic guiding principles of psychoanalytic therapy.

A defense is an attempt both to achieve a pleasure and to prevent its acknowledgment in consciousness. The strategy is of a particular kind of aim which is a means both to control and covertly to accomplish a wish. Thus intrastructurally a defense is part of the representation of a conflict. The defensive transformation of the schema consists of responsiveness to the establishment of new aims and circumstances which evoke the conflicting tendencies. The defense aspect of the schema in action and thought is essentially a strategy invoked in circumstances that trigger the conflict with which it is intended to deal. Schafer (1968b) has pointed out that every defense makes both a positive and a negative assertion: "Something is *not* so" and "something is gratified or gratifiable." To the extent that it is successful the defense actualizes in behavior the following: (a) It has made the clashing trends psychologically compatible; (b) it has eliminated the affective threat provoked by the conflict; (c) it has alleviated a ruptured sense of self through a restriction of both conscious awareness and volitional control of action.

The nature of defense can be illustrated by exploring the meaning of "isolation." Freud writes:

> But in thus endeavouring to prevent associations and connections of thought, the ego is obeying one of the oldest and most fundamental commands of obsessional neurosis, the taboo on touching. If we ask ourselves why the avoidance of touching, contact or contagion should play such a large part in this neurosis and should become the subject-matter of complicated systems, the answer is that touching and physical contact are the immediate aim of the aggressive as well as the loving-cathexis. . . . Since obsessional neurosis begins by persecuting erotic touching and then, after regression has taken place, goes on to persecute touching in the guise of aggressiveness, it follows that nothing is so strongly proscribed in that illness as touching nor so well suited to become the central point of a system of prohibitions [1926, pp. 121-122].

Here are the two aspects of defense which show its motivational function: it organizes behavior in respect to actions involving contact; it directs itself to the implied sexual wish to touch, also to the prohibition not to touch. "Not to touch" becomes a dictum of action on any occasion where both the wish and the constraint are active. At the same time, it is a reminder of the desirable pleasure embedded in the act of touching (and thereby not usually given up)—an important if not exclusive source of the resistance met in analyzing a defense.

A defense, then, is a strategy of behavior reflected in a patterned engagement with the environment, and in aims exhibited in respect to that environment; these aims reflect an effort at synthesis of incompatible tendencies—neither of which can be renounced.

The regressive or dissociative strategy of preserving self-unity can be implemented in a variety of ways. The achievement of the aims cited above often requires a rearrangement of functions and potentials, utilizing the person's existing abilities and capacities, which are adaptable to the requirements of different conflicts. The so-called defense mechanisms describe different means for accomplishing disassociation in different conflicts. The logic of psychoanalytic theory does not require us to assume that they take only the forms described by Anna Freud (1936) in her famous *The Ego and the Mechanisms of Defence.* She did not assume that there are specific "mechanisms of defense" in the sense of a triggered series of linked behaviors. In calling a particular pattern of behavior "defensive" we interpret a motivational *meaning,* that is, we try to figure out how a pattern of behavior reflects a defensive aim. This in turn rests on the assumption of a conflict between a desire and a counteractive attitude to which the defense is directed. Thus the actual variety of "defenses" is an empirical matter rather than a closed set of possibilities prescribed by the theory.

Defenses reflect one of the two main organismic strategies for preserving self-identity. The principle of repression and dissociation was at the heart of Freud's psychoanalytic theory, even its conception of normal development. The other dynamism postulated by Freud and heralded in his late recognition of an "active ego"—the principle we will call *active reversal*—is, however, an equally vital aspect of the dynamics of self-identity. Without it, the conception of self-identity and its development must remain incomplete and one-sided—a state, indeed, in which psychoanalytic conceptions of development have remained for many years. For if the principle of repression is the heart of what psychoanalysis has to say about the restriction of function in neurosis, active reversal is the heart of what it potentially has to say about growth through reconstruction, innovation, and integration—the difference between the resolution of incompatibility by retreat on the one hand and commitment and change on the other. Moreover, the interaction of the two principles is a necessary aspect of a complete psychoanalytic account of development, whether psychopathological or normal—a thought expressed by Erikson when he remarked: "It is always difficult to say where, exactly, obsessive symptomatology ends and creative ritualization begins" (1969, p. 157). These major principles by which self-identity is molded and sustained—repression and active assertion—will occupy three of the chapters that follow, but they are so inextricably an aspect of structure formation that a preliminary assay of the distinctions among them is inescapable.

In conflict, the essential locus of experienced incompatibility is an impasse concerning a desire. The crises of trauma or of developmental turning points concern a failure of a practiced code of behavior. In such acute crises and conflicts, a human being is "not himself" or "beside himself" before he is able to "come to himself." He is equally capable of senseless behavior or of repeating the same hopeless attempt to transcend his dilemma. From such experiences of turmoil emerge resolutions in the form of rules of action and thought, attempts to reinstate unity in that aspect of identity which is under strain—continuity, coherence, or integrity. The outcome is an internalization of conflict, along with a modification of cognitive structure reflecting the changes in the aims and motivation that constitute the resolution.

Thus one can "come to himself" from either of two directions—two alternative strategies, each of which modifies cognitive-affective structures, which in turn modify further action and thought. In one, the conflicted tendency or self-negating encounters are dealt with by dissociating the cognitive-affective components of the conflict from the mainstream of acknowledged tendencies and goals. It is on the presumption of such an integrative effort through disavowal that Freud observed and accounted for "screen memories," and tendentious memories and cognitions generally.

> We shall then form a notion that two psychical forces are concerned in bringing about memories of this sort. One of these forces takes the importance of the experience [e.g., a wish or, negatively, an intolerable assault—GSK] as a motive for seeking to remember it [i.e., to internalize it in a cognitive-affective representation—GSK], while the other—a resistance—tries to prevent any such preference from being shown. These two opposing forces do not cancel each other out, nor does one of them (whether with or without loss to itself) overpower the other. Instead, a compromise is brought about, somewhat on the

> analogy of the resultant in a parallelogram of forces. And the compromise is this. What is recorded as a mnemic image is not the relevant experience itself—in this respect the resistance gets its way; what is recorded is another psychical element closely associated with the objectionable one ... The result of the conflict is therefore that, instead of the mnemic image which would have been justified by the original event, another is produced which has been to some degree associatively *displaced* from the former one.... the substituted memory ... will seem incomprehensible to us because we are inclined to look for the reason for its retention in its own content, whereas in fact that retention is due to the relation holding between its own content and a different one which has been suppressed [1899, pp. 306-307].

Freud is here applying the model of dissociative splitting to a phenomenon of memory.[1] This same model lies at the basis of the meaning not only of repressed memories generally but symptoms and defenses as well. From this model, whose cornerstone is repression, are derived some of the most fundamental concepts about unconsciously active cognitive-affective structures, concepts which are used in clinical work for deciphering meaning in terms of motive; for example, unconscious fantasy, repetition, and transference.

Fundamental in all of these concepts is the assumption of a split-off cognitive-affective structure which exerts a selective influence on behavior.

Thus the strategy of dissociation gives rise to a distinctive class of aims dedicated to both the covert avowal and expression, and the overt disavowal and disengagement from, tendencies that have been in conflict. Many advances in psychoanalytic conceptualizations are elaborations of one or another implication of this model. The structural qualities are represented in such concepts as the inner world of unconscious fantasy, emotional syllogisms, defense, repressed memories, and negative identity. The behavioral manifestations of such repression-organized cognitions are conceptualized as parapraxes, repetitions of unconscious fantasy themes, symptoms, and transfer-

[1]He describes two kinds of "cover memories." One attempts to *correct* the past in a fashion that satisfies a wish ("If only I had . . .") in the present. The other attempts a correction in memory that hides an *earlier* wish that had to be foregone. The first one, therefore, screens a later event; the second screens an earlier event.

ence. All of these refer to regressive emphases on early pleasure sources, which state themselves in varied forms of tendentious falsification of actions and experience. The consequence of this strategy is stasis—maintenance of the existing self-identity which had provoked the experience of incompatibility.

Thinking of such internally represented conflicts and resolutions split off from self-identity as cognitive-affective schemata underscores the impact of such structures on behavior. The term schema is useful in referring to dispositions in a state of relationship to each other but is specifiable as a set of rules—acting as motives—which influence reasoning and action and are exemplified in varying configurations of thought and action.

A successful defense, for instance, combines two different sets of rules so that in respect to action and thought one lives on several planes at once. A defense is a structure in the sense that unrelated cognitive matrices are combined in such a way that a new level is added to the hierarchy of control—by containing previously separate structures in the new configuration of excitation. The defense is, in this sense, a synthesis of two frames of reference. It becomes a basis for organizing experience, a motive or disposition toward action in certain circumstances, and a basis of emotional appraisal. Such internalized representations of conflict and their defensive aspect are features of that created *inner environment* which serves as the person's notions of and dispositions toward the "real world," providing the means of encoding it and making it meaningful.

It is this structured inner world that the analyst, through his interpretations, attempts to reveal.

Franz Alexander (1935) called such unconsciously structured, repression-maintained schemata, *emotional syllogisms*. An emotional syllogism is an unacknowledged and unacknowledgeable (except through therapy) logic of a conflictual structure, which exhibits itself in interpersonal relationships. For example, a conflict between aggressive taking and passive receiving may take the form: "I cannot accept anything from the person whom I really want to rob." Or "giving" may stimulate hostility because the obligation to give may cause resentment of the recipient. Hence the inhibition of receiving may increase the urge to take. Such syllogisms code encounters, and shape actions and thoughts. The construction of such emotional syllogisms, and communication to the patient of their content and of the manner in which they code and symbolize action, is the basis of psychoanalytic efforts. Psychoanalytic therapy is to be construed in part as a kind of "vector-value" analysis of conflictual aims.

Since the original point of Freud's delineation of the repression-formation model was to account for neurotic developments, the activities of repression were viewed as deviations of development, *interruptions* of growth making for stasis, if not for actual regressions to and fixations on earlier emotional positions and pleasure sources. Loewald reminds us that defense is an attempt at reintegration on a *regressive* level: "Defense measures are regressive attempts to come to terms with experiences which cannot be integrated on the level of development reached by the ego in other areas of its integration of reality" (1952, p. 444).

A significant, and for psychology a liberating, advance occurred when Freud saw many phenomena of interruption of development in terms of crises that demanded resolutions for the preservation of selfhood and when he saw this process as an inevitable one in normal development as well as in neurosis. Without exception, the path of growth is marked by conflicts and their resolution, including repression, with its aim of holding fast to positions reached. It is not conflict itself that is pathological; rather, pathology is to be seen in the solutions that emerge from conflict, trauma, and stress. Conflict resolution may mean growth rather than stasis and regression.

But to sustain this view we must have concepts that reflect the growth aspects of solutions rather than the regression-promoting aspects. We must not try to squeeze these constructive aspects through the eyelets of "nothing but" formulae, i.e., regard them as forms of defense or varieties of symptoms. This need for concepts of growth-promoting solutions became especially evident in the development of ego theory, with significant assists by Erikson and Hartmann who began to speak of nonconflictual motives—"secondary autonomy."

The essential dynamic principle that emerged with ego psychology is embodied in Freud's recognition of an "active ego," a subject that will occupy us in the chapters ahead. It is enough for now to quote one statement of the point: "The ego, which experienced the trauma passively, now repeats it actively in a weakened version, in the hope of being able itself to direct its course. It is certain that children behave in this fashion towards every distressing impression they receive, by reproducing it in their play. In thus changing from passivity to activity they attempt to master their experiences psychically" (1926, p. 167). Here Freud is offering the principle of a strategy we will call "active reversal," a strategy that can be activated in any situation where "signal anxiety" (a cue of threatened identity) occurs.

This principle was a crucial advance in ego psychology and is the cornerstone of the broadened exploration of the activity of the "ego." It offers a principle of development that is coordinate with repression and provides another standpoint for observing the structural outcome of conflict, stress, and trauma. By implying that it is on a par with repression, Freud made explicit that there is a "normal," nonneurotic growth force in the resolution of conflict. Furthermore, this principle can encompass the nonneurotic aspects of the development of neurotics as well; indeed, it makes possible the recognition that neurotics are in many ways *non*neurotic. Just as Freud earlier posited a continuity between neurotics and normals in respect to conflict and repression, so this principle extends the conflict principle to normal people.

The structural outcomes of active reversal are not interruptions of development, nor are they function-limiting symptoms or inhibitions; on the contrary, they are additions that increase the scope of experience and relationships. Actions that stem from this strategy make the encounters of the conflict self-*syntonic*, rather than dystonic as in repression. The outcome is therefore *accommodative* in respect to self-identity, giving rise to an enlarged region of differentiation of what is "me" and "mine"—and a greater differentiation of motives that will deal with future events without feelings of estrangement and dissonance. This principle has significance for treatment: it widens its scope and introduces a new dimension of possibility of change, through a program of therapy that first attempts to crack the stasis of repression which the neurotic brings with him. From this issues the important implication that, in transference, models of *both* growth effort and of stasis will be exemplified and acted upon. For therapy, it is not enough now to "uncover" the "compromise" and its work; it is necessary to rework the isolated tendency to a new level of acknowledgment via a change in self-identity.

Both repression and active reversal generate significant transformations in existing structures. Repression leaves essentially unchanged the schemata of a conflict as well as the conception of self-identity; it *adds* a component of inhibition to the structure. The activity of the repressed structure is assimilative; it absorbs facts and events within the terms of the repressed tendencies. The strategy is a splitting process which disengages incompatible components from the self while the incompatible components themselves remain unchanged.

The resolutions that occur through active reversal contribute to new differentiations and consolidations of identity. Active reversal can lead to new *positive* identifications, in contrast to the negative or rejected identifications that persist as a negative identity. For example, Loewald points out that the outcome of the acute phase of the Oedipal conflict is not necessarily a regressive one. Meeting the anxiety involved is not limited to the alternatives of "remaining in or sinking back into the structureless unity from which the ego emerged" (1951, p. 15). Instead, the "powerful paternal force," a source of the experience of threat, is invoked to resolve the threat. Being at one with the father, joining him identifiably, involves a new level of differentiation and complication of the personality. This has the twofold advantage of producing a new level of unity within the self and removing the threat to selfhood. It is also the alternative to a regressive solution. Identification is a nondefensive solution to conflict, which produces a new level of self-identity.

Aiding the process of active reversal which makes this identification possible is the fact that the Oedipal crisis occurs in the same developmental period in which discovery through play is productive of a sense of initiative. "His learning now is intrusive; it leads him into ever new facts and activities" (Erikson, 1968b, p. 288). Moreover, the play during this period "relies on the existence of some form of basic family, which also teaches the child by patient example where play ends and irreversible purpose begins.... The 'oedipal' stage thus not only results in a moral sense restricting the horizon of the permissible, but it also directs the way to the possible and the tangible, which attract infantile dreams to the goals of technology and culture" (p. 289).

Active reversal manifests itself early, even in pre-Oedipal stages. Spock observes that a six- to nine-month-old child already exhibits a tendency to outgrow symbiotic relationships. The child's nature obliges him to detach himself from a totally dependent relationship with his mother. Thus it is wholly in keeping with this tendency for the baby to give up the breast and the bottle that the mother holds (1963, pp. 361-364). Spock describes a typical crisis of transition in this period—the weaning from the breast or bottle to the cup. He raises the question of why breast-fed babies are more easily weaned to the cup (6-9 months) than bottle-fed babies, particularly those who have been encouraged to hold and drink their own bottles. The *increasing* infatuation with the independently held bottle after six months and the reluctance to use the cup require explanation. Spock points out that as the child senses his own autonomy, the mother's breast begins to be restrictive because he cannot use it apart from her. When the bottle-holding baby takes the bottle to bed, he can have his sucking pleasure and his autonomy as well. But why the reluctance to take to the cup? Spock finds that the need for the bottle is greatest at bedtime, and presumes that the child, being separated from the mother at this point, is also experiencing the greatest dependency. The bottle then supplies the oral gratification that he *used to have,* and the soft object, the nipple, provides the tactile pleasure that he used to gain, without the necessity of relinquishing autonomy. Hence the increasing attachment to the bottle after six months. Spock concludes that weaning, properly conducted, is not a deprivation but a step in maturation. The "transitional object" at this point is reminiscent of the pleasure aspect of the mother and a substitute, but also an insurance against re-envelopment by the mother. The situation is analogous to the resolution of Oedipal stress through an active reversal process which uses "the powerful parental force"; through this transitional object, regression is invited but also limited.

While repression serves the self in "holding its ground," active reversal is regenerative; it involves a reorganization of self-conception and consequently of the standards of its own unity. The two strategies constitute a polarity, one producing isolation and segregation within the personality, the other constitutive *of* personality. Active reversal activates skills or dormant potentialities. While the activity of the repressed structure leads to repetitions which reproduce the conflict in behavior with the aim of satisfying the interdicted gratification, active reversal leads to repetition on another level: trying to modify the terms of the conflict to a condition acceptable to the self on a new level of integration. In the latter we have what Erikson has called creative re-enactment and what Loewald has called creative reconstruction.

Thus conflict is not necessarily disintegrative. It can lead to integration at new levels of articulation of the self's aims and identity. In an acute conflict, aspects of both repression and active reversal are likely to appear. An initial retreat to more primitive, more plastic, and less committed stages may be followed by a sudden turn in a new direction. The implications for psychoanalytic therapy are great. For the phenomena of transference can embody both the regressive aspects of repetition and the acting out of repressed structures, and the identificatory process of re-enactment. The distinction between the two kinds of transference manifestations becomes an important one for the analyst—one that gives new scope and brings new complexities to psychoanalytic therapy. Is it no longer possible to hold to the old familiar view of transference as wholly a matter of repression, regression, and defense.

Just as repression is manifested behaviorally and structurally in particular forms, so does active reversal have distinctive structural and process outcomes. Indeed, it is possible to see these outcomes as counterparts of each other. For instance, the internalized figures of a repressed structure are called "introjects." An introject is a schematized representation of a significant figure dissociated from selfhood. Its counterpart in active reversal is "identification," i.e., a relationship that emerges from a process which is not isolated from self-identity but on the contrary becomes a part of the structure of selfhood. It represents an accommodative change in self, the self's structure at a new level of differentiation. Similarly, "defense" and negative identity on the one hand, "cognitive style" and positive identity on the other, reflect aspects of personality dissociated from self-identity, and incorporated, differentiated aspects of self-identity.

The analytic model of therapy relies heavily on the view that many motivations come about as resolutions of experienced impasses. The identification of such impasses, their re-enactment through transference, the development of new motivations based on such recognition and re-enactment—all in one respect or another are referable to this basic psychoanalytic precept. Therapeutic effort and understanding are directed toward getting the patient to acknowledge the rule-conforming nature of his actions, the specifications of the rules, their origins, and the threats to selfhood that they reflect and which were the basis of his ignoring them. His symptoms are made intelligible as solutions that reflect an emotional syllogism. The therapist looks for evidence of regression or fixation to a particular developmental position. What it was that made this solution necessary becomes the focus of the therapist's effort. The analyst will look for repetitively stated themes of conflict and stress, above all in the manner in which the patient construes the relationships of themes. The gratifications involved could be sensual or aggressive, or, in the service of resistance, the designation of self as a moral victim, i.e., a defensive inclination to deflect responsibility. The principle, in short, is the basis of semantic encoding by which the analyst "understands" behavior. Working through the terms of the conflict in the context of transference leads, optimally, to a condition where the symptoms or the defense lose their "function" for the patient as effective resolutions. (The situation is not actually so simple, for the defense and the symptom may, in repeated life practice, have "justified" themselves in a variety of ways. Hartmann [1950], for example, describes the "secondary autonomy" of defenses.)

Although exploration of the principle of active reversal, or, in conventional terms, an "independently assertive ego," is still in the early stages, viewing behavior from the enlarged perspective of *two* strategies of self-integration has profoundly influenced therapeutic sensitivity. Loewald (1960), for example, has reinterpreted transference to allow for the importance of active reversal. In general, the view that therapy is not only an attempt to uncover repression but a growth process involving active reversal is coming more and more into prominence.

Repression and Reversal in Relation to Art and the Artist

The double perspective provided by repression and active reversal as molding principles gives renewed vigor to the attempt to penetrate the enigma of the motivations for the making of art and for an understanding of its constructive outcomes. Psychoanalytic studies have tended to remain within the confines of the principle of repression and defense, but, however useful the assumptions of unconscious fantasies, repetitive themes, and defenses in penetrating the motives of the artist and the meanings of his constructions, this single-minded approach has faltered before the problem of accounting for the creative aspects of an art form beyond its "projective-test" revelations about the artist himself. The close relation between self-realization and self-repair issuing from the basic precept that the resolution of incompatibility has structural consequences is underscored in both principles. From this standpoint, the art-making impulse originates in a context of experienced limitation—experiences involving the fracturing of selfhood and anxieties that herald the possibility of such a threat. Losses and severances, experienced as threats, are lived out in and inspire restitutive efforts through the making of art. In this process can be observed the same elements of undoing an old pattern and redoing into a new one. It involves breaking up rigid cognitive structures and reassembling them into a new synthesis. One aspect of creative activity, therefore, is a kind of do-it-yourself therapy—an attempt, through the improvisations of art-making, to come to terms with traumatizing challenges to selfhood through a created addition to the environment.

However, creation is not simply another form of repetition. Art is fantasy, but not all fantasy is art. The novel aspect of resolutions in art is the very reverse of defense. Defense involves a restriction of function; in art-making a function and a form of a talent become an instrument of re-enactment in which a new reality is shaped, one that is capable of being judged objectively by others. It carries the re-enactments of repression one step further, by "forcing," as it were, a change in the environment, but not a tendentious falsification of it. To the extent that falsification occurs, indeed, the art might be considered "unsuccessful." Indeed, to the extent that a creative work is not hemmed in by the requirements of defense, and does not transform defense itself into a style, it loses in freedom. What sustains the artist's incentive is the *pleasure* of creating a world that was not there but that contains the necessary revision to produce a more balanced internal state.

Thus in a work of art the artist's personal dilemma combines with a perception of a condition of his cultural climate in a constructive act of transposition. The product represents itself as a commentary on reality and offers itself as a cultural "fact." A perception of a cultural condition is the focal point of the re-enactment of a personally experienced dilemma. Behind the artist's hoped-for "approval" is his wish that the attempted integration has been achieved, that it is indeed a *"fact."* Creative change, then, is more a matter of regenerative construction, for it leads from the painful consciousness of one's position to a new version of reality molded from that position. This is always the case for the individual artist, but major art trends may have a cultural reverberation of the same sort. New trends in art shake theories and practices which have rigidified into assumed actuality; like scientific discoveries, they make nonsense of cherished assumptions about what is "real" and reveal them as mere beliefs.

The thematic output of an artist is selective; study will disclose the relationship between themes of the art to those of crises and conflicts which originated in a blow to or crisis of selfhood and that left a cognitive residue which is repeatedly enacted. In this respect, the aim of the creative artist is indistinguishable from what is simply "human" and characteristic of his less gifted fellows.

The question arises, Whence comes the attempt to effect such restitution through the making of art? Here, the discovery of a skill that can be turned to gratifying mastery of crises of selfhood is probably crucial in the genesis of an artist's commitment to the art-making process. Some skills are especially suited to the representation of internal states, e.g., painting, writing. Others are more suited to direct environmental control, e.g., machine skills, handicrafts. In either case the skill serves a reparative purpose in turning a blow passively experienced into an experience of environmental mastery. For example, words can turn a fantasied world into a new reality, and when the writer receives confirmation of its effectiveness, he is encouraged to more such efforts, a recognition that the new reality is in fact real—it has been approved. The novelist thus works his way through the experienced social impediment by reshaping it through words. Similar motivations prod the musically inclined and the painter. The early perception of the mastery thereby obtained, and the pleasure this experience evokes, are especially vivid in a context of social failure, or failure in interpersonal relations. This contrast would amplify the pleasure brought about by the ability and add an intense reinforcement to its further and repeated invocation. A child who follows this course will be "creative" in the art-making sense, because he has *emotionally* invested in a *means of invention* which is the basic ingredient of creating new forms. The informational returns of mastery (further reinforced by rewards and public notice) come to produce an autonomous reliance upon the skill itself, in a cycle of autonomous self-rewarding creation and re-creation. When this happens one is an "artist." Of course, the genesis of the skill itself is not encompassed by this conception.

The resort to a skill in circumstances of unsuccessful social or affiliative efforts and of losses is not, it should be said, the usual mode of attempted resolution. Most children work out social failures in social experiences and not through withdrawal or dependence upon the by-products of mastery via a skill. One senses that, in the nascent artist especially, the failure was accompanied by the feeling that such social efforts would be unavailing, and he tends to give up hope that he may find solutions through such a route, or at least it becomes secondary to the more manageable solutions and perhaps the more certain pleasurable reinforcements of effective control that are promised by a manipulative skill under his own governorship.

To sum up: The psychoanalytic emphasis on conflict is placed in the broader context of a principle of synthesizing efforts that are necessitated by the developing self which is responsive to crises of disunity. The preservation of the coherence, continuity, and integrity of selfhood is a basis of growth; crises of synthesis require modification of strategies and rules of behavior to reinstate self-unity. From such experiences of cleavage, whether of the nature of conflict, trauma, or developmental crises, arise efforts at solution in the form of a realignment of aims and goals. The more relevant a motivation is in bringing about a solution to a crisis of selfhood, the more lasting, generalized, and thereafter relied upon it is in the economy of personality. Thus the resolution of experienced incompatibility is the major basis of motivational structure. Motivations, rather than being regarded as arising from a "parallelogram of impersonal forces" defined in terms of intensity, are regarded as arising as resolutions of issues of self-integration and self-perpetuation.

Incorporating the emphasis of ego psychology upon an intrinsically active principle of self-identity, we have proposed two main organismic strategies of effecting self-unity. One is predicated on repression, in which the alien conflictual terms of incompatibility are dissociated from the mainstream of the self-identity structure. The strategy is that of preserving unity by limitation of function. The other, the principle of active reversal, follows the course of confrontation and re-enactment of the alien tendencies, leading to an integration that is in effect a differentiated enlargement of selfhood.

The principle of growth through a reconciliation of incompatibilities points to a normal phenomenon, not a pathological one. Certain forms of conflict are inevitable. Moreover, development is marked and defined by crises of transition or turning points that occur in the incompatibility of practiced modes of a given stage with emerging potentialities. In this view the outcomes of conflict or other forms of incompatibility are not necessarily debilitating and restrictive. It becomes comprehensible, also, in terms of the principle, that the outcome of disrupted selfhood can be creative effort as well as severe functional limitation.

Viewing conflict as one class of incompatibility determined by its context in self-identity gives us a broader and freshened perspective on a number of possible avenues of investigation. From this view derive conceptions about the formative influence of conflict, defense, and repetition of themes in the coding of action and thought, and the degree to which life functions are restricted by such processes. From it also derive concepts that enable us to envisage creative re-enactment in contrast to repetition, and self-differentiation via identification in contrast to functional stasis of self-identity. This perspective also has implications for psychoanalytic therapy. At the same time, it must be acknowledged that the principle and its implications are far short of fulfillment in their empirical underpinnings and in the exploration of their implications. In the form we have sketched, it is still only an open-ended directive for development rather than a systematic accounting of solidly established clinical experience.

There are great problems left open by this principle: When is a blow to selfhood likely to lead to repressive dissociation, inhibition of function, restriction and regression on the one hand, and when to active reversal and self-differentiation? Is the choice conditional on whether a blow is so "intolerable" that it is dealt with dissociatively? And what *is* an intolerable blow? When does a "defense" become a symptom? And what precisely distinguishes them? And, of course, the old issue of "choice of symptom" is no nearer solution.

CHAPTER 6

The Vital Pleasures

MAN'S ACTIVITY, Freud wrote, develops in two directions, according to whether it seeks to realize the experience of pleasure or the absence of pain.[1] For an organism that is without a preformed, adapted identity and subject to prolonged dependence, the capacity to feel pleasure, anxiety, and pain are critical safeguards of his adaptation. The structuring and education of the pleasure potential are at the heart of what Freud went on to call the "reality principle."

In the rendering of the "pleasure principle" to be followed in the pages ahead, the emphasis will be upon pleasure and unpleasure *experiences*—qualities of awareness. This emphasis is different from that of the more usual versions of the pleasure principle that have evolved in psychoanalytic theory. The version known as the constancy principle holds that an organism tends to maintain itself at an optimal level of tension: increases being states of unpleasure; return to the optimum, states of pleasure. The other version combines the constancy principle with a quasi-physiological model of drives pressing for discharge as "stimuli on the mind" (Jacobson, 1953). Indeed, theorists in either mold are likely to warn the reader not to equate their use of

[1]"[Human beings] strive after happiness; they want to become happy and to remain so. This endeavour has two sides, a positive and a negative aim. It aims, on the one hand, at an absence of pain and unpleasure, and, on the other, at the experiencing of strong feelings of pleasure. In its narrower sense the word 'happiness' only relates to the last. In conformity with this dichotomy in his aims, man's activity develops in two directions, according as it seeks to realize—in the main, or even exclusively—the one or the other of these aims" (Freud, 1930, p. 76).

the term pleasure with pleasure experience (see, for example, Rapaport, 1959; Schur, 1966).

In the drive-discharge version, pleasure is spoken of in the language of libido. How libido came to be an all-encompassing designation of pleasure is an intricate story that we can touch on here only in outline. It had its beginnings in Freud's revolutionary insight that the sexuality of adulthood is linked to infancy through a potential for sensual pleasure that evolves in different forms. Libido, referring to a hypothetical energy specific to this sensual development, was Freud's way of freeing considerations of sexuality from the traditional identification of sexuality with genital maturity and the procreative function, and of describing its diverse and extensive manifestations in thought, work, and morality, both normal and deviant (Freud, 1905b).

However, libido soon became more than simply a way of generalizing sensuality; it developed into a putatively explanatory *model,* which reified libido into an energic process pressing for *discharge,* and subject to transformations ("vicissitudes") under that pressure. Discharge was the key element of the process. The model accounts for diverse variations of sensuality by explaining them as deflected or inhibited discharges, or as transformations of libido via hypercathexes, fusions, defusions, sublimation, and, in a later addition by Hartmann (1952), neutralization. Taken as a model, the libido-drive-discharge theory is a quasi-physiological, hypothetical mechanism of causation, rather than an account of pleasure experience. Since the essential moving agent in motivation was not pleasure as experienced but the "push" of the drive energy, there was little need to consider the experiential nature of pleasure, which was taken to be mere description with little theoretical status.

Insofar as the experience of pleasure itself is considered at all, the tendency of the drive-discharge model is to equate all pleasure with sensual pleasure. The theory has no language for conceiving other than sensual pleasures, or of varieties of pleasure in other than the terms of the sexual theory. An analogous blurring occurs in the constancy version of the pleasure principle, which lends itself to collapsing all pleasure experiences into mere manifestations of a reduction of tension or of discharge.

The status of pleasure, then, in psychoanalytic theory presents the ironic picture of an initial emphasis upon man's consciousness of pleasure and unpleasure as a decisive factor in development undergoing sophistications of theory that steadily downgraded this very emphasis.

The difficulties of the constancy principle and the drive-discharge model are well documented and require no review here (see Herold, 1941-1942; Kardiner, Karush, and Ovesey, 1959; Kaufman, 1960; Holt, 1965, 1967; Apfelbaum, 1965; Klein, this volume, Chapter 3). But among the criticisms leveled at either of these meanings of the pleasure principle, none seems to me more important than that they lose the import of a crucial principle implicit in a number of Freud's formulations—namely, that the loss of instinctual adaptiveness makes man's survival contingent on the evolution of his *consciousness*. The point is precisely that they deflect attention from pleasure as a positive, causal, selective factor of conscious *experience* in the retaining or discarding of patterns of behavior—or, in contemporary parlance, as a reinforcer. By narrowly construing the classes of pleasure experiences, they also ignore the important possibility that motives may vary according to the variety of pleasure experience involved. This is suggested by Buchenholz's pioneering studies (1956, 1957). If pleasure is a basis for activities becoming desirable, then the emergence of sensibility to different conditions capable of exciting the pleasure potential is a significant facet of ego development.

It becomes important, then, to reassert the role of pleasure experience as an important contributor to a person's evolving identity and to the structuring of his motives. To return psychoanalytic theory to this base requires, first of all, that we free considerations of pleasure from the confines of the model of libidinal development, which tends to equate pleasure with sensual experience alone, and set aside assumptions of a hypothetical energy which waxes and wanes as states of tension; second, that we try to delineate prototypical conditions or contexts of pleasure—different pleasure modalities; third, that we take stock of the functional role of these different sources of pleasure in the structuring of relationships.

The schema offered in the pages that follow will include sensual pleasure in its adapted, as well as its conflictual and restitutive, role in ego development. But it is assumed that there are modalities of pleasure in addition to the sensual. The principle of developmental stages, usually restricted to sexuality, is applied to other classes of pleasure as well, allowing also for a dynamic interplay among them. Such an approach in terms of distinctive prototypical pleasures invites research curiosity rather than dulling it by comfortably relegating pleasure to a single line of physiological development and to one class of pleasure capacity.

My aim, in short, is to reorient psychoanalytic theory to the essential wisdom of the pleasure principle—that we act so as to maximize pleasure or gratification and to minimize unpleasure of all kinds, especially anxiety.

Let us first get our bearings by positioning pleasure at the executive center of behavior, the ego. In this view, pleasure, even sexual, does not reflect something essentially external to the ego, impinging on it as a "force" to be controlled, a "stimulus" to be dealt with, or something to be disposed of or reacted to. Rather, we should think of pleasure as reflecting a number of different forms of well-being experienced in the body, which are triggered by particular contexts of stimulation, and whose arousal and inhibition are further shaped by experiences of permissibility and restraint that come to be associated through learning with the arousal of the pleasure prototype.

It will be easier to think of pleasure as an ego experience if we consider that a precedent and a guide for doing so already exist in how anxiety has come to be regarded in psychoanalysis. At one time Freud regarded anxiety as he did pleasure—in the context of the model of drive discharge. Anxiety, in this view, resulted from either insufficient or overcontrolled discharge of libido, the extreme being the *Aktualneurose*. Later, Freud considered it more fruitful to regard anxiety as an ego function, reflected in experiences of actual or threatened helplessness and estrangement (Freud, 1926). With the present way of looking at anxiety, many previously worrisome issues have turned out to be insignificant or even pseudo problems. Few psychoanalytic theorists consider it important any longer to ask whether the energy of the anxiety signal is libidinal or not. Nor is it sufficient to regard anxiety solely as a quantitative problem of discharge. Although Freud put aside his model of libido and discharge in shifting from a purely quantitative conception of anxiety as an overflow of pent-up libido to the structural view, he did not give up that model where pleasure experience was concerned.

What Freud did with anxiety could well be done now with pleasure.

It seems a logical extension of the theory, as Eidelberg (1962), Kanzer and Eidelberg (1960), and Szasz (1957) suggest, to regard pleasure as complementary in function to anxiety. Seen in the same light, as an ego capability, pleasure can be usefully disengaged from the assumptions of the drive-discharge model, and we are thereby encouraged to consider various *qualitative* forms of pleasure experience and their motivational significance. Just as anxiety is informative experience with regard to events that forebode helplessness and estrangement, pleasure is an informative experience of accord and well-being, through which things and objects acquire values of approachability and desirability. Pleasure and anxiety thus designate states of self-experience—one of well-being, the other of experienced threat.[2] We can then also assume that pleasure experience, like anxiety, can have

CHART 1

PLEASURE AND ANXIETY VIEWED AS COMPLEMENTARY EGO EXPERIENCES

EGO STATE ⟶	SELF-EXPERIENCE ⟵	PROTOTYPICAL PLEASURE EXPERIENCES
cohesiveness continuity integrity	well-being	tension reduction sensual pleasure pleasure in functioning effectance pleasure in pleasing pleasure in synthesis
EGO STATE ⟶	**SELF-EXPERIENCE ⟵**	**PROTOTYPICAL PLEASURE EXPERIENCES**
fragmentation discontinuity conflict	helplessness estrangement	fear of suddenness fear of separation fear of loss of love, etc.

[2]In this formulation, the more useful antithesis of pleasure is anxiety rather than pain or "unpleasure." Pain is a special adaptive response to stimulation beyond physiologically tolerable limits (high and low). Nor is unpleasure, the experiential accompaniment of frustration, a general enough category to stand in polar contrast to pleasure. The polarity of pleasure and anxiety is exemplified by the contrast of motivations issuing from each. Motives of pleasure involve affiliative aims, which may even encompass tolerance of pain and unpleasure; motives generated by anxiety (e.g., defense) are pointed toward the alleviation of fantasied threats to self-identity.

an anticipatory as well as fully actualized aspect; that is, we can speak of "signal pleasure" as well as "signal anxiety."

To point up the relationship of ego and self to states of anxiety and pleasure we picture them together in Chart 1. Pleasure and anxiety are seen as major and contrasting states of feeling generated by the organism in response to contact with things, events, and people; the ego in anxiety is in a state of disjunction, fragmentation, conflicted encounter, these being experienced as estranging and threatening to one's identity. Pleasure experiences reflect and promote ego conditions of cohesiveness and continuity.

Seen as an ego potential, pleasure no longer is assumed to be, as in the drive-discharge model or constancy principle, simply a state of modulated stimulation defined negatively and wholly quantitatively as relief from pain, the diminished pressure of a drive, or relieved frustration. Pleasure and anxiety are qualitatively distinct processes, independently arousable. Correspondingly, anxiety and pleasure are motivating in distinctively different ways: motives arising from anxiety are designed to minimize experienced threat; those of pleasure to reinstate and to sustain contact. This is not to omit the possibility of states that complexly exemplify both anxiety and pleasure ("awe" is perhaps such a state, involving a feeling of helplessness before a dominating entity quickly followed by the pleasure of resignation and acceptance of one's position in relation to it).

The study of anxiety in psychoanalysis was much advanced by Freud's further attempt to specify *forms of anxiety* that are prototypical for different stages of development, e.g., fear of separation, fear of loss of love, fear of castration, fear of death. Freud called these forms of anxiety "motives of defense" (1926). From the standpoint of concern with the means or phenomenology of anxiety, it is more fruitful to speak of anxiety in the cognitive terms of *kind* or *quality* of threat, rather than in purely quantitative terms; it is much more important to know that anxiety occurs in the form, say, of "a fear of abandonment," than "how much" anxiety there is.[3]

Freud's view of anxiety offers the more clinically pertinent model for

[3]It may be noted that this meaning conception of anxiety has still not registered strongly in laboratory studies of anxiety, which usually focus on its physiological manifestations, as a phenomenon of goose pimples or GSR deflection, rather than on its different cognitive-affective meanings of subjectively experienced threats.

the study of pleasure. Rather than speaking of pleasure strictly as a sensation that one can have a "little" or a "lot" of, I shall speak of *prototypical varieties of pleasure* in their developmental and motivational aspect. Just as with anxiety, so we can assume about pleasure experiences that there are a limited number of prototypical forms, which retain importance throughout development but assume particular importance at different stages of development. Such sources of pleasure are primary in the sense of being innately given potentialities that are not further analyzable; however, they undergo continual cognitive elaboration in schemas. Just as "danger situations" are distinguishable in their internal representation as different kinds of threat, so relationships acquire an internally represented form in their pleasure aspect. Partial activation of such schemas can produce pleasure signals corresponding to anxiety signals.

The specification of pleasure prototypes should look to developmental models for clues of qualitatively distinguishable pleasure experiences and for a rationale of their adaptive utility. Here Erikson's conception of development offers a framework within which to conceive such prototypes and to relate them to psychological growth (Erikson, 1963, 1968a). It is one of the few conceptions that has been an attempt to articulate a logic of ego growth that is not limited to stages of psychosexual development, and indeed tries to encompass the entire life of a person. Especially important for a theory of pleasure is its sensitivity to the phenomenology of self-experience at different stages. At the same time, Erikson's model neither gives up nor slights considerations of crisis and conflict as formative factors in growth. He views these, rather, as manifestations of an ever-continuing effort to bring about a balance between internalized group values (group identity) and autonomous individuality (ego identity). He thus provides a dynamic context within which to consider the economy of pleasure experiences, their management, their miscarriages and pathology, as well as their adaptive involvement in the stage-specific tasks of development. Actually Erikson has extended Freud's qualitative view of anxiety by delineating the forms of anxiety experiences for all stages of the life cycle. He has not, however, carried this view to a consideration of pleasure.

Accordingly, I will describe six prototypes of pleasure experience. These are taken to be potentials for pleasure which appear in infancy, but thereafter undergo a cognitive-affective elaboration consistent with the developments in physical and cognitive capacity of different periods. We consider these pleasure prototypes to be vital in helping to affirm and crystallize the gains of each developmental stage, with its residue of "trust," "initiative," "competence," and the like. They are vital also in the sense that incapacity and miscarriage of these pleasure sensibilities will be permanent liabilities, restricting psychological growth. Although important at every life stage, the relative importance of each pleasure is assumed to vary with the tasks and crises of selfhood at different periods of life, particular classes of pleasure experience being especially pertinent at certain stages. In this sense of "vital" pleasure, the prototypes are specifically and collectively crucial in the delineation of self-identity.

Pleasure in Reduction of Unpleasant Tension

It was once commonly thought that the world of the baby was made up mainly of satisfiers and frustrators. Recent observations, however, suggest that the baby's experience is much wider in range than this. The world, for instance, often seems to be not so much satisfying or frustrating as interesting to him, holding his attention and perhaps provoking something akin to wonder. With the recognition of such states as "alert inactivity" (Wolff, 1959, 1966), the role of tension reduction has been somewhat downgraded as a factor in the development of the baby's attachments to things and people.

Frustration is, however, an inescapable fact from the very beginnings of postnatal life. Babies do experience tension at times; they look and feel tense as they strain over a bowel movement or howl in hunger and pain, and they seem more content as these states subside. Although an expressive capacity for conveying pleasure is not very evident in the very young infant, it is not farfetched to assume that the diminution of such tension and the "return to baseline" is experienced as a pleasurable state of well-being of some kind. We also assume, of course, that such early experiences are primitive in their cognitive elaboration.

In hypothesizing that tension reduction is a source of pleasure, we refer to an actual *experience* of tension and its relief, not to a hypothetical condition of energic pressure. It is part of the present hypothesis that the relief of bowel pressure or, or hunger, and later on the intermittent relief from teething, is not simply the elimination of unpleasure; the relief is itself experienced positively as pleasant.[4]

With developing attentional and conceptual capacity and increased options of response, the experience of tension and its pleasurable reduction becomes more and more removed from its original locus in bodily needs. A variety of cognitive conditions may create uncomfortable tension, e.g., incompleteness, interruption of a tendency (if the tendency remains active), unfamiliarity, failure of recognition. But this is not to say that the relief of somatic tensions ever loses its pleasurable aspect; for example, the cycle of anal retention-evacuation, including flatulation, is an underestimated source of pleasure.

The intimate connection of tension reduction to somatic or bodily state, and to sensual and functional pleasures as well, suggests that these pleasure sources make a particularly early appearance in development, and are vital to the sense of physical separateness, or "body ego," which is a crucial precursor of psychological separateness and the later sense of "I" or self. Bettelheim (1967) has described an autistic child who was extraordinarily impervious to harmful stimulation and who absorbed herself in a game of holding back and letting go in defecation, as if inviting the cycle of tension and relief as a test of being "alive."

It used to be thought that the pleasure of tension reduction was the crucial reinforcer of human attachments, e.g., that the reason a child becomes attached to a particular person is that she feeds him and removes his other bodily discomforts. Recent evidence suggests that this is an oversimple reduction: mere relief of hunger does not necessarily make for greater attachment to the source of gratification of food needs. The reason, says Bowlby (1969), is that for the hungry baby, the person who gives food is only a mediator, the bearer of the object that will relieve the tension. Once the infant learns this

[4]Commenting on this passage, my colleague R. R. Holt takes issue with the assumption that reduced tension is necessarily felt as pleasurable. He points out that the actual sources of the pleasure may be the means by which tension gets reduced—e.g., eating or defecating—not the relief of tension per se. The reduction of tension may be merely a state of tranquil inertness, felt neither as pleasant nor unpleasant. He concludes: "I'm afraid that you are simply trying to absorb the old view by granting tension reduction a minor place as one type of pleasure, whereas I think the implication of your paper, from the very first sentence, is that pleasure is *not* phenomenologically identical with less pain, less unpleasure, or less tension." Since at present the issue is not easily testable, I concede that it is debatable.

distinction, the mother is not herself the hungered-for object. Relationships seem to depend more on other forms of pleasure, shortly to be discussed, which lend themselves more naturally to and even require arousal conditions of mutual exchange and give and take.

Nevertheless, it is difficult to avoid the conclusion that the mother's appearance, which brings distress to an end and induces pleasure, does carry a powerful message of beneficence, affirming trust, and therefore contributes to a motive of attachment to the mother. That is why Murphy (1964), for example, insists that tension reduction *is* important in establishing the relationship of a child to its mother. It is likely, however, that this basis of attachment is stronger in infants than it is in older children. Certainly the reliability of care in infancy, registered through the experience of tension relief, would be a factor in producing what Erikson calls a favorable balance of trust over mistrust.

Developmentally advanced, more purely cognitive forms of tension experience and its reduction involve the circumvention of an obstacle. For example, Freud regarded this as an important basis for the enjoyment of a joke; tendentious jokes, as Freud refers to them, have, particularly, a twofold advantage: they satisfy a repressed tendency in some measure, but they also afford relief from the effortful work of inhibition. The convergence of these two sources of tension makes for a particularly intense pleasure (Freud, 1905c).

Freud suggested that such lifting of inhibition (experienced as the relief of tension) also explains the pleasure that children, and adults too, get from the games which deliberately create obstacles which are gotten rid of in "joyful acts of recognition." On the same assumption, Freud tried to account for the pleasure in certain games of nonsense.[5] He even goes so far as to offer the challenging hypothesis that in some disturbances of learning, the unconscious insistence upon bringing

[5]"Whatever the motive may have been which led the child to begin these games, I believe that in his later development he gives himself up to them with the consciousness that they are nonsensical, and that he finds enjoyment in the attraction of what is forbidden by reason. He now uses games in order to withdraw from the pressure of critical reason. But there is far more potency in the restrictions which must establish themselves in the course of a child's education and logical thinking and in distinguishing between what is true and false in reality; and for this reason, the rebellion against the compulsion of logic and reality is deep-going and long-lasting. Even the phenomena of imaginative activity must be included in this [rebellious] category. The power of criticism has increased so greatly in the later part of childhood and in the period of learning which extends over puberty that the pleasure in 'liberated nonsense' only seldom dares to show itself directly. One does not venture to say anything absurd" (Freud, 1905c, pp. 125-126).

about such pleasure in nonsense plays a part in the child's inefficiency in learning certain operations that require the *"inhibitive* control of reason."

To bring both infantile and later developments into a conception of this pleasure prototype, we may consider the critical criterion of tension-reduction pleasure to be the relief of an experience of inhibition. In this generic formulation, tension relief is not limited to the correction of an actual somatic deficit but covers all occasions when the bringing to an end of unpleasant tensions is experienced as pleasing.

These considerations raise the question of whether there develop motives specifically directed to *producing* the pleasure of tension reduction by the intentional creation of states of tension. Undoubtedly there are motives which deliberately court tension, and even anxiety and pain, for the sake of evoking the pleasure of relief. Usually, however, closer scrutiny of such instances suggests the presence as well of sensual pleasure and of pleasure derived from experiencing oneself as the intended agent of control (what we will call "effectance pleasure"). Even the thrill of a racing car, of the amusement park loop-the-loop, probably comes not only from the game of tension creation and its relief but also from admixtures of sensual arousal and effectance pleasure. For example, the counterphobic thrill may well be a mixture of anxiety and the self-reassurance that it is mastered.

Sensual Pleasure

Like the pleasure of tension reduction, sensual pleasure originates in bodily induced sensations. We could therefore expect the capacity for sensual pleasure also to be vital in affirming a sense of physical and psychological identity.

Earlier (see Chapter 3) I proposed that Freud's revolutionary perceptions regarding infantile sensuality and its developmental course are most clearly appreciated when they are uncoupled from the drive-discharge model, which requires us to assume a *vis-a-tergo* pressing for discharge.

Freud's innovations derived from several lines of evidence which compelled him to conclude that sexuality must have an earlier origin than in puberty—one, indeed, that affects how sexuality will appear in puberty. It became critical to identify this specific developmental factor, which manifests itself long before puberty, is independent of procreative sexuality, yet is continuous with it. From the standpoint of conscious experience, this prototypical sexuality (its time of first appearance is an empirical issue) reveals itself as a capacity for a distinctively pleasant experience, arousable through appropriately patterned stimulation of body surfaces; it has its own thresholds and its own qualities, compared with other forms of sensory experiences that are also associated with the same body regions and modes that elicit sensual pleasure. The nub of Freud's proposal was that this pleasure capability undergoes development: it changes in respect to the bodily conditions of its arousal and the cognitive-affective record left behind by its arousal, this record or schema coming in time to be a factor in the regulation of the pleasure.

In this view, sensual pleasure is not simply an outcome of the removal of unpleasure or of tension; it is tied to conditions of arousal specific to itself and it is different from the pleasant experiences of other forms of satisfactions or rewards. Sibylle Escalona (personal communication) points out that although the occasions of sensual pleasure very often involve tension relief, sensual pleasure occurs also in contexts of fairly high tension, e.g., tickling and cradle-rocking.

Surprisingly little is known as yet, however, about the conditions of sensual arousal, even less about the informational gains from sensual pleasure or about the first appearance in infancy of sensual pleasure as a motive; i.e., when activity is generated for the sake of its yield of sensual pleasure. Quite likely the capacity for sensual pleasure does not make its appearance at birth. After some weeks, however, we may assume the appearance of sensually specific activity; i.e., pleasure experience not contingent on preceding experiences of tension but directly aroused by appropriate bodily stimulations, either externally or endogenously produced. Evidence on all these matters is meager. We are not even far advanced in the first and critical task of validating the basic claim of Freud's hypothesis: of distinguishing sensual from other forms of pleasure in infancy.

Quite possibly an important characteristic of sensuality, as compared to other forms of pleasure, is the unique way in which consciousness is dominated by the pleasure experience during sensual arousal, so that the informational yield of sensual contact is secondary to the pleasure experience itself. Sensory avenues are of course critical sources of information, but in nonsensual, sensory contact the sensations themselves are not important most of the time, and we hardly attend to them; it is the information about the *source* of these sensations that is important. The case is different with contacts that arouse sensual pleasure; here the pleasure experience itself pre-empts consciousness. Nonetheless, it becomes a matter of great interest whether and to what extent the wafting movements, caressing, fondling, etc., which provoke sensual pleasure, provide the baby with some information about correlated internal states in the person who provokes it—of desiring, giving, offering, and the like—that is, social information concerning experiences of pleasure and intimacy in the other. Sensual experience in infancy may therefore be an important primary source of affiliation and attachment. At the age when such a perceptual capacity has matured enough to be said to operate in circumstances of sensual arousal, sensual contact can become one means of acquiring what Harlow (1958) calls "contact comfort."

At a recent concert I was struck by an incident of contact pleasure between parent and child that took the form of a playful ritual or game. A father was holding his little boy in his lap as the orchestra was playing. Respecting his father's insistence that he be quiet, the little boy listened in his own way. Taking the father's large hand, he pumped the fingers rhythmically this way and that with the music, moving now this finger, now that finger to his will, turning the palm up and then down, running the father's hand against his face and moving it over his lips. All the time, the father was attentively focused on the concert, passively assenting to the play with his hand. Then the father in turn took the boy's hand, closed it into a fist and drum beat it to the rhythm of the music; the boy passively, almost hypnotically, lent himself to the rhythmic movement of his limb with a rapt expression of quiet pleasure. Throughout, there was a sense of play structured by registrations of benign messages of acceptance and affirmation, communicated through bodily responses of pleasure.

A critical attribute of sensual arousal is its *plasticity*: arousal can be autoerotic, heterosexual, or homoerotic, through the activity of bodily zones and modes which are not specifically sensual in function. This plasticity makes sensuality uniquely serviceable to a variety of adaptive aims. For example, since it is arousable autoerotically, it can be a means of *controlling* the objects of sensuality in fantasy. But plasticity is also a vulnerable asset in that it renders sensual potential uniquely susceptible to conflict. Although in the exercise of every pleasure prototype there develops a range of discretion and indiscretion which bounds its arousal and implementation, none seems to match the firmness of regulation and the exactitude of rules of severance that govern sensual pleasure. The requirement that development be guided toward procreation and heterosexuality and away from societally destructive choices, notably incestuous ones, runs counter to the natural tendency during the early formative years to seek and expect gratification precisely from such incestuous contact (Lindzey, 1967). Being in this way an exceptional experience, sensuality is distinctively etched in memory and concept in an evolving record of what sensual pleasure furnishes for good and ill, and which affects its arousal and regulation.

Pleasure in Functioning

Very early it seems evident that gratification of bodily needs does not account for activities that an infant engages in spontaneously and which afford him pleasure: there are times when he seems to grasp, suck, babble, squeeze, and pull for no reason other than the pleasure of their repetition. Possibly included here are sensory pleasures and the exercise of distance receptors. A baby's fascination with a colorful mobile seems qualitatively different from his pleasure in having an erogenous zone stimulated. Wolff (1959, 1966) has discovered that this activity is typical of states that he calls "alert inactivity," when the body is not occupied with feeding or other homeostatic business. Awareness of emerging sensory and motor capabilities, such as ocular fixation, prehension, phonation, locomotion, generates interest and pleasure in demonstrating them, so to speak, to oneself, and such pleasing repetitive play continues until the particular manipulation is mastered—that is, the skill becomes available for other aims and other sources of pleasure. The repetitions then cease. Piaget (1951) believes such pleasure in functioning is the inherently motivating aspect of assimilative and accommodative activity, referring to it as "desirability." From such beginnings in repetitious, playful exercise of capacity develops a sense of and pleasure in skill itself.

One of the first to draw attention to pleasure in functioning was Karl Bühler (1928,[6] 1930). In the psychoanalytic literature it was Hendrick (1943a) who first described this distinctive category of pleasure, which he called a "work principle"—the principle that primary pleasure is sought by efficient use of the central nervous system for the performance of well-integrated ego functions.

Hendrick spoke of his work principle as a "drive." Hartmann (1952) was considerably more influential in gaining acceptance for essentially the same idea when he read into ego psychology the proposal that there is an autonomous line of conflict-free development of perceptual and cognitive functions which is fostered by associated experiences of pleasure in functioning. Such conflict-free activity and its attendant pleasure is evident in the infant who is exploring, examining, and playing with various parts of his body, fingering his toes and his hands, pulling his ears, etc.

That there should be pleasure in functioning, leading to sharpened awareness of one's capabilities, is consonant with what embryologists have pointed to as an important factor in growth—the idea that a new function emerges as a state of "readiness" or potential "competence" requiring prompt exercise within a critical period. That is, if a specific chemical inductor hits the developing embryo, it will produce an effect if the competence or readiness is there; if it is not, the effect will not occur. The capacity for pleasure in functioning would seem to aid this process of provoking or serving the emergence of function.

Conversely, were pleasure in functioning impeded, it would stultify awareness of function, probably with deleterious effects. Not only does such pleasure in functioning affirm a sense of capacity and skill, it aids in the development of a sense of physical separateness and autogenous control which is the necessary precursor of ego autonomy. Indeed, the sensory pleasures that are incidental to or anaclitic on the satisfaction of basic needs, along with sensual pleasures, help create the basic sense that life is good and the world a pleasant place, on which a sense of "basic trust" rests.

[6]"Indeed, the facts concerning children's activity in play are not to be explained by the supposition of a general libido and this formula alone.... Think of the movements themselves as endowed with pleasure, and we have formulated a fundamental, a central knowledge concerning children's play. I call it *Function Pleasure.* The fact is, certain forms of movements are themselves pleasurable.... In the phase of development where the child learns to grasp, the grasping movements of arms, hands, and fingers are endowed with function pleasure—and so in other phases the movements of walking, or talking, etc." (Bühler, 1928, p. 197).

The Pleasure in Experiencing the Self as an Effective Agent of Change: Effectance Pleasure

The pleasure of effectance (White, 1959, 1963) resides in the perception that through one's own interference one has changed and can change the course of events once set in motion. Psychological autonomy has its beginnings in this awareness, and the practicing of this awareness becomes itself pleasurable. When the baby starts to grasp articles, sits up, crawls, tries to walk, he begins a process that eventually yields the sense that the locus and origin of these achievements is in himself. When the child thus feels the change as originating with himself, he begins to have a sense of *being* himself, a psychologically, not simply physically, autonomous unit.

Such a sense of control has an early precursor in the responsiveness that even babies show to imposed versus autogenously initiated movements of the body. For example, Piaget (1951) describes the reflex resistance with which a baby reacts to restrictive obstacles to his movements; the baby is clearly sensible to the operant movements of his own body.

Effectance pleasure can be for the infant a powerful self-affirming experience in surmounting psychological stress. Weaning, for example, is assisted by the potential for effectance pleasure. As Spock points out (1963), the infant experiences stress in the change-over of feeding routine, but the stress is alleviated by the pleasure of mastering bottle and spoon. This pleasure in effectiveness may be more than compensating, for it brings something of the environment under *his* control and initiative.

The component that distinguishes effectance from pleasure in functioning is the pleasure in observing the successful correspondence of *intention* and effect. It differs from pleasure in functioning in that, in effectance, the focus is not simply upon the exercise of skill or function per se, but on pleasure derived from the instrumental power of skill as a tool of one's intention.

White (1960) was the first to show that the developments traditionally characterized as psychosexual stages owe much to effectance pleasure. For instance, defecation can provide an elemental form of satisfaction in "doing the job" well. Ample evidence indicates that the period of "latency," which has been left somewhat anonymous in the emphasis on psychosexual development, is actually one of aimful activity. In this period, described by Erikson as involving a dominant emphasis upon a sense of industry, a need to feel useful, to make things of significance, and exploratory identifications with those who know how to do things, the potential for effectance pleasure is an important experience that abets these facets of self-identity.

The pleasure that comes with effectance is especially important not so much in the sense of motivating adjustment to the environment as in motivating changes of the environment. If one thinks of growth as an active process, not simply of adjusting, but of creating adaptive variations in the environment to promote a balanced "fit" with it, one can hardly exaggerate the importance of effectance pleasure as an affirming, supportive experience that abets the process. In the child this begins with the pleasure of making "traces," as Arnheim (1954) suggests, perhaps left on the floor or on the wall by dirty hands and feet. These activities are pleasurable, Arnheim explains, not only because "they involve the exciting experience of bringing about something visible that was not there before" (p. 136), but also because of the child's perception of the trace as a sign of himself. Moreover, such actions control the *viewer*, a further bonus in effectance pleasure. If this is what the sign means to the child, then the creation and making of signs, of categories, of artifacts, and this sense of identity may be closely related: the making of these is a means by which one identifies oneself. Even when making traces has turned toward the higher stakes of making "art," the affirming pleasure in self-generated solutions remains powerfully motivating.

Threatened self-autonomy is likely to stimulate rage and aggression. For the ego in such a state, motives of effectance pleasure can acquire ruthless intensity, reflecting the insistent, not-to-be-denied assertion of such autonomy. On the other hand, chronic deprivations in the child of a kind in which effort brings feedback only of failed influence are mortifying to selfhood and self-respect, and may result in a resigned yielding to complete passivity. Bettelheim (1967) points out that harm can come not merely from chronic absence of opportunity for effectance experiences but also from pushing the child too soon into reliance upon psychological independence, which too may produce returns only of failure, so that in time even extraordinary events may not reach the child's attention because he can really do nothing about them.

Bettelheim's account of what he believes to be the essential deficit in autistic children seems to come down to a failure to experience effectance. The exaggerated rituals of order often seen in such children would appear to be symptomatic indicators of this. "It seems generally true," he writes, "that the less we are able to act where the results are important to us the more we predict. And the less we can act and predict, the more inclined we are to order" (p. 21).[7]

The Pleasure in Pleasing

An infant tends to become attached to persons who initiate interaction with him. A key factor in the attachment is the pleasure aroused in the mutuality of interaction—an interaction that seems to involve a sensibility in the baby to the pleasure he is bringing about in the other. The pleasure felt is in the pleasure created. The mother seems to be communicating *her* pleasure in his activity; the baby's rejoinder of pleasure may hardly be called as yet a message of his own, but it provokes a kind of positive amplification of those maneuvers of mutuality in baby and mother that brought about this shared pleasure. Whether consciously or not, the mother seems to behave as if she senses that she is communicating her feelings to the baby by the way she responds. Surely it is not long before the infant can react to whether her emotions are mainly positive, negative, or ambivalent.

Call (1964) has drawn attention to the infant's subtle capacity to determine and adapt to the optimum stimulus configuration of bottle or breast, using the kinesthetic sensations derived from the mother's holding position. It is not farfetched to infer from this capacity that a

[7]He continues: "This is why artificial feeding times, arranged according to the clock, can dehumanize the infant. The reason is not just that time-clock feeding is contrary to the natural rhythms of the body, or that it signifies a mechanical ordering of time and of the mother-child relation. More important here is that it prevents the infant from feeling that *his* actions (crying, smiling) have a significant effect on this important life experience of being fed.

"What humanizes the infant is not being fed, changed, or picked up when he feels the need for it, though they add greatly to his comfort and feeling of well-being. . . . It is rather the experience that *his* crying for food brings about *his* satiation by others according to *his* timing that makes it a socializing and humanizing experience. It is that *his* smile, or facial grimacing, evokes a parallel or otherwise appropriate response in the mother.

"Conversely, the experience that his own actions (cry or smile) make no difference is what stops him from becoming a human being, for it discourages him from interacting with others and hence from forming a personality through which to deal with the environment" (p. 25).

pleasure experience of the kind just described may arise in the baby from recording, in a primitive way, that his actions and movements bring pleasure to the mother. This sensibility is perhaps within the infant's capacity from a quite early age. According to Bowlby (1969), a predictable outcome of the baby's smile is that "the baby's mother (or other figure smiled at) responds in a loving way that prolongs social interaction between them and increases the likelihood of her exhibiting maternal behaviour in future . . . and . . . that the function of a baby's smile is that of increasing interaction between mother and baby and maintaining them in proximity to each other" (p. 280). The pleasure he obtains in *her* reaction further enhances his efforts to foster the same behaviors that brought that reaction about in the first place—a circular process of mutually amplified maneuvers designed to sustain pleasure in the other.

There is experimental evidence to suggest the early appearance of such a prototypical potential for pleasure. Bowlby writes: "There is good evidence that when a baby's smile is responded to in a loving sociable way he smiles thereafter more strongly" (1969, p. 287). Brackbill (1958) demonstrated this with three-month-old babies. When the baby smiled, she smiled back, stroking and cuddling him. This response in turn brought on another smile from the baby and with several such exchanges the role of smiling increased. Bowlby's comment seems an apt description of the shared experience: "In all this each partner seems to be expressing joy in the other's presence and the effect is certainly one of prolonging their social interaction" (p. 246). Conversely, when the experimenter stopped responding to the baby's smile, its smiling became more and more infrequent and eventually died out. Rheingold, Gewirtz, and Ross (1959) reported in another study that, if similar responses of pleasure are directed to a three-month-old baby's vocalizations, babbling will increase. After two "rewarded" days in which they responded to the infants' vocalizations with gestures of pleasure, the infants' vocalizations had almost doubled. It is reasonable to suppose, then, that pleasure in the pleasure one provokes in another can become an early basis of actions expressly calculated to please another; that generating pleasure in another is early recognized as an occasion for being approved, for being affirmed in one's being. A potential for pleasure experience in this affiliative context may be one of the factors that justifies Scott's belief (1968) that a critical period for primary socialization exists in human development.

The fact that pleasure arises from such a source tells us too that the affiliative requirement has roots just as deep as those pleasure potentials that are more directly localized and originate in the "body ego." But perhaps an equally important inference to be drawn from this early appearing, qualitatively distinct pleasure prototype is that distinctions between self-interest and interest in the other are probably less clear-cut than has been assumed in the past. We may remind ourselves here that feeling onself a needed part of a larger, more encompassing affiliative entity is, after all, a continuing requirement of a developing self-identity. The pleasure in pleasing can therefore be vital in helping to affirm both one's psychological autonomy and one's need for an accepted status in a social entity: "I am not only that which enables me to control the environment, but I am also what another is pleased at me for being." The capacity to feel pleasure in pleasing helps growth to proceed from reaction to *interaction*, into a self that can both affirm and be affirmed by others.

The active responsiveness to another's pleasure that even infants seem capable of also is one more indication that in mother-child relationships the child has less need for passive reception than was once thought to be the case. The requirement to "belong" certainly makes an early appearance, but as something *sought*.

Pleasure in Synthesis (Aesthetic)

By pleasure in synthesis I mean the delighted contemplation of *restored* or *discovered* order. Substitute "lingering over" or "attending to" for the word "contemplating," and it is not difficult to maintain that something of the sort is seen quite early in development. The evidence is impressive that there are in very young children, and indeed even in primates, preferences for certain forms and shapes, and standards of "rightness" and "fit." Even in the first year and a half of life, we see the beginnings of a sensibility to order, of operations of making order, of correction of error, of perceiving order emerging from disorder, of distinguishing match from mismatch, and for such recognitions to be accompanied by pleasure. Morris's descriptions (1962) of the paintings and scribblings of the chimp Congo seem to disclose not simply the "pleasure in functioning" of exercising visual-motor coordinations; they reveal primitive conceptual preferences and compositional control. Particularly striking was the indication that Congo seemed to appreciate when a picture was finished. Children's "art" (Kellogg, 1969) shows similar indications of archetypical representations and formal preferences. Erikson (1963, p. 100) notes that children take pains that their play constructions be "just right." He also shows that the preferred configurations of boys and girls seem to be tied in with respective differences in the ground plan of their bodies.

The pervasive sensibility to order is well expressed by Huizinga's (1950) description of children's play. Play, he writes,

> . . . creates order, *is* order. Into an imperfect world and into the confusion of life it brings a contemporary, a limited perfection. Play demands order absolute and supreme. The least deviation from it spoils the game, robs it of its character and makes it worthless. The profound affinity between play and order is perhaps the reason why play. . . seems to be to such a large extent in the field of aesthetics. Play has a tendency to be beautiful. It may be that this aesthetic factor is identical with the impulse to create orderly form, which initiates play in all its aspects. The words we use to denote the elements of play belong for the the most part to aesthetics, terms with which we try to describe the effects of beauty: tension, poise, balance, contrast, variation, solution, resolution, etc. . . . It is invested with the noblest qualities we are capable of perceiving in things: rhythm and harmony [p. 10].

If something akin to aesthetic sensibility is demonstrable in apes, the question arises what adaptive usefulness this has for development. Clearly, if an aesthetic potential does exist in apes they have not taken it very far, whereas the case is different in man. The answer perhaps lies in the necessity in man, distinguishing him from the ape, of having to create a self-identity. From childhood on throughout life the effort to be at one with oneself, and to find an acceptance in and to accept a place within a social context, is a pervasive and dominant focus of motives and actions. Since self-identity is a continuing achievement, wrought out of adjudicating and resolving incompatibilities, it is fitting that a sensitivity to dissonance, cleavage, and finiteness, and a corresponding pleasure in discovering order, in restoring order, and in ordered complexity will not only have early beginnings but be of continuing importance throughout life.

When, because of accidental developmental shifts or conflicts, one loses a sense of essential wholeness, efforts at restructuring it in a design that re-establishes it define motivational direction. As Erikson (1963) points out, among the earliest and most sobering lessons of limitation are the experiences of falling, of *sudden* loss of support, of suddenness generally, which can lead to a fear of sudden change. He also suggests that the baby may very early acquire some continuing sense of loss from experiencing the mother's withdrawal of the nipple. But such sensibility to limitation and finiteness, and the distaste for it, whets the appetite for order; experiences of limitation hint and offer an inducement for a principle of order to be learned. And we do in fact learn our body's limitations without having to be taught them formally: for instance, early experiences tell us that we cannot walk on water, or fly. Being able to sense our finiteness converts fear into thoughtful respect—a condition for pleasure in order. Familiar things that have served the efforts to achieve self-related synthesis become "right," "good," "preferred"; novel things that promise to create a sense of rectifying mismatch and disorder become valued, "worthwhile," "beautiful," in their proven utility. Both the familiar and the novel come to be endowed with properties of pleasingness for their restitutive capacity or in closing the gaps of incompleteness. From this standpoint, even the uniformities of children's art are images of wholeness and integration.

With cognitive and physiological development, the sensibility to cleavage and dissonance becomes even more complex; correspondingly, the appreciation of meaning and of the limits of tolerable error becomes more charged with self-consciousness, urgency, and even anxiety. It reaches its crest, perhaps, as a need, in those twilight years when irreversible finitude is finally to be faced and the effort to bring together past, present, and a shrinking future into a self-justifying meaning is especially poignant and difficult.

From this perspective the capability and requirement for experiencing pleasure in achievements of synthesis are present in all men; they are not the exclusive province of the professional aesthete, nor are they confined to the ritualized aesthetic play afforded by museums and the "art world." Pleasure in things that fit and that re-establish wholeness is a vital self-affirming experience, serving to accredit as "real" or "true" those conditions, objects, relationships, and symbols that help sustain a sense of coherence and continuity of self. Preoccupation with issues of making things fit and with establishing and re-establishing a sense of wholeness is one of serious engagement, although it may be specifically actualized and sought in the contexts of fantasy, play, and art.

The conditions of aesthetic pleasure are more purely cognitive than those of tension reduction and sensual pleasure. At stages of cognitive immaturity it is possible, therefore, that the occasions of pleasurable syntheses are indistinguishably linked to the reduction of tension. With maturing cognitive capacities, the aspect of pleasure derived from perceiving and closing a gap with the *right* fit comes to be discernible, and deserves to be designated as a pleasure prototype in its own right. If experienced tension is involved at all in aesthetic pleasure (and it need not be), it is *tolerated* tension; indeed, the aesthetically pleasurable solution may itself be experienced as tension, but as a satisfying kind of tension—a state of active tension in balance, felt as things "falling into place."

An important aspect of aesthetic pleasure is that it involves an active integration. It would belie our understanding of aesthetic pleasure experience in its adaptive utility to regard it as implying an attitude of passive receptiveness. Rather it would seem to be more in the service of what Freud (1926) called a mental mechanism of turning passive into active, which he regarded as central to the maintenance of man's individuality and wholeness. The conditions of what we call pleasure in synthesis derive from this momentum. This tie-in with a requirement for an actively sustained identity is what links aesthetic pleasure so much more closely to the act of discovery than to sensual contact and tension reduction.

This completes the inventory of the vital pleasures. In delineating these classes of pleasure, I have considered it more useful to specify *distinguishable contexts* of pleasure experience rather than to try to delineate varieties of pleasure "sensation" itself. Traditional views of pleasure as a "sensation" (see, for example, Beebe-Center, 1932) have led to futile efforts to develop criteria for measuring it at the expense of designating its cognitive context. Yet, as Kenny (1963) and Peters (1969) point out, even efforts at simply setting up criteria for the sameness of sensations encounter the inescapable need to take into account the conditions in which they occur and what people do about them. Following Kenny's lead, therefore, the present focus has been on the circumstances of pleasure arousal, the kinds of encounters people engage in for the pleasure they afford, as distinct from habitual actions or things done for some extrinsic reason, unaccompanied by pleasure.

The six classes of pleasure refer, accordingly, to contexts of stimulation and action that seem to be inherently pleasurable. From the standpoint of motivation, they refer to the intrinsic motivational aspect of an action. When we argue that pleasure is in the category of a motive we are in agreement with Peters (1969), who speaks of the intrinsically motivating aspect of actions, the pleasure aspect in respect to which things are "wanted," and "needed." Certainly a large part of motivation is searching for and doing things for the sake of a pleasure aim. Situations and encounters and relationships become important for having proved themselves as occasions for such pleasures; they are thereafter wanted for that very reason. The pleasures do not themselves require rewards in order to be aroused, they are not themselves reinforced, but become "reinforcers."

The study of such inherently pleasurable classes of activity, or different pleasure aims, is important for education. We need to know what particular gain in pleasure frames the context of learning, how it becomes a basis of incentive to learn, and indeed, for what is learned. Knowing *what* pleasure gain is intrinsically motivating for a person, and the conditions of action and encounter that foster and inhibit it, are important for encouraging learning. If we knew more about this we might come to know better how to offer knowledge to children. Different pleasure aims can lead to learning that is appropriate to the situation as viewed by a teacher. What an anatomy book offers for learning to a sexually preoccupied adolescent may be very different from what it offers to a medical student. To assume, as has been done in the past, that learning itself must be made pleasurable (or is the outcome of "reinforcement") is merely a crude beginning.

What we are saying about pleasure as motive is in sympathetic accord with what we hear these days from those (White, 1963; Hunt,

1965; Koch, 1956, 1969b) who point to such intrinsically motivating dispositions as the tendencies to explore, to master, etc., which are indulged in for their own sake.

We depart, however, from Hunt and others when they take the evidence of intrinsically motivated action as the whole story of motivation, when they caustically criticize psychoanalysis for explaining one aim in terms of another extrinsic one. They ignore the possibility that inherently pleasurable activity can be extrinsically motivated as well. It is true that psychoanalysis has tended to slight the causative and self-perpetuating influence of a pleasure experience. But the "intrinsic motivation" view neglects the understanding opened to us by psychoanalysis—that there are motives *for* pleasure seeking and thus that the different pleasures can themselves acquire *functions*, and indeed be sought and *selectively* emphasized for *unconscious* aims. It is not only necessary to know that certain conditions have the meaning for a given person of affording an opportunity for a particular kind of pleasure; it is also necessary to understand the selective emphasis he is giving to that rather than to another source of pleasure. The assumption, for example, that the different classes of pleasure can be serviceable to *defense* helps to account for repetitive insistence upon one or another form of pleasure, for extreme avoidance of certain pleasure opportunities on the one hand and for extreme hedonism (in one or another pleasure source) on the other. It also allows for the possibility of arrests and regressions in respect to pleasure seeking. The developmental record of the vital pleasures will vary in respect to the relative claims and dominance that each class of pleasure has in a person's life, including such variations, for example, as desiring too much of a particular pleasure or of expecting too little. Clinical therapeutic exploration consists in part of examining the relative selective emphasis on the different forms of pleasure in the patient's history.

I shall close my discussion by considering some developmental implications of the notion of pleasure prototypes.

As a means of accenting these implications I have pictured the different vital pleasures in an Eriksonian "epigenetic" chart, which tries to reflect their relation to other schedules of development, physical and cognitive (Chart 2).

Chart 2

THE VITAL PLEASURES AND CRITICAL PERIODS OF ASCENDANCE

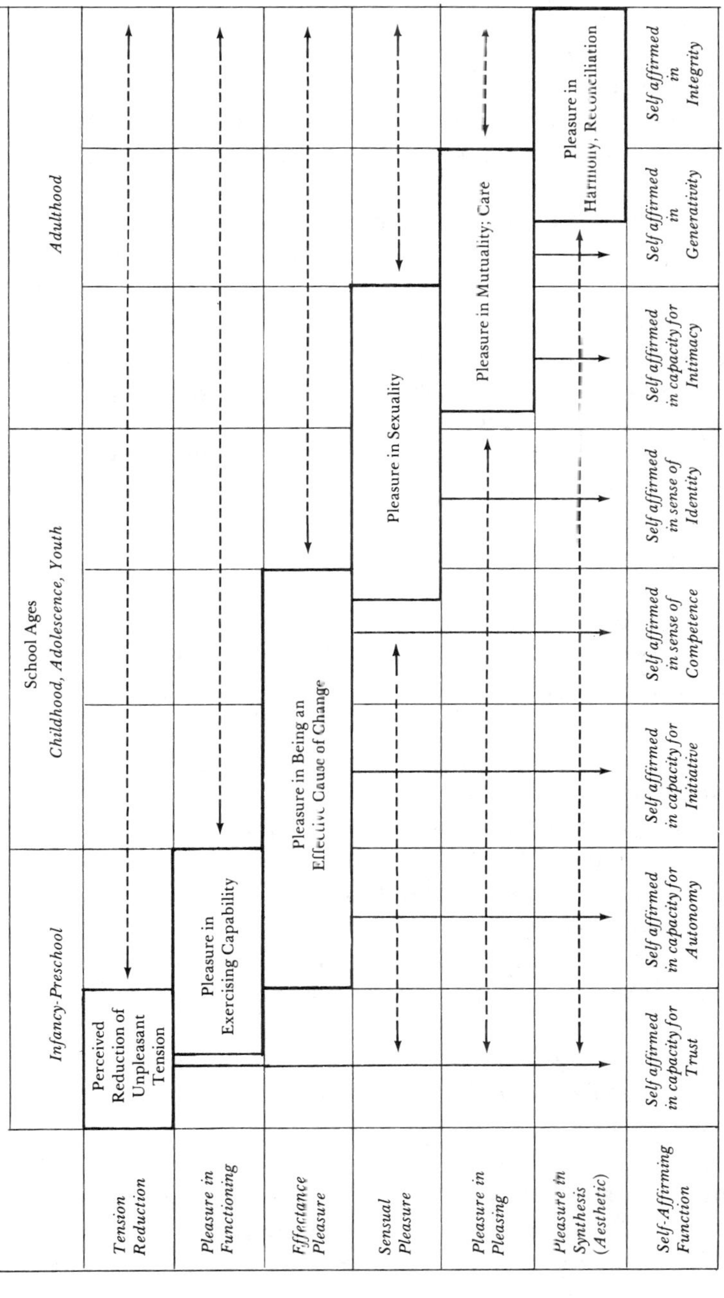

It goes without saying that this scheme is extremely tentative. My intention is only to suggest some fresh and possibly fruitful leads that open up to us when considerations of pleasure are viewed in this way.

The various pleasure capacities are assumed to have early origins. For example, a baby may show something like autonomy from the beginning, in the particular way in which he angrily tries to wriggle his hands free when tightly held, although his capability for responding with pleasure to conditions of effectance, and of specifically *seeking* this source of pleasure, will come only much later. The pleasure prototypes are shown to have a continuing development, as well as a time of special pertinence to a phase of ego growth. The forward-pointing horizontal arrows suggest that a given pleasure prototype undergoes modifications that reflect the ego developments of a given stage. By far the most elaborated conception of a prototypical pleasure is, of course, Freud's description of psychosexual stages. Each of the empty boxes can be thought of as qualitative varieties of each of the pleasure prototypes, and remains to be filled in.

The diagram tells us that the study of any of the pleasure prototypes should be oriented to specifying its qualitative characteristics at different stages. For example, each life stage produces and requires norms of order and balance that condition aesthetic pleasure—a projected expression of the tasks of the stage, imagined in an ideal resolution and exhibited in the form of play, fantasy, and activity. For the child, it may be the recognition of the mother in all her "perfection"; for the growing boy, the hero ideal. In advanced years, the occasions for aesthetic pleasure may be symbols, in which images of the past are reconciled with those of the present and with premonitions of irreversible finitude.

The heavily outlined boxes that form the diagonal indicate periods in which the pleasure prototype seems especially relevant to the tasks and crises developmentally specific to that period. Thus pleasure experiences associated with reduction of tension will help create an orientation of trust. In the periods of early and middle childhood, when issues of psychological autonomy, work initiative, and industry become paramount, the pleasure in functioning and effectance pleasure are particularly vital reinforcements. It is reasonable that feeling one's body in action and the effectiveness of the parts of one's body that work, and taking pleasure in so doing, will promote a sense of physical autonomy. Discovering his ability to give *intentional* sound-signs is a pleasure that leads the child to exercise it for its own sake.

The diagram should not be taken to imply that there is necessarily an even and progressive development of each pleasure prototype. A more likely possibility is that all or some reach an asymptote, as, for example, sensual pleasure at the genital stage. It should also be pointed out that the heavily outlined box does not imply that development of the pleasure prototype stops at that point, or that its importance for ego development was minimal before or wanes thereafter. Effectance pleasures, for example, would seem to be important at all ages. At the same time, it would appear that with increasing and changing potentialities of conflict, the potential for aesthetic pleasure undergoes continuing change throughout the life cycle.

The horizontal arrows pointing both ways suggest the possibility of regression as well as of progression. Development of a prototype may be arrested at a given stage, and there may also occur regression to pleasure forms of an earlier stage. Such occurrences would characterize pathological developments in a given period.

The vertical arrows of the chart tell us that experiences of pleasure in the different prototypes are important to the emergence of what Erikson calls the *ego strengths* of different periods. Pleasure nourishes self-affirmation. Different pleasure experiences seem especially relevant in consolidating these gains of ego strength. Correspondingly, we may infer that pleasure incapacity, or the failure to activate the different sources of pleasure at appropriate points of development, whether because of conflict, frustration, insufficient opportunity, or deprivation, may contribute to chronic anhedonia and to a residue of ego vulnerability and insufficiency. Thus, following the arrows downward and in a progressive course, we find that a rich pleasure life in infancy, particularly in respect to the prompt alleviation of tension, reinforces the emerging ego strength of trust; adequate experiences of pleasure in functioning and effectance help affirm a sense of autonomy, initiative, and industry; pleasure in genital mutuality helps actualize a sense of intimacy; and, at the later stages, pleasure in pleasing and aesthetic pleasures are especially relevant to consolidating achievements of "generativity" and "integrity."

In describing pleasure we face the age-old problem of how to penetrate a private experience. Pleasure is that, of course; nevertheless, I have chosen to avoid the temptation of distinguishing pleasures by variations in experienced sensation, and to specify them instead by aim and by the configuration of circumstances that elicit and reinstate them. On this basis I have delineated six prototypical classes of pleasure. Although several of and even all these pleasures may be interactively present in particular occasions of pleasure, they are still distinguishable conceptually; the distinctions are important in the way in which height and weight are different, though indivisibly associated.

I have preferred not to face the question whether these pleasures, defined on the basis of cognitive context, are accompanied also by distinctive pleasure sensations, although I grant the importance of this issue. For example, sensual pleasure may indeed be unique in respect to the quality of sensation, and this may have something to do with the tenacious hold of this pleasure on consciousness, as compared with others, and with the peculiarly pre-emptive clarity of sensual experiences.

Nevertheless, viewing pleasure from the standpoint of aim has enabled us to keep in focus the adaptive significance of pleasure as an ego resource supportive to an evolving self-identity. Especially for the human organism, confronted as it is with complexity of choice, pleasure is the most immediate and intimate testimony of beneficent engagement with the world. It is as vital to development to be responsive to messages of adaptive beneficence, provided by different forms of pleasure experiences, as to experience opposite ones—varieties of estrangement evoking anxiety.

CHAPTER 7

The Principle of Repression and the Activity of the Repressed

ONE OF FREUD'S seminal principles, stated in its most general form, is that internal as well as external events are responded to selectively, that responsiveness is connected with cognitive schemata (knowledge), and that without the person's awareness of that knowledge its effects are evident. This conception differs from pre-Freudian psychology, and even from many theories that followed Freud, according to which most memories are dormant and uninfluential until activated. Freud brought to light this "dynamic knowledge" beyond awareness, and revealed that it can decisively influence our behavior. This is the essence of the principle of repression or of the "dynamic unconscious."

The discovery of unconsciously dynamic ideas was not a proposal for a redefinition of mental concepts; it was a discovery of a *new range of facts* that had enormous social-psychological import. The discovery of "unconscious purposes" implied that we are less free than we had supposed, because we are less fully self-conscious than we had believed. It implied that we very commonly misrepresent to ourselves what we are trying to do. To this core idea are linked the distinctions among conscious, preconscious, and unconscious activities and thoughts which underlie a good many psychoanalytic conceptions.

A related but independently seminal idea is Freud's emphasis *upon the pre-emptive power of primary-process ideation, especially fantasy, over secondary-process thought and behavior.* It is an interesting historical fact that psychoanalysis did not begin with a drive theory, but with the notion that ideas themselves have a force component that affects behavior (Rapaport, 1959). The first and central elements of the psychoanalytic theory of neurosis were psychical trauma and conflict among ideas, and the consequences for behavior of conflicting ideas. In Freud's early statements of the theory, the critical ideational component of conflict was the memory of a real event which was incompatible with the main body of a patient's consciously acceptable ideas. The assumption that unacceptable, repressed ideas owed their unique power to sexual involvement contributed, of course, to Freud's eventual emphasis on drives as the motive power of conflict and unconscious ideation.

Unfortunately, the implications of the principle of repression, and perhaps its most crucial clinical meanings, have been obscured by the energy conceptions of cathexis and anticathexis and, especially, by metapsychological distinctions between *consciousness* and *unconsciousness.* These confusions unfortunately originated in Freud's early formulations, which reflected the general immaturity of the theory at that time, and in the failure to bring cognitive considerations into relationship with experience and consciousness. It would be useful to disengage this principle from these accretions of theory and to restate it in the language of a conception of meaning.

The essence of the principle of a dynamically "unconscious" idea is illustrated in an example cited by Freud:

> I was called in to a consultation last year to examine an intelligent and unembarrassed-looking girl. She was most surprisingly dressed. For though as a rule a woman's clothes are carefully considered down to the last detail, she was wearing one of her stockings hanging down and two of the buttons on her blouse were undone. She complained of having pains in her leg and, without being asked, exposed her calf. But what she principally complained of was, to use her own words, that she had a feeling in her body as though there was something 'stuck into it' which was 'moving backwards and forwards' and was 'shaking' her through and through: sometimes it made her whole body feel 'stiff'. . . . The girl herself had no notion of the bearing of her remarks; *for if she had, she would never have given voice to*

> *them*. In this case it had been possible to hoodwink the censorship into allowing a phantasy which would normally have been kept in the preconscious to emerge into consciousness under the innocent disguise of making a complaint [1900, p. 618; italics added].

The critical statement is "for if she had, she would never have given voice to them." It implies the salient accomplishment of repression —which is to maintain *a gap in comprehension*, or, as Freud put it, to keep something at a distance from consciousness (1905b, p. 203) *without necessarily impeding its expression in behavior*. The example refers to (a) a meaning schema that is dissociated from the person's self-conception, (b) yet has an organizing—i.e., motivating—influence on conscious thought, experience, and behavior, (c) but of which the effects—i.e., the feedback from action—are *uncomprehended*; (d) the uncomprehended meaning having certain affective and value connotations that are themselves the motives for instituting the repression in the first place, as well as for the noncomprehension.

These critical precepts of dynamic unconscious activity will be the main concern of this chapter. The principle of repression tells us that

> . . . there occur psychological events or states which exert control over behavior, which are not under ordinary circumstances of reflective introspective attention reportable (as to their character or even their existence), and whose causal properties are such as to justify us in attributing to them an *internal structure and content* which includes those features of intentionality that have ever since Brentano been considered definitive of the "mental" [Meehl, 1966].

All that Freud said about substitutive ideas, and about fantasies which are repressed but nonetheless capable of organizing activity, is derivable from these characteristics of the principle of uncomprehended, unconsciously active schemata. The unconscious schema provides a code for internalizing experiences and sensations, but this code is not comprehensible in the self's domain of experience; the action it impels are so organized as to preserve such an exclusion (see Klein [1967] for a more detailed treatment).

1. *Dissociation from self*. The core of the principle of repression is an unconsciously active idea which is dissociated from the person's

self-experience. Reactions to experience are always anchored in self-reference. Response to experience takes two main forms: active *integration to the self-schema*, and *disengagement of the self*. (The latter may take the further form of splitting off the observing self [Arlow, 1966].) Repression, according to Freud (1926, p. 153), is fundamentally an "attempt at flight," and the flight is from a *meaning*. The uncomprehended meaning is the organizing principle which lends logic to behaviors which may appear to possess contradictory qualities of both approach and avoidance. In Freud's example, the patient cannot avow the meaning of certain impulses, and in this sense impulses are being *avoided*. The impulses are nevertheless being acted upon, and in this sense being gratified. Thus repression is the refusal to acknowledge the *meaning* of a tendency, but not the tendency itself; the gratifying aspect of the tendency has not been renounced.

The exclusion of a cognitive schema from the self-organization is a critical aspect of repression, and the key to understanding the condition of "motives" for which the repressive solution is adopted. Also critical is the activity of the repressed structure, which includes a variety of means of perpetuating this segregation.

A dynamically unconscious idea is denied the attributes of self-relatedness, is excluded from the self as *agent*, self as *object*, and self as *locus*. Through repression, a meaning or tendency is taken outside these limits: disowned. Refusal to accept such a schema means that the impulse in question is never experienced as self-initiated or self-connected.

Thus the proper focus in the concept of repression is not simply that an impulse has been inhibited. It is, rather, that an impulse, or an associated value of an action, wish, encounter, or relationship, is inadmissible to a schema of acknowledgeable self-identity. Repression produces an incapacity to attend to and comprehend the meanings of one's actions and creates a gap between meanings that are acknowledged by the self and meanings that are "lived out" *without* comprehension. The activity or potential activity of an internal representation that exists in such a relation to a self-structure is what we mean by a "repressed impulse."

2. *Failure of comprehension*. Conventional discussions of repression emphasize the issue of accessibility of an idea to consciousness. For a

conception of meaning, however, the critical *accomplishment* of repression is the inducing of a *failure to comprehend* an enacted idea. In repression, attention is deflected from the meaning of a pattern of behavior, and thus ignorance of an event that is relevant to a tabooed wish or pleasure is enforced. The processes affected in bringing about such a condition are those that ordinarily assist *approach, choice,* and *action*—particularly awareness and attention. Failure to comprehend conceptual, perceptual, or instrumental links of a wish serves the *defensive* aspect of the repression.

But it is only comprehension that is removed, not a sought-after satisfaction. Understanding is inhibited, but appropriate substitute gratification is not precluded. A successful repression rather ingeniously allows choice and behavior that simultaneously embody both commitments. Repression is therefore by no means a wholly "negative" suppressive event, as is commonly supposed. A person may act in terms of a wish if he avoids painful affects by not realizing it as such. Some forms of acting out, indeed, have this property. The failure of comprehension can come about through one or another ego function (not necessarily through failures of memory alone): through a *perceptual failure*, by *breaks in awareness of causal sequences*, by miscarriages of *judgment* (producing attitudes of naïveté), etc.—according to whichever best suits the circumstances. Various strategies of interfering with comprehension form the main features of many defenses and symptoms arising from repression. Thus a phobia is a behavioral pattern in which repression through the *induction of a fear* insures the failure to comprehend a wish and a course of action necessary to satisfy it.

Freud's emphasis on the inhibitions of awareness in repression documents his respect for the central importance of *conscious* processes in guiding action. Freud assumed that to be focally aware increases the likelihood of acting upon what we are aware of. One means of warding off temptation, therefore, is through the control of awareness and attention. The inhibition stirred by *anticipatory* anxiety affects functions which contribute to conscious experience and produces cognitive failure, e.g., misconceiving, forgetting, misjudging, etc.

When a repressed wish is activated, then, incoming information related to its satisfaction triggers an inhibition of awareness of intent. In extreme form, this inhibition makes unacceptable any perception, action, or memory, including their verbal links, that would open the way toward a gratifying but pain-associated fulfillment; less extreme forms of inhibition involve at least a failure to comprehend behaviors that do accomplish this substitutively. Perceptual or other clues that might signal an unwelcome consummation are dealt with by diverting awareness from connections to the wish and its associated pleasure.

However, the possibilities of *unconscious* gratification are clearly within the scope of the principle of repression. A person may know that he wants or fears something but he does not know what. The inhibition of conscious comprehension is a crucial aspect of the repressive process. Indeed, a principle weapon for combatting repression in psychoanalytic treatment is to focus or even *force* attention on clues of relevant meanings—attempts to redirect attention and awareness precisely to those gaps of understanding that were created by repression (Freud, 1916-1917), attempts that may be fiercely resisted.

3. *Unresponsiveness to feedback.* This is another way of stating the aspect of noncomprehension in the activity of a repressed schema. Because it shows how the schema is *active*, even though repressed, it deserves separate emphasis.

In contrast to intentional thought, thought related to a repressed schema precludes responsiveness to information concerning its meaning. In Piaget's terms, such a train of thought is *assimilative* but not *accommodative*; it is impervious to change by feedback from action. Vital for accommodative thinking is the capacity to respond to the consequences of self-generated activity (see Klein, 1962, 1965; also Held and Hein, 1958). For instance, the successes that a child experiences in taking action, and the modifications his successes and failures produce in his schemata of action, are critical to his development. Experiences of *passive* satisfaction are not enough, says Bettelheim, reporting on his work with autistic children: "They came to life only when we were able to create the conditions. . . that induced them to take action in their own behalf" (1967, pp. 16-17).

These characteristics of conscious, intentional thought are not part of the activity of a repressed schema. Like all activated schemata, an activated repressed idea produces output: a communication, an approach, an aversive action. But it is the condition of a repressed idea that the cognitive schema which these activities represent remains unresponsive, its arousability and persistence unmodified, and that the person be oblivious to an understanding of consequences that would constitute a *regulating feedback* to the schema. The "preconsciously" recorded feedback that is so much a part of the subsidiary awareness of an intentional (nonrepressed) train of thought is denied to a repressed schema.

The result of such assimilation without accommodation of feedback is *gaps in the person's comprehension of the significance for the self of an acted-upon idea.* The critical core of the repressive process is the loss of responsiveness to one's own actions and ideas. In extreme form, repression may cut off an idea from all realizability. However, repression does not necessarily mean that complex affective properties and actions are not part of the experiences that are provoked in the activity of the repressed schema, e.g., guilt and anxiety. More critical is that the expression of *responsibility* for such affects and actions is disowned.

To restate the main principle: both conscious and unconscious ideas affect behavior, but only the consequences of behavior issuing from intentional thinking affect choice—a high-level, conscious, accommodative operation. Behavior that originates in an unconscious activated schema is not shaped by the feedback of behavior—rewards and consequences. Loevinger (1966) has termed this the "law of no effect."

Responsiveness to the feedback from one's actions is critical for maneuverability and change. There are two kinds of feedback: *general arousal* and *cue* feedback. In the general-arousal category is the stabilizing feedback that is constantly present in our activity on the environment, such as the effects of gravity, and the auditory return of one's own voice. It is not experienced as such or as a specific "meaning," but as part of the subsidiary awareness (Polanyi, 1958) that surrounds activities which require such information for the maintenance of basic adaptational levels. It constitutes the background against which it is possible to have *focal* experience. In the category of cue feedback is what has specific content meaning which reinforces an experienced focal meaning. When feedback has a cue function, the experience is that of a *signal* which is linked to a motor response; here one becomes aware of whether a particular result of an action is consonant with an intention or not. The meanings given by both types of feedback converge in what is experienced focally.

A *sine qua non* of responsiveness to feedback is *awareness of experiencing this feedback* (see Klein, 1965). Why do we need to be aware of the effect of an action for it to be learned? One critical factor is that awareness develops in the context of a *mode* of expression—as a perception, a memory, an image, and the like—and that possibilities of action are inherently associated with such modes of awareness. For instance, the perception of an apple increases the potentiality of taking a bite of it; the image of an apple does not normally provoke such an act. Experience or awareness is no epiphenomenon; it has direct implications for the nature of action to follow. Attention is also clearly tied to experiencing feedback. Modes of experience are, therefore, means of knowing.

Studies of the auditory return from one's own voice demonstrate that experienced feedback and attention to mismatches are critical for the maintenance of voluntary control. The more something is repeatedly effective, the less does it require continued experience of informational returns; it is awareness of mismatch that mobilizes attention.

The latter point discloses an additional source of importance of consciously experienced feedback. It is when we encounter obstacles that we become aware of incompatibility; and the self as agent becomes a more focal experience. When there is synchrony of behavior, intent, and environment, we are aware, but not self-consciously so: events go on in subsidiary awareness, or preconsciously; we do not have to be focally conscious of what we are doing. Only when there is a disruption is self-consciousness aroused and attention mobilized. When emotional conflict is experienced at the same time that awareness of the core meaning is inhibited by repression, self-consciousness may grow to pathological proportions. The neurotic is often the most self-preoccupied and self-conscious of persons: he is constantly turning the adaptive function of awareness over to areas of contradiction and noncomprehension.

4. *Repression as a motivational state*. Repression has come to suggest *forgetting*, but to view repression in such negative terms overlooks equally important motivational properties. Freud asserted that its very status as repressed gives a train of thought special impetus and unique properties. The impulse, though blocked, can be activated; and, like any other activated train of thought, activated repressed ideation compels sensorimotor adjustment. This second side

of repression—its consequences for action—is sometimes neglected even in psychoanalytic discussion.

> . . . we are inclined . . . to forget too readily that repression does not hinder the instinctual representative from continuing to exist in the unconscious, from organizing itself further, putting out derivatives and establishing connections. Repression in fact interferes only with the relation of the instinctual representative to *one* psychical system, namely, to that of the conscious.
>
> . . . it is not even correct to suppose that repression withholds from the conscious *all* the derivatives of what was primarily repressed [Freud, 1915, p. 149].

An unconsciously active motivational schema, then, is the schema of an affectively colored relationship subjected to an inhibition of the functions associated with intentional thinking. It nevertheless particularizes all sorts of thoughts and actions in relation to objects in the environment that are consistent with the leading element of the idea. In short, the activity of such a dissociated schema is purely assimilative.

Take away intentionality and its conscious accompaniments of comprehension, Freud said, and you still have meaningful behavior. This idea had interesting repercussions in the history of psychology. The proposition that choice and decision are made possible by consciousness had, before Freud, led to the notion that there is no behavior without consciousness; to understand behavior, therefore, we must emphasize introspection as a method. With Freud came the realization that meaningful behavior without consciousness is possible. This tenet was eagerly embraced by behaviorism and carried to an extreme conclusion: that the study of consciousness is unimportant for understanding behavior. The behaviorists ignored the heart of Freud's discovery of repression; that uncomprehended meanings can be active and have a positive impact on behavior. Such a train of thought is "unconscious" in the sense that it is uncomprehended, its activity is involuntary, and its behavioral manifestations are not subject to control by feedback.

The principle of repression brought into psychoanalytic theory a peculiar duality of motivational determinants: passively "suffered" "unconscious" events and volitional, self-initiated "conscious" events. The activity of a repressed—unconscious—schema may parallel, or even intersect, a focal—conscious—line of thought. So far as thought products are concerned, we may call this parallel processing or coding. A repressed schema shows its effects in the subsidiary or preconscious context of a focal train of thought (see Klein, 1967).

The association of repression with two conceptions in particular has confused its fundamental meaning and significance and has drawn psychoanalytic theorizing into futile detours and misplaced emphases. In one version of repression, it is identified exclusively with memory, in particular with forgetting. This linkage of repression with memory stems from Freud's early—and later discarded—theory that neurosis originates in an actual occurrence, the *memory* of which is repressed. In the other version, repression is identified with the basis for drawing a fundamental distinction between consciousness and unconsciousness, and with a more abstract conception of consciousness and unconsciousness as "structures," to which repression became subordinate. In different ways, both emphases have obscured the power and importance of repression in psychoanalytic theory.

5. *Repression and memory.* A lingering residue of Freud's early theory that repressed memories underlay neuroses was that the undoing of repression, in this sense alone, is the main task of analytic therapy. Freud's later account of repression (1915) expanded the concept far beyond the domain of memory, however, and today we recognize that undoing a repression is more than uncovering a memory. Recalling an event does not necessarily undo repression; indeed, recall may be *facilitated by* the removal of a repression, as memories are seen in a new light and are *therefore* remembered. It is not a memory, but the *meaning* of a memory, that was condemned (see Fingarette, 1963, p. 149). To undo a repression means to bring about comprehension of the terms of a previously uncomprehended relationship, the perception of a causal link to which the person had been impervious, and a new level of understanding.

Moreover, even when repression does involve specific memories, the nonrecallability instituted by repression is not the same as forgetting. Repression may be regarded as a gigantic process of *preserving data* as well as of suppressing it. Generally, when a memory is repressed, Freud supposed, permanent forgetting seems to be prevented: ". . . ideas which have become pathological have persisted with such freshness and affective strength because they have been denied the normal wearing-away processes by means of abreaction and reproduction in states of uninhibited association" (Breuer and Freud, 1893-1895, p. 11).

The "forgetting" that occurs in repression is quite different from the ordinary kind, and ideas that are repressed have quite a different status than do those subject to ordinary forgetting. It is obvious that the process by which a repressed memory remains unconscious is quite different from the quiet and passive fading undergone by impressions of insignificant events. When, for instance, a repressed wish produces a powerful compulsion, a blatant error or a slip of the tongue, we cannot believe that it has lost its basic organization. As Schlesinger (1964) summarized the matter, "Repression is as much a form of *memory* as it is a form of forgetting. It implies a form of memory storage which violates all the usual logical principles of memory organization." Not being recalled or recallable, repressed memories are not corrected and assimilated, and, moreover, are retained in a motivating (and inhibitory) capacity.

Consciousness and Unconsciousness

The division of psychic life into conscious and unconscious contents was originally bound up with the dynamic aspect of psychic organization and specifically with the theory of repression. Elements present latently or "unconsciously" in the psyche do not necessarily remain in a state of impotence; they can intervene actively in behavior. The reason why such contents are barred from consciousness is that they arouse tendencies that are opposed by other processes which control attention and awareness.

From this meaning of a dynamic factor of human behavior, the word "unconscious" came to have a further meaning: it designated a part or *structure* of personality, not simply a *property* of active elements of psychical life. It came to be viewed as a "sector," as in the "topographic point of view," which contained "unconscious content." From the principle of repression, then, Freud *abstracted a theory of the unconscious.* The distinction between unconscious and conscious became a means of classifying psychic events, and occupied much of his theoretical interest. He dealt with the facts of repression by viewing the unconscious and the conscious as *systems*, each distinguished by unique properties of thought.

A variety of considerations led him to give up this conception (see Klein, 1959; Rapaport, 1959; Gill, 1963; Arlow and Brenner, 1964). Later he referred consciousness to awareness made possible by an energic quantity, whose "deployment" made conscious experience possible; unconsciousness referred to the "withdrawal" of this quantity. Throughout Freud's speculations about the nature of consciousness there are traces in Taine's idea of consciousness as a beam of light, an internal sense organ which dispenses light upon existing associations resulting from resemblances and integrations between unconscious memories. Both of these conceptions—consciousness conceived as a system, and consciousness as an organ for dispensing energy —erect barriers to the understanding of cognitive activity; the principle of repression is best disengaged from both of them. *The theory of repression does not rest upon or require either of Freud's conceptions of consciousness and unconsciousness.*

The disposition to speak of unconsciousness and consciousness as systems is still popular in psychoanalytic discussions. But there is little profit in so bifurcating thought processes or in asserting that each is characterized by special thought operations, the unconscious by primary process, the conscious by secondary process. It is certainly not necessary to see repressive activity as "primary process." All behavior occurs in the context of a state of consciousness. States of consciousness vary in complex ways, not, however, in respect to the presence of consciousness per se, but in respect to the status of intentionality, volition, and particular functions. In different states of consciousness, the status of functions—their activity and inactivity—is reflected in the thought products that appear in awareness. In this functional view, there is only one set of thought processes and its variations and properties are not distinguishable for "conscious" and "unconscious" events. What is critical is the condition of activation and inactivation of these functions, and how such activation and inactivation contribute to repression, either in the occurrence of repression or in its maintenance and persistence.

In considering repression in relation to issues of consciousness-unconsciousness, Rycroft points out that the mind acts as a whole; it is not *thought* that is unconscious, but a *person* who is unconscious of a thought product—a cogent reminder, when nonconscious processes are at issue, of the need to ask whether a repressive intent is evident anywhere in the pattern of behavior.

Merleau-Ponty (1945) has pointed out that to live out meaning is always to live it consciously. Not all such "lived" meanings are *understood*, i.e., cognitively represented; some may have representation but be segregated from understanding, i.e., *dissociated from the self.* Such dissociation, not the fact of unconscious content or activity, is the essence of repression. The fact to be stressed is that failure of comprehension may be dynamically induced without preventing behavior, and even conscious activity, emanating from the repressed train of thought. In the latter case, consciousness is not eliminated but *enlisted.* The *products* of the activity of the repressed schema are always manifested in conscious form. We might say that repression "uses" consciousness for its purposes.

To say that a meaning is being lived out "unconsciously" can only mean that comprehension of the leading element of a schema is lacking. Specific aspects of the schema's activity are of course being experienced: the *statement* of a schema in action is within the context of conscious, intelligent (in Piaget's sense), selective experience. It is wrong to think of the repressed schema as causing or producing conscious effects; it is being lived out and in that sense is accompanied by consciousness. What is lacking is self-relatedness, ownership, responsiveness to feedback that would lead to experiencing the *meaning* of the behavior. In this interpretation, it follows that the expression "unconsciously living out a meaning" can be misleading. Any activity proceeds from a body in some state of animation; it states itself in a condition of consciousness, within conditions that give a sense of realness to behavior. (That is why it seems fruitless to search for a "center" of consciousness, since consciousness has so many parameters or manifestations.)

Thus, although living out a meaning always takes place through modes of experiences—that is, encounters and products of thinking—these experiences may not include comprehension of their meaning. Comprehension may be limited by the status of functions within the state of consciousness, as well as by repression. For example, conceptual capacity may be restricted by developmental level (e.g., an infant cannot know the meaning of its behavior; a child may act aggressively but not recognize his aggression as such).

From the standpoint of the dynamics of repression, "unconsciousness" is not a quality of experience; rather, it refers to a gap in understanding, to the condition of a cognitive schema in relation to an observer-self. In this special sense we cannot say that all failures of knowing are unconscious.

It is always in the context of a state of consciousness that any kind of behavior occurs; the fact that a repressed idea may manifest itself in one rather than another state of consciousness becomes an indicator of differences among states of consciousness. Some states may foster primary-process modes of thinking more than do others. Consequently a repressed idea may manifest itself in a certain way because of the prevailing state of consciousness. The effects differ not because of the nature of the repressive activity itself but because of the characteristics of functions in that state. Thus repressed ideas may show themselves in different forms accordingly. Although different manifestations of the repressed idea are allowed in each state of consciousness, this does not indicate that repression is less in one state than in another, assuming failure of comprehension in both.

For instance, we may contrast the conscious orientation that characterizes a subject in an experiment on psychophysical judgment with the consciousness prevailing in the dream state. In the former, thinking is purposeful; intention is at the service of veridical outcome; and matching in terms of standards of reality testing is the dominant orientation, which includes, too, a heightened distinction between self and object and an emphasis on logical connection. In such a state the threat to the maintenance of a loss of comprehension is particularly great, and the inhibiting processes that maintain it are especially active in view of the dominance of the intentional train of thought. In such a state, unconsciously active ideas maintained in the state of repression are necessarily producing activities that are unresponsive to the feedback of their effects, in contrast to intentionally guided ideation. In a dream state of consciousness, in contrast, intentionality and volition are in abeyance; by and large distinctions between self and observer are weakly or erratically maintained; there occur fusions that have the imprint of primary-process transformations. The keynote is a condition of passivity—a surrender of purposefulness. The dreamer does not necessarily experience the passivity per se; it is evident mainly in the manner in which his thinking is organized. There are other states where dreamlike thinking occurs, but in a context of *ex-*

perienced passivity: absence of volition is experienced as part of the state of consciousness itself. In such a state the experience of "thoughts happening to me," intrusive ideas, strange affects, may be acute, even intolerable.

The critical distinction among these states is not one of the quality of consciousness per se, but has to do with the status of intentionality, volition, and particular functional possibilities. A repressed idea may manifest itself in all of these states of consciousness. The schema states itself in action in the characteristic manner of a repressed idea, impervious to feedback from the actions that are generated by it. Distinctions between sign and symbol are lost, e.g., a content as "standing for," or the distinction between focus and instrumentality, of "serving as," or of cause and effect. Certain states of consciousness are presumably especially conducive to the maintenance or dissolution of repression. The critical issue about repression, then, is that of the status of functions that are contributing to a failure of comprehension and of functions that are facilitating the living out of meanings involved in the repression.

Research is badly needed on these issues; it is by no means obvious how a repressed idea manifests itself in different states of consciousness. Different states of consciousness may bring about breaches in repression or changes in the manifestations of the schema and in the comprehension of it. While behavior is always occurring in a context of awareness or consciousness, "states of consciousness" may be characterized by the extent to which they allow or are conducive to the primary process or the secondary process.

In this discussion consciousness is taken to mean an experienced integration of a meaning. Consciousness always implies consciousness *of something*. In the same fashion, unconsciousness refers to being unconscious of meaning, but not all failures to experience meaning imply repressive activity. The products of thinking may include the activity of conceptual and action schemata that are unconscious simply in the sense that they are not experienced. Automatized instrumental actions are in this category. The structural properties of trains of thought whose aspects are *actually experienced* may vary considerably in respect to the primary- and secondary-process features categorizing them; in either case it is not the quality of consciousness or awareness per se which distinguishes them.

Repression as Primary Assimilation

Rather than using the distinction between consciousness and unconsciousness as the frame of reference for repression, it seems more appropriate to think of repression in terms of the distinction between the assimilative and the accommodative activities of a schema. This brings into the foreground the functional aspects and accomplishments of repression, as well as the fact that repressive activity can code encounters while being unresponsive to corrective feedback. Stimuli may acquire meaning in terms of unconsciously active ideas; the repressed cognitive-motor schema provides an assimilative basis for the coding and recording of experienced stimuli. In this sense, dynamically unconscious activity is assimilative.

It is characteristic of the peremptoriness created by contradictory excitations of the repressed ideation (e.g., incipient approach and perhaps even anticipatory pleasure, and contradictory avoidance and anticipatory anxiety) that it is *primarily* assimilative in its behavioral effects, rather than accommodative. Accommodation would mean *comprehension*. For Piaget, the conscious implementation of a wish is an important accompaniment, even a requirement, of accommodative behavior. But a repressed train of thought is usually impervious to changes wrought by interactions with the environment; it colors encounters with objects and events with its own meanings—the "pull of the repressed," as Freud referred to it—rather than itself being modified by such encounters. In other terms, the activity of the repressed train of thought is peculiarly resistant to extinction: ". . . the instinctual representative develops with less interference and more profusely if it is withdrawn by repression from conscious influence. It proliferates in the dark, as it were, and takes on extreme forms of expression" (Freud, 1915, p. 149).

In accounting for the varieties of assimilative activity induced by repression, it must be remembered that the principal taboo is not necessarily on the pleasure itself, but on the *content* or *object* of pleasure. Through displacement, therefore, a person can achieve a pleasure while failing to comprehend what his good feeling really refers to. Conversely, a frigid, hysterical patient who indulges in promiscuous sexual behavior associated with incestuous fantasies may find that the sexuality is somehow not enjoyable. The act is dissociated from pleasure and hence is permissible.

It is the nonaccommodative quality of repressed ideation that distinguishes its peremptoriness from the kind of urgency that can be experienced in an intentional train of thought. In intentional thinking, urgency may be experienced as such in direct proportion to the obstacles the action tendencies encounter. When we make our way with determination toward an object, anticipation of the outcome is part of the "forceful" property of the idea. In the case of a repressed train of thought, the all-important objective of resolving the pleasure-unpleasure impasse may override realistic thinking; it may include symbolic transformations, if by this means the resolving feedback is achieved. Moreover, *experienced* force or tension is not the measure of the peremptoriness of the repressed idea. In fact, action instigated by a repressed idea is often characterized by an apparent absence of intentionality and of the experience of forcibleness (see Klein, 1967).

Implications

The principle of the motivational activity of repressed schemata has been an enormously generative one in psychoanlytic thought and has led to a number of vital analytic propositions; e.g., the notion of an inner reality of unconscious fantasy in which introjected relationships hemmed in by contradictory affects and conflicts are nonetheless active in producing and responding to replicas of such relationships in interpersonal encounters. The notion of unconscious fantasy stems from the basic proposition that repressed schemata can induce responsiveness to internal and external stimuli without the effects of this responsiveness being evident to the person.

A curious and paradoxical feature of unconscious fantasy, consistent with the principle of repression in its clinical usage, is that the components of such a fantasy are assumed to be highly organized, yet its leading elements—gratifications sought after and feared, dangers past and potential—are all dynamically unconscious. Yet the term fantasy seems appropriate to designate a state of affairs that exists only internally, with the person behaving as though he believes it were true.

Such a conception seems to make good clinical sense if we view this unconscious activity as the existence in cognitive form of a dilemma grounded in contradictory impulses and affects that are pressing toward solution through rearrangements of thought and action. The activated unconscious fantasy sets a complex problem for "discharge" or expression because of the contradictory forms of excitation of which the fantasy consists. Such a cognitive schema must take behavioral forms that are realistically permissible yet do not intolerably activate the affective and dispositional facilitations that make up the activated fantasy structure.

When aroused, such a fantasy is motivational; it includes directives of approach and avoidance, of goal relevance and irrelevance, of behavioral selectiveness generally. It has properties that Tolman (1948) has described as a "cognitive map," acting as a guide to scanning and encoding. There ensues a search for behavioral and perceptual conditions that will repair conditions of potential threat that are part of the fantasy. In this sense unconscious fantasies induce the creation of symbols. Symbolism would be in the nature of environment made relevant to the coding tendencies of the components of the fantasy. Clearly, the coding and programming activities produced by unconscious fantasy could present a continuing problem for maintaining veridical and accommodative contact with the environment. This derives from the possibility that in the emergency created by a profoundly injured self-esteem, a peremptory fantasy can provoke defensive and symbolic transformations of environmental encounters. In such symbolic activity the environment is made relevant to the particular tendencies of wish, danger, and defense which make up the fantasy. It potentiates the environment for action not hitherto associated with it. It produces behavior designed to be accurate not in the sense of veridical portrayal of the world by intellectual activity but in the sense of representing an inner world of emotional events (and their representational structure) that is every bit as real as the other.

The principle of repression also has much to do with understanding the concept of transference—that peculiar mixture of overestimation and affective evaluation bestowed on people in significant positions without consideration of the context of the relationship. The principle of repression also implies the view that psychological discovery is promoted in certain ways by irrational involvements of the observer in a phenomenon or observation.

The fact that motor tendencies in a repressed schema may be activated without comprehension of their consequences helps to account for many forms of *repetition* phenomena. (This issue will be discussed in more detail in the next chapter.) As Kubie has put it,

"Unsatisfied cravings continue to make demands; there is no compulsion to repeat for the sake of repeating, but for the sake of consummating it."[1] Loewald (1955) has stressed the same point: "Traumatic experiences are merely laid down as unconscious memory traces. Repression, as a defense, is a regressive repetition of this nonarrival at consciousness" (pp. 205-206).

Since there is no feedback, the behavior is repeated. As the motor aspect of the wish is repeatedly activated, so repeatedly must be the functions of "superego" or the inhibiting process associated with manifestations of the wish. Thus one type of repetition derives from the clamor for "expression" that occurs in conjunction with defensive tendencies that inhibit comprehension of the meaning of the activity. Repression, by interrupting the ideomotor system through the input of inhibitory excitation, jams the switch-off mechanism of the schema; the system continues to operate, like the sorcerer's apprentice as it were, but with additional "power" provided by the activation of negative affect. This is one basis for understanding the "repetition compulsion' without recourse to a self-destructive or death instinct. According to this model of repression, one would expect the phenomena Freud conceptualized as the repetition compulsion to appear whenever dynamically unconscious ideational systems are primed.

A most important implication of the repression principle as formulated here is that all forms of *defense* are seen as variants of repression. This notion is a frank "regression" to an early view of Freud's that he later relinquished. Yet I believe there is economy in a single-process conception of defense: blocked wish, associated with anticipatory pleasure and unpleasure, such as anxiety, which lead to activities in part corresponding to what have been construed as defenses, and in part are surrogate forms of expression of the wish itself. In this view, defenses are a means of implementing a repression: for instance, an intellectualizing defense at work in the psychoanalytic situation, as Freud describes it (1916-1917, p. 288). In the unaccustomed position of lying on the couch and committed to free association, the patient feels the stirrings of unwelcome thoughts; these are automatically blocked by a flood of farfetched, irrelevant ideation, operating as a kind of sanctuary. Other varieties of defense as well become understandable as meeting the requirements of repression.

[1]*Editors' note.* We have been unable to locate the source of this quotation.

Finally, the principle of repression has developmental implications. Viewed as a structure-developing process, that is, as a process whose activity produces an internalized representation of object relationships, its cumulative effects in adaptation are a facet of psychoanalytic theory not yet systematically explored. We will have more to say on this implication of repression in a later chapter.

CHAPTER 8

The Principle of Self-Initiated Active Reversal of Passive Experience[1]

IN *Beyond the Pleasure Principle* Freud (1920) puzzled over the phenomenon of normal play; it seemed to him that certain aspects of play contradicted the dominance of the "pleasure principle" in the regulation of behavior. His observations deserve quotation at length:

> Without wishing to include the whole field covered by these phenomena, I have been able, through a chance opportunity which presented itself, to throw some light upon the first game played by a little boy of one and a half and invented by himself. . . .
>
> The child was not at all precocious in his intellectual development. At the age of one and a half he could say only a few comprehensible words; he could also make use of a number of

[1]Several authors have centered on one or another aspect of this principle, notably Balint, Bibring, Erikson, Fenichel, Hartmann, Hendrick, White, and especially Loewald and Loevinger, whose formulations are the most explicit and systematic. The present statement distinguishes two aspects merged in Loevinger's (1966) discussion, the self-initiated repetition of an experience, and its by-products in accomplishments of mastery. White's (1959, 1960, 1963) contribution is also relevant. However, he offers his principle of "competence" as an addition to psychoanalytic theory, whereas the effort here is to bring it into continuity with other dynamic principles of the theory.

> sounds which expressed a meaning intelligible to those around him. He was, however, on good terms with his parents and their one servant-girl, and tributes were paid to his being a 'good boy'. . . . This good little boy, however, had an occasional disturbing habit of taking any small objects he could get hold of and throwing them away from him into a corner, under the bed, and so on, so that hunting for his toys and picking them up was often quite a business. As he did this he gave vent to a loud, long-drawn-out 'o-o-o-o', accompanied by an expression of interest and satisfaction. His mother and the writer of the present account were agreed in thinking that this was not a mere interjection but represented the German word *'fort'* ['gone']. I eventually realized that it was a game and that the only use he made of any of his toys was to play 'gone' with them. One day I made an observation which confirmed my view. The child had a wooden reel with a piece of string round it. It never occurred to him to pull it along the floor behind him, for instance, and play at its being a carriage. What he did was to hold the reel by the string and very skilfully throw it over the edge of his curtained cot, so that it disappeared into it, at the same time uttering his expressive 'o-o-o-o'. He then pulled the reel out of the cot again by the string and hailed its reappearance with a joyful *'da'* ['there']. This, then, was the complete game—disappearance and return. As a rule one only witnessed its first act, which was repeated untiringly as a game in itself, though there is no doubt that the greater pleasure was attached to the second act.
>
> The interpretation of the game then became obvious. It was related to the child's great cultural achievement—the instinctual renunciation . . . which he had made in allowing his mother to go away without protesting. He compensated himself for this, as it were, by himself staging the disappearance and return of the objects within his reach [pp. 14-15].

Freud concludes:

> On an unprejudiced view one gets an impression that the child turned his experience into a game from another motive. At the outset he was in a *passive* situation—he was overpowered by the experience; but, by repeating it, unpleasurable though it was, as a game, he took on an *active* part. These efforts might be put down to an instinct for mastery that was acting independently of whether the memory was in itself pleasurable or not. . . . It is

> clear that in their play children repeat everything that has made a great impression on them in real life, and that in doing so they abreact the strength of the impression and, as one might put it, make themselves master of the situation [pp. 16-17].

Freud was here stating a dynamic principle of activity that is usually associated with the ego. Indeed, it is a key principle of ego psychology and central to phenomena of "ego autonomy." Together with the principle of repression it makes up a substantial segment of the dynamics of internalization and structure formation in development.

In the passage quoted, Freud singled out three aspects that are at the heart of the principle: (1) There is a tendency to recreate in an active mode an event that has been passively experienced as in some respect unacceptable, unrelated, or alien to the self. Such events can be experienced as meaningless, hence anxiety evoking, unfamiliar, and even as profoundly traumatic and alienating blows. The response in such circumstances is of the nature: "What I have experienced as being done to me, *I* must make happen." (2) The same experience may be reproduced or the recipient of the "blow" may be reversed, i.e., "What he does to me, and I experience as unpleasant, I must do to him (or it)." (3) The reversal may occur in action or in fantasy, through a substitute in either.

The principle of "reversal of voice," as Loevinger (1966) terms it, captures the essential distinction between activity and passivity which Rapaport (1953) intuitively felt to be one of the fundamental foci of psychoanalytic theory generally and of a dynamic conception of ego organization in particular. I believe it is the essential dynamic aspect of what is usually encompassed by the term "will." The principle encompasses such diverse phenomena as play, novelty, curiosity, repetitive working through of traumatic experiences, interruption phenomena, and certain aspects of art-making. From a developmental standpoint it encompasses phenomena that White (1959, 1960, 1963) has described as competence motivation; perhaps most important of all, it provides a dynamic basis for identification. In psychoanalytic therapy the positive or adaptive aspects of transference, as Loewald (1960) has emphasized, are explainable in its terms. Some of these implications will be dealt with in this chapter and the next.

From a psychoanalytic standpoint, the focal references of the principle are interpersonal experiences. The principle covers encounters which are passively felt as impositions, engendering efforts to *re-experience* them so as to make them self-syntonic. A *relationship* is re-experienced so that, in relation to the self, it is changed from an imposed experience to one that, even if painful, is self-generated; it is made part of "my" experience.

In the first phase of restructuring the experience self-syntonically, the aim is not necessarily retaliatory but simply to make the *experience of the blow itself* a controllable *self*-experience. This self-initiated re-experiencing can take the form of a fantasy in which I act submissively, have others dominate me, act uncontrolled so others will have to dominate me—I retaliate, reverse roles, I make him, or myself, do it to me. The functional importance of such repetition of experience is that it produces a form of control or integration; the self is able to make the experience happen. The basic aim is to "own" the experience; its alien status and disconnectedness from the self are reduced by a self-governed re-experiencing of it.

Balint (1931) offers a good illustration of the process:

> Uncle Doctor arrives and looks down the child's throat with a spoon. On a first such occasion most children react violently against the assault and make it absolutely clear that the whole thing is very far indeed from pleasing them. But, strange to say, instead of forgetting the unpleasant business as quickly as possible, they almost without exception begin soon afterwards to play at doctor. Thus the child behaves after the doctor's visit just as he does after parting from an object that he likes. . . . This is all the more peculiar because, according to what we have hitherto found, a child identifies himself with an absent object in order to replace it and so get rid of his longing for it. But children do not long for the doctor: so what can the meaning of the identification here? The child dislikes what the doctor does to him but he is compelled to submit to it. Then, afterwards, the child becomes the doctor, looks down everyone's throat, applies compresses, gives medicine, and so on. *Thus he does actively what he suffered passively* [italics added]. We know how much it injures a child's narcissism if he is obliged to put up with something against his will [pp. 120-121].

Though often allotted great importance in clinical formulations, the reversal of voice principle has not had comparable status in systematic psychoanalytic theory. Freud's own doubts about it probably had much to do with this state of affairs: the force of his clear initial assertion of the principle as independent of the pleasure principle was dissipated when he later viewed it as a manifestation of a distinctive motive—the "repetition compulsion" (which in turn carried him on a divergent path of theorizing to the "death instinct"). Turning away from those aspects of play that seemed clearly to show the reversal of passivity into activity, Freud instead focused on the fact of repetition as the primary datum. He linked the "compulsion to repeat" to the constancy principle—that is, to an energic state "preferred" by the organism, which gives rise to a motive to reinstate a *previous* state. He went on to view this propensity for constancy as a spontaneous manifestation of the "Nirvana principle" which asserts itself through destructive urges. He further dulled the edge of his observations by proposing an alternative explanation of play, one consistent with the "pleasure principle," namely, that it expresses the "wish to be grown up" or "the wish to satisfy an aggressive impulse toward the mother." However, the assertion that one is acting upon a wish is merely a description, not a dynamic explanation. The paramount question remains: Why the wish? And why the anxiety connected with it? In this respect the necessity for reversing a "blow" is not an *alternative* explanation, but may account for the origin of either wish. Mastering the experience entails a tendency frustrated, a blow experienced, and the control of an aggressive wish thus aroused.

Thus the antinomy Freud saw between his alternative explanations is more apparent than real, and is a matter to be regretted, because had he stayed with his initial formulation the outline of a truly dynamic ego psychology might have evolved from *Beyond the Pleasure Principle*. Instead, his conclusion was equivocal: "We are therefore left in doubt as to whether the impulse to work over in the mind some overpowering experience so as to make oneself master of it can find expression as a primary event, and independently of the pleasure principle" (1920, p. 16). Thereafter psychoanalytic theorists (except for Hendrick, 1942, 1943a) tended to accept the validity of Freud's doubts and pursued his efforts to resolve the problem of "compulsive repetitions" in terms of the pleasure principle, or through Freud's postulation of an aggressive instinctual drive pressing toward discharge.

Perhaps Freud's most misleading step here was his conception of the nature of the "reinstatement" in "compulsive repetitions," for the facts of play that he cited seem to be not so much matters of reinstatement or reproduction as of recreation with the aim of *resolution* or mastery. The difference is critical, for on it rests the decision to remain on the level of explaining development as the by-product of the discharge requirements of instinctual drives, or to move in a direction of a psychology centered on identity and self.

One might go further, and suggest that the principle accounts *for* aggression. Activities of reversal of voice could be considered synonymous with the "aggressive drive"—not in the sense of a specific aggressive *motive* to destroy but as manifestations of an instinctual aggressive potential. In a narrower sense of aggression, the principle would account for conditions in which specific hostility is aroused, namely, circumstances where a passive experience is also experienced as an assault.

In the security of hindsight we may say that Freud failed to see that he had in hand two principles with which to account for phenomena of the "repetition compulsion": efforts at *reversal of voice;* and the repetitiveness which is the inevitable consequence of activated schemata that are in a state of *repression.* Freud's feeling that the mastery principle was insufficient to account for all phenomena of repetition was justified. As we have seen, a powerful source of repetition is inherent in the activity of repressed ideas. But the role of the principle of mastery as a source of repetition is obscured by thinking of it as an explanation in terms of "drives" pressing toward gratification. The principles of repression and active reversal are not contradictory but coordinate, and both are critical in accounting for what Freud dealt with as the repetition compulsion.

Although in *Beyond the Pleasure Principle* Freud seemed doubtful about the reversal of voice principle, later on he again resorted to it, in *Inhibitions, Symptoms and Anxiety* (1926), this time to account not for play but for repetitions of traumatic experiences. It is noteworthy that in this context he did not explain traumatic experience in terms of a "compulsion to repeat," which had been one of his conclusions in *Beyond the Pleasure Principle.*

> Let us call a situation of helplessness of this kind that has actually been experienced a *traumatic situation.* We shall then have good

> grounds for distinguishing a traumatic situation from a danger-situation. . . . Let us call a situation which contains the determinant for such an expectation a danger-situation. It is in this situation that the signal of anxiety is given. . . . Taking this sequence, anxiety—danger—helplessness (trauma), we can now summarize what has been said. A danger-situation is a recognized, remembered, expected situation of helplessness. . . . The ego, which experienced the trauma passively, now repeats it actively, in a weakened version, in the hope of being able itself to direct its course. It is certain that children behave in this fashion towards every distressing impression they receive, by reproducing it in their play. In thus changing from passivity to activity they attempt to master their experiences psychically [1926, pp. 166-167].

It is interesting that Freud proposed this principle without noting that he had previously rejected it. And it is equally interesting that the principle was quite in accord with the conception of an autonomously active ego that was beginning to take shape at this time, a conception in which Freud seems to have given more importance to what Hartmann calls the "synthetic function." However, to attribute a "synthetic function" to the ego is not to state a dynamic principle; what the integrative *aims* themselves are is not indicated—a gap in ego psychology which the reversal of voice principle helps to fill.

Two points must be noted. First, reversal of voice clearly concerns the relationship of an encounter to the *self,* and in the present version emphasis is moved from the ego to the *self* aspect of ego organization. Second, the motivational aspect of the principle is not construed simply as a "need for mastery" which must be "gratified."

In its various formulations, the reversal of voice principle is generally viewed as an ego activity. Except for Erikson's version (see 1963, Chapter 6), the subject for the reversal tendency is commonly considered to be the "ego." The ego has multiple referents, and to think of the principle in terms of the workings of the ego tends to obscure something essential, namely, that reversal behaviors concern experiences that threaten self-continuity.

While in recent years the concept of the ego has certainly broadened, it is only gradually being recognized that among its autonomous aspects is a personal, continuous identity in terms of which a great deal of behavior is selected, pressures are responded to, and a personal environment is created; that self-identity is a distinctive aspect of the organism's development, having phenomenological as well as non-phenomenological aspects; and that in relation to this identity there develop crises and conflicts which call for resolution (see Erikson, 1963, 1968a). In this view it is the *self,* rather than an impersonal ego agency, that is a center to which activity is referred. The perceived self is held to be responsible or not for an encounter; as such, the self has its own requirements of balance and integrity at each age. This assumption of a developing selfhood is central to the principle being formulated here. Reversal of voice is not a principle of "drive control" or "delay"; rather, it is one of control in the form of the self experienced as an initiator of action. Experience and automatized control are possible without their being self-related. This distinction is crucial in understanding the phenomena incorporated in this principle, and it is quite consistent with the capacities Freud came to attribute to the ego in his later theory.

Thus a basic assumption of the principle is that to "make sense out of" things and to bring them into connection with a continuing self-identity is a fundamental tendency of development. We "own" our experiences as we own an object. Conversely, an object may be perceived as strange or uncanny, with an accompanying feeling of "not making sense," of discontinuity. Just as the hammer in one's hand to make a table is a tool experienced as an extension of the self, so can the table be experienced as "my table" as against a "table made for me." When events have been thoroughly self-accommodated they are no longer focally experienced. It is when discordance appears—experiences that cannot be "placed," that "don't fit," in short, that have no ready reference point to the self—that we have a condition for focal awareness, with consequent efforts toward making the discrepancy self-syntonic.

It is assumed that bringing experience into relationship with the self is a basic condition for the development of motives. Continuity of ego experience and consistency with self-identity is a critical phenomenon of growth. With it go experiences of responsibility, of ownership. Such motives accomplish control of a phenomenon, by linking it cognitively to a body of self-identified meanings. "In finding [a niche in his society] the young adult gains an assured sense of inner continuity and social sameness which will bridge what he was as a child and what he is about to become, and will reconcile his conception of himself and of his community's recognition of him" (Erikson, 1956, p. 111).

The crucial aspect of the principle is not a "need for mastery" per se but the self-provoked effort to bring an experience into syntonic relationship with the self by restitution, differentiation, or rejection. Mastery is viewed as a by-product of efforts to make the unfamiliar familiar and controllable. Thus the motivational aspect of the principle is centered in the maintenance of self-integrity, feelings of sameness and oneness, rather than upon arousal of a "need for mastery." Mastery is an expression and consequence of this integrative tendency in which first the body and then self-conception are the reference points for organizing experience.

Both affective experiences and sensory information about the environment may become dissonant with self-identity. A passively experienced event in either sphere has perceptual reality—for example, an unfamiliar moving object crossing our view, or the startle and pain of an interpersonal encounter. In relation to self-identity, affect may become structured in the form of what Kubie calls an "affective position" which has become so closely associated with the self as to be unnoticed—it is completely self-syntonic. Kubie offers the example of one of his patients:

> Throughout his life a physician of high and well-earned repute had been lost in a profound depression, of which he had remained wholly unaware until after he had been in treatment for a long time.... Because this had been with him always, he had come to take depression for granted as he took the air he breathed. He had never known what it was to feel any other way. Therefore he had never thought of himself as chronically depressed.... yet the depressive color of his whole life was not under repression. It was not unconscious in the technical analytic sense [Kubie, 1963, pp. 106-107].

We would say it was unconscious not in the dynamic sense, but in the sense that walking movements are "unconscious"; it was self-syntonic. The self-syntonicity achieved was of course unadaptive, but it was not a *repressed* affective position dissociated from the self.

Reversals of passively experienced encounters have several important aspects, three of which deserve to be singled out.

1. The self-initiated activity leaves an internal record. A by-product of reproducing an experience is knowledge about objects encountered. The knowledge gleaned in altering experience is now also part of a self-associated conceptual organization. Now assimilated to the self, this internalized knowledge brings about an additional nuance concerning the environment; it is knowledge connected with the self *about* the environment. For example, in the play of disappearance and return, the child also learned facts about the environment; the "game" produced not only a fact about a human relationship (a mother who disappears can be made to return) but facts about physical conditions that are associated with perceptual experiences of appearance and disappearance of an object.

2. Another effect of reversal is a differentiation of the self-schema. The assimilative structuring becomes itself an extension of the self, in the form of "knowledge about." This has often been called "incorporation"—somewhat misleadingly, since the knowledge that becomes "part of self," or "my knowledge," persists as an internal differentiation. Balint refers to this "assimilation" as an "extension of the ego":

> It is a remarkable fact, for instance, that the essence of a small child's play consists in the child itself becoming a dog or a motor-car or a railway-train though the corresponding toys are close at hand. Until this mental incorporation has been achieved, the toy remains something alien and frightening. The preference felt by children for a piece of paper or wood, for an empty box or a bit of string, is easily explained by the fact that these things can assume a greater diversity of shape and consequently afford wider possibilities for identification [1931, p. 96].

This contrasts with the structural product of repression, where an "incorporation" is dissociated from the self-schema; and the structures emanating from the operation of the two principles influence behavior in critically different ways.

3. Repeated recreation of the passively experienced is directly tied to some form and degree of *voluntary motor* activity. Mediation by self-initiated motor control is perhaps the most critical reason why re-experiencing an encounter can soften the impact of an alien experience and bring about congruence with self. In this connection words are an extremely important means of achieving control and

producing such self-syntonicity. For example, patients, especially at the beginning of therapy, often feel a "pressure" to talk about the analytic goings-on outside the therapy hours. Similarly, people in trouble often experience a relief from pressureful talk. Such behavior was once commonly explained as "tension discharge," but the reversal of voice principle provides a more illuminating view of its motivational basis. By *verbalizing*, one connects an experience with the self and in this respect makes it manageable; connecting the experience to words makes it possible to work it over in reflective consciousness and thereby help the accommodative process.[2] "When a word is attached to an experience, there is an increase in cognitive and referential precision which may, in some instances, amount to becoming 'aware' of what was previously only vague and undefined" (Laffal).[3] In large measure, what becomes conscious is what can be *named;* words make it possible to experience events that are not otherwise in our grasp.

The importance of vocalization and language in the development of voluntary control has been a matter of considerable interest in recent years (see especially Luria, 1961). Laffal (1964) reminds us, for example, of the importance Freud attached to the infant's cry; at first this is only a diffuse "discharge"—a motor expression of need—but it quickly yields an informational return in the responses of a caretaker. Vocalization is not only associated with bodily tensions generally, but becomes an early means of social communication of these bodily states, a way of sharing them with others. Mediation via language and words works both ways: language also becomes a means of evoking associated bodily states and the awareness of them.

Mastery as a By-product of Reversal of Voice

The cognitive-motor events that are entailed in self-initiated repetition turn the experience of "it controls me" into "I control it." Part of the structural yield of such repetition is more delineated schemata of environmental events. Self-initiated repetition brings a feeling of having "made sense out of"; alienation turns to familiarity, accom-

[2]The equally common experience of mutism does not really contradict this point: in such instances one does not want to *hear* the troublesome thought (see Klein and Wolitzky, 1967). Words make the thought more tangible, more like an "object."

[3]*Editors' note.* We have been unable to locate the source of this quotation.

panied by experiences of controlling through knowledge. This is mastery, a by-product of reversal of voice. (See in this connection Held's work on the importance of feedback from self-initiated motor events in bringing about structural changes in perception [Held and Hein, 1958; Held and Schlank, 1959].)

It is useful to separate the experience of recreating an event from controls that are consequent to it, and from adaptive mastery: these are not synonymous. Some of the phenomena that Bibring (1943) has referred to as "working-off mechanisms" (in contrast to defenses) are of the nature of self-syntonic repetitions that fall short of actual mastery, consisting mainly of eradicating experiences of being controlled or manipulated. Certain forms of stereotyped play, repetitive anxiety dreams, and certain transference phenomena are also of this nature.

But the reversal of voice principle does provide a basis for saying how motives for mastery originate, i.e., behavior undertaken *for the sake of* mastery. Activities leading to mastery always originate in efforts to make alien experiences self-syntonic, to undo passive intrusion and experienced dissonance. The experiences of gratification emanating from successful repetitions of encounters and from bringing feedback under voluntary control contribute to making the experience of mastery itself a *value* to be achieved and in this sense a basis of independent motivation.

These comments are made to dissociate the reversal of voice principle from an "instinct for mastery." The critical event is the self-initiation of the experience, not the impulse for mastery itself, which is a derivative of such efforts. As Wolff points out, mastery itself has to be accounted for, and concepts like the instinct for mastery, need-achievement, or competence motivation do no more than describe the behavior in general terms; they tell us little, for instance, about the direction that action will take when a novelty is encountered, and little about the origin of the "need" which directs this action (1963, p. 236). They are in the same category of explanation as Freud's "compulsion to repeat," which he presented as a primary "drive" which is beyond the pleasure principle. The present principle accounts for mastery by a dynamic principle rather than by a specific drive that needs to be "gratified." The function of reversal of voice is that of bringing dystonically experienced events into relationship with the self.

Reversal of voice also takes account of the phenomena that White

(1959, 1963) has described as "effectance" motivations. White's conception of "competence" has the characteristic of a drive which must be "gratified." He is content to remain within the drive framework, using his evidence to show that "competence" motivation deserves equal status with "libidinal drives," and proposing a "neutral energy" of nonlibidinal, nonaggressive origin. His valuable account of competence behavior has the appearance of a graft upon psychoanalytic theory rather than of an integration with dynamic conceptions of psychoanalytic clinical theory. It is not especially illuminating to point out that the principle of reversal of voice has drive*like* qualities or that an impulse for mastery "seeks its own gratification." It seems more important to speak of the conditions that evoke it. Rapaport (1960) was also critical of White's attempt to add to the lexicon yet another drive that must be satisfied, and on this basis distinguished between "motives" and "causes," placing competence motivations, as well as Piaget's "function motivations," in the category of causes. However, if competence motivation is dubiously characterized as a "drive," it is clearly *motivational* in the sense of having a directional and organizational influence on behavior. Therefore accounting for this class of motivations by a dynamic principle seems a more useful approach than reclassifying it in a category of "causes." Elsewhere Rapaport (1953) did strongly imply such a dynamic principle in his distinction between activity and passivity as organizing factors in behavior, but did not use it to account for the phenomena of competence to which White draws attention.

Infantile Precursors

In the above account the central focus of the reversal of voice principle was seen to be the relating of experiences to a sense of self-identity. This appears to be an issue that arises only at a fairly advanced stage of development. Our account obviously presupposes an established self-schema. However, it seems justified to assume infantile precursors of this organizing tendency before an explicit self-conception has developed. Indeed, these precursors of reversal of voice are perhaps themselves a condition for the eventual development of a distinction between self and other.

A precursor possibly occurs at the stage of development in which the infant is capable of experiencing consequences of autogenous movements and of associating the message "received" with the movements that provoked it (Freud [1895] noted something of the sort in the infant's cry). The infant is capable of responding to frustration and interruption of activity with actions that in turn produce a message that they *have been responded to*. From the first, the infant's responsiveness to such feedback from his own actions seems to be critical in development, and there seems to be a tendency to be able to take some action in his own behalf. Referring to a film produced by Mittelmann, Malkenson, and Monroe, Bettelheim comments on a remarkable scene in which an infant attempts to feed himself, requiring a give and take between infant and mother—"a perfect example of how good relations between mother and infant permit both of them to find a solution that implies respect for the child's autonomous decisions while still assuring him of dependent care" (1967, p. 22).

From this primitive condition arises the person's tendency to reproduce unintegrated experience actively. Piaget has described such a prototype of passivity turned into autogenous activity in what he terms the "primitive assimilative tendency" of infants. He remarks that one of the essential tasks of primitive assimilation is the coordination of the heterogeneous worlds of tactile, visual, and auditory schemas so that, for example, the hand can be simultaneously a visual object and a source of tactile, kinesthetic impressions. Thus, if one holds an infant's hand outside his vision, he is conscious of tactile-kinesthetic sensations, but he looks all around him for a *visual* situation corresponding to his impression—that is, a point of resemblance.

The early importance of responsiveness to informative consequences of experience is implied in Wolff's (1963) description of infantile activity:

> When the child discovers for the first time that a ball will roll down an inclined plane all by itself, he repeats this experiment out of the need to explore the causal properties of objects that he now experiences as being *independent of himself* [p. 231; italics added].
>
> He appears to act in order to repeat events which are independent of his action [p. 234].
>
> In contrast to intellectual adaptation proper, the child does not assimilate the spatial properties of the object to his thought

> schemata of space and causality, in order to understand them, but imitates the model as he has perceived it. His primary aim appears to be to reconstitute the novelty to himself, to conserve it without seeking to comprehend it [p. 238].

Such a tendency in early childhood is perhaps fundamental to the development of the self-other distinction, and facilitates reliance upon the reversal of passively endured experience through activity.

Experiences of autoinitiated activity have not been sufficiently emphasized as critical in infant development. Bettelheim points out, for example, that psychoanalytic accounts of gratification and frustration of oral needs have tended to ignore the multiple happenings around the feeding process—the action and reaction between mother and child which is a prelude to the full development of self-initiated action. In Bettelheim's view, neither mother love, nor food, nor the skin contact between mother and child account for the relationship between breast feeding and a sense of trust; in his view, the child's sense of trust depends vitally on the mutual communications provoked by the infant's autogenously generated and experienced movements. Certainly the kind of autocontrolled action connected with feeding does not lie solely in its being an "oral" gratification related to the stimulation of a particular mucous membrane or specific erogenous zone, though all of these "help the experience along" (Bettelheim, 1967, p. 19).

> This is why artificial feeding times, arranged according to the clock, can dehumanize the infant. The reason is not just that time-clock feeding is contrary to the natural rhythms of the body. . . . More important here is that it prevents the infant from feeling that *his* actions (crying smiling) have a significant effect on this important life experience of being fed.
>
> What humanizes the infant is not being fed, changed, or picked up when he feels the need for it, although they add greatly to his comfort and feeling of well-being. Nor does irregular care necessarily dehumanize, though it will tend to make him dissatisfied with life or may cause poor development or sickness. It is rather the experience that *his* crying for food brings about *his* satiation by others according to *his* timing that makes it a socializing and humanizing experience. It is that *his* smile, or facial grimacing, evokes a parallel or otherwise appropriate response in the mother [1967, p. 25].

It is possible, then, that infantile experiences of the effectiveness of autogenously initiated actions are crucial precursors of the development of the self-schema, and for the emergence of the principle of reversal of voice in the development of control.

Developmental inadequacy in this respect may be ruinous to self-development. Bettelheim sees this as fundamental in the psychopathology of the autistic child:

> For our own part, we have found, as we worked more intensively with autistic children, that at the core of their disturbance was not . . . that they lacked for any passive satisfactions. Those satisfactions were very easy for us to provide. Some autistic children accepted the offered satisfactions and remained autistic; others rejected them. None moved out of the autistic position because of them. This they did only if and when we were able to activate them. . . . They came to life only when we were able to create the conditions, or otherwise be the catalysts, that induced them to take action in their own behalf [1967, pp. 16-17].

So long as confronting an experience—no matter with how much anxiety—produces messages which are coordinate with the passively experienced "blow," there exists, as it were, "hope" for active management of it. But if the encounter is also experienced as inescapable, the situation is otherwise. "Consistent nonreward for being active may even lead to his giving up trying to shape his interactions" (p. 17). One is then at the mercy of forces experienced as beyond one's control, for responses are "unanswered" by any evidence that repetition is effective.

Thus the seeds of self-initiated reversal of passive experience are present in infantile life. It is manageable frustration that makes the infant aware that an outer world exists. If the experience is of complete ineffectuality and helplessness, the alternative strategy of repression may also have its genesis in primitive attempts to "disown" the experience.

A Few Applications of the Principle

The scope of the principle of reversal of voice is better appreciated by comparison with the principle of repression, and we will consider them jointly in the following chapter. However, a few applications briefly touched upon in the above discussion can be highlighted.

1. *Repetitive Behavior*

Encounters which produce an experience of cleavage with the self give rise to efforts to reduce such discrepancies by repetitive reversal. Continually renewed contact with conditions that produce such discrepancies are part of an effort to make them self-syntonic. In this respect the outcome of this process has much in common with what Piaget has described as activities which produce a balance of assimilation and accommodation.

However, this is not the sole dynamic context of repetition. As Kubie (1941) has pointed out, it is the nature of a repressed impulse to be repetitively active. A repressed schema is unresponsive to feedback but the repressed tendency is not inactive, and this activity reverberates in whichever motor channels permit its expression in a cognitive format that does not threaten the repression.

Thus repetitions may reflect the workings of reversal of voice, of repression, or both. In either case, however, repetition is not a "compulsion to repeat" for the sake of repetition. In both cases, efforts at control are involved—assimilative in repression, accommodative mastery as well in reversal of voice. Certain repetition phenomena may have a basis in both principles: for example, a reversal of voice may be a secondary consequence of an early repression, in which evoking experiences of self-initiated control is a response to the repressed traumatic experiences. And a repressed feeling of "I was (or am) made helpless" could stimulate a need for power, for recognition, for reassurance of love.

2. *Activity-Passivity*

The reversal of voice principle, again in conjunction with the principle of repression, allows interpretation of activity and passivity in dynamic terms. In this view, activity has to do not with mere motor activation, but rather with subjective experiences of the relation of action to what is valued and acceptable in self-conception. Activity experiences would be those in which the self as initiator is a dominant aspect: i.e., "I am doing, am responsible for making." Passivity would be reflected in experiences of "being done to," "suffering," "being made to happen," "driven." The production of active experience would therefore be synonymous with behavioral efforts of reversal of voice. Attempts to gratify needs per se may be subjectively accompanied by either active or passive experiences. An "active role" is made synonymous with self-initiated repetitive experience and its by-products of experienced self-responsibility, ownership, and continuity.

It follows from our description that activity and passivity are not directly specifiable in strictly behavioral terms; it is rather the *experienced* meanings of behavior in relation to selfhood that are crucial; the same behavior can have meaning either at the active or the passive pole. Centrality of self in time and space is the crucial frame of reference. A sense of freedom of choice accompanying behavior marks it as "active"; its absence stamps behavior as "passive." "Men cannot tolerate to have . . . [a sense of freedom of choice] questioned beyond a certain point, either as an individual among his fellow men, or as a member of a group among other groups" (Erikson, 1964, pp. 148-149). The experiential aspects of self-relatedness provide the primary criteria for asserting whether behavior is active or passive.

3. *Play*

Erikson points out that to grow means to be divided into different parts which move at different rates. This process creates issues of synthesis, of inadequacy in one area and adequacy in another. Play assists integration in enabling a person to experience the effects of obeying himself. Play synchronizes bodily and social processes within the self in accordance with the requirement of preserving a sense of the self's capabilities as an initiating agent, of controlling choice, and of being continuous. Play helps the child gain synthesizing power through involvement and disengagement. At each stage play is a valued means of enlarging and reaffirming self-identity through mastery experiences. The activities of play range from the control and integration of inexplicable, not yet meaningful experiences, to traumatic, self-alienated experiences. Normal play and the special kind of intense play that occurs in emotional crises have essentially similar dynamic aims. Play in which emotional crises are worked through has special qualities, notably an affiliation between its themes and the themes of personal crises, in its creation of model situations that incorporate the particular alienating encounters that must be dealt with. Thematic content appears not to be so crucial a component in other occasions of play. In the context of traumatic experience, play is an attempt to incorporate the experience through self-initiated, active engagement;

thus playful involvement and engagement can have considerable therapeutic value.

Accounting for play in terms of the reversal of voice does not contradict the tendency in recent years for psychoanalytic theorists to broaden the "pleasure principle" to include recognition that children and animals do many things not in order to reach a "goal" but for the sheer *pleasure in functioning* itself. However, "pleasure in functioning," while a useful descriptive term, has scant explanatory value. To recognize that behavior is exhibiting the gratification of a "need" is not explanatory; more important are the conditions that brought out the need. This is why speaking of a "need" for mastery is not sufficient. Such a "need" is the expression of efforts to maintain syntonicity when self-dissonant experiences have been provoked by a passively experienced event. The operative principle, as Loevinger (1966) says, is to account for the origin of such needs or wishes, not for the fact that the impulse, once aroused, "seeks gratification"—which says no more than that it exists.

That "pleasure in functioning" is not explanatory is evident in the difficulty of accounting for the selection of the activity that yields "pleasure"; the child's choice is usually highly specific. As Waelder put it, "interchangeability of content does not exist. . . . a particular game is given preference at a particular time. The content is not a matter of indifference" (1933, p. 212). Moreover, experiences that yield pleasure vary from one developmental stage to another, and seem to be correlated with mastery problems arising at specific ages. Finally, it is difficult to distinguish conditions where pleasure in functioning is sought from occasions when the person's preference is definitely to preserve a previous state rather than to seek a new one. For instance, the adult or the child may tenaciously cling to specific ways of acting in spite of the fact that they have repeatedly brought pain, frustration, and defeat. In short, the occasion when "the need for pleasure in functioning" produces its own basis for motivation must itself be incorporated within a more general principle that embodies reasons why the need itself arises.

From a dynamic standpoint, pleasure in functioning would refer to organizing efforts that arise from conditions which, though not conflictual in the psychoanalytic sense, still pose a requirement for self-syntonic, assimilative activity. To the extent that it functions like a "drive" and is motivational, its satisfaction gives "pleasure."

4. *Transference*

Both repression and the reversal of voice contribute to the workings of transference, that most extraordinary and inevitable phenomenon of therapeutic procedures. In transference, the perceptions, beliefs, and attitudes of which a patient's relationship to his therapist consists mirror conflicts born of unconsciously active cognitive schemata (unconscious fantasies). Therapy is especially conducive to such manifestations, given the nature of the therapeutic situation, which encourages activation of unconscious repressed schemata for releasing what Kubie has called the inherent repetitive momentum of repressed ideation. In this context the therapist is "incorporated" assimilatively, in terms of prototypical elements of unconscious fantasy. Dynamically unconscious meanings in interpersonal relationships are re-enacted in behavior toward the therapist; such expressions of repressed schemata are encouraged to appear. The inaccessibility or "resistiveness" of such schemata to the conscious evaluation of their consequences is, of course, the point and focus of psychoanalytic therapy.

It is precisely because such promptings are *passively experienced*—without a sense of control, with a growing awareness of the self as "suffering" them rather than as "causing them to happen"—that repetition with the aim of self-syntonicity is engendered, again with the therapist's encouragement. A patient's behavior in therapy has a peculiar duality in that he is impelled by unconsciously active schemata which, being unconscious, produce nonaccommodative repetitions; yet, being also experienced as self-dystonic, such repetitions need to be mastered. As long as they remain dynamically unconscious they cannot be mastered, and the cycle continues. With the therapist's encouragement and through enforced confrontations of self-dystonicity, the process of "undoing the repression" by the reversal of voice comes into play.

Important components of the reversal of voice process in therapy are those efforts which seem to incorporate the therapist as an *identification model.* In this aspect of transference the therapist is not only the focus for the repetition of unconscious prototypical relationships but also a model for achieving a modified self-identity capable of nullifying the unconscious prototypes and their passively endured clamorings. This aspect of therapeutic transference differs from acting out and from interpersonal encounters outside the therapeutic situation, which also afford opportunities for the assimilative activity of unconscious fantasy. In short, therapeutic transference in the psychoanalytic situation is intended (a) to foster awareness of self-dystonic aspects of unconsciously induced repetitions; (b) to encourage converting the passively experienced promptings of introjected schemata into the active voice; and (c) to remodel the self-schema in terms of an identification with the therapist. Self-initiated activity directed to the reversal of the passively experienced unconscious event is made possible by the revised self-conception promoted by this identification.

With these functions, therapeutic transference reproduces an aspect of normal growth, an aspect given insufficient attention in the psychoanalytic theory of therapy, as Loewald (1960) has pointed out. Just as the young boy "borrows power" by identification with his father, the value identifications of a patient with his therapist provide him with a protective position from which to confront relationships split off from understanding and, through the terms set by a revised self-concept, to deny them further influence. The identificatory "presence" of the therapist, his influence as a value-inducing figure, is a powerful, perhaps the most compelling, aspect of the therapeutic process. It must be noted, of course, that the impact of the therapist, like that of the father on his boy, is not didactic in nature; it is that of an identificatory incorporation which becomes salient at just those points in therapy where repressed ideas are to be dealt with.

CHAPTER 9

Two Developmental Principles: Fractionation and Identification

THE PRINCIPLES OF repression and of active repetition of a passively experienced event, identifying different means of internalizing interpersonal meanings, are equally important in the internal representation and symbolizations of interpersonal relationships.

Their functional center is the "grade" of ego organization called *self* and its experiences of self-identity. Self-identity enables one to experience responsibility and irresponsibility as subjective events, and the setting of goals in terms of which actions acquire meaning. From the first emergence of a self-schema, preservation of its identity and continuity is a prominent organismic concern. The strategies of repression and of reversal of voice have to do with the maintenance of the self-schema.

As the infant develops, his experiences of discomfort proceed from the diffuse to the localizable. This differentiation is accompanied by a feeling of self. Following Schafer (1968a), we may think of the self-structure as including three parameters: the self-as-agent (e.g., as knower or doer), the self-as-object ("I see myself torn in different directions"), and the self-as-locus (i.e., location of experience in the body). Self-identity refers to a persisting quality of continuity in these three aspects of the self. In large measure, the self is a subsidiary presence in awareness (Polanyi, 1958) rather than directly experienced: we locate an object in relation to the self, but we are not focally aware of the self in doing so. Nevertheless, such subsidiary awareness of the self is critical for adaptation; for example, it makes possible judgments of the position of an event in space and time.[1] The self serves as a frame of reference for behavior and thought.

A variety of phenomena speak for the importance of a self-schema located in, but not identical with, the body. Held (Held and Hein, 1958; Held and Schlank, 1959) has demonstrated the crucial role played by return afferentation of self-initiated action. Holzman, Rousey, and Snyder (1966) and Klein and Wolitzky (1967) have described the role of the auditory return from one's voice as a support for rational thinking. Clark and Graybiel (1957) have described what they call a "break-off" phenomenon that occurs in pilots at high altitudes: the self is experienced as detached or fluid, or as merging with the aircraft, with other objects in space, or with space itself (see Hebb, 1960, p. 741). The self as the locus of experience may shrink or expand. One may experience a limb as a foreign element, as "not mine." These phenomena have much in common with what Federn (1929) conceptualized as ego boundaries which are capable of expansion and contraction.

The background of stimulation provided by self-initiated movements seems to be essential for distinguishing between experiences connected with self and experiences external to self. Such experiences have much in common with what Piaget called the "egocentric" orientation, present in infancy before the emergence of a clear sense of self, and having the experiential quality of perceptual reality without distinctions between inner and outer. With the development of the self-schema there emerge standards that make possible judgments of what is "foreign to me," what is "synchronous" or "dissonant" with what one is. Self-syntonic movement becomes purposive, "forward-looking." When movements are disconnected from the self there is no grasp of means, no apprehension of their significance to the self.

Anxiety always involves issues of identity and selfhood: it appears when behavior is at odds with self-identified standards, or when an

[1]This is not to say that localization is exclusively dependent upon a self-concept. But there is good reason to believe that it is a crucial factor (see Gaffron, 1956).

encounter is experienced as meaningless, or difficult to position in relation to self. Experiments have confirmed the motivational impetus of interrupting a task in which one's self is invested, of situations of "cognitive dissonance" and novelty. Even the pursuit of a "why" problem is a reflection of a requirement to maintain continuity in the self's grasp of the environment (Berlyne, 1965, p. 286). As Balint (1931) has expressed it, "the intellectual working over of a problem . . . implies that knowing is always *re*-knowing, that is, that we are able to know the external world only as something akin to the ego" (p. 97). The spatial and temporal ordering of experience also seems to have some element of self-reference.

In the development of the self-schema, therefore, experienced *dis*unity and *dis*continuity come to be a source of distress, and a basis of motivations aimed at reducing this dissonance. The self-schema responds to the absence of integration in ways designed to restore it—ways which range from the delusional to the accommodative, the latter bringing about a change in the self-schema itself.

In Piaget's terms, the self-schema comes to be the focus of assimilation and accommodation, of motivational activity, and of the ordering of sensorimotor feedback. A sense of continuous selfhood seems, then, to be a developmental requirement and objective.

In psychoanalytic thinking, the self-schema was implied in Freud's earliest theory of an ego which controlled the flow of stimulation, opening and closing lines of transmission and "discharge." Over the years, the ego concept became rigidly embedded in a hypothetical model of autoregulation which failed to give specific recognition to the "me" or "I" experience as an organizer, or to give it a distinctive role within the system of controls and operational principles that make up the "ego." The notion of ego structure as a distinctive line of development has always been vexed with the question of what is the "rewarding" force in its structural formations—what are the motives of activities that propel and consolidate psychical change. Here the striving for "competence," hedonic gratification, and the like, come to mind. Ego psychology has failed to confront this question in distinctively psychoanalytic terms. The dynamic principles which account for the emergence of "ego controls" remain unclear. These principles appear in bolder relief against considerations of the emergence of structures that have developed from confrontations with issues of sameness, continuity, and discontinuity in selfhood. The ego as the "agent" of responsibility takes on meaning when it implies a self-schema to which actions "belong." It then becomes easier to delineate "ego development" as distinct from intellectual, sensorimotor, affective, and psychosexual development. In this view psychological growth concerns differentiation of the self-schema. It may reveal Freud's (1933, p. 80) adage, "Where id was, there ego shall be," as a moral appeal, based on standards of responsibility that develop in relation to a self that is always seeking meaning—that is, seeking to make experiences syntonic, to preserve continuity in this syntonicity, to integrate societal claims and expectations to that end.

The importance of self-identity, and its developmental continuity in the phenomenology of self-experience were implied in Freud's theorizing, but until Hartmann drew attention to them they were vague in psychoanalytic theory. Perhaps the most significant work in this area has been done by Erikson. Instead of an impersonal ego or "organ," subjective experiences of self are crucial in the development of structures. Erikson asserts that the ego is the guarantor of self-continuity; he realigns the entire emphasis of ego psychology by viewing the operational principles and dynamics of ego organization in terms of their role in the structuring and development of the self-schema.

Freud pointed out that growth is a continuity, but he also pictured it as a series of qualitatively distinct victories of each stage over the one just past. The infant's original experience of unity (Fairbairn, 1952)—self undifferentiated from not-self—dissipates with the inevitable frustrations and impasses which require resolution. Developmental crises occur when the standards and structures of self-identity at one developmental stage are confronted by the internal and environmental events which usher in the next stage. Growth is not simply the surmounting of action structures inappropriate to these new circumstances; a sense of continuing identity requires an enlarged, more differentiated self-conception. The preservation of identity, unity, and continuity is an extremely important psychological objective—an important reason for the pervasive search for meaning that characterizes human enterprise, a search not so much for adaptation per se as for consonance with what one "is." This view qualifies the tendency nowadays to think of the "ego" as an impersonal means of achieving environmental adequacy. In the view expressed here, experienced continuity as self is not synonymous with what is adaptationally effective.

From this standpoint, adaptive "functions" (the so-called "ego functions") are not per se the central concern of ego psychology; rather, they are interesting only in their role of preservers of self-continuity and integrity. Given biological growth as a differentiation of parts which occurs in a given sequence, such functions are the means by which experiences of selfhood become possible, integrated contact with the social milieu accomplished, and continuity achieved in a manner which bridges one stage and the next. Psychological functions are enlisted in the resolution of such identity crises,[2] and themselves develop in relation to the nature and degree of this involvement.

Seen in relation to the requirement for unity and continuity of selfhood, the principles of reversal of voice and repression described earlier stand out as organismic means of insuring unity of the self-schema. Both are rooted in the proposition that the self-schema cannot tolerate more than a certain level of imposition and victimization. Both processes involve the internalization of relationships: in one case, an aspect of the self-schema is modified; in the other, a schema is split or fractionated from the self-structure. However, having different relationships to the self-schema, the motivational consequences of the principles differ in critical ways. It is upon these differences that the present discussion will center.

Turning first to the principle of reversal of voice: through repetition, a frustrating encounter becomes syntonic with the self-schema that has "incorporated" it. The self-schema remains unified but becomes *differentiated;* the unification is achieved through the self itself becoming to an extent an image of the restraint—accommodation. Freud said that overwhelming stimuli have to be "bound" before they can be dealt with. The reversal of voice principle is a dynamic substitute for this energic concept: "binding" is the process of self-initiated re-experiencing.

The process of reversal of voice operates very much like a "drive"; each step of growth involves the child in new experiences that must be mastered. Much remains to be learned about what makes an event a

[2]I do not follow Erikson in relating the identity crisis so closely to the stage of adolescence. I think, rather, that each stage has its identity crisis.

passively experienced "blow" that must be re-experienced in reverse, as well as about the characteristics that provoke this course of action. Presumably such experiences have various sources—biological changes, environmental claims or deprivations. But with each new level of mastery through the reversal of voice, the child acquires new vulnerabilities; the structures require new opportunities for stimulation, which increases the likelihood of new frustrations—and the process repeats itself. Such is the momentum of growth.

Certain characteristics of the process of reversal of voice distinguish it as a principle of structure formation.

Experiences of Self-Initiated Action

The heart of the principle is that when a passively endured encounter or relationship is affectively coded, a search for information is stimulated, toward two ends: (a) to make the experience understandable in relation to self; (b) to position the internalized relationship within the self-schema as usable information related to the self-as-agent. When something is perceived as informative in the context of such self-participation, it becomes part of the self because it yields differentiated information. A crucial distinction between reversal of voice and repression is that in the former responsiveness to such information is made part of the effort of integration, whereas in the latter it is denied.

There is no greater contribution to controlling an alien experience—and to this extent making it a more tolerable one—than its being *self*-initiated and experienced as such. As Erikson puts it:

> A child who has just found himself able to walk, more or less coaxed or ignored by those around him, seems driven to repeat the act for the pure delight of functioning, and out of the need to master and perfect a newly initiated function. But he also acts under the immediate awareness of the new status and stature of "one who can walk," with whatever connotation this happens to have in the co-ordinates of his culture's space-time—be it "one who will go far," "one who will be able to stand on his own feet," "one who will be upright," or "one who must be watched because he might go too far." The internalization of a particular version of "one who can walk" is one of the many steps in child development which (through the coincident experience of physical mastery and of cultural meaning, of functional pleasure and of

> social prestige) contribute on each step to a more realistic self-esteem. This self-esteem grows to be a conviction that one is learning effective steps toward a tangible future, and is developing into a defined self within a social reality. The growing child must, at every step, derive a vitalizing sense of actuality from the awareness that his individual way of mastering experience (his ego synthesis) is a successful variant of a group identity and is in accord with its space-time and life plan [1963, p. 235].

Behaviors yielding such experiences are favored and so repeated. The experience is no longer alien; although negative, it is now part of "my" experience. The act reinforces the self-as-agent aspect of the self-schema ("I make it happen; I control the conditions of its happening"). Wolff's (1965) description of the attentional process in infants gives us a clue to the early importance of self-initiated activity. Hunger and bowel discomfort, external overstimulation, and sensorimotor feedback of diffuse activity produce changes in the attentional state of the organism, i.e., in how it *experiences* stimuli. Cognized loss itself becomes a stimulus to activity, and experiences of responses to self-initiated expressions of such loss become vital. An early preference for social objects adds importance to the self-initiated experiences that accompany the infant's transactions with the mother (p. 825).

Repeated thwarting of self-initiated activity, even in the infant, can be catastrophic. Bettelheim (1967) has proposed that in the most intractable form of autism the child had "given up" in infancy the possibility of self-initiation of action in the seeming belief that it was either impossible or to no avail. In his classic study of concentration-camp survivors, Bettelheim (1943) had earlier noted that survival seemed to depend on this possibility; the hardiest survivors were those who constantly sought out at least one area, no matter how small, in which they could "beat the game," one that offered the experience of the self as controller rather than as controlled, e.g., successfully stealing a scrap of food or a moment of rest. The total elimination of such possibilities resulted in despair and hopelessness.

Development of Cognitive Controls

The structural outcomes of behavior stemming from the reversal of voice are facts which are now internalized as the self's knowledge of the environment. The registration of information and the capacity to distinguish self from other are mutually reinforcing. To know himself as separate, the child must develop information about separateness. For example, in Freud's (1920) illustration, the child in repeating his game has learned something about the perceptual conditions of "absence" and "presence." The child totters and falls when learning to walk, destroys the tower he has built, but in doing so learns what it takes to make a tower stand.

One outcome of the informational coding and "incidental learning" that goes on in reversal-of-voice activities may be strategies of response that have been described as *cognitive controls:* field dependence-independence, leveling-sharpening, scanning, etc. Such strategies may be structuralized means developed by the person to deal with self-dystonic experiences, means that have proved effective for him over a range of circumstances. They represent tolerable adaptational levels that are serviceable in situations calling for integrative efforts.

While there is little in the way of tested information to link cognitive style to the dynamics of reversal-of-voice activity, a finding by Barclay and Cusumano (1967) is suggestive. They found that boys reared without fathers tended to be more field-dependent than were boys whose fathers were present. The authors relate the former tendency to a more "passive-receptive" reliance on the environment and a closer identification with the available maternal model "which usually includes an expressive rather than instrumental orientation to the environment" (p. 248).

Considerations of the origin of cognitive controls have usually dealt with whether they are "autonomous" or emerge from "defenses," usually construed as manifestations of repression. In the present view, not all cognitive controls originate in the context of repression.

Interpersonal Controls: Conversion of External Control to Self-Syntonic Control

Developmentally, perhaps the most interesting aspect of the reversal-of-voice principle is its usefulness in accounting for the internalization and structuring of interpersonal relationships. Loevinger (1966) has pointed out that one is controlled simultaneously or in turn by one's impulses and one's parents. One therefore needs to control something in return, if not one's parents then one's impulses. What one does in this respect becomes what one is. Interpersonal encounters involve the interplay of impulse and response to impulse, impulse experienced as self-syntonic or not, impulse and response as socially syntonic or not.

Reversal of voice *internalizes* such relational patterns, i.e., converts an *interpersonal* model into an *intrapersonal* schema which becomes an integral aspect of selfhood.[3] The paradigm of the development of internalized controls through successive reversals of voice is as follows:

1. He (she) does to me—I suffer what he (she) is doing to me.
2. I put myself (him) (her) in a replica situation—I make happen the experience (via play, substitute object, etc.).
3. What did or could happen to me—I do to my impulse (moral structure).
4. I control my impulse—part of "me"—as an ethical principle.

Through the reversal of voice there comes about the inner perpetuation of the child's subordination to the will of his elders, a development Freud called the "superego."

Erikson (1964, p. 223) has commented: ". . . the moral proclivity in man does not develop without the establishment of some chronic self-doubt." The child experiences enforced obedience to external authority as a passively endured, self-dystonic "blow." Wishing to destroy the restraint, but appreciating the danger of doing so, the child comes to turn his vengeance on that part of the self—the impulse—that provoked the restraint. This phase may have substages. At first, repetition of the experience may actually be tried out on the primary authority—but the child is likely to find this course too dangerous. He then assumes the role of the parent and treats part of himself as the parent treated him. At this stage the child often either takes out on other children what was done to him by the parent, or is more severe with himself than the parent would be in restraining the same action. Finally, the child reaches the point where "I no longer try to do to him what was done to me" but "I do to my impulse what was done to me," thus producing in himself a relationship of obedience to authority as a means of controlling both the passively experienced restraint and the impulse. The child has become internally differentiated, using an interpersonal relationship both as a model and as an impetus.[4] Shame and guilt become the responding signaling system of this internalized moral schema.

[3]Failure of reversal is experienced as rage in the infant and later as shame and humiliation.

[4]Freud has described the chronological sequence as follows: "First comes renunciation of instinct owing to fear of aggression by the *external* authority. (This is, of course, what fear of loss

Fundamentally, then, the internalizations that lead to moral values are the product of successive reversals of voice.

Moral development is here pictured as proceeding from internalized restraints in the form of moral strictures (associated with guilt and dread of punishment) to the level of ethical principles (associated with conscience and acceptance of responsibility for the action) which are so taken for granted as to be felt as "part of me" or "what I am." In the above account, identification with authority is pictured as an earlier phase of this process. At this stage, awareness of the commission of a wrong is not synonymous with conscience: arousal of guilt is associated simply with accepting authority's restraint of the impulse. Integration of the impulse in relation to self takes the form of accepting the moral stricture against it while disowning the impulse itself. Moral restraint is not yet on the level of self-criticism (see Freud, 1930, pp. 125-126).

Although we have stressed the role of reversal of voice in the development of superego controls, repression also has an important part in moral development. In the sequences described above, the two principles are cooperatively involved. In repression the internalization is accompanied by segregation from self accomplished in a variety of ways. Such efforts at dissociation seem evident at different stages of superego development. Anna Freud (1936), in her account of how a child internalizes adult criticism, seems to suggest that the two principles work alternately. In the early stage of superego formation, self-criticism is dissociated from the child's reprehensible acts and turned against the world. Criticism of the act is internalized, but the offense is not acknowledged as "one's own." Vehement indignation is directed at someone else's transgression, and this is the precursor of the guilt that later accompanies breaches of an ethical precept.

---

of love amounts to, for love is a protection against this punitive aggression.) After that comes the erection of an *internal* authority, and renunciation of instinct owing to fear of it—owing to fear of conscience. In this second situation bad intentions are equated with bad actions, and hence comes a sense of guilt and a need for punishment. The aggressiveness of conscience keeps up the aggressiveness of the authority" (1930, p. 128). ". . . the original infantile stage of conscience . . . is not given up . . . but persists. . . . Fate is regarded as a substitute for the parental agency. If a man is unfortunate it means that he is no longer loved by this highest power; and, threatened by such a loss of love, he once more bows to the parental representative in his super-ego—a representative whom, in his days of good fortune, he was ready to neglect. . . . It is remarkable how differently a primitive man behaves. If he has met with a misfortune, he does not throw the blame on himself but on his fetish, which has obviously not done its duty, and he gives it a thrashing instead of punishing himself" (pp. 126-127).

Identification

Identification refers to a reversal of roles in an interpersonal relationship that is brought into syntonicity with the self-schema. It seems to evolve in stages—from an initial stage where the role is associated with a specific figure to a final stage where the mode or role is an indistinguishable aspect of self-definition. Identification with a model is commonly associated with "imitation," and with a capacity for, as Balint (1931, p. 25) has described it, "identificatory thinking." While this emphasis on identification as a cognitive process is helpful, it must still be asked what the motives of identification are, what instigates the process.

The essential elements of and occasions for such incorporation of a model have been variously construed: as imitation of the father (or mother) in an early stage of constitutionally guided object relationships; as a mechanism of response to "lost object cathexis"; as the internalizing of parental values; as a reaction formation against sibling rivalry; as an aim-inhibited tender tie among group members; as a defense against aggression. But invoking identification to explain motives does not account for why the identification process itself was evoked. White (1963), for instance, speaks of identification as model-copying based on the admiration of "competence." But why the "admiration"? Moreover, imitation in which there is no important issue of self-integration and no sign of ensuing structural residue is not always distinguished from imitation in emotionally invested occasions which *does* leave a structural residue (as, for example, identification with the aggressor) and leads to a stabilized "incorporation" and accommodation of the self-schema.

The various occasions for incorporating a model listed above in fact share a common dynamic theme which simplifies the motivational context in which identification occurs: they all seem to be passively imposed, self-dystonic experiences. In childhood, identification implements *reversal* activities when the unity and autocracy of self are threatened—and for the growing child such circumstances are numerous.[5]

[5] Balint's comment is apropos: "What children so often sigh for—'when I'm grown up'—means, as we all know, 'when I can do everything I want to'. Thus identification is a means by which they seek to recapture their old position of autocracy; and this hope is increased by parents who, while being strict with their children, allow themselves every sort of indulgence. Most parents believe

Within this motivational context identification becomes a means of accomplishing the re-enactments and repetitions involved in reversals of passive experience. In this view, identification is not a principle which explains mastery or reversal of voice; it is itself accounted for by the reversal of voice principle. In identification with the parent, the parent's admonition (i.e., a pattern of relationship) is turned not upon the parent, but upon the impulse: the child is not only taking over the adult's criticism, he is making it part of what he is. Where superego issues are involved, identification is an instrument of control.

The nature of the passive experience, the requirements of control, can vary, and constitute the "motives" of reversal; identifications accordingly have differing significance as "solutions." For instance, the child must passively endure sexual changes that become especially clamorous at adolescence. Parental figures very early become active perpetrators and participants in many of these experiences. Through identification the force of such experiences is mitigated. Identification then becomes a shoring up of "narcissistic supplies." Narcissistic mortification and passive frustration are compensated for by the sense of power borrowed from the father and surrogates.

The "wish to be grown up" is similarly accounted for as a passively suffered "blow," giving rise to counteractions that lead to a sense of expanded control, a process which operates like a "drive" seeking "gratification" in alternative ways.

As Balint puts it:

> We know how much it injures a child's narcissism if he is obliged to put up with something against his will [p. 121].
>
> By way of summary, it may be said that identification never fails to reveal itself as a direct derivative of narcissism. Even though it sometimes looks as though it were a means towards doing without something and making an adaptation, it turns out in the end that it is clinging obstinately to its original aim, the defence of narcissism [p. 126].
>
> Thus, . . . in the last resort a child wishes to meet only its own beloved self [p. 98].

---

that they are educating their children for the tasks of life by exacting unquestioning obedience and limitless faith from them. But the facts are just the other way, and children are brought into closer contact with reality if they learn that even their parents are neither omnipotent nor infallible" (1931, p. 126).

Identification can also implement reversal of voice when the essential aim is reparation of self-esteem. In the example given above, the child expresses his anger at the doctor through playing doctor. The fact that the event is re-enacted more mercilessly in the game than in the child's actual experience suggests the reparative quality of the entire sequence. Identifications may occur, too, when a child profoundly dissatisfied with self draws sustenance from those who love him in spite of his imperfections.

In short, identification, through which the values, manners, and interpersonal modes of others are brought into relation to one's self, occurs when there is an experience of: (a) an uncontrolled impulse, (b) inadequacy of self-initiated control, (c) inability to control aggressive intent, (d) depletion produced by failures in love—all contexts of a passively suffered blow, insufficiency, or felt limitation requiring rectification. In all these instances of actively repeating what one has passively experienced, the structural products have to do with an extension of self.

> The attachment that we form with the external world by means of identification is far better described as . . . an extension of the ego. . . . [a] means of our making a larger and larger portion of the external world into a portion of our ego. . . .
>
> All this leads us to what will undoubtedly seem a paradoxical conclusion, namely, that a child is driven to have recourse to identification above all when he is overcome by painful impressions from which he has no other means of escape. And since running away or getting rid of a disturbing phenomenon is the least practicable method of defence in earliest childhood, identification is incomparably more important at that period of development than at any other time of life [Balint, 1931, pp. 96, 98, 99].

By such identifications, accommodation—differentiation of the self-schema—occurs. Experientially, when an identification is successful, there is no separation between "where I got this particular role from" and the role as distinctively "mine." Ego identity in no small measure comprises identifications, the motive power of which was active, continually applied, reversal of voice in the service of self-syntonicity. What one has done has become what one is. This conception of identification as deriving from reversal of voice is quite in keeping with

Freud's late view of identification not as a defense mechanism but as a crucial structuring *process* in ego and superego development.

Within this framework of the dynamics of self-development it is possible, for example, to see the Oedipal drama as a repetitive theme that occurs throughout life. Although Freud consigned the drama entirely to the ages of three or four, Erikson remarks on the difficulty of ascribing the power of the Oedipus myth solely to this infantile stage of life. From the perspective of the reversal-of-voice principle, both the infantile sexual aspect and the social significance of the Oedipus complex are accounted for within the larger theme of a self-schema that repeatedly needs to test this solution in encounters having a father-mother prototype. In Erikson's theory of personal identity, development is always social, always involves father and mother surrogates in some fashion. The original problem as well as the solutions once worked out reverberate throughout life. The Oedipus complex, then, is not a special phase but occurs in different forms throughout the life cycle. Its main efflorescence may be in the period that Erikson sees as dominated by the issues of "initiative." In this phase it can be a pervasive existential problem, rather than a merely "dynamic" one, as it would be in other periods. That is, the pre-adolescent's consciousness may be dominated by issues of how to surmount the frustrations and restraints of parental figures; and the guilt aroused by this struggle can block initiative at a critical phase of life. The essential theme, however, is repeatable throughout life—the father being replaced by the son, younger generations replacing the old. This really is the larger significance of the Oedipus myth; this is why it has such a hold on us.

Repression and Introjects

We have emphasized resolutions of crises which take the form of an accommodative revision of the self-schema through the reversal of voice. Repression is also related to the control of dystonic experience, and to issues of integrity and self-continuity. The strategy of control here is different, however, as are its consequences for development. Where reversal of voice takes the form of confrontation through re-experiencing, repression is condemnatory. Issues of self-continuity and integrity are resolved through dissociation from self; a relationship is internalized but disowned. From this standpoint, interpersonal schemata differ in their status as fractionated from or as in consonance with the self-schema. A repressed idea is not exposed to the organizing activity of conscious experiencing: this is the very means of preserving the integrity of the self-schema. Such a split-off, dissociated schema of interpersonal relationship we call an introject, as contrasted with an identification, which is the structural product of reversal of voice. We think of an introject as an organized schema with three components: image of the object; image of the self in interaction with that object; affective coloring of the object, image, and self-image at the time of interaction (e.g., rage and aggression). This last affective component is a critical aspect of the structure.

Like an identification, an introject has to do with the development and maintenance of self-unity. The question arises: When does one resort to reversal of voice, and when to repression? In general, repression is resorted to when experienced dissonance is of traumatic proportions, i.e., when the experience cannot be "re-enacted" by reversal of voice because of overwhelming fear and anxiety. Of course, what is traumatic in the experience is its *meaning*—its connotations of inescapable danger and fear of destruction, which are probably the crucial circumstances of repression (see Niederland, 1965). Crises experienced at traumatic intensity, events which evoke intense experiences of helplessness and blows to self-esteem, interpersonal encounters involving wishes accompanied by intense fear, anxiety, ambivalence, and rage—such emergencies requiring immediate control are likely to be met by the solution of ejection via dissociation, i.e., repression.

Anger, if accompanied by fear and anxiety, is an important instigator of repression. The most common occasion of anger is an experienced restraint. Responsiveness to anger becomes a crucial determinant of whether the restraint will be dealt with by reversal of voice or by repression. The mounting of anger into rage is especially important, for rage provokes anxiety. Fear of direct confrontation with the consequences of rage, and the increase of fear to the point of debilitating anxiety or panic, can provoke repression: the person believes he cannot act to reduce the danger and the accompanying anxiety. More benign affective signals may instigate a reversal of voice.

Thus the critical factor is the traumatic nature of the experienced encounter: terror, anxiety, helplessness. Quantitative differences in the "stimulus load" and probably constitutional differences of tolerance determine whether the person will resort to repression.

Why preserve such a traumatically experienced relationship as an internal construction? Surely not *every* painful experience is given internal representation. It may be that internalization provides a safety valve in case of recurrence. Preserving an encounter in a schematized form, as a dissociated prototype, makes possible the coding of related encounters in the future—events that may be more easily recognized and dealt with even if not anticipated.

Thus what is repressed is not an "object" but an interpersonal mode—a traumatically experienced relationship. An introject refers to a relationship associated with danger, anxiety, and fear. While from the point of view of an observer, an introject is a relational mode, from the subjective phenomenological (not necessarily conscious) point of view the introject is experienced as an alien presence (Schafer, 1968a). It is an inner presence "with which one feels a continuous or intermittent dynamic relationship." It presents itself as a person or part of a person, but in the manner of an "object"; it is felt as part of the body, or one's thought, but not as part of the self. It is felt as influencing, but not as capable of being influenced by, one's self. It may therefore be dealt with as one deals with an object or thing. Its valence may be positive, in the sense of a wished-for gratification, but a negative valence is more likely because the introjection took place under conditions that traumatically involved the self.

From this standpoint, defenses are viewed as maneuvers associated with introjected object relationships. Defensive activities in relation to an introjected figure may vary, e.g., in the ways described by Melanie Klein for dealing with "bad objects." Here the purpose is to master the "bad object" inside, because one cannot do so in reality. One has an interpersonal relationship with the figure on the level of defense, dissociated from self.

But the cognitive activity of the introject schema consists of more than "defense"; it also deals with or actively finds replicas in interpersonal encounters. The self-conception of one patient ran thus: "If I am to have my mother's love, I must be like her in all ways; and I must be stupid and illiterate." The schema is acted upon, but it is alien to the accepted self-identity. One might visualize displacement, condensation, and other primary-process operations linking different repressed systems to each other under the guiding principle of a common affective valence.

The same person may be the object of both identification and introjection, some aspects of the relationship being internalized in one form and some in the other. The child who "borrows" his father's power by being like him in one respect may also have an unconscious fantasy of him as a terrifying and castrating figure toward whom the child feels murderous impulses. Obviously the coexistence of a fractionated schema and a self-syntonic identification involving the same person can create a persistent conflict in identity formation. Through secondary accompaniments of guilt and shame, the activities of a segregated schema can be a constant source of anxiety.

Motivational Attributes of a Fractionated Schema

To appreciate the developmental implications of dissociated schemata, we must pause over how such schemata can be motivational. "Accepting" reality means making it self-related. Acceptance of a tendency into the self-schema via identification means accommodation, that is, response to the consequences of action, and the constant referral of such feedback to standards of self-syntonicity.

It is precisely accommodation that is absent in repression. A repressed idea is not amenable to correction by feedback. It involves messages sent but without a return, i.e., comprehension. In that respect, repressive behavior is "unthinking" behavior: impulses "act themselves out," so to speak, without comprehension. Indeed, the subjective experience accompanying behavior dominated by a repressed schema often has an aspect of "unthinkingness," of helplessness. (A good example of the purely assimilative activity induced by repression is Segal's [1963] description of a case of impulsive sexuality.) The repressed schema includes a tendency (e.g., a wish) which, like all tendencies once aroused, seeks an opportunity for "perceptual identity" (Freud): it states itself in action. While its affective aspects are uncomprehended, the schema is still very much an organizing influence in behavior. The "language" in which the introjected relationship states itself is that of symbolism, much like the essentially egocentric mode that Freud described for the dreamer and the child—an imaginary incorporation of the external world, and suppression of the consciousness of ego or self, with no subsidiary awareness of self as a responsible participant.

In this condition of assimilative activity, the schema operates: (1) as a code, i.e., circumstances are recognized and given conceptual status in terms of similarity to the schema (Piaget calls this aspect of a schema's motor activity "recognitive assimilation"). (2) As a scanning and searching structure. In the latter capacity, wishful aspects of the schema seek out, as it were, "nutriment" ("reproductive assimilation"), on the principle that all internal tensions require appropriate motoric release. Although unconnected to the self-schema, the fractionated schema seeks perceptual "support" or a perceived origin. In this respect the activity resembles the dreamer's search for points of resemblance in external images—in Piaget's terms, an assimilation of the imagined reality to the internal bodily sensations. (3) As a disguised substitute, i.e., a symbol, wherein actions take on meaning, not in a sign function but in producing an identity of the prototype of the schema—similar to the prototype, yet its similarity to the core meaning of the repressed relationship is incapable of being comprehended or recognized. Symbolic expression is indeed the only means of translating the schema into behavior which does not upset the required inhibition of comprehension. Thus the complexity of a relationship is "acted out" but not comprehended, and any cognitive expression it might receive is developed on the level of fantasy through substitute, disguised, symbolic identities.

Repetitive and persistent activity of repressed schemata may lead to further structural modifications of personality. For example, modes of gratification which previously brought satisfaction may be sought directly or substitutively, and become a highly generalized disposition. In this view, what Freud called "libidinal types," in which oral, anal, and genital modalities are prominent, would be not forms of "drive reduction" but motor symbolisms in which unconsciously schematized forms of interpersonal relationships are repeatedly expressed in symbolic behavior. (I bypass the question of the appropriateness of subdivision according to alleged instinctual stages.)

Although lack of comprehension is a critical accomplishment of effective repression, that does not mean that an activated repressed schema does not give rise to conscious experience. There has been confusion about the role of consciousness in repression. A difficult repression actually requires the collaboration of consciousness for its completion—experiences that implement acting out as well as other subjective accompaniments.

Experiences that reverberate from the activity of introjects are either devoid of understanding or are accompanied by delusion or illusion. The experience may be one of "being caused" rather than of "intending," of an inchoate need to solve without knowing what it is that has to be solved, of gaps in meaning, of despair. At the same time, the "recognitive assimilation" of encounters in the terms of an introject has a particularly intense realness, such as is possible only when consciousness and responsiveness to meanings have been denied to one's actions. Divorce from self-relatedness and its tool of conscious reflection—as occurs in the dreamer and in the egocentrically oriented child—entails the kind of belief that precludes any possibility of doubt. The reflective assessment of an introject which would make it comprehensible as a fantasy rather than as a reality is prevented by the dissociative process. Nothing seems more real or actual than a transference-produced characteristic of the therapist. He is what the patient experiences him to be.

It is when experiences can be admitted and positioned within the regions of self-as-agent, self-as-object, or self-as-locus of control that the "real" can be distinguished from illusion. How "real" an experience feels, and its mode or quality as a reality, depends upon bringing it into relationship to a parameter of self. On this basis one distinguishes illusion from fact, the implausible from the plausible, hallucination from actuality.

The qualities that characterize subjective experiences of introjects are distinctively different from those involving identifications. The avoidance of comprehension can take many behavioral forms and conscious attitudes, such as naïveté, oversensitivity (in order to avoid consequences), forgetting, pseudo stupidity, rationalization, and even delusional understanding. Such conditions of failed comprehension make possible "acting out."

In such acting out in terms of introject activity, self is experienced in the passive voice, as if it were in the vise of an alien presence—"of being done to"—a phenomenological fact that led to a tendency for theories to reify the personal or object aspect of introjection in such expressions as "good and bad objects," and to an unfortunate subordinating of the essential aspect of introjection as having to do with interpersonal relationships. The critical point is that in the introject relationship the self's relation to another is that of an "object"; the relationship is experienced as "outside," influencing "me." The self as an agent is denied, and an experiential split has occurred between the observing and experiencing aspects of self.

No such split is discernible in identification. There is synchrony between the self and the incorporated aspects of a relationship with another person. Actions in terms of this relationship are accompanied by feelings of intention—of wanting them to happen. They are seen as an appropriate aspect of self-continuity, this being produced by an equally appropriate accommodation of the self-schema. Where an imitated action is truly an identification, it is not felt *as* imitation. The young boy who repeats his father's words does not view this action as a repetition, but as his *own*, in his own voice. It is a relationship, in Piaget's terms, which has produced an equilibrium in the self-schema.

Unconscious Fantasy

Cognitively, the activity of an introject is an unconscious fantasy. Unconscious fantasy refers to the activity of internalized relationships that have the status of schemata dissociated from the self. The assimilation of a repressed interpersonal mode of relationship results in a repressed interpersonal schema which replicates the dilemma, conflicts, and wishes of that relationship.

When such a schema—an unconscious fantasy—gives meaning to an event or an encounter, defining it as useful or harmful, loving or unloving, these attributes ascribed to the environment are not merely coded but potentiated in the terms of the schema. The environment is endowed, so to speak, with the significance of the unconcious fantasy. In the organizing grip of unconscious fantasy, the person can be said to be living out his lies—living in a world of "invented situations populated with nonexisting figures." He behaves as if imaginary events, figures, and relationships were true. In Angyal's words, "This mythical conception usually attaches to certain selected people—e.g., to all those in authority, or to all women—and becomes the basis for irrational attitudes toward them. Much of the neurotic's implicit philosophy, which provides guidelines for his conduct, consists of similarly fantastic images and assumptions" (1965, p. 84). If, in therapy, this underlying philosophy is articulated to or by the patient in an abstract, generalized fashion, it will not mean much to him. But if he is confronted with a sufficient number of cases in which he has behaved as if he believed certain false things to be true, these "as ifs" gradually add up, and the patient reaches a point where he can himself discover the general pattern of his fantastic beliefs and the hierarchy of emotional syllogisms that constitutes his unconscious fantasy.

We have tended to equate assimilative, unconscious fantasy with passivity, but we must reiterate that only the subjective experience of being inexplicably "driven" is passive, in the sense that no responsibility for the acted-out message is admitted. The behavior-inducing activity of an unconscious fantasy is very potent; it has far-reaching effects in structuring reality for the person.

Among the behavioral indicators of unconscious fantasy, one of the most reliable is the inadequacy of a person's emotional responses to a situation: excessive or inappropriate responses, or an absence of an expected response, or repetition of certain responses. Perhaps most telling is that the person seems to live in a world of counterfeit images of himself, from which he seems to be peculiarly alienated. These indications may be accompanied by a sense of self-betrayal, a feeling that one is pretending, and profound despair.

Infantile Precursors

As in the case of reversal of voice, it is likely that repression too has infantile precursors, in this case, in the form of a primitive externalization process.

We earlier alluded to a possible infantile prototype of repression: in conditions of traumatic stimulus overload, and helplessness where stimulus messages are sent but none are received, the intolerable experience is dealt with by a kind of splitting. The infant, lacking a firm capacity for self-nonself distinctions, cannot distinguish the origins of his experiences. When such experiences are painful and terrifying, the source is condemned along with the experience. Such condemnation may occasion a massive withdrawal from experience. For example, Bettelheim points out that in autistic children, the extinction of all feeling, including pain, is heralded by a total repression of the hostility that develops from a profound "giving up" of any hope that messages will be responded to. This progress may begin extremely early, before actual attachment to a particular person has taken place.

Balint's (1931) summary of the development from externalization to a capacity for repression is worth quoting:

> Let us take as our starting point those cases in which a child feels as something alien to him a part of his body which is causing him pain. We see children holding an injured finger far away from them, being angry with it and not wanting to look at it. Or they talk about the organ that is tormenting them in the third person—'that naughty tummy'—and wish someone would buy them another one, and so on. It is as though this behaviour meant: 'I'm fond of myself; but what hurts me is naughty and I don't like it; that's not me at all'. On the one hand, therefore, everything that is not part of the ego is, to begin with, bad and alien, while on the other hand, there is an inclination to project into the external world everything in the ego that is disturbing [pp. 102-103].
>
> Thus in the splitting of the ego two forces play a part . . . one of these is identification with the behaviour of the environment and the other is projection of the portion of the ego which has become disagreeable precisely owing to that identification. It is probably only later, in connection with the development of the sense of reality, that there sets in repression—that is, a complete elimination from consciousness—of the affects and wishes which were in the first instance projected. For to begin with a child makes no distinction between his world of phantasy and reality. At that stage of development he is quite content with the fiction that the guilty foot does not belong to him. It is not until this notion becomes untenable that he is obliged to have recourse to repression. For something of which I know nothing can surely not be 'I': even the grownups must see that. Accordingly, it would be a necessary precondition of repression that we should have identified ourselves with the adult idea of reality [pp. 115-116].

When cognitive development has advanced to the stage where the child can experience conflict with self-conception, his natural tendency—to externalize the painful—becomes a capacity for repression in dealing with threats to the self-conception. Such threats must be denied accommodation—must not be allowed to modify the self-conception—for accommodation involves awareness of the meaning of the organizing terms of an encounter. Just such an occurrence must have taken place in instances of "primary repression"; accommodation encountered difficulties, whether through anxiety, fear, or associated punishment, or through persistent nonresponsiveness.

A replica of the encounter which produced these reactions is internalized as a schema, serving thereafter to subject analogous encounters to a process which denies them entry or acceptance into the self-schema.

I have delineated two principles of internalization through which interpersonal encounters acquire intrapersonal structuring; they are viewed as dynamic principles in having motivational consequences for behavior. Both principles are directed to requirements of self-continuity and integrity, but they differ critically in their impact on interpersonal experiences. Their structural products therefore deserve to be distinguished. The internalized representatives arising from the reversal of voice have the essential character of converting passively experienced, alien encounters into self-syntonic experience, and are called identifications. In the other case—repression—the internalized relationship is called an introjection.

My usage of these terms departs in certain respects from psychoanalytic convention. Introjection is commonly considered an aspect of identification, or vice versa. But if we keep in mind the essential difference in their dynamic origins, the distinctions between introjection and identification are more than semantic.

	A	*B*
Principle of Control	repression	reversal of voice
Structural Product	fractionated schema; introjection	self-syntonic schema; identification
Motivational Aims	defense; substitute gratification	self-congruent intention; purpose

In *A*, motivations remain centered on the objects of impulse and wish; in *B*, motivations are related to self-acknowledged interests and self-conception.

Although separate discussion of these principles has perhaps misleadingly given the impression that they develop independently, certain developmental formations are best viewed as the structural products of both. In clinical discussion, emphasis upon one principle to the exclusion of the other has tended to distort understanding of certain phenomena. For instance, it seems evident that "stages of superego formation" should be viewed not as exclusively the outcome of one or the other, but as a matter of varying emphasis, at different stages of childhood, on repression or on reversal of voice. In the following discussion we will look at three sets of phenomena in regard to which the orientation given by both principles can increase our understanding. Taking self as the critical center, it is useful to consider repression and "active repetition" as alternative and sometimes interacting means of preserving self-integrity and continuity throughout development.

Defense

Both repression and reversal of voice give rise to modes of control, but those in which repression is pre-eminent are particularly close to the meaning of defense. In this view, defense "mechanisms" are different modes of implementing repression, and secondarily of providing consummation of the repressed wish—strategies designed to ensure noncomprehension of unacceptable meanings, wishes, and affects.

When development has reached the stage where the preservation of self-unity has become an organismic requirement and repressive dissociation is possible, there develop a variety of means of meeting this requirement, all designed to maintain a repression. This is the essential meaning of defense and is in accord with the principle that anxiety and guilt are major "motives" of defense. It is also in keeping with Hartmann's (1939, p. 63) point that defenses actually prevent "assimilation" by cognitive means (Hartmann uses the term assimilation in a fashion that is identical with Piaget's meaning of accommodation). The essential aim of defense—to prevent an intolerable understanding of a critical meaning—may be accomplished in various ways. Defensive strategy may focus on intellection, emotion, or motor activity, separately or together. Within each of these spheres, the result is that of achieving unresponsiveness to feedback having to do with an alienated meaning of a repressed schema. In this view, a defense like "undoing" would be an attempt at reintegration and synthesis through a motor reaffirmation of the dissociation constituting the repression. (Freud in fact once referred to it as "motor repression.") It would be regarded not as a defense "mechanism" but as a defensive motivation, a behavioral pattern which implements the aim of repression. The presence or absence of consciousness can assist in certain forms of defense, as, for example, in rationalization and intellectualization.

Certain defensive maneuvers may also be throwbacks to behaviors and modes that were self-syntonic and effective at an earlier stage of development. Thus in certain circumstances the assimilative strategies of an earlier time will come into play again in a time of crisis—will be reapplied to new circumstances. Overeating or other oral emphases in certain circumstances may have the meaning of an earlier mode of defensive pleasure.

How different defensive modes actually develop is far from being well understood in psychoanalysis. A perhaps important principle of "choice" of means is that instrumentalities most easily available to the developing child either by maturation or inclincation ("gifts") are enlisted for defensive purposes. Sensory abilities, talents, skills, verbal capacities, motor aptitudes, and the like, may form the instrumental core of defensive patterns.

Although repression is at the basis of defenses whose central functional objective is a failure of comprehension, it is not contradictory to suppose that some defenses are compounded of both repression and reversal of voice: obsessional tendencies, for instance, can be interpreted as such a phenomenon. Obsessional behavior on the one hand reflects the repetitive assimilative type of thinking induced by the activity of a repressed idea in which there is also a notable absence of insight into the meanings of the thoughts and repetitions. However, according to the reversal-of-voice principle, all passively experienced stimulation leads to efforts to make it self-syntonic. This aspect seems to be reflected in the positively amplified self-preoccupations that accompany obsessional experience. The obsessive rumination, *felt* as self-alien, evokes repetition by virtue of this self-dystonia. The result in subjective experience, reflecting both principles, is self-preoccupation without resolution, a prominent condition of the neurotic generally.

Repetition Compulsion

A persistent problem for psychoanalytic theory has been the group of phenomena referred to by Freud as compulsive repetitions. It was earlier thought that such phenomena are manifestations of instinctual drives pressing for "discharge." More recently, the emphasis has been on the "ego's" participation in such repetitions (Hartmann, Bibring, Mahler). However, to speak of the ego's "use" of the repetition compulsion seems to say little about the origin of such motivation. It fails to distinguish the repetitions induced by repression per se from the repetitive behaviors described by Piaget as emanating from the search for "aliment," the achievement of competence.

The problem of repetition would benefit from a revised perspective in which self, rather than an impersonal ego, is the structural focus of explanation. In going into the motives of repetition, one asks what is the essential dynamic locus of behaviors that have the character of active repetition; in this regard, ego explanations which speak simply of "control" are insufficiently explicit. For example, defenses associated with repression are also "controls" and in that sense are of the "ego," but defenses are by no means synonymous with those "controls" emanating from reversal of voice activities.

To explain repetition phenomena, then, it seems to me that two considerations should be held in mind: first, the importance of centering explanations on the relation of repetition to self-identity and unity; second, that the roles of reversal of voice and repression be distinguished as contributing to repetition; repetitive behaviors are induced by both, but are functionally quite different. The need to reduce dissonances in respect to self-identity and self-continuity is an essential motivational source of active repetitions. As we have seen, this seems to be especially important in the development of superego controls, moral concern, and guilt. Here considerations of "What I am," "What I was," What I ought to be"—aspects of the self-schema —are directly involved in what Loewald (1971) has properly emphasized as a moral component in certain active, repetitive behaviors.

As for the second point: to account for repetitive phenomena, the dynamic processes described in this chapter must be distinguished—symbolic replications of an active unconscious fantasy, and the repetitive efforts toward ego-syntonicity and mastery in the reversal of voice. In general, repetitions engendered by reversal of voice have the character of actions of responsibility, of conscious avowal and reorganization, what Loewald calls active, re-creative repetition; the primary aim of repetition from this source is to make an experience syntonic, as, for example, in repeatedly talking about an experience which has involved anxiety or a loss of self-esteem. These are different in aim and quality from repetitions of the compulsive type. The latter are dramatic clinical reminders that repressed ideas are not inactive, that repressed schemas induce behaviors of a passive, repetitive kind. Kubie (1939, 1941) was among the first to point out that regarding the "compulsion to repeat" as a distinctive motivational force is something of a pseudo issue. It is of the nature of a repressed impulse to clamor continually for expression and behavior; this will be accomplished, and repeatedly, by whatever means do not threaten the repression. Compulsive, passive repetition, then, is simply the manifestation of repressed ideation denied feedback from conscious organization.

The "repetition compulsion," then, is not a single phenomenon—what is repeated, toward what end, and in what form are critical considerations. The two principles described in this chapter provide a guide for interpretation as well as for distinguishing among a variety of repetition phenomena. In this light, we list some varieties of repetition:

1. Those that reflect a repressed wish or unconscious fantasy which is stating itself repeatedly either through symbol or action. If there is no response to feedback, an activated impulse or wish is repetitively manifested.

2. Replica induction, e.g., the repeated manifestations of an introjected, unconscious relationship which reproduces the dynamically unconscious prototype.

3. Automatism occurring in states of dissociation.

4. Interruptions of "ego-involved" tasks which give rise to incentives for completion and repetition (e.g., phenomena of the Zeigarnik type).

5. "Pleasure in functioning" repetition, as, for example, when the child repeats his efforts to walk in the wake of success experienced with his first steps.

6. The "working-off" of anxiety by repetitive, e.g., counterphobic, behavior (Bibring, 1943).

7. Imitative internalizations of a model's behavior via identification.

8. Transference repetitions which combine both acting out and mastery via identification with the therapist.

9. Symbolic repetitions in art-making: the art-making process itself, and its other aspect, the repetition of significant repressed contents through art.

To account for these varieties of repetition it is helpful to ask what each means for self-identity, for the aims of repetition are to be understood in relation to this aspect of the ego, and in terms of whether the repetition exhibits activity of the repressed on the one hand and efforts at reversal of voice on the other. For example, when we encounter repetition in therapy it is important to consider whether it is simply acting out (in the old metapsychological terminology, "discharge"), or whether it indicates efforts—in a new, uncertain step toward mastery—at self-governed re-creations and evaluations of what before was passively suffered. This is in fact what we encourage in therapy, but it is an arduous process not always welcomed by the patient, and a source of considerable resistance. It is the contemporary interpretation of the classical therapeutic aim of "undoing a repression."

Transference Repetitions

In the last paragraph, our discussion of the repetition compulsion alluded to the fact that transference phenomena express both reversal of voice and repressed introject activity. Besides the passive repetitions by which unconscious prototypes are experienced and acted out in relation to the therapist, transference also involves the creation of similar relationships on a "higher level of organizing potential," as Loewald (1971, p. 60) put it, which lead to self-syntonic differentiations, novel configurations, and novel resolutions in which identification with the therapist itself plays a crucial part. This aspect of transference is actually a critical criterion of growth in therapy. The aims of these forms of transference repetition differ. For example, the Oedipus problem is not "settled" and left behind in early childhood; it is reactivated in adolescence, and flares up again in analysis, but here the therapeutic path steers it to repetition in an active manner, at a "higher level of organizing potential," involving novel, self-syntonic resolutions. The repetition is not simply the reviving of the repressed schema in the therapeutic situation, but an active confrontation of the self with the feelings, mourning, fears, and anxieties experienced earlier in the Oedipal situation. This is creative repetition, concentrated in the person of the therapist.

In viewing transference in terms both of passive, reproductive repetitions which mirror unconscious fantasies, and of active, creative repetitions which occur via identification with the analyst, Loewald has made an important advance in the theory of transference. He refers to passive transference repetition as reproductive and absorptive—what we termed the primacy of assimilation, the activity of a repressed schema. Reconstruction of this schema is for him accomplished in recreative repetition, or what we have called accommodation. In summary, to quote Loewald:

> Psychoanalysis has always maintained that the life of the individual is determined by his infantile history, his early experiences and conflicts; but everything depends on *how* these early experiences are repeated in the course of life, to what extent they are repeated *passively*—suffered again even if "actively" rearranged, —and to what extent they can be taken over in the ego's organizing activity and made over into something new—a re-creation of something old as against a duplication of it. In such re-creation the old is mastered, where mastery does not mean elimination of it but dissolution, and reconstruction out of the elements of destruction [1971, p. 60].

Therapeutic Implications

We have remarked that progress mirrors normal processes of growth. If re-experiencing is important in self-differentiation and mastery, so is it a vital element of therapeutic progress. Thus the principle of reversal is used in dealing with repression. The analyst capitalizes on the principle that passively experienced blows can lead to efforts at reversal. The first task is that of confronting the patient with self-dissociated patterns through their repetitions in transference. From the stage of reproductive acting out, the patient is urged toward active, creative re-experiencing of the meaning of these repetitions. This is the stage of derealization, spoken of earlier, and from it develops, optimally, dissolution or reconstitution of interpersonal schemata within the self-schema. In this context of self-integrative (in contrast to reproductive) repetitions (acting out) of conflicts of psychosexual development, early object relationships, and traumatic experiences, the prototypical unconscious relationships attain assimilative and accommodative restatement.

If bringing unconscious patterns to light in analysis is effective, it is not simply because it is abreactive in the sense of a release of an energic quantity of "strangulated affect." As Loewald says, "The patient is not merely to be made aware of the existence of such contents in his psyche, but he is asked . . . to own up to them as *his* wishes and conflicts and defences, to re-experience them as psychic activity of a non-automatic nature" (1971, p. 62). Experienced ownership and responsibility are the key objectives. Freud's adage, "Where id was, there ego shall be," comes to be construed as an appeal to standards of responsibility in which experience is related to a self which seeks meaning and continuity and an altered perspective toward the future. One repeats in order to anchor one's self in the present; but the repetition is endowed not with unconscious fantasy but with selfhood enlarged by newly developed identifications with the therapist. This is of course the essential aspect of identification, and it is in relation to these crises of growth in therapy that identification, as in normal development, also occurs in therapy. Here too identification does not occur simply for the sake of mastery but for the sake of achieving self-unity through extending the region of effective control consonant with self-identity.

It is in this sense of bringing about repetitions that lead to self-syntonic control and differentiation that emotional comprehension becomes a primary objective in therapy. The phrase implies experiencing a meaning at the level of its unconsciously effective core—namely, as an emotional syllogism. "Acting out" an unconscious fantasy reiterates an affective value in action in terms of which behaviors have acquired their significance. Comprehension involves experiencing this syllogism in its emotional aspect, appreciating its self-dissociated aspect, and daring to confront the turmoil that accompanies conscious appreciation of its dissonant relations to the self-schema. Thus the value aspect of an unconscious syllogism is its affective significance. This is the condition for bringing about accommodation of the schema and resolving its status vis-à-vis self-identity. Understanding of an introjected relationship is not a matter of verbal articulation; it is an experiential matter. Conceptualization of a relationship is not enough; it must be re-experienced in its feeling aspect, for the feeling aspect is a vital part of the intrinsic meaning of the action parts of the schema; it defines the value aspect of an idea for the self. Since the emotional aspect of the unconscious syllogism gives it its cohesion, meaning, and intensity, it is this emotional aspect that can be comprehended only be being directly experienced in the process of therapeutic accommodation. Of course, affective experience lends itself to separation from the verbal and intellectual, and this provides an all-too-easy escape from affective reiterations to pseudo understanding. Analysis as yet has no easy answers to this difficulty.

Toward a Theory of Art and Creativity

Together, the two principles provide a framework for viewing the origins and development of impulses that go into the making of art. An essential dynamic of the art-making process would be that it converts the clamor of unconscious fantasies, passively experienced, to self-initiated versions accomplished through the creation of forms. In this interpretation, art-making would be, in an important sense, reparative. It is a manifestation of reversal of voice achieved through the symbolic re-experiencing of fractionated fantasies. The artist is born in the discovery of a skill that he intuitively senses as capable of producing structural outcomes that have bearing upon and utility for re-experiencing the replica-inducing symbols of unconscious fantasy. An incentive for commanding a medium such as paint is joined to such an effort, and those who have made this discovery are the potential artists. In this view, resort to art-making through an expressive medium would have its genesis especially in circumstances where social and interpersonal failure is intensely experienced, to the extent of its being a profound assault on self-conception. The successes of practice and the mastery experienced over recurrent activations of fractionated repressed schemata further encourage the process. The issue of how much these principles are involved by the form-making activity of art must be deferred to other occasions for exploration.

The two organizing principles compared in this chapter present the paradox that repression, no less than the reversal of passive experience into activity, has the essential aim of confronting threats to self-integrity and continuity. But, inevitably, the simultaneous operation of the principles promotes conflict and even pathology. The same person who figures largely as an object of identification in respect to certain sectors of relationships may be introjected in other relational aspects, hemmed in by fear and anxiety, which are internalized in a fractionated condition. The father identified with in one respect is in other respects internalized via introjection. In this fashion are difficulties and ambivalence created. Harassment from the dissonant schema can create poignant conditions of conflicted identification, and pathological motives may arise from efforts to resolve impasses created by this source.

REFERENCES

Adams, D. K. (1954), Learning and Explanation. In: *Learning Theory, Personality Theory, and Clinical Research:* The Kentucky Symposium, by D. K. Adams et al. New York: Wiley, pp. 66-80.

Adrian, E. D. (1946), The Mental and the Physical Sources of Behavior. *Internat. J. Psycho-Anal.*, 27:1-6.

Alexander, F. (1935), The Logic of Emotions and Its Dynamic Background. *Internat. J. Psycho-Anal.*, 16:399-413.

Allport, G. W. (1964), The Fruits of Eclecticism—Bitter or Sweet? *Acta Psychol.*, 23:27-44.

Angyal, A. (1965), *Neurosis and Treatment: A Holistic Theory*. New York: Wiley.

Apfelbaum, B. (1965), Ego Psychology, Psychic Energy, and the Hazards of Quantitative Explanation in Psycho-Analytic Theory. *Internat. J. Psycho-anal.*, 46: 168-181.

______ (1966), On Ego Psychology: A Critique of the Structural Approach to Psycho-Analytic Theory. *Internat. J. Psycho-Anal.*, 47:451-475.

Arlow, J. A. (1963), Conflict, Regression, and Symptom Formation. *Internat. J. Psycho-Anal.*, 44:12-22.

______ (1966), Depersonalization and Derealization. In: *Psychoanalysis—A General Psychology*, ed. R. M. Loewenstein et al. New York: International Universities Press, pp. 456-478.

______ & Brenner, C. (1964), *Psychoanalytic Concepts and the Structural Theory*. New York: International Universities Press.

Arnheim, R. (1954), *Art and Visual Perception*. Berkeley: University of California Press.

Baldwin, A. L. (1967), *Theories of Child Development*. New York: Wiley.

Balint, A. (1931), *The Early Years of Life. A Psychoanalytic Study*. New York: Basic Books, 1954.

Barclay, A., & Cusumano, D. R. (1967), Father Absence, Cross-Sex Identity, and Field-Dependent Behavior in Male Adolescents. *Child Devel.*, 38:243-250.

Bartlett, F. C. (1932), *Remembering: A Study in Experimental and Social Psychology*. Cambridge: Cambridge University Press.

Beebe-Center, J. G. (1932), *The Psychology of Pleasantness and Unpleasantness*. New York: Van Nostrand.

Berlyne, D. E. (1965), *Structure and Direction in Thinking*. New York: Wiley.

Bettelheim, B. (1943), Individual and Mass Behavior in Extreme Situations. *J. Abnorm. Soc. Psychol.*, 38:417-452.

______ (1967), *The Empty Fortress*. New York: Free Press.

Bibring, E. (1943), The Conception of the Repetition Compulsion. *Psychoanal. Quart.*, 12:486-519.

_____ (1953), The Mechanism of Depression. In: *Affective Disorders,* ed. P. Greenacre. New York: International Universities Press, pp. 13-48.

Bowlby, J. (1969), *Attachment and Loss,* Vol. 1. New York: Basic Books.

Brackbill, Y. (1958), Extinction of the Smiling Response in Infants as a Function of Reinforcement Schedule. *Child Devel.*, 29:115-124.

Breuer, J., & Freud, S. (1893-1895), Studies on Hysteria. *Standard Edition,* 2. London: Hogarth Press, 1955.

Bruner, J. (1968), Report at Colloqium on Affect and Cognition. Meeting of the American Psychoanalytic Association, May.

Brunswik, E. (1956), *Perception and the Representative Design of Psychological Experiments.* Berkeley: University of California Press.

Buber, M. (1929), Dialogue. *Between Man and Man,* trans. R. G. Smith. London: Routledge & Kegan Paul, 1947, pp. 1-39.

Buchenholz, B. (1956), The Motivating Action of Pleasure. *J. Nerv. Ment. Dis.*, 124:569-577.

_____ (1957), The Pleasure Process. *J. Nerv. Ment. Dis.*, 125:396-402.

Bühler, K. (1928), Displeasure and Pleasure in Relation to Activity. In: *Feelings and Emotions,* ed. C. Murchison. Worcester, Mass.: Clark University Press, pp. 195-199.

_____ (1930), *The Mental Development of a Child.* New York: Harcourt, Brace.

Call, J. D. (1964), Newborn Approach Behavior and Early Ego Development. *Internat. J. Psycho-Anal.*, 45:286-294.

Clark, B., & Graybiel, A. (1957), The Break-Off Phenomenon: A Feeling of Separation from the Earth Experienced by Pilots at High Altitude. *J. Aviat. Med.*, 28:121-126.

Dahl, H. (1972), A Quantitative Study of a Psychoanalysis. *Psychoanalysis and Contemporary Science,* 1:237-257. New York: Macmillan.

Edelheit, H. (1967), Binswanger and Freud. *Psychoanal. Quart.*, 36:85-90.

Eidelberg, L. (1962), A Contribution to the Study of the Unpleasure-Pleasure Principle. *Psychiat. Quart.*, 36:312-316.

Eissler, K. R. (1965), *Medical Orthodoxy and the Future of Psychoanalysis.* New York: International Universities Press.

Erikson, E. H. (1954), The Dream Specimen of Psychoanalysis. *J. Amer. Psychoanal. Assn.*, 2:5-56.

_____ (1955), Freud's "The Origins of Psycho-Analysis." *Internat. J. Psycho-Anal.*, 36:1-15.

_____ (1956), The Problem of Ego Identity. In: Identity and the Life Cycle. *Psychol. Issues,* Monogr. No. 1. New York: International Universities Press, 1959, pp. 101-171.

_____ (1958), *Young Man Luther.* New York: Norton.

_____ (1963), *Childhood and Society,* 2nd ed. New York: Norton.

_____ (1964), *Insight and Responsibility.* New York: Norton.

_____ (1968a), *Identity: Youth and Crisis.* New York: Norton.

_____ (1968b), Life Cycle, *International Encyclopedia of the Social Sciences,* 9: 286-292. New York: Macmillan & Free Press.

_____ (1969), *Gandhi's Truth.* New York: Norton.

_____ (1970), Reflections on the Dissent of Contemporary Youth. *Internat. J. Psycho-Anal.*, 51:11-22.

Fairbairn, W. R. D. (1952), *Psychoanalytic Studies of the Personality.* New York: Basic Books.

Federn, P. (1929), The Ego as Subject and Object in Narcissism. *Ego Psychology and the Psychoses*. New York: Basic Books, 1952, pp. 283-322.
Fingarette, H. (1963), *The Self in Transformation*. New York: Basic Books.
Fisher, C. (1966), Dreaming and Sexuality. In: *Psychoanalysis—A General Psychology*, ed. R. M. Loewenstein et al. New York: International Universities Press, pp. 537-569.
Ford, C. S., & Beach, F. A. (1951), *Patterns of Sexual Behavior*. New York: Harper.
Fraiberg, S. (1967), The Origins of Human Bonds. *Commentary*, 44(6):47-57.
Freud, A. (1936), *The Ego and the Mechanisms of Defence* New York: International Universities Press, 1946.
Freud, S. (1895), Project for a Scientific Psychology. *Standard Edition*, 1:295-397. London: Hogarth Press, 1966.
______ (1896), The Aetiology of Hysteria. *Standard Edition*, 3:191-221. London: Hogarth Press, 1962.
______ (1898) Sexuality in the Aetiology of the Neuroses. *Standard Edition*, 3:263-285. London: Hogarth Press, 1962.
______ (1899), Screen Memories. *Standard Edition*, 3:301-323. London: Hogarth Press, 1962.
______ (1900), The Interpretation of Dreams. *Standard Edition*, 4 & 5. London: Hogarth Press, 1953.
______ (1905a), Fragment of an Analysis of a Case of Hysteria. *Standard Edition*, 7:7-122. London: Hogarth Press, 1953.
______ (1905b), Three Essays on the Theory of Sexuality *Standard Edition*, 7:130-243. London: Hogarth Press, 1953.
______ (1905c), Jokes and Their Relation to the Unconscious. *Standard Edition*, 8. London: Hogarth Press, 1960.
______ (1909), Analysis of a Phobia in a Five-Year-Old Boy. *Standard Edition*, 10:5-149. London: Hogarth Press, 1955.
______ (1911), Formulations on the Two Principles of Mental Functioning. *Standard Edition*, 12:218-226. London: Hogarth Press, 1958.
______ (1912), The Dynamics of Transference. *Standard Edition*, 12:99-108. London: Hogarth Press, 1958.
______ (1914), On the History of the Psycho-Analytic Movement. *Standard Edition*, 14:7-66. London: Hogarth Press, 1957.
______ (1915), Repression. *Standard Edition*, 14:146-158. London: Hogarth Press, 1957.
______ (1916-1917), Introductory Lectures on Psycho-Analysis. *Standard Edition*, 15 & 16. London: Hogarth Press, 1963.
______ (1920), Beyond the Pleasure Principle. *Standard Edition*, 18:7-64. London: Hogarth Press, 1955.
______ (1923), Two Encyclopaedia Articles. (A) Psycho-Analysis. *Standard Edition*, 18:235-254. London: Hogarth Press, 1955.
______ (1924), The Economic Problem of Masochism *Standard Edition*, 19:159-170. London: Hogarth Press, 1961.
______ (1925), An Autobiographical Study. *Standard Edition*, 20:7-70. London: Hogarth Press, 1959.
______ (1926), Inhibitions, Symptoms and Anxiety. *Standard Edition*, 20:87-172. London: Hogarth Press, 1959.
______ (1930), Civilization and Its Discontents. *Standard Edition*, 21:64-145. London: Hogarth Press, 1961.

______ (1933), New Introductory Lectures on Psycho-Analysis. *Standard Edition,* 22:5-182. London: Hogarth Press, 1964.

______ (1940), An Outline of Psychoanalysis. *Standard Edition,* 23:144-207. London: Hogarth Press, 1964.

Gaffron, M. (1956), Some New Dimensions in the Phenomenal Analysis of Visual Experience. *J. Pers.*, 24:285-307.

Gibson, J. J. (1967), The Mouth as an Organ for Laying Hold on the Environment. In: *Symposium on Oral Sensation and Perception,* ed. J. E. Bosma. Springfield, Ill.: Charles C Thomas, pp. 111-136.

Gill, M. M. (1963), Topography and Systems in Psychoanalytic Theory. *Psychol. Issues,* Monogr. No. 10. New York: International Universities Press.

______ & Paul, I. H. (manuscript), The Differential Effect of Paired Appropriate and Inappropriate Interventions in Psychoanalysis.

Gottschalk, L. A., & Gleser, G. C. (1969), *The Measurement of Psychological States through the Content Analysis of Verbal Behavior.* Berkeley: University of California Press.

Harlow, H. F. (1958), The Nature of Love. *Amer. Psychol.*, 13:673-685.

Hartmann, H. (1939), *Ego Psychology and the Problem of Adaptation.* New York: International Universities Press, 1958.

______ (1948), Comments on the Psychoanalytic Theory of Instinctual Drives. *Essays on Ego Psychology.* New York: International Universities Press, 1964, pp. 69-89.

______ (1950), Comments on the Psychoanalytic Theory of the Ego. *Essays on Ego Psychology.* New York: International Universities Press, 1964, pp. 113-141.

______ (1951), Technical Implications of Ego Psychology. *Essays on Ego Psychology.* New York: International Universities Press, 1964, pp. 142-154.

______ (1952), The Mutual Influences in the Development of Ego and Id. *Essays on Ego Psychology.* New York: International Universities Press, 1964, pp. 155-181.

______ (1956), The Development of the Ego Concept in Freud's Work. *Essays on Ego Psychology.* New York: International Universities Press, 1964, pp. 268-296.

______, Kris, E., & Loewenstein, R. M. (1945-1962), Papers on Psychoanalytic Psychology. *Psychol. Issues,* Monogr. No. 14. New York: International Universities Press, 1964.

Hebb, D. O. (1960), The American Revolution. *Amer. Psychol.*, 15:735-745.

Heider, F. (1926-1959), On Perception, Event Structure, and the Psychological Environment: Selected Papers. *Psychol. Issues,* Monogr. No. 3. New York: International Universities Press, 1959.

______ (1958), *The Psychology of Interpersonal Relations.* New York: Wiley.

Held, R., & Hein, A. V. (1958), Adaptation of Disarranged Hand-Eye Coordination Contingent upon Re-afferent Stimulation. *Percept. Motor Skills,* 8:87-90.

Held, R., & Schlank, M. (1959), Adaptation to Disarranged Eye-Hand Coordination in the Distance-Dimension. *Amer. J. Psychol.*, 72:603-605.

Hendrick, I. (1942), Instinct and the Ego during Infancy. *Psychoanal. Quart.*, 11: 33-58.

______ (1943a), Work and the Pleasure Principle. *Psychoanal. Quart.*, 12:311-329.

______ (1943b), The Discussion of the "Instinct to Master." *Psychoanal. Quart.*, 12:561-565.

Hernández-Peón, R. (1964), Attention, Sleep, Motivation and Behavior. In: *The Role of Pleasure in Behavior,* ed. R. G. Heath. New York: Hoeber-Harper.

Herold, C. M. (1941-1942), Critical Analysis of the Elements of Psychic Functions. *Psychoanal. Quart.*, 10:513-544; 11:59-82, 187-210.

Hochberg, J. (1964), *Perception*. Englewood Cliffs, N. J.: Prentice-Hall.

Holt, R. R. (1965), A Review of Some of Freud's Biological Assumptions and Their Influence on His Theories. In: *Psychoanalysis and Current Biological Thought*, ed. N. S. Greenfield & W. C. Lewis. Madison: University of Wisconsin Press, pp. 93-124.

______ (1967), Beyond Vitalism and Mechanism: Freud's Concept of Psychic Energy. In: *Science and Psychoanalysis*, 11:1-41. New York: Grune & Stratton.

______ (1968), Sigmund Freud. *International Encyclopedia of the Social Sciences*, 6:1-12. New York: Macmillan & Free Press.

Holzman, P. S., Rousey, C., & Snyder, C. (1966), On Listening to One's Own Voice: Effects on Psychophysiological Responses and Free Associations. *J. Pers. Soc. Psychol.*, 4:432-441.

Home, H. J. (1966), The Concept of Mind. *Internat. J. Psycho-Anal.*, 47:42-49.

Huizinga, J. (1950), *Homo Ludens: A Study of the Play Element in Culture*. Boston: Beacon Press, 1955.

Hunt, J. McV. (1965), Intrinsic Motivation. In: *Nebraska Symposium on Motivation, 1965*, ed. D. Levine. Lincoln: University of Nebraska Press.

Jacobson, E. (1953), The Affects and Their Pleasure-Unpleasure Qualities in Relation to the Psychic Discharge Processes. In: *Drives, Affects, Behavior*, ed. R. M. Loewenstein. New York: International Universities Press, pp. 38-66.

______ (1963), *The Self and the Object World*. New York: International Universities Press.

______ (1967), *Psychotic Conflict and Reality*. New York: International Universities Press.

Jones, E. (1953), *The Life and Work of Sigmund Freud*, Vol. 1. New York: Basic Books.

Kanzer, M., & Eidelberg, L. (1960), The Structural Description of Pleasure. *Internat. J. Psycho-Anal.*, 41:368-371.

Kardiner, A., Karush, A., & Ovesey, L. (1959), A Methodological Study of Freudian Theory: II. The Libido Theory. III. Narcissism, Bisexuality and the Dual Instinct Theory. *J. Nerv. Ment. Dis.*, 129:133-193, 207-221.

Kaufman, I. C. (1960), Some Theoretical Implications from Animal Behavior Studies for the Psychoanalytic Concepts of Instinct, Energy, and Drive. *Internat. J. Psycho-Anal.*, 41:318-326.

Kaufmann, W. A. (1961), *The Faith of a Heretic*. Garden City, N Y.: Doubleday.

Kellogg, R. (1969), *Analyzing Children's Art*. Palo Alto, Cal.: Natural Press Books.

Kenny, A. (1963), *Action, Emotion and Will*. London: Routledge & Kegan Paul.

Klein, G. S. (1959), Consciousness in Psychoanalytic Theory: Some Implications for Current Research in Perception. *Perception, Motives, and Personality*. New York: Knopf, 1970, pp. 235-263.

______ (1962), Blindness and Isolation. *Perception, Motives, and Personality*. New York: Knopf, 1970, pp. 310-321.

______ (1965), On Hearing One's Own Voice: An Aspect of Cognitive Control in Spoken Thought. *Perception, Motives, and Personality*. New York: Knopf, 1970, pp. 322-353.

______ (1967), Peremptory Ideation: Structure and Force in Motivated Ideas. In: Motives and Thought: Psychoanalytic Essays in Honor of David Rapaport, ed. R. R. Holt. *Psychol. Issues*, Monogr. No. 18/19:80-128.

______ & Wolitzky, D. L. (1967), Occluding Audible Feedback from One's Own Voice. In: *The Organization of Human Information Processing*; Report of the

Symposium of the XVIII International Congress of Psychology, Moscow, 1966, ed. F. Kliz. Berlin: Akademic-Verlag, pp. 157-174.

Koch, S. (1956), Behavior as "Intrinsically" Regulated: Work Notes toward a Pre-theory of Phenomena Called "Motivational." In: *Nebraska Symposium on Motivation, 1956*, ed. M. R. Jones. Lincoln: University of Nebraska Press, pp. 42-87.

______ (1961), The Allures of Ameaning in Modern Psychology: An Inquiry into the Rift between Psychology and the Humanities. In: *Science and Human Affairs*, ed. R. Farson. Palo Alto, Cal.: Science and Behavior Books, 1965.

______ (1969a), Psychology Cannot Be a Coherent Science. In: *Readings for an Introduction to Psychology*, ed. R. A. King. New York: McGraw-Hill, 1971.

______ (1969b), Value Properties: Their Significance for Psychology, Axiology, and Science. In: Toward a Unity of Knowledge, ed. M. Grene. *Psychol. Issues*, Monogr. No. 22:251-279. New York: International Universities Press.

Koestler, A. (1968), *The Ghost in the Machine*. New York: Macmillan.

Kohut, H. (1959), Introspection, Empathy, and Psychoanalysis: An Examination of the Relationship between Mode of Observation and Theory. *J. Amer. Psychoanal. Assn.*, 7:459-483.

Kris, E. (1932-1952), *Psychoanalytic Explorations in Art*. New York: International Universities Press, 1952.

______ (1951), Ego Psychology and Interpretation in Psychoanalytic Therapy. *Psychoanal. Quart.*, 20:15-30.

Kubie, L. S. (1939), A Critical Analysis of the Concept of a Repetition Compulsion. *Internat. J. Psycho-Anal.*, 20:390-402.

______ (1941), The Repetitive Core of Neurosis. *Psychoanal. Quart.*, 10:23-43.

______ (1952), The Place of Emotions in the Feedback Concept. In: *Cybernetics: Circular, Causal and Feedback Mechanisms in Biological and Social Systems*, ed. H. von Foerster. Transactions of the Ninth Conference, March 20-21. New York: Josiah Macy, Jr. Foundation, pp. 48-72.

______ (1963), The Central Affective Potential and Its Trigger Mechanisms. In: *Counterpoint: Libidinal Object and Subject*, ed. H. S. Gaskill. New York: International Universities Press, pp. 106-120.

Kuhn, T. (1962), *The Structure of Scientific Revolutions*. Chicago: University of Chicago Press.

Laffal, J. (1964), Freud's Theory of Language. *Psychoanal. Quart.*, 33:157-175.

Laing, R. D. (1960), *The Divided Self: An Existential Study in Sanity and Madness*. Baltimore: Penguin Books, 1965.

______ (1961), *The Self and Others*, 2nd ed. Baltimore: Penguin Books, 1969.

Lichtenstein, H. (1961), Identity and Sexuality. *J. Amer. Psychoanal. Assn.*, 9: 179-260.

______ (1964), The Role of Narcissism in the Emergence and Maintenance of a Primary Identity. *Internat. J. Psycho-Anal.*, 45:49-56.

Lindzey, G. (1967), Some Remarks concerning Incest, the Incest Taboo, and Psychoanalytic Theory. *Amer. Psychol.*, 22:1051-1059.

Loevinger, J. (1966), Three Principles for a Psychoanalytic Psychology. *J. Abnorm. Psychol.*, 71:432-443.

Loewald, H. W. (1951), Ego and Reality. *Internat. J. Psycho-Anal.*, 32:10-18.

______ (1952), The Problem of Defence and the Neurotic Interpretation of Reality. *Internat. J. Psycho-Anal.*, 33:444-449.

______ (1955), Hypnoid State, Repression, Abreaction and Recollection. *J. Amer. Psychoanal. Assn.*, 3:201-210.

______ (1960), On the Therapeutic Action of Psycho-Analysis. *Internat. J. Psycho-Anal.*, 41:16-33.

______ (1962), The Superego and the Ego Ideal. *Internat. J. Psycho-Anal.*, 43: 264-268.

______ (1971), Some Considerations on Repetition and Repetition Compulsion. *Internat. J. Psycho-Anal.*, 52:59-66.

Luborsky, L. (1964), A Psychoanalytic Research on Momentary Forgetting during Free Association. *Bull. Philadelphia Assn. Psychoanal.*, 14:119-137.

______ (1967), Momentary Forgetting during Psychotherapy and Psychoanalysis: A Theory and Research Method. In: Motives and Thought: Psychoanalytic Essays in Honor of David Rapaport, ed. R. R. Holt. *Psychol. Issues*, Monogr. No. 18/19:177-217. New York: International Universities Press.

Luria, A. R. (1961), *The Role of Speech in the Regulation of Normal and Abnormal Behavior*. New York: Pergamon.

Lustman, S. (1963), Some Issues in Contemporary Psychoanalytic Research. *The Psychoanalytic Study of the Child*, 18:51-74. New York: International Universities Press.

Meehl, P. E. (1966), Comments on Two Examples of Psychoanalytic Research. Discussion at Symposium, A Psychoanalyst and a Methodologist Look at Two Examples of Psychoanalytic Research. Meeting of the American Psychological Association, September.

Merleau-Ponty, M. (1945), *Phenomenology of Perception*. New York: Humanities Press, 1962.

Michotte, A. E. (1963), *The Perception of Causality*. New York: Basic Books.

Morris, D. (1962), *The Biology of Art*. New York: Knopf.

Murphy, L. B. (1964), Some Aspects of the First Relationship. *Internat. J. Psycho-Anal.*, 45:31-43.

Murray, H. A. (1938), *Exploration in Personality*. New York: Oxford University Press.

Niederland, W. G., rep. (1965), Memory and Repression. *J. Amer. Psychoanal. Assn.*, 13:619-633.

Peller, L. (1965), Biological Foundations of Psychology; Freud versus Darwin. *Bull. Philadelphia Assn. Psychoanal.*, 15:79-97.

Peterfreund, E. (1971), Information, Systems, and Psychoanalysis. *Psychol. Issues*, Monogr. No. 25/26. New York: International Universities Press.

Peters, R. S. (1956), Freud's Theory. *Brit. J. Phil. Sci.*, 7:4-12.

______ (1960), *The Concept of Motivation*, 2nd ed. London: Routledge & Kegan Paul.

______ (1969), Motivation, Emotion and the Conceptual Schemes of Common Sense. In: *Human Action: Conceptual and Empirical Issues*, ed. T. Mischel. New York: Academic Press, pp. 135-165.

Pfaffman, C. (1960), The Pleasures of Sensation. *Psychol. Rev.*, 67:253-268.

Piaget, J. (1951), *Play, Dreams and Imitation in Childhood*. New York: Norton.

Pine, F. (1970), On the Structuralization of Drive-Defense Relationships. *Psychoanal. Quart.*, 39:17-37.

Polanyi, M. (1958), *Personal Knowledge: Towards a Post-critical Philosophy*, rev. ed. New York: Harper Torchbooks, 1964.

______ (1965a), On the Modern Mind. In: Scientific Thought and Social Reality. *Psychol. Issues*, Monogr. No. 32:131-149. New York: International Universities Press, 1974.

______ (1965b), The Structure of Consciousness. *Brain*, 88:799-810.

______ (1966), *The Tacit Dimension*. New York: Doubleday.

Pribram, K. (1965), Freud's Project: An Open, Biologically Based Model for Psychoanalysis. In: *Psychoanalysis and Current Biological Thought*, ed. N. G. Greenfield & W. C. Lewis. Madison: University of Wisconsin Press, pp. 81-92.

Rapaport, D. (1951), The Conceptual Model of Pyschoanalysis. *Collected Papers*. New York: Basic Books, 1967, pp. 405-431.

______ (1953), Some Metapsychological Considerations concerning Activity and Passivity. *Collected Papers*. New York: Basic Books, 1967, pp. 530-568.

______ (1957), Cognitive Structures. *Collected Papers*. New York: Basic Books, 1967, pp. 631-664.

______ (1958a), The Theory of Ego Autonomy: A Generalization. *Collected Papers*. New York: Basic Books, 1967, pp. 722-744.

______ (1958b), A Historical Survey of Psychoanalytic Ego Psychology. *Collected Papers*. New York: Basic Books, 1967, pp. 745-757.

______ (1959), The Structure of Psychoanalytic Theory: A Systematizing Attempt. *Psychol. Issues*, Monogr. No. 6. New York: International Universities Press, 1960.

______ (1960), On the Psychoanalytic Theory of Motivation. *Collected Papers*. New York: Basic Books, 1967, pp. 853-915.

Rheingold, H. C., Gewirtz, J. C., & Ross, A. W. (1959), Social Conditioning of Vocalizations in the Infant. *J. Comp. Physiol. Psychol.*, 52:68-73.

Ricoeur, P. (1970), *Freud and Philosophy: An Essay on Interpretation*. New Haven: Yale University Press.

Riviere, J. (1936), On the Genesis of Psychical Conflict in Earliest Infancy. *Internat. J. Psycho-Anal.*, 17:395-422.

Rogers, C. (1947), Some Observations on the Organization of Personality. *Amer. Psychol.*, 2:358-368.

Rubinstein, B. B. (1967), Explanation and Mere Description: A Metascientific Examination of Certain Aspects of the Psychoanalytic Theory of Motivation. In: Motives and Thought: Psychoanalytic Essays in Honor of David Rapaport, ed. R. R. Holt. *Psychol. Issues*, Monogr. No. 18/19:20-79. New York: International Universities Press.

______ (1968), On the Inference and Confirmation of Clinical Interpretations. Manuscript.

Schafer, R. (1968a), *Aspects of Internalization*. New York: International Universities Press.

______ (1968b), The Mechanisms of Defence. *Internat. J. Psycho-Anal.*, 49:49-62.

______ (1970), The Psychoanalytic Vision of Reality. *Internat. J. Psycho-Anal.*, 51: 279-297.

Schlesinger, H. J. (1964), The Place of Forgetting in Memory Functioning. Presented at panel on Memory and Repression. Midwinter Meetings of the American Psychoanalytic Association, Dec.

Schur, M. (1966), *The Id and the Regulating Principles of Mental Functioning*. New York: International Universities Press.

Scott, J. P. (1968), *Early Experience and the Organization of Behavior*. Belmont, Cal.: Brooks/Cole.

Scriven, M. (1964), Truisms as the Grounds for Historical Explanations. In: *Theories of History*, ed. P. Gardiner. New York: Free Press, pp. 443-475.

Segal, M. M. (1963), Impulsive Sexuality: Some Clinical and Theoretical Observations. *Internat. J. Psycho-Anal.*, 44:407-418.

Spock, B. (1963), The Striving for Autonomy and Regressive Object Relationships. *The Psychoanalytic Study of the Child*, 18:361-364. New York: International Universities Press.

Steiner, G. (1969), The Language Animal. *Encounter*, 33(2):7-24.

Szasz, T. S. (1957), *Pain and Pleasure*. New York: Basic Books.

Tolman, E. C. (1948), Cognitive Maps in Rats and Men. *Psychol. Rev.*, 55:189-208.

Waelder, R. (1933), The Psychoanalytic Theory of Play. *Psychoanal. Quart.*, 2: 208-224.

______ (1936), The Principle of Multiple Function: Observations on Over-determination. *Psychoanal. Quart.*, 5:45-62.

______ (1966), Adaptational View Ignores "Drive." *Internat. J. Psychiat.*, 2:569-575.

______ (1967), Trauma and the Variety of Extraordinary Challenges. In: *Psychic Trauma*, ed. S. Furst. New York: Basic Books.

White, R. W. (1959), Motivation Reconsidered: The Concept of Competence. *Psychol. Rev.* 66:297-333.

______ (1960), Competence and the Psychosexual Stages of Development. In: *Nebraska Symposium on Motivation, 1960*, ed. M. R. Jones. Lincoln: University of Nebraska Press, pp. 99-140.

______ (1963), Ego and Reality in Psychoanalytic Theory. *Psychol. Issues*, Monogr. No. 11. New York: International Universities Press.

Wolff, P. H. (1959), Observations on Newborn Infants. *Psychosom. Med.*, 21: 110-118.

______ (1963), Developmental and Motivational Concepts in Piaget's Sensorimotor Theory of Development. *J. Amer. Acad. Child. Psychiat.*, 2:225-243.

______ (1965), The Development of Attention in Young Infants. *Ann. N. Y. Acad. Sci.*, 118:815-830.

______ (1966), The Causes, Controls, and Organization of Behavior in the Neonate. *Psychol. Issues*, Monogr. No. 17. New York: International Universities Press.

Yankelovich, D., & Barrett, W. (1970), *Ego and Instinct*. New York: Random House.

INDEX

Index

Index